LIBRARY OF NEW TESTAMENT STUDIES
547

Formerly Journal for the Study of the New Testament Supplement Series

Editor
Chris Keith

Editorial Board
Dale C. Allison, John M.G. Barclay, Lynn H. Cohick, R. Alan Culpepper,
Craig A. Evans, Robert Fowler, Simon J. Gathercole, John S. Kloppenborg,
Michael Labahn, Love L. Sechrest, Robert Wall, Steve Walton,
Robert L. Webb, Catrin H. Williams

WRITTEN TO SERVE

The Use of Scripture in 1 Peter

Benjamin Sargent

LONDON • NEW YORK • OXFORD • NEW DELHI • SYDNEY

T&T CLARK
Bloomsbury Publishing Plc
50 Bedford Square, London, WC1B 3DP, UK
1385 Broadway, New York, NY 10018, USA

BLOOMSBURY, T&T CLARK and the T&T Clark logo are
trademarks of Bloomsbury Publishing Plc

First published in Great Britain 2015
Paperback edition first published 2018

Copyright © Benjamin Sargent, 2015

Benjamin Sargent has asserted his right under the Copyright, Designs and Patents Act,
1988, to be identified as Author of this work.

All rights reserved. No part of this publication may be reproduced or
transmitted in any form or by any means, electronic or mechanical,
including photocopying, recording, or any information storage or
retrieval system, without prior permission in writing from the publishers.

Bloomsbury Publishing Plc does not have any control over, or responsibility for,
any third-party websites referred to or in this book. All internet addresses
given in this book were correct at the time of going to press. The author and
publisher regret any inconvenience caused if addresses have changed or
sites have ceased to exist, but can accept no responsibility for any such changes.

A catalogue record for this book is available from the British Library.

ISBN: HB: 978-0-56766-085-5
PB: 978-0-56767-245-2
ePDF: 978-0-56766-084-8

Sargent, Benjamin, 1983-
Written to serve : the use of scripture in 1 Peter / by Benjamin Sargent.
    pages cm. – (Library of New Testament studies; 547)
ISBN 978-0-567-66085-5 – ISBN 978-0-567-66084-8 (epdf) 1. Bible. Peter, 1st, I, 10-12–
Criticism, interpretation, etc. 2. Bible. Old Testament–Criticism, interpretation, etc. I. Title.
    BS2795.52.S27 2015
    227'.9206–dc23
    2014045838

Series: Library of New Testament Studies, volume 547

Typeset by Forthcoming Publications Ltd

To find out more about our authors and books visit
www.bloomsbury.com and sign up for our newsletters.

CONTENTS

Abbreviations	ix
INTRODUCTION	1
1. The Use of Scripture in 1 Peter from Selwyn to the Present	7
2. Plan of the Present Study	16

Chapter 1
1 PETER 1.10-12: A HERMENEUTICAL STATEMENT?   18
  1. 1 Peter 1.10-12 as a Hermeneutical Statement   18
  2. Form and Setting of 1 Peter 1.10-12   19
  3. Commentary on 1.10-12   21
      a. Verse 1.10   21
      b. Verse 1.11   24
      c. Verse 1.12   30

Excursus: A Comparison of 1 Peter 1.10-12 with 2 Peter 1.20-21   33

  4. Theological Narrative in 1 Peter 1.10-12   40
  5. Paraenesis and Kerygma in 1 Peter 1.10-12   44

Chapter 2
FORMAL CITATION OF SCRIPTURE IN 1 PETER   50
  1. What Is a Citation and How Many Are There in 1 Peter?   51
  2. Analysis of the Citations in 1 Peter   54
      a. 1 Peter 1.16 and Leviticus 19.2   54
      b. 1 Peter 1.24-25 and Isaiah 40.6b and 8   58
      c. 1 Peter 2.6-10: Stone *Stichwört* Catena
         and Associated Allusions   64
      d. 1 Peter 3.10-12 and Psalm 34.12-16 (OG 33.13-17)   78
      e. 1 Peter 3.14-15 and Isaiah 8.12 and 13   85
      f. 1 Peter 4.8 and Proverbs 10.12   88
      g. 1 Peter 4.14 and Isaiah 11.2   91
      h. 1 Peter 4.18 and Proverbs 11.31   93
      i. 1 Peter 5.5 and Proverbs 3.34   96
  3. Conclusion   98

Chapter 3
ALLUSION TO SCRIPTURE IN 1 PETER — 100
1. What Is an Allusion and How Many Are There in 1 Peter? — 101
   a. 1 Peter 1.1 and διασπορᾶς — 105
   b. 1 Peter 1.2 and ῥαντισμὸν αἵματος — 107
   c. 1 Peter 1.6-7 and Zechariah 13.9 — 109
   d. 1 Peter 1.10-12 and the Prophets — 110
   e. 1 Peter 1.19 and ὡς ἀμνοῦ ἀμώμου καὶ ἀσπίλου — 111
   f. 1 Peter 2.1 and Psalm 34.14 (OG Psalm 33.14) — 112
   g. 1 Peter 2.3 and Psalm 34.8 (OG Psalm 33.9) — 112
   h. 1 Peter 2.5 and οἶκος πνευματικὸς — 114
   i. 1 Peter 2.5 and εἰς ἱεράτευμα ἅγιον ἀνενέγκαι πνευματικὰς θυσίας — 118
   j. 1 Peter 2.9 and Isaiah 43.20b-21, Malachi 3.17 or Exodus 19.5-6 — 119
   k. 1 Peter 2.10 and Hosea 1.6, 9; 2.23 (OG 2.25) — 122
   l. 1 Peter 2.12 and Isaiah 10.3 — 124

Excursus: The Definition of 1 Peter 2.22-25 as Allusion — 125

   m. 1 Peter 2.21-25 and Isaiah 53.4, 5, 6, 9 and 12 — 126
   n. 1 Peter 3.5-6 and the ἅγιαι γυναῖκες of Israel's History — 131
   o. 1 Peter 3.19-21 and Noah and the Spirits in Prison — 136
   p. 1 Peter 3.22 and Psalms 110.1 (OG 109.1) and 8.6-7 — 141
   q. 1 Peter 5.8 and Psalm 22.14 (OG 21.14) — 142
2. Conclusion — 143

Excursus: Sectarian Exegesis in 1 Peter and the New Testament — 144

Chapter 4
THE EXEGETICAL BACKGROUND TO THE USE OF SCRIPTURE IN 1 PETER — 147
1. 1 Peter and Apocalyptic Judaism — 147
2. 1 Peter and Biblical Exegesis at Qumran — 148
   a. Qumran in Scholarship on 1 Peter — 149
   b. Biblical Hermeneutics in the Dead Sea Scrolls — 156
   c. Determinate Meaning at Qumran and in 1 Peter — 160
3. Conclusion — 162

Excursus: The Use of Scripture in 1 Peter and the Letter's Historical Setting — 163

Chapter 5
1 PETER AND THEOLOGICAL INTERPRETATION OF SCRIPTURE   170
  1. The Use of 1 Peter in Hermeneutical Discussion   172
  2. Determinate Meaning in Biblical Hermeneutics   177
  3. Determinacy in 1 Peter and Today   186

CONCLUSION   192

Bibliography   195
Index of References   209
Index of Authors   222

ABBREVIATIONS

AB	Anchor Bible
AJBI	*Annual of the Japanese Biblical Institute*
ANTC	Abingdon New Testament Commentaries
ASNU	Acta Seminarii Neotestamentici Upsaliensis
AsSeign	*Assemblées du Seigneur*
BBR	*Bulletin for Biblical Research*
BECNT	Baker Exegetical Commentary on the New Testament
BeO	*Bibbia e Oriente*
Bib	*Biblica*
BIS	Biblical Interpretation Series
BSac	*Bibliotheca Sacra*
BZ	*Biblische Zeitschrift*
BZNW	Beihefte zur Zeitschrift für die neutestamentliche Wissenschaft
CBOTS	Coniectanea Biblica: Old Testament Series
CBQ	*Catholic Biblical Quarterly*
CI	*Critical Inquiry*
DSD	*Dead Sea Discoveries*
ErIs	*Eretz-Israel*
EvQ	*Evangelical Quarterly*
ExpTim	*Expository Times*
HeyJ	*Heythrop Journal*
HNT	Handbuch zum Neuen Testament
HThKNT	Herders Theologische Kommentar zum Neuen Testament
HTR	*Harvard Theological Review*
ICC	International Critical Commentary
IJST	*International Journal of Systematic Theology*
JBL	*Journal of Biblical Literature*
JETS	*Journal of the Evangelical Theological Society*
JJS	*Journal of Jewish Studies*
JQR	*Jewish Quarterly Review*
JSNT	*Journal for the Study of the New Testament*
JSNTSup	Journal for the Study of the New Testament: Supplement Series
JSOTSup	Journal for the Study of the Old Testament: Supplement Series
JSS	*Journal of Semitic Studies*
JTS	*Journal of Theological Studies*
LD	Lectio divina
LNTS	Library of New Testament Studies
MT	*Modern Theology*

NA²⁷	Novum Testamentum Graece, Nestle-Aland, 27th ed.
NIDNTT	The New International Dictionary of New Testament Theology
NIGTC	*The New International Greek Testament Commentary*
NovT	*Novum Testamentum*
NovTSup	Supplements to Novum Testamentum
NTS	*New Testament Studies*
RB	*Revue Biblique*
ResQ	*Restoration Quarterly*
RevQ	*Revue de Qumran*
RHPhR	*Revue d'Histoire et de Philosophie Religieuses*
RThL	*Revue Theologique de Louvain*
SBLMS	Society of Biblical Literature Monograph Series
SBLSCS	Society of Biblical Literature Septuagint and Cognate Studies
SBLSP	*Society of Biblical Literature Seminar Papers*
SBLWGRW	Society of Biblical Literature Writings of the Greco Roman World
SDSSRL	Studies in the Dead Sea Scrolls and Related Literature
SPA	*Studia Philonica Annual*
SJT	*Scottish Journal of Theology*
SwJT	*Southwestern Journal of Theology*
TDNT	*Theological Dictionary of the New Testament*. Edited by G. Kittel and G. Friedrich. Translated by G. W. Bromiley. 10 vols. Grand Rapids, 1964–76
TLNT	*Theological Lexicon of the New Testament*. C. Spicq. Translated and edited by J. D. Ernest. 3 vols. Peabody, Mass., 1994
TS	*Theological Studies*
TynBul	*Tyndale Bulletin*
WBC	Word Biblical Commentary
WUNT	Wissenschaftliche Untersuchungen zum Neuen Testament
ZNW	*Zeitschrift fur Neutestamentliche Wissenschaft*

INTRODUCTION

Until relatively recently, it was customary to justify new 1 Peter research by referring to John H. Elliott's famous article 'The Rehabilitation of an Exegetical Step-Child: 1 Peter in Recent Research'.[1] At the end of his study, in which he laments the failure of the third edition of Beare's popular commentary to reflect more recent advances in research on the epistle, Elliott concludes that,

> First Peter, together with the historical figure to whom it was ascribed, has for quite some time been the victim of biased oversight and benign neglect. There are lively indications, however, that both apostle and letter have passed their latest exegetical *peirasmos*.[2]

Thankfully, in many areas of 1 Peter research this trend towards interest in the epistle has borne a great deal of fruit, not least due to the scholarship of Elliott himself. However, in one particular area of research a detailed recent study is lacking. This is in spite of a considerable interest in the subject both in 1 Peter research and in New Testament studies more generally. As is often noted, 1 Peter, for its size, has the highest density of explicit references to the Scriptures of Israel out of all the books of the New Testament.[3] Not only that, but study after study suggests intriguing possibilities for how Scripture functions in the epistle: texts which exercise a silent influence over large swathes of 1 Peter,

---

1. *JBL* 95 (1976), pp. 243–54. Reprinted in *Perspectives on First Peter* (ed. Charles H. Talbot; Macon, Ga.: Mercer University Press, 1986), pp. 3–16. References in this study are to the latter.

2. Elliott, 'The Rehabilitation of an Exegetical Step-Child', p. 16. Like Elliott, most scholars recognise that this period of neglect has passed; see, e.g., M. Eugene Boring, *1 Peter* (Nashville: Abingdon, 1999), p. 13; J. Ramsey Michaels, *1 Peter* (WBC 49; Nashville: Thomas Nelson, 1988), p. xxxi; William L. Schutter, *Hermeneutic and Composition in 1 Peter* (WUNT 30; Tübingen: Mohr Siebeck, 1989), p. 1.

3. This study will generally refer to the sacred texts referred to in 1 Peter as 'Scripture', rather than 'Old Testament', for no other reasons than those offered, in relation to Paul, by Christopher D. Stanley, *Arguing with Scripture: The Rhetoric of Quotations in the Letters of Paul* (London: T&T Clark International, 2004), p. 1 n. 1. Similarly, the designation 'Hebrew Bible' is unhelpful since the texts Peter employs are Greek.

leitmotifs that reveal the complex relationships between scriptural references and intriguing possibilities for sources behind scriptural references. Much of the complex uses of Scripture and the possible sources for references were detailed in the late 1980s by William Schutter, though Schutter had little scholarship to draw upon. However, since then, there has been a significant growth of scholarship on the use of the Old Testament in the New Testament in general, the nature of early rabbinic scriptural interpretation as well as the use of Scripture in 1 Peter, though there are few detailed monographs specifically on the latter.[4] Of particular importance has been the growth of interest in the theological narrative provided by Scripture which is both assumed and articulated in 1 Peter. Often without a citation and only with very loose or general allusion to Scripture, interest in such narratives marks a significant departure from previous areas of investigation.

Yet despite this recent growth of interest in the use of Scripture in 1 Peter, no study has yet attempted to offer a definition of 1 Peter's general approach to Scripture. No study has attempted to examine the various recent shorter studies on the use of Scripture in the whole of the letter with a view to distilling a clearer understanding of the author's scriptural hermeneutic.[5] Hitherto, the attempt to characterise the author's

---

4. Whilst there have been no book-length studies on the general use of Scripture in 1 Peter since Schutter, a number of unpublished doctoral theses have been devoted to the use of Scripture in 1 Peter. Dan Gale McCartney, 'The Use of the Old Testament in the First Epistle of Peter' (Ph.D. diss., Westminster Theological Seminary, 1989), concentrates on the 'hermeneutical goal' of the use of Scripture in 1 Peter, arguing that Scripture was understood as focused upon the particular situation of the communities. Gregory Ray Robertson, 'The Use of Old Testament Quotations and Allusions in the First Epistle of Peter' (Ph.D. diss., Anderson University, 1990), defines the use of Scripture in 1 Peter as addressing two ends: to establish relationships between the Church and society and rulers, and to give hope during a time of tribulation. Robertson defines 1 Peter as 'an epistle of hope'. Eric James Gréaux, '"To the Exiles of the Dispersion…from Babylon": The Function of the Old Testament in 1 Peter' (Ph.D. diss., Duke University, 2003), argues specifically that the original literary context of scriptural references is important to their use in 1 Peter.

5. This study reflects contemporary agreement that 1 Peter is a letter, rather than liturgical material with later epistolary prescript and postscript. See Lutz Doering, 'First Peter as Early Christian Diaspora Letter', in *Catholic Epistles and Apostolic Tradition: A New Perspective on James and the Catholic Letter Collection* (ed. K-W. Niebuhr and R. Wall; Waco: Baylor University Press, 2009), pp. 215–36. Cf. David G. Horrell, 'The Themes of 1 Peter: Insights from the Earliest Manuscripts (the Crosby-Schøyen Codex ms 193 and the Bodmer Miscellaneous Codex containing P^{72})', *NTS* 55 (2009), pp. 502–22.

scriptural hermeneutic has been somewhat subordinated to the task of characterising exegetical style. Whilst Schutter's study, as will be suggested, broke new ground in investigating prior assumptions about the use of Scripture in the epistle, a case can now be made for another detailed study which reflects the great development of interest in the subject which can possibly be traced to Schutter. Throughout this study, the debt which scholarship on the use of Scripture in 1 Peter owes to Schutter will be abundantly clear. As this study attempts to move beyond Schutter, it will seek to answer the following research questions:

1. How might the biblical hermeneutic or hermeneutics of the epistle be characterised? This study will seek to formulate an understanding of how Scripture is used in 1 Peter, developing a clear description of the author's scriptural hermeneutic. Following Schutter's work, an investigation of 1 Pet. 1.10-12 will be crucial, perhaps attributing greater importance to that passage than in Schutter. The extent to which the passage expresses a theological narrative of continuity or discontinuity will be explored. This research question will be addressed in Chapter 1.
2. How does the apparent scriptural hermeneutic of 1.10-12 relate to use of Scripture in the epistle? This study will discuss the various uses of scriptural allusions and citations in 1 Peter, drawing upon the most recent scholarship. It will attempt to define the apparent hermeneutic of 1 Peter further in relation to 'practical' usage. In addition to this, the nature of citation and allusion will be discussed in relation to the use of Scripture in 1 Peter as well as research on forms of scriptural reference in the New Testament published since Schutter's study. This research question will be addressed in Chapters 2 and 3.
3. Where does Peter's use of Scripture come from? What exegetical culture does 1 Peter operate within? This study will explore the possible exegetical backgrounds to the hermeneutic and use of Scripture in 1 Peter, drawing particularly upon recent research into scriptural interpretation at Qumran. This research question will be explored in Chapter 4.
4. What are the implications of Peter's use of Scripture for contemporary biblical scholarship? Given the recent trend towards re-establishing distinctively Christian theological hermeneutics, what contribution might a study of the use of Scripture in 1 Peter add to this debate? The final chapter of this study will attempt to relate the hermeneutic applied to Scripture in 1 Peter to questions discussed in contemporary biblical hermeneutics, particularly in

the area of theological hermeneutics. A chapter such as this would perhaps have been unusual at Schutter's time of writing, yet the relationship between the nature of biblical scholarship and early Christian interpretation of Scripture is perhaps one which has fuelled much of the growth of interest in the interpretation of Scripture in the New Testament.

In response to the first research question, this study will argue that 1 Pet. 1.10-12 is of considerable importance in explaining both Peter's understanding of Scripture and his scriptural hermeneutic, offering a detailed analysis of these verses. It will be argued that Peter viewed Scripture as fundamentally oriented towards Jesus Christ and the Christian community. This is grounded in Peter's view of the Prophets, whom he understood to have anticipated Christ as the climax of salvation history and who acted to serve the community brought into being by the proclamation of the Gospel. Here the work of Christ and his community are seen as being at the climactic pinnacle of time. This climax is a moment the Prophets yearned to know, yet were ignorant of: a climax which the very angels desire to peer down into. It will be argued that there are two dominant aspects to Peter's view of the prophetic witness to Christ. First, the Prophets wrote or spoke to describe the time and circumstances of the sufferings of Christ and the glories after. They are seen to offer kerygmatic and predictive testimony to the significance of Christ. Secondly, the Prophets wrote or spoke to serve the communities to which the epistle is addressed. It is argued that this assumption explains the direct paraenetic use of Scripture in the epistle. In addition to the kerygmatic and paraentic *functions* of the Prophets and hence of Scripture suggested in 1 Pet. 1.10-12 (and these two aspects are often combined), the passage also enables characterisation of a biblical hermeneutic. It will be argued that interpretation of Scripture in 1 Peter, based on the author's understanding of the relation of the prophetic witness to the communities to which he writes, is primitive and sectarian. It is 'primitive' insofar as Scripture is understood to have a single meaning focused upon a particular set of people and events. There is no evidence that the author is aware of other interpretations of the texts he employs. Because of this, he is able simply to cite them or allude to them as though they were unambiguous. In addition to this, use of Scripture is 'sectarian', owing to the evident assumption that Scripture relates exclusively to a single group of people. The character of Peter's scriptural hermeneutic as well as the functions he ascribes to Scripture will be demonstrated in the analysis of particular uses of Scripture in the epistle.

This study will depart from the current trend in research on the use of Scripture in 1 Peter of viewing the epistle as dominated by a theological narrative emphasising the continuity of the people of God, both past and present. It will be argued that 1 Pet. 1.10-12 posits a radical disjuncture between the ignorance of the past and the glories of the present as the climax of salvation history. It will be argued that typological interpretation which assumes a significant status for the things of the past in their own right is not a feature of the use of Scripture in 1 Peter.

Regarding the possible exegetical background or influences upon 1 Peter, this study will argue that the letter is best understood within an apocalyptic Jewish milieu. This can be seen in the priority given to the needs of the Christian communities in 1.10-12, in which those who have heard the Gospel stand at the climax of history and are served by the Prophets of the past. This tendency to place the community at the centre of exegesis is much closer to the exegetical practice of Qumran than it is to rabbinic scriptural commentary. Whilst rabbinic reading of Scripture typically demonstrates an understanding that a multiplicity of interpretations of the same passage are held, even if one interpretation is to be preferred, scriptural interpretation at Qumran, to the extent that it may be simply characterised, has much more in common with the primitive and sectarian character of the use of Scripture in 1 Peter. This character helps to locate the letter as perhaps reflecting an earlier date than is often thought. Certainly, 1 Peter lacks the exegetical sophistication of, for example, the Epistle to the Hebrews or the Acts of the Apostles.

In response to the third research question stated above, it will be argued that the determinacy of Peter's use of Scripture ought to be considered as part of a genuinely theological approach to biblical hermeneutics. This presents something of a challenge to contemporary trends in biblical hermeneutics, particularly in theological interpretation of Scripture, in which determinacy (as a theory of limited potential meaning) is ignored despite its importance (or because of its importance) in historical criticism. It will be shown that determinate meaning has a significant historical pedigree, not least in the New Testament. Furthermore, it will be suggested that 1 Peter offers a stimulus to a theologically conceived account of determinacy on the basis of salvation history and ecclesiology.

Before progressing to a brief account of scholarship on the use of Scripture in 1 Peter, two issues relating to the language of this study need to be mentioned: the use of the term 'Peter' to refer to the author of 1 Peter and the most appropriate means of referring to the Greek scriptural traditions upon which 1 Peter depends. The authorship of 1 Peter has been debated extensively. Whilst the identity of the author of 1 Peter has little bearing upon a study of this sort (especially since so little is known of the historical Peter), it must be said that many of the arguments employed in the authorship debate are deeply problematic philosophically. This is particularly true of many of the arguments against Petrine authorship which typically depend on an assumption of the normativity of the post-Enlightenment worldview, especially in relation to the limits of the historical Peter's education. Such a worldview comes with severe and, perhaps, unrealistic limitations on such things as Peter's ability to learn and communicate in Greek. Such assumptions are often seen as no longer philosophically warranted or self-evident,[6] leaving the issue of authorship far from settled. At the same time, the dating of 1 Peter is a significant factor in discussion of authorship. This too is an almost impossible task since so little is known of early Christian history that the meagre suggestions of *Sitz im Leben* in 1 Peter itself cannot be related to known events with any certainty. This is particularly the case when deciding on the referent of the 'persecution' mentioned in 1 Pet. 4.12. References to persecution have often been seen to relate to one of the official persecutions under particular Roman emperors for which there is some literary evidence in the letters of Pliny, for example. But this rests on the assumption that what is known now represents all that scholars need to know to understand early Christian history and plot certain texts in places within that history. This assumption rules out the possibility of local persecution for which there is little specific extant written evidence, yet which has gained broad support. There is simply not enough information available about the historical Peter or the setting of 1 Peter to dismiss the possibility of Petrine authorship, nor is there enough information on such matters to confirm it beyond reasonable doubt. Because of this, and for sheer convenience of expression, this study will refer to the author of 1 Peter as 'Peter' throughout.

In the past, it was commonplace to identify the origins of the scriptural texts cited in the New Testament by comparing citations with extant Greek and Hebrew texts. From such comparisons, scholars felt able to discern how New Testament authors had adjusted texts to suit a particular use. However, as has been demonstrated in more recent studies,

---

6. Craig G. Bartholomew, 'Uncharted Waters: Philosophy, Theology and the Crisis in Biblical Interpretation', in *Renewing Biblical Interpretation* (ed. Craig G. Bartholomew, Colin Greene and Karl Möller; Grand Rapids: Zondervan; Carlisle: Paternoster, 2000), pp. 1–34. Cf. Benjamin Sargent, 'Chosen through Sanctification (1 Pet 1,2 and 2 Thess 2,13): The Theology or Diction of Silvanus?', *Bib* 94 (2013), pp. 117–20.

such comparison is deeply problematic due to the evident complexity of Greek Scripture in the first century. Because of this, this study will follow the recent practice of employing the designation OG (Old Greek) instead of LXX (Septuagint) so as to recognise something of this complexity.[7]

1. The Use of Scripture in 1 Peter from Selwyn to the Present

Edward Gordon Selwyn, whose commentary is foundational for contemporary 1 Peter research, along with that of F. W. Beare, characterised the use of the Scripture in 1 Peter as typical of a general tendency within the New Testament:

> It needs no saying that for all the Christian writers of the first two centuries the Jewish Scriptures were a primary source of information as to the meaning of Christ and Christianity; for in Him they were fulfilled. The author of 1 Peter is deeply steeped in them, as he shews both by direct quotation and by frequent indirect allusions; and he knows them in the LXX form.[8]

Selwyn had a confidence in the extant LXX text which must now be regarded as unfonded. He suggested that in cases where 1 Peter's scriptural citations disagree with extant Old Greek readings, this reflects either a failure in the author's memory of the text or else the catechetical or liturgical adjustment of the text prior to its use in 1 Peter.[9] Furthermore, he noted that Peter demonstrates a familiarity with Jewish apocalyptic literature, employing vocabulary common in intertestamental literature such as *Sirach* and the *Maccabees*. Whilst Selwyn made useful observations regarding the use of particular references to Scripture in 1 Peter, his introductory remarks about the use of Scripture in the letter are very brief and are of little value. This is surely due to Selwyn's time of writing prior to the emergence of the use of the Old Testament in the New as a special scholarly interest. Beare's commentary, which in its

---

7. As suggested by R. T. McLay, *The Use of the Septuagint in New Testament Research* (Grand Rapids: Eerdmans, 2003), p. 6. Cf. R. A. Kraft, 'Para-mania: Beside, Before and Beyond Bible Studies', *JBL* 126 (2007), pp. 11–17, and Wolfgang Kraus and R. Glenn Wooden, 'Contemporary "Septuagint" Research: Issues and Challenges in the Study of the Greek Jewish Scripture', in *Septuagint Research: Issues and Challenges in the Study of the Greek Jewish Scriptures* (ed. Wolfgang Kraus and R. Glenn Wooden; SBLSCS 53; Leiden: Brill, 2006), pp. 1–13.

8. Edward Gordon Selwyn, *The First Epistle of St. Peter: The Greek Text with Introduction, Notes and Essays* (London: Macmillan, 1958), p. 24.

9. Selwyn, *Peter*, p. 25.

various editions is roughly contemporary with Selwyn (though the first edition is considerably older), is similar in its rather limited description of 1 Peter as employing the LXX. Beare's analysis of the use of Scripture in 1 Peter is offered as part of his discussion on the epistle's authorship. Beare contends that the author of 1 Peter demonstrates only a 'literary knowledge' of Greek Scripture:

> Moreover, this knowledge of the Scriptures which he exhibits is a literary knowledge, not that of one who has himself practised the religion of the Old Testament before becoming a Christian. To the Jew, the Torah was the heart of the religion in which he was reared; but to this writer, the substance of the earlier revelation lay in its testimony to 'the sufferings of Christ and the glory that should follow', and there is never a suggestion that he is troubled by the problem that so strongly occupied the mind of Paul, the problem of showing how a faith which made constant appeal to the Old Testament could at the same time reject the fundamental principle which based the whole religious life upon obedience to the divinely-given Law.[10]

Whilst the designation 'literary' does not seem to do justice to the depth and sophistication of the use of Scripture in 1 Peter, it is notable that Beare uses 1 Pet. 1.11 to define the understanding of Scripture in the epistle, something that Selwyn does not do.

Other commentators between Selwyn and the late 1980s typically included some limited discussion of the use of Scripture in 1 Peter to introduce the epistle. Like Selwyn, their description was often limited to an acknowledgement that references are derived from the 'LXX' and that 1 Peter displays christological interpretation of Scripture.[11] To some extent, the short studies by Jacques Schlosser and Thomas P. Osborne (both of which attempt to provide a general account of the use of Scripture in 1 Peter) added little to these observations.[12] Ernest Best

---

10. F. W. Beare, *The First Epistle of Peter: The Greek Text with Introduction and Notes* (3d ed.; Oxford: Blackwell, 1970), p. 46. Cf. idem, 'The Sequence of Events in Acts 9 to 15 and the Career of Peter', *JBL* 42 (1943), pp. 295–306.

11. See, e.g., Bo Reicke, *The Epistles of James, Peter and Jude* (AB 37; New York: Doubleday, 1964), 70. Cf. the analysis provided by Abson Prédestin Joseph, *A Narratological Reading of 1 Peter* (LNTS 440; London: T&T Clark International, 2012), p. 3, which argues for a general consensus on the use of Scripture in 1 Peter from Selwyn to 1976.

12. Jacques Schlosser, 'Ancien Testament et Christologie dans la Prima Petri', in Charles Perrot, *Etudes sur la Première Lettre de Pierre* (LD 102; Paris: Cerf, 1980), pp. 65–96, argued that Scripture was the primary source for the Christology of 1 Peter yet that Peter read his christological themes back into the Scriptures (seen most clearly in 1 Pet 1.10-12 in Peter's understanding of the Prophets as focused upon

attempted to outline something of the use of the Old Testament in 1 Peter, though his discussions are limited to a desire to shed light on issues of authorship and the place of 1 Peter in the development of early Christian thought.[13] A slightly more detailed introduction to the use of Scripture in 1 Peter was offered by J. Ramsey Michaels.[14] Michaels identifies only four examples of formal citation of Scripture within 1 Peter, with many other less formal references, and describes 1 Peter as relating Scripture to Christology and the Christian community.

The most significant work to this date, William L. Schutter's *Hermeneutic and Composition in 1 Peter*, appeared in 1989. Schutter argues that previous 1 Peter research had largely ignored the use of Scripture in the epistle. Several studies, he notes, had explored the use of a particular text or set of texts in a portion of 1 Peter, but none had attempted a general study of the use of Scripture in the epistle as a whole.[15] Schutter makes a determined effort to define a scriptural hermeneutic, derived from 1.10-12, in which Scripture is understood to focus upon the 'sufferings and glory' of Christ. Schutter was the first to attempt to define different modes of scriptural reference (or in his own terms, levels of 'literary dependence') in 1 Peter, organising references into explicit and implicit citations; explicit, implicit, incipient and iterative allusions and, finally, Biblicisms.[16] For Schutter, citations require a citation formula.

Christ), manipulating them to express his Christology. Thomas P. Osborne, 'L'Utilisation de l'Ancient Testament dans la Première Épître de Pierre', *RThL* 12 (1981), pp. 64–77, argues for the dependence of 1 Peter upon the Greek Scriptures by comparing six identified scriptural citations with both Greek and Hebrew equivalents. Osborne notes that structural importance of the citations he discusses and the theological and paraenetic importance of Isa. 53 in particular.

13. Ernest Best, *1 Peter* (NCBC; Grand Rapids: Eerdmans, 1971), pp. 47, 49–50 and 57.

14. Michaels, *1 Peter*, pp. xl–xli.

15. Schutter, *Hermeneutic and Composition*, pp. 2–3. Notable studies include J. H. Elliott, *The Elect and the Holy: An Exegetical Examination of 1 Peter 2.4-10 and the Phrase βασίλειον ἱεράτευμα* (NovTSup 12; Leiden: Brill, 1966), and Klyne R. Snodgrass, '1 Peter II. 1-10: Its Formation and Literary Affinities', *NTS* 24 (1978), pp. 97–106.

16. Schutter, *Hermeneutic and Composition*, pp. 35, 37 etc. Schutter describes the relation between 1 Peter and Scripture as one of 'literary dependence'. As Schutter notes, 1 Peter contains a significant number of 'biblicisms', suggesting that the language of the epistle is heavily indebted to Scripture. Yet does reference to a text indicate dependence? Literary dependence suggests the conscious imitation of another text. It is not clear that this is what Peter is attempting to do when he cites or alludes to Scripture. The use of biblicisms in 1 Peter is quite different from, for example, the 'septuagintalisms' of Acts, noted by W. K. L. Clark ('The Uses of the

The most explicit citations are introduced with a formula featuring διότι, whilst implicit citations are introduced with either ὅτι or καὶ.[17] Elliott and Moyise, perhaps rightly, reject Schutter's view that a midrashic type of exegesis is employed in 1 Peter, noting that 1 Peter does not demonstrate any interest in expounding or explaining a particular text, nor is the meaning of any text discussed.[18] In addition to this, Moyise notes that 1 Peter tends to employ texts which had a considerable degree of popularity in the early Church, rather than showing a sophisticated and detailed knowledge of Scripture, and suggests that Schutter tries too hard to promote 1 Pet. 1.10-12 as a hermeneutical statement explaining the use of Scripture in 1 Peter, particularly in his attempt to embrace the application of Scripture to 'the sufferings of Christ and the subsequent glories'. Moyise suggests that Schutter makes these ideas too all-embracing, able to accommodate each use of Scripture in 1 Peter.[19]

Since Schutter, several commentaries have offered more substantial introductory discussion of the use of the Old Testament in 1 Peter, going beyond mere statement of debt to the LXX and the use of christological interpretation.[20] Elliott's commentary offers a much more extensive

---

Septuagint in Acts', in *The Beginnings of Christianity*, vol. 2 [London: Macmillan, 1922], pp. 66–103), which suggest to Jacob Jervell ('The Future of the Past: Luke's Vision of Salvation History and Its Bearing on His Writing of History', in *History, Literature, and Society in the Book of Acts* [ed. Ben Witherington; Cambridge: Cambridge University Press, 1996], pp. 104–206 [110]) that Luke is attempting to write 'Scripture'. Cf. Max Wilcox, *The Semitisms of Acts* (Oxford: Clarendon, 1965).

17. Schutter, *Hermeneutic and Composition*, pp. 35–7. Schutter regards ὅτι as a formula due to its possible relation to διότι, whilst γάρ in 1 Pet. 3.10 is regarded as a citation device because of 'what can only be the explicit quotation of Psalm 34 in 3.10-12'.

18. John H. Elliott, *1 Peter: A New Translation with Introduction and Commentary* (AB 37B: New Haven: Yale University Press, 2000), and Steve Moyise, 'Isaiah in 1 Peter', in *Isaiah in the New Testament* (ed. Steve Moyise and Maarten J. J. Menken; The New Testament and the Scriptures of Israel; London: T&T Clark International, 2005), p. 187.

19. Steve Moyise, *Evoking Scripture: Seeing the Old Testament in the New* (London: T&T Clark International, 2008), p. 93. Cf. Joseph, *Narratological Reading of 1 Peter*, p. 15, who suggests that Schutter often relies on an exaggerated emphasis upon particular details in the use of a scriptural text to support the hermeneutical significance of the 'sufferings' and 'glories' of 1 Pet. 1.11.

20. Though many simply repeat the simple observations popular prior to Schutter. For example, Paul J. Achtemeier, *1 Peter: A Commentary on First Peter* (Philadelphia: Fortress, 1996), p. 12, notes only the different types of citation formula used in 1 Peter and discusses the use of Scripture only insofar as it relates to questions of authorship.

overview than any earlier commentary, drawing heavily upon Schutter. Elliott presents his readers with a helpful chart of citations (divided into those with a citation formula, those with a simple preceding term and those without either), allusions (with text, without text, incipient allusions, iterative allusions and possible iterative allusions) and Biblicisms. To a large extent these follow the analysis of Schutter.[21] Like Schutter and earlier commentaries, Elliott outlines possible sources for the scriptural references in 1 Peter, noting some differences from extant sources. Elliott also notes certain technical features of the use of Scripture in 1 Peter, including telescoping of texts, conflation, the use of scriptural catenas and the use of the wider text plot of scriptural references. Furthermore, Elliott characterises the use of Scripture in 1 Peter as emphasising the identity of the reading communities with 'God's covenant people' so as to explain the alienation they face in their 'diaspora' contexts. In addition to this, Elliott notes that Scripture provides an important resource for the epistle's Christology, soteriology and paraenesis: both when applied directly as paraenetic as well as when providing examples of good behaviour, as with Sarah in 3.6.

Joel B. Green's commentary reflects upon the use of Scripture in 1 Peter to engage with some issues in contemporary biblical hermeneutics.[22] Green is particularly interested in the nature of the Old Testament as Christian Scripture and uses Peter's approach to Scripture, based largely upon 1 Pet. 1.10-12, to shed new light on this as a problem raised by historical criticism and the development of contemporary Theological Interpretation of Scripture.[23] Green argues that the use of Scripture in 1 Peter is characterised by the theological narrative or *fabula* expressed in the epistle. The *fabula* features an understanding that the communities addressed by the epistle are the people of God in continuity with Israel. For this reason, scriptural descriptions of Israel are applied to the communities, as in 2.9-10. This aspect of Green's analysis witnesses to the growth of interest in theological narrative in scholarship on the use of Scripture in 1 Peter.

In addition to the work on this subject in commentaries, several short studies of the use (or particular uses) of Scripture in 1 Peter have been published, mostly in very recent years. Richard Bauckham offered a

21. Elliott, *Commentary*, pp. 12–17.
22. Joel B. Green, *1 Peter* (Grand Rapids: Eerdmans, 2007).
23. Cf. Betsy Bauman-Martin and Robert L. Webb, 'Reading First Peter with New Eyes: An Introduction', in *Reading First Peter with New Eyes: Methodological Reassessments of the Letter of First Peter* (ed. Robert L. Webb and Betsy Bauman-Martin; LNTS 364; London: T&T Clark International, 2007), pp. 1–7.

small but significant contribution to the study of the use of Scripture in 1 Peter in 1988: too late to feature in Schutter.[24] Unfortunately, Bauckham's discussion of 1 Peter is tightly limited to two principal passages on which, however, he displays considerable insight. His general characterisation of the use of Scripture in the letter is helpful too. Bauckham notes considerable parallels between Peter's use of Scripture and that of the Qumranic pesharim, seen particularly in the similarity between 1 Pet. 1.10-12 and 1QpHab 7.1-8 and the use of *Stichwörten*, text selection and adaptation in 1 Pet. 2.4-10. This Qumranic parallel is maintained despite Bauckham's initial claim that the epistle, along with 2 Peter, belongs to an early Roman Christian, rather than Palestinian context.[25] Bauckham's characterisation of two types of use of Scripture – prophetic and paraenetic – is also helpful and features prominently in the analysis below.

A most comprehensive study of the use of the Old Testament in 1 Peter is offered by D. A. Carson in the *Commentary on the New Testament Use of the Old Testament*, published in 2007.[26] Part of Carson's purpose is to explore the extent to which the use of Scripture in 1 Peter coheres with historically reconstructed accounts of the original meaning of such Scripture. Carson generally argues that the use of Scripture in 1 Peter is in harmony with the probable original meaning of the texts quoted or alluded to, reflecting good translation and some awareness of a text's literary context. This conclusion seems forced and apologetic in tone to some scholars.[27]

Also of considerable significance are the recent studies published in The New Testament and the Scriptures of Israel series, edited by Maarten J. J. Menken and Steve Moyise. To date, volumes in this series have been published on the use of Genesis, Psalms, Isaiah and the Minor Prophets in the New Testament, each of which has a chapter on 1 Peter. Sue Woan provides a stimulating discussion of the use of the Psalms in 1 Peter, beginning with a helpful discussion of the use of terminology to indicate

---

24. Richard Bauckham, 'James, 1 and 2 Peter, Jude', in *It Is Written: Scripture Citing Scripture: Essays in Honour of Barnabas Lindars* (ed. D. A. Carson and H. G. M. Williamson; Cambridge: Cambridge University Press, 1988), pp. 309–12.

25. Cf. Bauckham, 'James, 1 and 2 Peter, Jude', p. 303.

26. D. A. Carson, '1 Peter', in *Commentary on the New Testament Use of the Old Testament* (ed. G. K. Beale and D. A. Carson; Grand Rapids: Baker; Nottingham: Apollos, 2007), pp. 1015–45.

27. Cf. the discussions in G. K. Beale, ed., *The Right Doctrine from the Wrong Texts? Essays on the Use of the Old Testament in the New* (Grand Rapids: Baker, 1994).

scriptural reference, such as 'quotation' and 'allusion'.[28] Woan supports and develops Bornemann's thesis[29] that Psalm 34 exercises a dominant influence over 1 Peter, arguing that the long citation from the psalm in 1 Pet. 3.10-12 structures the various themes on either side of it. Steve Moyise offers a substantial study of the use of Isaiah in 1 Peter with plenty of material to work with in terms of citations and allusions to Isaiah in the epistle.[30] This is a valuable study with some detailed consideration of 1 Pet. 1.10-12 as an expression of Peter's approach to Scripture. Moyise argues that the use of Isaiah is of considerable importance in the argument of 1 Peter, principally as proof texts supporting central notions of Christ's forbearance under suffering, the Christian duties of proclamation and reverence and the promise of the Spirit to those who suffer on account of Christ. A possible weakness of Moyise's study might be a tendency to explain too much of 1 Peter's composition, textual variants from extant Old Greek scriptural texts and choice of words with reference to Scripture. This is not exclusive to Moyise: Elliott and Schutter display this tendency too. Whilst it is no doubt obvious that Peter's mind is saturated with Scripture, it may not be possible to see as much of a relation to Scripture as Moyise does. Karen H. Jobes, writing on the Minor Prophets in 1 Peter, certainly has the least material to consider and this paucity results in some detailed examination of possible allusions which Jobes herself concedes to be exegetical dead-ends. Yet she addresses some issues of verbal similarity and allusion with helpful clarity with an unusually clear vision of a general approach to Scripture within the epistle.[31] In addition to her commentary published in 2005, which contains many valuable insights for the study of the use of Scripture in 1 Peter, Jobes has also produced a detailed study of the Old Greek texts employed in the epistle and their differences compared to extant versions of the same texts.[32] Here, Jobes draws attention to the

---

28. Sue Woan, 'The Psalms in 1 Peter', in *The Psalms in the New Testament* (ed. Steve Moyise and Maarten J. J. Menken; The New Testament and the Scriptures of Israel; London: Continuum, 2004), pp. 213–29.

29. W. Bornemann, 'Der erste Petrusbrief – eine Taufrede des Silvanus', *ZNW* 19 (1920), pp. 143–65.

30. Moyise, 'Isaiah in 1 Peter', pp. 175–88.

31. Karen H. Jobes, 'The Minor Prophets in James, 1 & 2 Peter and Jude', in *The Minor Prophets in the New Testament* (ed. Maarten J. J. Menken and Steve Moyise; LNTS 377; The New Testament and the Scriptures of Israel; London: T&T Clark International, 2009), pp. 135–6 and 142–6 Cf. idem, *1 Peter* (BECNT; Grand Rapids: Baker, 2005), p. 52.

32. Karen H. Jobes, 'The Septuagint Textual Tradition in 1 Peter', in Kraus and Wooden, eds., *Septuagint Research*, pp. 311–33.

substantial agreement between the scriptural citations in 1 Peter and their extant Old Greek counterparts, noting that in the majority of cases where ambiguity exists, Peter agrees with the Old Greek versions against extant Hebrew versions.

In general, these studies, along with that of Carson, represent the traditional concerns of scholarship on the use of Scripture in the New Testament: the form of texts, mode of citation, the precise referents of allusions, the relation of different references and their origins.[33] Yet many recent studies, particularly in the early years of the twenty-first century, have shown a primary interest in theological narrative, as seen in Green's commentary. For example, Eugene Boring, whose commentary says relatively little on the general use of Scripture in 1 Peter (though it gives plenty of helpful insights into the use of particular texts), argues that the paraenesis of the epistle is dependent upon a theological narrative derived from a reading of Scripture. Boring's later study, 'Narrative Dynamics in 1 Peter: The Function of Narrative World', expands certain observations in the appendix of his commentary on the role of theological narrative in 1 Peter.[34] In this study, Boring discusses the advantages and problems associated with the application of narratology to a non-narrative text such as 1 Peter. He argues that the act of letter writing, if it is directed towards a known audience, assumes a shared narrative between the audience and writer on two levels: the historical narrative which grounds the relation of the writer to the audience (perhaps involving visits from the author to the audience) and, in the case of 1 Peter, a shared theological narrative.[35] Letters like 1 Peter, Boring argues, project a narrative world. The theological narrative projected by the text involves and is conditioned by Scripture. Boring suggests that 1 Pet. 1.10-12 is a particularly clear expression of the theological narrative in 1 Peter.

Perhaps the most important study to embody this approach is Abson Prédestin Joseph's *A Narratological Reading of 1 Peter*. This study could be regarded as the second in-depth and general major piece of published research on the use of Scripture in 1 Peter, though it engages

---

33. The same can be said of Samuel Bénétreau, 'Évangile et Prophétie: Un Texte Original (1 P 1, 10-12) Peut-il Éclairer un Texte Difficile (2 P 1, 16-21)?', *Bib* 86 (2005), pp. 174–91, which reaches many of the conclusions already seen in Schutter, such as the hermeneutical function of 1 Pet. 1.10-12 and christological nature of this hermeneutic.

34. Eugene Boring, 'Narrative Dynamics in 1 Peter: The Function of Narrative World', in Webb and Bauman-Martin, eds., *Reading First Peter*, pp. 7–40.

35. Boring, 'Narrative Dynamics in 1 Peter', pp. 9–15.

with quite different issues from Schutter. It could be argued that, despite the title of Schutter's study, Joseph comes closer to defining the hermeneutic employed by Peter. Joseph claims a close affinity with Dryden's study, extending his connection of narrative and ethics to consider Peter's 'theological interpretation of Scripture' on the basis of the narrative.[36] Joseph argues that the narrative both emerges from and controls Peter's interpretation of Scripture and is evident throughout the epistle. The narrative, according to Joseph, is a christological understanding of the history of issues featuring four important emphases which Joseph studies in turn: election, suffering, steadfastness and vindication. These emphases are seen to be significant in the theological identity of Israel and the communities addressed by 1 Peter who are seen to stand in continuity with Israel because of Jesus Christ. Peter's hermeneutic is seen in the narrative substructure of the epistle. Because this narrative involves the incorporation of the communities addressed by 1 Peter into the people of God, Scripture is seen to address them too, quite directly.[37]

In addition to these recent studies which are explicitly interested in the use of Scripture in 1 Peter, other recent studies of various themes in the epistle often have significant implications for an understanding of its use of Scripture. For example, Andrew M. Mbuvi argues that 1 Peter reflects a tradition of eschatological expectation of a restored temple beginning in Second Temple Judaism.[38] For Mbuvi, the perhaps dominant theme of suffering reflects the purification of the communities to whom 1 Peter is addressed as the new temple: the house of God. Arguments such as these, because 1 Peter is so thoroughly imbued with scriptural references, depend upon the reassessment of scriptural references and the scriptural background to significant concepts in the epistle. This is seen in Mbuvi's argument that the use of the language of exile in 1 Peter reflects the restoration tradition seen in Isa. 11.11-17, Ezek. 29.21-29, Hag. 1.1-5, *Jub.* 1.15-17 and *T. Benj.* 9.2. Yet arguments such as this, which posit unattested background texts which are not clearly referred to in the epistle, are weak. As Mbuvi continues,

36. Joseph, *Narratological Reading of 1 Peter*, p. 23.
37. Joseph, *Narratological Reading of 1 Peter*, pp. 29–31.
38. Andrew M. Mbuvi, *Temple, Exile and Identity in 1 Peter* (LNTS 345; London: T&T Clark International, 2007). More specifically, Mbuvi sees 1 Peter as expressing interest in the fulfilment of the four apocalyptic Jewish hopes recognised by E. P. Sanders, *Judaism: Practice and Belief, 63 BCE–66 CE* (London: SCM; Philadelphia: Trinity Press International, 1994), pp. 279–303: the restoration of the twelve tribes of Israel, the inclusion of the Gentiles, a renewed and purified temple and the renewal of the people, albeit with the communities of 1 Peter understood as Israel.

> Given that Isaiah provides the largest share of OT passages quoted, echoed or alluded to in 1 Peter, it is significant to note that Isaiah closely associates the eschatological temple with Gentiles who stream into the temple, are gathered with the scattered of Israel, and bring their wealth to adorn the temple (Isa. 2.2; 56.7; 60.4-13). 1 Peter takes over this Isaianic theme and not only allows for the possibility of Gentiles entering the eschatological temple but also goes a step further to integrate Gentiles into the spiritual eschatological temple (2.4-10). In so doing, 1 Peter reshapes and reconstitutes both the identity of the temple and that of believers.[39]

Yet if one believes, as many scholars do, that Peter's primary access to Isaiah was through the testimonia collections to which he refers, this rich scriptural background suggested by Mbuvi becomes difficult to support.

2. Plan of the Present Study

This study will differ significantly from the approach taken by Schutter. Schutter begins by attempting to define the use of sources in 1 Peter quite generally in relation to the author's compositional technique:

> Because the Scriptures represent but a portion of the letter's formal sources, oral and written, to approach them in isolation from the rest would be methodologically unsound. Not only would it be arbitrary, but in that case it would also be impossible to say for certain whether any distinctive relationship exists with the Scriptures that does not exist with any other sources.[40]

Whilst Schutter is, of course, right that a study of the use of one kind of source can only be truly productive when the use of that source is considered in relation to other sources used, there is so little evidence of which other sources are deliberately employed in 1 Peter that this kind of comparison is more or less impossible. Apart from the *Haustafel* material in 1 Pet. 3.1-7, there can be little certainty of literary or oral sources for 1 Peter, and even in the case of the *Haustafel*, there is no clear textual tradition which 1 Peter uses: the sort of source criticism conducted on the scriptural citations in the epistle is not possible with this material, for example. Indeed, Schutter's analysis of the general use of sources in 1 Peter seems to prove this. Schutter cautiously notes the possibility that

---

39. Mbuvi, *Temple, Exile and Identity*, p. 44. Cf. Leonhard Goppelt, *Typos: The Typological Interpretation of the Old Testament in the New* (trans. Donald H. Madvig; Grand Rapids: Eerdmans, 1982), p. 154, who similarly associates 'spiritual house' with the temple.

40. Schutter, *Hermeneutic and Composition*, p. 19.

1 Peter may have been influenced by Pauline letter composition and his treatment of 'non-biblical formal sources' is remarkably brief, rightly noting that most possible non-biblical sources are oral.[41] These are therefore not extant and not significantly subject to scholarly speculation.

The first chapter of this study offers a detailed examination of 1.10-12 as a witness to the theological narrative substructure of the epistle which determines its use of Scripture. It is argued, contrary to recent assessment, that 1 Peter operates upon a narrative of essential discontinuity in which the communities to which the letter is addressed stand at the climax of the author's theological narrative, dramatically elevated above God's people of the past. Because of this, the Prophets and their Scriptures are understood to be fundamentally oriented towards the communities.

The second chapter provides an examination of the formal citations in 1 Peter. This chapter seeks to advance discussion of each citation whilst exploring the extent to which the author's theological narrative is evident in the treatment of particular texts. It is argued that in practice, the narrative contributes towards a hermeneutic that is essentially determinate, treating texts as though they unambiguously refer to the communities and events of significance to them, either as paraenesis or kerygma.

The third chapter, for reasons explained below, examines the use of allusion to Scripture in 1 Peter, likewise exploring the role of the author's theological narrative.

Chapter 4 examines the exegetical background to the use of Scripture in 1 Peter and argues that the author's hermeneutic reflects a sectarian ideology akin to certain Qumran texts which similarly assume a narrative in which the community is given an exclusive status.

The final chapter relates the findings of the study to contemporary debate regarding biblical hermeneutics. It discusses the hermeneutic of 1 Peter as possessing a theologically conceived version of determinate meaning. This is discussed in relation to theological critiques of historical criticism which assume indeterminate meaning as a necessary element of any theological hermeneutic.

---

41. Schutter, *Hermeneutic and Composition*, pp. 19–32 and 32–5.

Chapter 1

1 PETER 1.10-12: A HERMENEUTICAL STATEMENT?

1. 1 Peter 1.10-12 as a Hermeneutical Statement

1 Peter 1.10-12 discusses the nature of prophecy in relation to the death of Jesus and the glory which follows it. It talks of the meaning of the prophetic writings and how they were inspired. It is perhaps surprising, then, that this passage has not been considered to be of more importance in discussing how Peter interprets Scripture. It is notable, for example, that 1.10-12 does not feature in the recent treatment of the use of the Old Testament in 1 Peter by D. A. Carson, nor does it feature in Selwyn and the majority of older commentaries. In contrast, 1 Pet. 1.10-12 is extremely important in Schutter's analysis of the use of Scripture in 1 Peter. For Schutter, the most significant hermeneutical assertion here is that the Scriptures are oriented towards the sufferings and glories of Christ, which he argues is reflected in the actual use of Scripture in 1 Peter. Jobes and Green perhaps come the closest amongst recent commentators, using the phrases 'hermeneutical principle' and 'theological hermeneutic' respectively, in relation to 1.10-12, though Jobes seems to refer simply to the prophet's direction by the 'Spirit of Christ' rather than the other claims made about the Prophets in these verses.[1] This chapter will attempt to offer a detailed study of 1 Pet. 1.10-12 with a view to providing a new understanding of its significance for the use of Scripture in the epistle. Whilst several scholars have considered this passage to be a hermeneutical statement, none have provided an in-depth study of it prior to exploring its relation to Peter's use of Scripture. This chapter

---

1. Jobes, 'Minor Prophets', p. 142, and Green, *1 Peter*, p. 251. Cf. Jobes, *1 Peter*, p. 51; Paul A. Hines, 'Peter and the Prophetic Word: The Theology of Prophecy Traced through Peter's Sermons and Epistles', *BBR* 21 (2011), p. 234; Schlosser, 'Ancien Testament et Christologie'; Bénétreau, 'Évangile et Prophétie'; Joseph, *Narratological Reading of 1 Peter*; J. Herzer, 'Alttestamentliche Prophetie und die Verkündigung des Evangeliums: Beobachtungen zur Stellung und zur hermeneutische Funktion von 1 Petr 1, 10-12', *BThZ* 14 (1997), pp. 14–22.

will attempt to define more closely the theological narrative alluded to in these verses, arguing against many recent assessments that the narrative is one of discontinuity which positions the communities addressed by 1 Peter at the climax of God's eternal plan, enjoying a status which those from the past (including the prophetic authors of Scripture) longed for but failed to find. The Prophets of the past are seen as the servants of the communities in the present. Because of this, Scripture is understood to be exclusively oriented towards Christ and the communities, both as kerygma and paraenesis. Both of these elements are important equally to the hermeneutic of 1.10-12 as to the actual interpretation of specific scriptural texts in 1 Peter. Whilst Schutter's emphasis is upon the importance of the 'kerygmatic' witness of Scripture to the suffering and glories of Christ, it will be argued here that perhaps more significant is the paraenetic function of Scripture in its personal address to the eschatological communities to whom 1 Peter is addressed.

2. Form and Setting of 1 Peter 1.10-12

David W. Kendall makes an impressive case for regarding the opening 'pericope' (1.3-12) of 1 Peter as setting the agenda for the rest of the letter, demonstrating that themes of the opening are developed systematically in 1.13–4.11. Given the efforts Kendall goes to demonstrate the significance of the opening of the letter as laying out the concerns discussed later in the epistle, it is somewhat surprising that 1.10-12 is perceived by him as having little significance beyond its mention of the sufferings of Christ, which he understands to be developed in 2.24-25 and 3.10-17.[2]

This passage occurs within the long introductory period of 1 Peter, before the first paraenetic in 1.13.[3] This introduction takes the form of a

---

2. David W. Kendall, 'The Literary and Theological Function of 1 Peter 1.3-12', in Talbert, ed., *Perspectives on First Peter*, p. 112. Cf. Beare, *Peter*, p. 25, who regards 1.3-12 as a 'comprehensive exordium'. However, in the same volume, Charles H. Talbert, 'Once Again: The Plan of 1 Peter', in Talbert, ed., *Perspectives on First Peter*, p. 142, suggests that 1 Pet. 1.3–2.10 is the introduction to the epistle.

3. There are various views regarding the length of this period. Best, *1 Peter*, p. 78, suggests 1.6 and 1.8 as possible endings, arguing that a doxological period ought to finish with thanksgiving, as in the use of ἀγαλλιᾶσθε in these two verses. J. T. Sanders, 'The Transition from Opening Epistolary Thanksgiving to Body in the Letters of the Pauline Corpus', *JBL* 81 (1962), p. 357, concludes that the period proper finishes in 1.12, though a subsidiary eulogaic period finishes in 1.7. Cf. Hans Windisch, *Die Katholischen Briefe* (HNT 4/2; Tübingen: Mohr Siebeck, 1911), pp. 46 and 51–2, for structure of the period.

long doxology or salutation, beginning at 1.3, praising God for the heavenly inheritance he has provided for his people through the resurrection of Jesus Christ. Within the context of this inheritance, Peter introduces the theme of his audiences' suffering, a significant theme of the epistle in general.[4] Suffering is explained as something which refines faith and results in glory and honour at Jesus' Parousia. Though Jesus has not yet been revealed visually to the audiences of the epistle, they are praised for their love of him and trust in him, through which they are currently receiving salvation. It is this salvation which is further defined in 1.10-12 from a somewhat salvation-historical perspective. The free-flowing, associative introduction is designed to encourage Peter's audiences by presenting something of the significance of their privileged position as followers Jesus Christ. Whilst 1.3-9 explores the future significance of what these scattered audiences have gained through their faith, 1.10-12 explores these gains from the perspective of the past. Peter's audiences are prompted to see something of the majesty of their salvation through the extent to which the Prophets looked forward to the time of Christ and the glory known by his followers. This historical perspective on the suffering and achievements of Christ is of significance to an attempt to understand how 1 Peter employs and interprets Scripture. The idea that the Prophets' writings or utterances referred not to their own times but to one time or circumstance in particular represents something of a Petrine theory of Scripture. Subsequent interpretation of Scripture in the epistle broadly follows this tendency to view Scripture as something written to serve followers of Jesus Christ and to speak of him. Michaels describes 1.10-12 as a chiasm as follows:

Introduction	Περὶ ἧς σωτηρίας
A	ἐξεζήτησαν καὶ ἐξηραύνησαν προφῆται οἱ περὶ τῆς εἰς ὑμᾶς χάριτος προφητεύσαντες,
B	ἐραυνῶντες εἰς τίνα ἢ ποῖον καιρὸν ἐδήλου τὸ ἐν αὐτοῖς πνεῦμα Χριστοῦ προμαρτυρόμενον τὰ εἰς Χριστὸν παθήματα καὶ τὰς μετὰ ταῦτα δόξας.
A¹	Οἷς ἀπεκαλύφθη ὅτι οὐχ ἑαυτοῖς ὑμῖν δὲ διηκόνουν αὐτά, ἃ νῦν ἀνηγγέλη ὑμῖν διὰ τῶν εὐαγγελισαμένων ὑμᾶς ἐν πνεύματι ἁγίῳ ἀποσταλέντι ἀπ'οὐρανοῦ, εἰς ἃ ἐπιθυμοῦσιν ἄγγελοι παρακύψαι.

---

4. J. N. D. Kelly, *A Commentary on the Epistles of Peter and of Jude* (London: A. & C. Black, 1969), pp. 5–11, accords priority to suffering, suggesting that it is the dominant theme of 1 Peter.

A is dominated by the use of aorist verbs, as is A¹, which also addresses and answers the 'searching' of the Prophets in A with a divine revelation. B is dominated by participles and imperfect verbs.⁵ The passage as a whole is loosely midrashic, reflecting upon various unidentified traditions. In this respect it is akin to the historical glosses of Wis. 10.1–11.1 and Heb. 11.35-38, which both allude to events in so vague a manner as to allow readers to imagine a variety of events to which the author could be referring.⁶

3. Commentary on 1.10-12

a. Verse 1.10

Περὶ ἧς σωτηρίας. The relative pronoun in this clause indicates a continuation from 1.9, which features salvation as the τέλος τῆς πίστεως ὑμῶν.⁷ The following verses are seen to define something of the nature of this salvation.⁸

ἐξεζήτησαν καὶ ἐξηραύνησαν προφῆται οἱ περὶ τῆς εἰς ὑμᾶς χάριτος προφητεύσαντες. The two aorist verbs here imply a determined and wholehearted quest and are used together in 1 Macc. 9.26 to describe the search for Judas' friends as well as in OG Ps. 119.2, though, as Achtemeier points out, it is unlikely that these two terms are intended to allude to 1 Macc. 9.26.⁹ In addition to this, the similarity of the terms is

---

5. Michaels, *1 Peter*, p. 39.
6. Michaels, *1 Peter*, p. 40.
7. The argument of Gerhard Dautzenberg, 'Σωτηρία ψυχῶν (1 Petr 1, 9)', *BZ* 8 (1964), pp. 262–76, that this salvation is eschatological and essentially future is problematic in the light of what follows. Given that this salvation is portrayed as equivalent to the subject of the prophetic witness in 1 Pet. 1.10, the more nuanced view of Selwyn, *Peter*, pp. 132–3, in which salvation in 1.9 is regarded as both present and future, is to be preferred. Cf. Karl Hermann Schelkle, *Die Petrusbriefe, Der Judasbrief* (HThKNT, 13; Freiburg: Herder, 1961), p. 38.
8. Indeed, Michaels, *1 Peter*, p. 38, describes this clause as a 'heading' for 1 Pet. 1.10-12. Cf. Elliott, *Commentary*, p. 345.
9. Achtemeier, *1 Peter*, p. 108. Cf. Beare, *Peter*, p. 90, Schelkle, *Petrusbriefe*, p. 39 n. 2, and Schutter, *Hermeneutic and Composition*, p. 41, who regards the use of these terms in 1 Macc. 9.26 as 'profane and spatial' in contrast to 'esoteric and cognitive' use in 1 Pet. 1.10. Goppelt, *Erste Petrusbrief*, p. 108 n. 81, suggests a parallel with 1QS 5.11 (כיא לוא החשבו בבריתו כיא לוא בקשו ולוא דרשהו בחוקוהי לדעת הנסתרות אשר תעו), which A. R. C. Leaney, *The Rule of Qumran and its Meaning: Introduction, Translation and Commentary* (London: SCM, 1966), p. 172, identifies as an allusion to Zeph. 1.6. However, as Schutter, *Hermeneutic and Composition*, p. 101, notes, the OG forms of Zeph. 1.6 differ too much from 1 Pet. 1.10 to be worth considering as the potential subject of an allusion.

often noted, as is the rhetorical function of that similarity and the use of assonance here.¹⁰ The use of ἐξεζήτησαν is well-attested in the OG Scriptures (Deut. 4.29; Hab. 2.1; 2 Esd. 4.51) and is also used in Lk. 11.50. 1 Peter 1.10 represents the only use of the verb ἐξηραύνησαν in the New Testament. The object of the verb may be what is searched for or the place that is searched (1 Sam. 23.23; Prov. 2.4; Judg. 17.2; Ps. 119.69).¹¹

The referent of προφῆται has been the subject of quite some discussion. The traditional and dominant view is that the term refers to the Prophets of the Hebrew Scripture who searched for the full meaning of their own prophetic utterances. This interpretation typically views 1 Pet. 1.10 as similar to Mt. 13.17 (whose aorist verbs place the activity of the πολλοὶ προφῆται καὶ δίκαιοι firmly in the past) and the very similar Lk. 10.24, as well as Jn 8.5b, 12.41, Heb. 11.13 and certain Pauline texts.¹² In addition to this, the understanding that the Prophets of Israel's past searched Scripture can be seen in 1QS 5.11: כיא לוא החשבו בבריתו כיא לוא בקשו ולוא דרשהו בחוקוהי לדעת לדעת הנסתרות אשר תעו. Likewise, something of the Prophets' ignorance of the precise time of the

---

10. Selwyn, *Peter*, p. 133, regards the use of these terms as an allusion. However, given the essentially negative purpose of the 'search' in 1 Macc. 9, this is unlikely. On the rhetorical value of these synonymous terms, see Michaels, *1 Peter*, p. 40; Achtemeier, *1 Peter*, p. 108, and David Horrell, *The Epistles of Peter and Jude* (Peterborough: Epworth, 1998), p. 28. On assonance, see Elliott, *Commentary*, p. 345.

11. Michaels, *1 Peter*, p. 40 notes that forms of the verb are used in Jn 5.39 (ἐραυνᾶτε τὰς γραφάς) and 7.52 (ἐραύνησον) to refer to searching in a written text of Scripture but suggests that that is not the meaning here.

12. See, e.g., Hort, *St. Peter*, pp. 49–50; Charles Bigg, *A Critical and Exegetical Commentary on the Epistles of St. Peter and St. Jude* (Edinburgh: T. & T. Clark, 1902), pp. 3 and 108; C. E. B. Cranfield, *The First Epistle of Peter* (London: SCM, 1950), p. 28. The most substantial differences between Mt. 13.17 and Lk. 10.24 are the Lukan use of βασιλεῖς in place of Matthew's δίκαιοι and the use of ἠθέλησαν in place of ἐπεθύμησαν, though, of course, it is impossible to say who is doing what to the common Q material. Interestingly, the Matthean text in D reads...ἐπεθύμησαν ἰδεῖν ἃ βλέπετε καὶ οὐκ ἠδυνήθησαν ἰδεῖν, which, perhaps, enhances the sense in which the Prophets and righteous ones are cut off from the events which Jesus refers to because of their situation in the past. John Nolland, *The Gospel of Matthew: A Commentary on the Greek Text* (NIGTC; Grand Rapids: Eerdmans; Bletchley: Paternoster, 2005), pp. 537–8, notes that this idea of Scripture as 'forward-looking' is important in Matthew with its emphasis upon fulfilment. Nolland notes an interesting comparison between the pericope and *Pss. Sol.* 17.50 and 1 Pet. 1.10-12.

Best, *1 Peter*, pp. 80–1, compares Peter's assumption that the Prophets wrote for the benefit of a later generation (seen particularly in 1 Pet. 1.12) with Rom. 4.23; 15.4; 1 Cor. 9.10; 10.11.

fulfilment of their own prophecies can be seen in 1QpHab 7.1-8, a text frequently compared to 1 Pet. 1.10-12. However, Selwyn famously argues that the term refers to Christian prophets living and ministering contemporaneously with 1 Peter, largely due to the description offered of their ministry in this verse.[13] He suggests that the verb ἐξηραύνησαν corresponds more closely with early Christian 'searching' of the Scriptures than earlier conceptions of the Prophets' function, since the use of the term in Jn 5.39 and 7.52 implies the searching of texts already written. However, this interpretation has been broadly rejected in more recent scholarship.[14] J. N. D. Kelly argues that it is unlikely that προφῆται refers to Christian prophets since their work appears to be firmly associated with the past, as noted above.[15] Bauckham supports this position, arguing that προφῆται ought to be understood to refer to Old Testament figures other than those typically described as such, noting that David is referred to as a prophet in Acts 2.30.[16] This observation, if truly applicable to 1 Peter, is of some importance given the widespread use of the Psalter in 1 Peter.

---

13. Selwyn, *Peter*, pp. 134–5. Schutter, *Hermeneutic and Composition*, p. 103 suggests that this view (which he rejects) is not particularly problematic for an understanding of 1 Pet. 1.10-12 as a hermeneutical statement, claiming that Peter could be seen to understand the writings of the Christian prophets as equivalent to those to which he refers from the Scriptures.

14. Achtemeier, *1 Peter*, p. 108, notes that the use of ἐξεραυνᾶν in OG Ps. 119.2 implies searching *for* the testimonies of the Lord, rather than searching *within* them. Selwyn's view is also taken by Julian Price Love, 'The First Epistle of Peter', *Int* 8 (1954), p. 69; Duane Watson, 'The Prophets of 1 Peter 1.10-12', *RestQ* 31 (1989), pp. 5–6 and J. D. G. Dunn, *Unity and Diversity in the New Testament: An Enquiry into the Character of Earliest Christianity* (London: SCM, 1977), p. 116.

15. Kelly, *Peter*, p. 59, and Elliott, *Commentary*, p. 345. Cf. Best, *1 Peter*, pp. 83–4, who notes that νῦν in 1.12 emphasises this chronological distinction. Moreover, the habits of 'searching' and 'inquiring' do not seem to relate to prophets described in the New Testament in Acts 11.28; 21.10; Rev. 1.3 and 22.18, any more than they relate to descriptions of prophetic activity in the Scriptures of Israel.

16. Bauckham, 'James, 1 and 2 Peter, Jude', p. 310. Interestingly, Bauckham describes 1 Pet. 1.10-12, here, as 'a fine statement of the early Christian view of the OT'. On the early tradition of regarding David as a prophet, see 11QPsa 27.11, *Tg. Ps.* 49.16, *Ep. Barn.* 12.10 and Josephus, *Ant.* 6.8.2, and in the secondary literature, Joseph Fitzmyer, 'David, "Being therefore a Prophet…" (Acts 2.30)', *CBQ* 34 (1972), pp. 332–39 (332); Peter W. Flint, 'The Prophet David at Qumran', in *Biblical Interpretation at Qumran* (ed. Matthias Henze; Grand Rapids: Eerdmans, 2005), pp. 165–6.

b. Verse 11

ἐραυνῶντες εἰς τίνα ἢ ποῖον καιρὸν. The meaning of τίνα in v. 11 has attracted considerable attention, since it is unclear whether it functions as an interrogative pronoun or an interrogative adjective. Notably, several scholars suggest that the term refers here to an unspecified person as well as a time, reading the term as a pronoun and translating 'what person and what time'.[17] However, G. D. Kilpatrick suggests instead that τίνα functions adjectivally, modifying καιρὸν, thus translating 'which or what manner of time'.[18] The use of καιρός here is utterly consistent with its eschatological character elsewhere in the New Testament and Jewish apocalyptic, referring to a decisive point of fulfilment or exposure. This might suggest that the latter, adjectival, view is most plausible, since eschatological interest in apocalyptic literature is primarily oriented towards a complex series of events, rather than a single person.[19] What is evident from this clause is that the prophetic utterances, writings or oracles referred to something unclear which was unclear to the Prophets themselves.[20] Their meaning had to be sought with some effort. This notion is certainly in agreement with post-exilic assumptions about the

---

17. Best, *1 Peter*, p. 81, and Elliott, *Commentary*, p. 345. Cf. Acts 8.34, which uses τίς substantively, as suggested here.

18. G. D. Kilpatrick, '1 Peter 1.11: ΤΙΝΑ 'Η ΠΟΙΟΝ ΚΑΙΡΟΝ', *NovT* 28 (1986), pp. 91–2. This interpretation is taken by Moyise, 'Isaiah in 1 Peter', p. 187; Goppelt, *Erste Petrusbrief*, p. 107; Michaels, *1 Peter*, p. 41, and Achtemeier, *1 Peter*, p. 109.

19. Hort, *St Peter*, p. 51 lists similar New Testament uses as follows: Mt. 16.3; Mk 1.15; 8.33; Lk. 12.56; 21.8, 24; Acts 1.7; 3.19; 17.26; Eph. 1.10; 1 Thess. 5.1; 1 Tim. 6.15; Titus 1.3; Heb. 9.10; Rev. 1.3; 11.18; and 22.10. Cf. Gerhard Delling, 'καιρός', *TDNT*, vol. 3, pp. 455–62 who notes that the term typically has this eschatological sense in the New Testament. Michaels, *1 Peter*, p. 41, agrees with Hort and translates the passage 'what or what kind of time'. Furthermore, he notes that the interest not only in time of fulfilment but also the nature of fulfilment is a feature of Jewish apocalyptic, as in Dan. 12.5-13; *4 Ezra* 4.33, 45; Hab. 2.1-4; and 1QpHab 7.1-8. This is supported by Jobes, *1 Peter*, p. 102, and Achtemeier, *1 Peter*, p. 109.

20. Schelkle, *Petrusbriefe*, p. 39; John H. Elliott, *A Home for the Homeless: A Social-Scientific Criticism of 1 Peter, Its Situation and Strategy* (Eugene, Ore.: Wipf & Stock, 2005), p. 156 n. 74; Kelly, *Peter*, p. 59; Boring, *1 Peter*, p. 66; Jobes, *1 Peter*, pp. 97–8; Reinhard Feldmeier, *The First Letter of Peter: A Commentary on the Greek Text* (trans. Peter H. Davids; Waco: Baylor University Press, 2008), p. 94; Best, *1 Peter*, p. 80 (who relates the quest of the Prophets here to Dan. 12.6-13); Norman Hillyer, *1 and 2 Peter, Jude* (Peabody: Hendrickson, 1992), p. 39. Green, *1 Peter*, p. 31, argues that the Prophets are not regarded as completely ignorant since at least the idea that their utterances were 'forward-looking' was made known to them.

nature of prophecy in Dan. 9; 12.4-13; 2 Esd. 4.33–5.15; *4 Ezra* 4.33-52 and 1QpHab 7.1-8. These texts suggest that the assumption, made by Peter, that the Prophets looked to events in the future for which they searched fervently, was a significant feature of Palestinian Jewish apocalyptic.[21] It will be argued below in Chapter 4, that this cultural milieu is of some importance in explaining the nature of the use of Scripture in 1 Peter.

ἐδήλου τὸ ἐν αὐτοῖς πνεῦμα Χριστοῦ προμαρτυρόμενον τὰ εἰς Χριστὸν παθήματα καὶ τὰς μετὰ ταῦτα δόξας. There are at least three significant complexities in this clause which have attracted considerable scholarly attention. Firstly, it is unclear what the object of the verb ἐδήλου is: either the phrase τίνα ἢ ποῖον καιρὸν or τὰ εἰς Χριστὸν παθήματα καὶ τὰς μετὰ ταῦτα δόξας, which is also the object of προμαρτυρόμενον. The verb itself is unusual. Ἐδήλου is used in connection with the work of the Holy Spirit in Heb. 9.8 and as part of the explanation of Hab. 2.6 in Heb. 12.27.[22] The former view is preferred by Achtemeier, who suggests that the Spirit of Christ's revelatory activity is meant to be understood as a counterpart to the searching activity of the Prophets.[23] However, Michaels argues that since the verb is imperfect it is most likely to refer to τὰ εἰς Χριστὸν παθήματα καὶ τὰς μετὰ ταῦτα δόξας, since that represents the incompleteness of the action as the Prophets experienced it, whereas the activity of the Prophets themselves is firmly in the past, indicated by the aorists.[24]

The second significant complexity in this clause is the precise meaning of πνεῦμα Χριστοῦ. The notion of the Spirit of Christ inspiring the words of the Prophets is certainly unusual in the New Testament, though it has many parallels in other early Christian writings as well as in Jewish apocalyptic (*Ep. Barn.* 5; *2 Clem.* 17.4; Ignatius, *Mag.* 8.2; Justin, *Apol.* 1.31-33; *Dial.* 56; Irenaeus, *Ad. Haer.* 4.20.4; Hermas, *Sim.* 9.12).[25] The

---

21. Indeed, as Achtemeier, *1 Peter*, p. 108, suggests, it is a widespread assumption in the New Testament generally, one implied on most occasions in which Scripture is cited in support of a statement in the New Testament. Cf. Dautzenberg, 'Σωτηρία ψυχῶν', pp. 266–7, and Schutter, *Hermeneutic and Composition*, p. 102, who notes the particular importance of ascertaining knowledge of an eschatological secret in such literature.

22. Moyise, 'Isaiah in 1 Peter', p. 186, suggests that this latter use established the term as exegetical, as it is in 1 Peter.

23. Achtemeier, *1 Peter*, p. 109.

24. Michaels, *1 Peter*, pp. 41 and 43.

25. Achtemeier, *1 Peter*, p. 106, notes that the concept of a revealing spirit or supernatural source of information is common, along with pseudonymity in Jewish apocalyptic. Cf. John J. Collins, 'Introduction: Towards the Morphology of a Genre', in *Apocalypse: The Morphology of a Genre* (ed. John J. Collins; Semeia 14; Missoula:

principal discussion here relates to whether the Spirit of Christ is synonymous with the Holy Spirit or whether it represents some sort of pre-incarnate activity of Christ as originally argued for by Anthony Tyrrell Hanson.[26] Best suggests that it is synonymous with the Holy Spirit, noting that in Rom. 8.9 the 'Spirit of God', the 'Spirit of Christ' and the 'Spirit' appear to be used to refer to the same Spirit.[27] Other scholars have followed Hanson.[28] In favour of the option of synonymity, it must be noted that the Holy Spirit is accorded a similar revelatory purpose in 1 Pet. 1.12, if indeed the dative here is to be understood instrumentally.[29] It may be unlikely that the same role is attributed to two distinct spirits, suggesting instead synonymy. The notion of the Spirit of Christ provides an important argument in favour of Selwyn's view that the Prophets referred to here are Christian, insofar as it is the Spirit of Christ which inspires them, suggesting to Selwyn that this activity must

---

Scholars Press, 1979), pp. 6–8, and Geert W. Lorein, 'The Holy Spirit at Qumran', in *Presence, Power and Promise: The Role of the Spirit of God in the Old Testament* (ed. David G. Firth and Paul D. Wegner; Nottingham: Apollos, 2011), pp. 371–95.

26. Anhony Tyrrell Hanson, *The Living Utterances of God: The New Testament Exegesis of the Old* (London: DLT, 1983), p. 141. The alternative suggestion of Beare, *Peter*, p. 192, that πνεῦμα Χριστοῦ refers to the spirit received by Christ in his baptism has attracted little support, nor has a possible view mentioned by Schutter, *Hermeneutic and Composition*, p. 104, that it refers to 'some spirit or other whose task is to testify to Christ'.

27. Best, *1 Peter*, p. 81 (Rom. 8.9 – ὑμεῖς δὲ οὐκ ἐστὲ ἐν σαρκὶ ἀλλὰ ἐν πνεύματι, εἴπερ πνεῦμα θεοῦ οἰκεῖ ἐν ὑμῖν. Εἰ δέ τις πνεῦμα Χριστοῦ οὐκ ἔχει, οὗτος οὐκ ἔστιν αὐτοῦ). Cf. Beare, *Peter*, p. 92. A significant difficulty with this argument is the paucity of uses of 'Holy Spirit' in relation to the Old Testament Prophets, which typically favour (as Daniel I. Block, 'The View from the Top: The Holy Spirit in the Prophets', in Firth and Wegner, eds., *Presence, Power and Promise*, pp. 175–6, points out) רוח יהוה (Isa. 11.2; 40.13; 61.1; 63.14; Ezek. 11.5; 37.1; Mic. 3.8), רוח אלוהים (Ezek. 11.24) or simply variously suffixed forms of רוח (Isa. 30.11; Joel 3.1; Zech. 4.6; 7.12).

28. Boring, *1 Peter*, p. 66, argues that the 'Spirit of Christ' here refers to Christ himself as an eternal being, associated with God's activity in the past in the New Testament in 1 Cor. 10.4. Cf. Windisch, *Katholischen Briefe*, p. 51; Horrell, *Peter and Jude*, p. 29; Achtemeier, *1 Peter*, p. 109, and Jobes, *1 Peter*, p. 101. The principal piece of evidence for this interpretation is the idea of Christ's pre-existence indicated in 1 Pet. 1.20 – προεγνωσμένου μὲν πρὸ καταβολῆς κόσμου φανερωθέντος δὲ ἐπ' ἐσχάτου τῶν χρόνων. As Michaels, *1 Peter*, p. 38, notes, B omits 'Christ' here, possibly because it implies pre-existence. Cf. Elliott, *Commentary*, p. 346.

29. Michaels, *1 Peter*, p. 47, regards this as an associative dative, suggesting that the Holy Spirit makes possible the proclamation, rather than providing the exclusive source of revelation. Cf. Achtemeier, *1 Peter*, p. 112, who suggests that no clear distinction can be drawn here.

take place after the death of Christ.³⁰ However, though it is certainly an unusual term,³¹ προμαρτυρόμενον implies inspiration prior to 'the sufferings of Christ and the glories after'.³² Yet the meaning of this latter phrase has proven problematic, largely due to the preposition εἰς, but perhaps also because so little is known of the verb itself.

The use of εἰς is the third significant area of discussion in this clause: how does one understand a phrase most simply translated as 'the sufferings *for* Christ'. Perhaps the majority of commentators regard the phrase προμαρτυρόμενον τὰ εἰς Χριστὸν παθήματα as referring to the sufferings Christ himself suffered. There is good reason for this interpretation. The belief that Christ's sufferings are predicted by the Prophets is reasonably well attested in other New Testament literature (Lk. 24.25-27; Acts 3.18; 1 Cor. 15.3). In addition to this, the sequence of Christ's sufferings and subsequent glory found in 1 Pet. 1.11 is also seen in Lk. 24.26, Phil. 2.9-12 and Heb. 2.9. At the very least, it can be said that if 1 Pet. 1.11 refers to the sufferings experienced by Christ himself, it is saying nothing unusual. Yet εἰς is still problematic, suggesting the meaning 'for'. Hort favoured 'destined for the Messiah', and this position has also been taken by Kelly, Best, Michaels, Hillyer, Elliott, Feldmeier, Jobes and others, and perhaps represents the dominant view.³³ Jobes, for example, notes that a similar use of εἰς is found in 2 Cor. 1.1 and 11.3. In addition to this, the phrase εἰς Χριστὸν appears to parallel εἰς ὑμᾶς in v. 10, which more easily bears the meaning 'destined for'.³⁴ However, some commentators

30. Selwyn, *St Peter*, pp. 135–6.
31. This is the only example of its use in the New Testament. F. J. A. Hort, *The First Epistle of St Peter* (London: Macmillan, 1898), p. 53, notes that the earliest extant use of the term is in Theodorus Metochita and suggests that its meaning is similar to that of μαρτύρομαι in Josephus, *War* 3.8.3; Acts 20.26, and Gal. 5.3: to 'declare'. For such a short work, 1 Peter contains an unusual number of *hapax legomena*, many of which are related to its use of OG Scripture. Indeed, 34 or 35 of the 61 *hapax legomena* in 1 Peter can be found in OG texts of Scripture. Yet, as Elliott, *Commentary*, p. 63, argues, many of these also relate to the particular semantic fields employed in 1 Peter, such as hostility, alienation and conduct.
32. Achtemeier, *1 Peter*, p. 108. In addition to this, as Best, *1 Peter*, p. 80, notes, the use of ὑμᾶς in 1.10 draws a distinction between the Prophets and the communities to which the epistle is addressed.
33. Hort, *St Peter*, p. 54; Kelly, *Peter*, p. 60; Best, *1 Peter*, p. 81 (who suggests that this expression betrays the manner in which Christians regarded the death of Christ as predestined with hindsight); Michaels, *1 Peter*, p. 44; Elliott, *Commentary*, p. 348; Jobes, *1 Peter*, pp. 99–100; Hillyer, *1 and 2 Peter*, p. 42, and Feldmeier, *Letter of Peter*, p. 94.
34. Beare, *Peter*, p. 91; Michaels, *1 Peter*, p. 44, and Achtemeier, *1 Peter*, p. 108. Cf. *de Vita Mos* 2.188 (ἀφικνοῦνται δ' εἰς σταθμὸν δεύτερον).

read the phrase as subjective: referring to the sufferings of believers on account of Christ. These include Selwyn, Cross and Boring. Selwyn's suggestion that Χριστὸν παθήματα refers to the Christian experience of suffering as a consequence of Christian discipleship (in a manner similar to a common 'Messianic Woes' interpretation of τῶν θλίψεων τοῦ Χριστοῦ in Col. 1.24[35]) is difficult to appreciate given his own particular view of the prophets as first-century Christians. It seems rather odd to imagine such prophets within the communities themselves, predicting sufferings which are apparently an expected consequence of Christian discipleship (familiar enough to be referred to simply as Χριστὸν παθήματα), yet about which the Prophets themselves are ignorant. A similar interpretation of Χριστὸν παθήματα as a consequence of 'mystic union' with Christ is offered by F. L. Cross.[36] Likewise, Boring relates the phrase to the experience of the communities' sufferings on account of Christ. In a particularly impressive argument, Boring lists nine factors in support of this position.[37] He notes that in Acts 3.24 prophets are regarded as predicting the sufferings of Christians, that grace and suffering in 1 Pet. 1.11 could be parallel aspects of the Christian experience (rather than references to an event in the life of Christ and its significance as grace) and that the general context of 1 Pet. 1.3-12 is the experience of the communities. In addition to this, the idea that the 'Spirit of Christ' (understood as the pre-incarnate Christ) would predict his own sufferings is awkward, the construction τοῦ Χριστοῦ is used in 1 Pet. 4.13 to refer to the suffering experienced on behalf of Christ and of

---

35. An interpretation featuring the 'Messianic Woes'. This reading is taken by Richard J. Bauckham, 'Colossians 1.24 Again: The Apocalyptic Note', *EvQ* 47 (1975), p. 170; Eduard Lohse, *Colossians and Philemon* (trans. William Poehlmann and Robert J. Karris; Philadelphia: Fortress, 1971), p. 70, and James D. G. Dunn, *The Epistles to the Colossians and to Philemon* (Grand Rapids: Eerdmans, 1996), p. 115. Cf. Andrew Perriman, 'The Pattern of Christ's Sufferings: Colossians 1.24 and Philippians 3.10-11', *TynBul* 42 (1991), pp. 62–9 (63). A rather persuasive 'mimetic' alternative is offered by Jerry L. Sumney, '"I fill up what is lacking in the afflictions of Christ": Paul's Vicarious Suffering in Colossians', *CBQ* 68 (2006), pp. 664–70.

36. F. L. Cross, *1 Peter: A Pascal Liturgy* (London: Mowbray, 1954), p. 22, who regards 'suffering' as 'a sort of Ariadne thread for [Peter's] whole work' (p. 14), sees this phrase as example of the priority of suffering in the epistle, suggestive of its original *Sitz im Leben* as a paschal liturgy. However, as T. C. G. Thornton, '1 Peter: A Paschal Liturgy?', *JTS* 12 (1961), pp. 16–17, shows, these terms do not appear to have a paschal connection prior to Melito of Sardis. Cf. Mbuvi, *Temple, Exile and Identity*, p. 135.

37. Boring, *1 Peter*, pp. 67–8, and Elliott, *Home for the Homeless*, p. 137.

the 42 times εἰς is used in 1 Peter, at least 16 rather unambiguously mean 'for'. Furthermore, the pattern of suffering before glory does not simply refer to Jesus in 1 Peter: in 1.7 and 4.14 the communities' suffering is seen to lead to glory. The time contrast in which the Prophets of the past speak about the present does not function if the Prophets are understood to refer to the experience of Christ, which is also in the past, and the plural term δόξας makes more sense in association with the sufferings of Christians rather than the single figure, Christ. Some of these arguments represent more of an obstacle to the view that Χριστὸν παθήματα refers to sufferings experienced by Christ than others. The use of the plural δόξας is explained by Best as referring to the succession of events following Jesus' death: his resurrection, ascension, session and return, each of which could be described as 'glorious'.[38] As Achtemeier notes, τὰ εἰς Χριστὸν παθήματα καὶ τὰς μετὰ ταῦτα δόξας are by implication portrayed as the content of the proclaimed 'good news' in 1.12.[39] This makes it more likely that they refer to the experience of Christ himself, rather than that of his followers.

The meaning of τὰ εἰς Χριστὸν παθήματα καὶ τὰς μετὰ ταῦτα δόξας is of considerable significance to any discussion of the use of Scripture in 1 Peter. As will be noted below, the practical use of Scripture in the epistle appears to fall into two distinct types: kerygmatic and paraenetic. If the focus of the Prophets in 1.11 is the experience of Christians, rather than the events in the ministry of Jesus Christ, then this 'hermeneutical statement' gives support to the paraenetic type alone. It might be concluded that, according to 1 Pet. 1.10-12, Peter understands Scripture to be focused principally on the challenges faced by the communities, as they encounter the 'messianic woes', rather than offering descriptive teaching about Christ and his significance. Since it is clear from the 'Stone Catena' in 1 Pet. 2.6-8 that Scripture is used for a kerygmatic purpose (even though this teaching is within the context of a broader paraenesis), an exclusively paraenetic focus in 1.10-12 would suggest that there is less of a relation between this passage and the interpretation of Scripture in the epistle as a whole.

---

38. Best, *1 Peter*, p. 81, and Beare, *Peter*, p. 92, who notes that Christ' suffering and glory are often held together in the New Testament, as in Lk. 24.25-27; Acts 17.3, and 1 Cor. 15.3 and 4. Cf. Achtemeier, *1 Peter*, p. 109, and Michaels, *1 Peter*, p. 45, who regards the term as equivalent to the use of τὰς ἀρετάς in 1 Pet. 2.9.

39. Paul J. Achtemeier, 'Suffering Servant and Suffering Christ in 1 Peter', in *The Future of Christology: Essays in Honor of Leander E. Keck* (ed. A. J. Malherbe and W. A. Meeks; Minneapolis: Fortress, 1993), p. 183.

c. Verse 12

Οἷς ἀπεκαλύφθη ὅτι οὐχ ἑαυτοῖς ὑμῖν δὲ διηκόνουν αὐτά. If there was any doubt that the Prophets did not belong to a different period of time from the initial audiences of 1 Peter, this clause appears to assert just such an historical separation, especially as the subsequent clause begins with a contrasting νῦν.[40] The Prophets served not themselves by their utterances about the sufferings of Christ and the glories after but a later generation: the dispersed disciples of Jesus.[41] As Goppelt notes, whilst there appears to have been a tradition of regarding the Prophets as in some way ignorant of the details regarding the fulfillment of their messages (see the comment on 1.10), the notion that the Prophets spoke to *serve* a later generation represents a distinctive contribution made by 1 Peter.[42] Goppelt tentatively suggests that the origin of this notion might be Dan. 9.2, 22-27 and 12.6-13 in which the prophetic referent is understood to be in the future, though these texts do not feature an idea of prophetic service. In addition to this apparent innovation, whilst the notion that the Scriptures were written for the benefit of later readers is well attested in St Paul, this idea that the Prophets spoke *only* for the later generation is unprecedented.[43] It is argued below that this principle is put into practice as Peter applies Scripture in the epistle as though it were written precisely for the benefit of the communities.[44] For Peter, the Prophets yearned for the unknown climax of history. The work of Jesus Christ, his message and the community of his followers represent something so significant that those who lived before it longed for it. They are things which even angels long to know more of. This view of history as climaxing with the

---

40. Beare, *Peter*, p. 94. Cf. Cross, *Paschal Liturgy*, p. 30, who argues that νῦν in 1.12, along with other instances in 2.10, 25 and 3.21, indicates that a paschal rite is now in progress. Cf. Mbuvi, *Temple, Exile and Identity*, pp. 131–2.

41. As Kazuhito Shimada, 'A Critical Note on 1 Peter 1, 12', *AJBI* 7 (1981), pp. 146–50, points out, αὐτά in this verse is the antecedent of ἅ in each case in the remainder of the verse and refers back to τὰ εἰς Χριστὸν παθήματα καὶ τὰς μετὰ ταῦτα δόξας in v. 11. Cf. Feldmeier, *Letter of Peter*, p. 94.

42. Goppelt, *Erste Petrusbrief*, p. 107. Cf. Elliott, *Home for the Homeless*, p. 120, who suggests that the contrast drawn here between the Prophets and the communities serves to construct the sectarian ideology of 1 Peter.

43. Elliott, *Commentary*, p. 352. The term διηκόνουν with the accusative as here, is unusual. Where it occurs in *Ant.* 6.298 it refers to the delivery of a message. Michaels, *1 Peter*, p. 46, suggests that the same meaning is meant here.

44. Moyise, 'Isaiah in 1 Peter', p. 186, makes this point, arguing that the use of Isaiah in 1 Peter agrees with the principle that the Prophets were 'serving not themselves but you', though he suggests that the use of Isaiah goes beyond the principle that the Prophets spoke of 'the sufferings destined for Christ and the glories after' (against Schutter, *Hermeneutic and Composition*, p. 144).

message and people of the Gospel provides Peter's essential framework for interpreting Scripture. This focus on the present generation receiving 'salvation' is expressed rather wonderfully by Karl Hermann Schelkle:

> Von allen Geschöpfen wird deises Heil ersehnt. Die Alten haben es erwartet. Die Propheten haben von ihm geweissagt. Die Engel begehren, es zu sehen. Die jetzige Generation aber ist die gesegnete, der es im Heiligen Geist verkündet wird.[45]

Because the Prophets 'served not themselves but us', Scripture is viewed by Peter as primarily describing things of importance to the early Church: typically, either the Church itself or the significance of Jesus Christ. As Best notes, the Prophets are regarded here as 'ministers to the church' and the Scriptures they wrote are 'subordinated...to the life of the church'.[46] This description of the Prophets as essentially lacking in some respect, compared to what the community know and have experienced, may explain why the author fails to identify himself using the prophetic language found in James, 2 Peter and Jude.[47]

ἃ νῦν ἀνηγγέλη ὑμῖν διὰ τῶν εὐαγγελισαμένων ὑμᾶς ἐν πνεύματι ἁγίῳ ἀποσταλέντι ἀπ'οὐρανοῦ. The community which the Prophets served as they spoke is one which has heard a message of good news. The message proclaimed as good news is of the utmost importance, defining the community in the present that the Prophets served.[48] The description of

---

45. Schelkle, *Petrusbriefe*, p. 38. Cf. J. de Waal Dryden, *Theology and Ethics in 1 Peter: Paraenetic Strategies for Christian Character Formation* (Tübingen: Mohr Siebeck, 2006), p. 80; Cranfield, *Peter*, pp. 28–9; Horrell, *Peter and Jude*, p. 29; Feldmeier, *Letter of Peter*, p. 93, and Boring, *1 Peter*, p. 65, who writes 'The author of 1 Peter concludes the thanksgiving by portraying the eschatological existence of Christian believers who live in the climactic time of God's plan for history as the envy of both the biblical prophets and the angels'. Also Reicke, *Peter*, p. 81, who describes the communities as occupying an 'exceptionally favoured position'.

46. Best, *1 Peter*, p. 82.

47. Jobes, 'Minor Prophets', pp. 135–6, suggests that the authorial designation as δοῦλος Ἰησοῦ Χριστοῦ in various forms in Jas 1.1; 2 Pet. 1.1, and Jude 1 (but not in 1 Pet. 1.1, which uses ἀπόστολος Ἰησοῦ Χριστοῦ, and also lacks the 'prophetic tone, language and images of judgement' found in the former) represents an attempt to identify with the prophetic role in the Scriptures. She suggests that this identification exists because these writers address their audiences 'as if they were a reconstituted Israel' whereas 1 Peter is concerned with the issue of how Christian communities are to relate to the rest of society. However, there is significant evidence to suggest that 1 Peter, too, sees its audiences as 'reconstituted Israel', particularly in 2.9-10.

48. Torrey Seland, 'Resident Aliens in Mission: Missional Practices in the Emerging Church of 1 Peter', *BBR* 19 (2009), pp. 565–89 (580), argues that this reference to the manner in which the communities came into being serves as an important element in the epistle's encouragement to outward witness.

the proclamation of the Gospel as 'in/by the Holy Spirit' might suggest that the earlier reference to the 'Spirit of Christ' is indeed a synonym for the 'Holy Spirit', since a common revelatory function is ascribed to both. However, as the complex 'pneumatology' of the Qumran literature demonstrates, it is quite possible that these descriptions of the Holy Spirit's work pertain to different persons.[49]

εἰς ἃ ἐπιθυμοῦσιν ἄγγελοι παρακύψαι. Παρακύψαι literally means 'to bend over'.[50] As Michaels suggests, the use here probably serves to create an image of angels peering down from the heavenly places.[51] As Best points out, the notion that angels have, in some respects, lower status than the people of God is quite well attested in the New Testament (1 Cor. 6.1; Heb. 1.14; 2.16) and related literature (*1 En.* 16.3; *2 En.* 24.3; Ignatius, *Eph.* 19.1), as is the idea that the people of God are privy to knowledge which the angels lack (1 Cor. 2.9; Eph. 3.10).[52] Whilst the majority of scholars take ἄγγελοι to refer to heavenly beings who do the will of God, Boring argues that it could refer to the 'bad' angels represented in 1QS 3.13–4.14, 4QAmram and *1 Enoch* 6–16.[53] The evidence for this is the possibly negative use of ἄγγελοι in 1 Pet. 3.22, in

---

49. The Qumran Scrolls demonstrate remarkably diverse understandings of רוח קדוש. In the earliest Scrolls, such as 4Q416 (בכל הון אל תמר רוח קודשכה כי אין שוה), the 'holy spirit' is seen as a feature of the human person. Cf. J. Coppens, 'Le Don de l'Esprit d'après les textes de Qumran et le Quatrième Évangile', in *L'Évangile de Jean: Études et Problèmes* (ed. F. M. Braun; Bruges: Desclée De Brouwer, 1958), pp. 209–23. At other times, such as in 1QS 8.15-16 (היאה מדרש התורה אשר צוה ביד מושה לעשות ככול הנגלה עת בעת וכאשר גלו הנביאים ברוח קודשו) the 'Holy Spirit' is seen as the inspiration of the Prophets and at other times the 'Holy Spirit' represents a divine revelatory presence in the human person, as in 1QH 17.32 (ובאמת נכון סמכתני ונרוח קודשכה תשעשעני). Lorein, 'The Holy Spirit at Qumran', helpfully documents this as something of an historical progression.

50. Wilhelm Michaelis, παρακύπτω, *TDNT*, vol. 5, pp. 814–16. In this context, Michaelis suggests that the term either implies 'inquisitive peeping' or a desire for 'genuine perception'.

51. Michaels, *1 Peter*, p. 49.

52. Best, *1 Peter*, p. 83. Cf. Ignatius, *Eph.* 19.1, and *1 En.* 16.3. Cf. also Michaels, *1 Peter*, p. 48, on the similarity with Heb. 2.2-3, in which the 'age to come' belongs not to the angels but to Christ and his brothers (Heb. 2.12). Yet, as Achtemeier, *1 Peter*, p. 112 n. 93, observes, the dominant tradition is that angels are superior to humankind. See Dan. 7.16; Zech. 1.9; *1 En.* 1.2; 72.1; 108.5-7; and *Fug.* 203.

53. Boring, *1 Peter*, p. 66. This is the same background which Bo Reicke relates to the πνεύματα in 1 Pet. 3.19. See below. Cf. Hans Dieter Betz, *Galatians: A Commentary on Paul's Letter to the Churches in Galatia* (Hermeneia; Philadelphia: Fortress, 1979), p. 168.

which they are grouped with 'authorities' and 'powers' in submission to the exalted Christ. In addition to this, a negative view of angels in seen in Pauline literature. Here, angels are depicted as both hostile to God's plan (Rom. 8.38) and ignorant of it (1 Cor. 2.9; Eph. 3.9-10). Boring also notes that ἐπιθύμεω can have 'evil overtones', as in the OG of Gen. 6.1-6 and in 1 Pet. 3.19-20.[54] However, Boring's suggestion has not witnessed a great deal of scholarly support. For example, Jobes argues that the introduction of the envy of fallen angels would make little sense to this setting and would provide a poor accompaniment to the prophets mentioned here. Jobes contends that the purpose of 1 Pet. 1.10-12 is to encourage the audiences by telling them of their exalted status, standing at the climax of salvation history. This is achieved to greater effect if the angels who long to see what is going on are the very angels who themselves are God's servants, looking down in envy.[55] Not only do the Prophets peer excitedly through history to see the message of the Christ and the glories which follow him, angels long to know more of it. The general effect of these verses is to emphasise the importance of the scattered Christian communities. Though they may be strangers in the world, the Prophets who eagerly awaited the Christ they follow are their servants. The event these Christians are a part of represents the climax of history. Even the angels long to hear what they have been told. Peter suggests to his readers that as they read the Scriptures of Israel, they are reading things which pertain directly to themselves. They pertain to themselves not because they speak to each generation in the same way. They do so because Scripture is *for* them in an exclusive sense. The Prophets served those who would hear the good news proclaimed by the Holy Spirit sent from heaven, not previous generations and not those who have now refused to obey the Gospel of God.

* * *

Excursus: A Comparison of 1 Peter 1.10-12 with 2 Peter 1.20-21

Whilst it is not particularly common to compare 2 Peter with 1 Peter, it is significant that both epistles contain material on the value of the prophetic witness from Israel's past. These two passages are worthy of comparison and this will not be the first attempt to do so.[56] Each can be found at the opening of the epistle in which it is set and can be seen to have some sort of introductory role. Each makes explicit the

54. Boring, *1 Peter*, p. 66.
55. Jobes, *1 Peter*, p. 105.
56. Cf. Kelly, *Peter*, p. 320; H. C. C. Cavallin, 'The False Teachers of 2 Pt as Pseudo-Prophets', *NovT* 21 (1979), p. 265, and Bénétreau, 'Évangile et Prophétie', pp. 174–91.

relationship between the implied scriptural texts (which are not mentioned, though 2 Pet. 1.20 does refer to προφητεία γραφῆς) and the audiences. Each involves some relation to eschatology. Whilst 1 Pet. 1.10-12 focusses upon the referent of the prophetic ministry, 2 Pet. 1.20-21 emphasises inspiration.

Paul A. Hines offers an analysis of 'Petrine' treatment of prophecy, cautiously encompassing Peter's Pentecost and Temple speeches in Acts with 1 Pet. 1.10-12 and 2 Pet. 1.19-21.[57] Hines notes the importance of prophecy in the Pentecost speech, both as a description of Joel in 2.16 and as a description of David in vv. 29-31, and draws attention to its predictive function of prophecy. Likewise, in the Temple Speech, the prophetic witness to the suffering of Christ is emphasised in 3.22-25. In 2 Peter, Hines draws attention to the broad aim expressed in the epistle to provide confidence in knowledge about Christ and notes that this theme provides the basis for the description of prophetic inspiration in 1.20-21, which thus implies the christological focus of prophecy. Hines argues that a 'Petrine' use of Scripture features an understanding that texts are predictive, an assumption that they refer to Christ and a sense that they directly challenge contemporary readers. These observations are certainly appropriate as a characterisation of the scriptural hermeneutics of 1 Peter, but there seems to be less warrant to regard them as universally Petrine. For example, the challenge provided by Scripture in Acts 2 is not that clear. Acts 2.36-37 appears to imply that it is the speech itself and its closing remark suggesting the crowd's complicity in the crucifixion of Jesus (identified by Scripture as the Christ) which motivates the crowd to respond. It is not clear that Scripture is seen to do this. In addition to this, the treatment of David as a prophet in Acts 2 is quite different from the type of exegetical reasoning one finds in 1 Peter. The Davidic authorship of Psalm 16, as well as the identity of David as a prophet, is of fundamental significance to Peter's argument in the Pentecost speech. At no point in 1 Peter is the identity of a human author of Scripture seen to be of any importance. Indeed, at no point in 1 Peter does Peter explain his interpretation of Scripture as is done in Acts 2. Yet one area of similarity not noted by Hines is the broad scope of prophetic

---

57. Hines, 'Peter and the Prophetic Word', pp. 229–41. Hines suggests that there is enough similarity between these texts to make their comparison worthwhile, even if they simply belong loosely to a Petrine 'school' rather than share a common authorship. Whilst this argument is extremely tentative if one were to relate, as Hines does, the 'Petrine' speeches in Acts with the Petrine epistles, a stronger case for camparison between 1 and 2 Peter can be made on the basis of shared tradition. Michael J. Kruger, 'The Authenticity of 2 Peter', *JETS* 42 (1999), pp. 645–71, demonstrates how many questions related to the authorship of 2 Peter ought to be regarded as unanswered, suggesting that many of the grounds for rejecting common authorship with 1 Peter are quite uncertain. Principally, Kruger notes the extreme difficulty in establishing 'Petrine' style, to the extent that the stylistic differences between 1 and 2 Peter are not as conclusive as often thought. Kruger also notes how little is known about the status and use of pseudepigraphy in the first century. He argues, against Bauckham and others, that there is some evidence suggesting that pseudepigraphy was not considered proper, such as 2 Thess. 2.2 and the reference in Tertullian's *On Baptism* 17 to the dismissal of the author of the pseudonymous *Acts of Paul and Thecla*.

reference in the Pentecost Speech. In 1 Pet. 1.10-12, the Prophets are seen to speak of not only the sufferings of Christ but the glories after. Whilst it has been noted that many take these 'glories' as purely christological events (the resurrection, ascension and session of Christ), they could equally refer quite generally to the blessings enjoyed by the community subsequent to Christ's suffering. In the same way, the citations in the Pentecost Speech refer both to Christ (in the case of Pss. 16 and 110) and to the blessings enjoyed by the community as the Spirit is poured out (in the case of Joel). The understanding of Scripture as paraenesis in 2 Peter is less clear than in other examples of 'Petrine' interpretation of Scripture, though Steven J. Kraftchick suggests that the phrase ᾧ καλῶς ποιεῖτε προσέχοντες in 2 Pet. 1.19 is a paraenetic exhortation.[58] However, in this case it is still the author, rather than the Scripture itself, which is seen to offer the imperative.

A significant difference between 1 Pet. 1.10-12 and 2 Pet. 1.19-21 concerns the nature of the prophetic witness. In 2 Pet. 1.20 the 'prophetic message' is referred to as προφητεία γραφῆς, a written text.[59] Carson argues that the phrase ὡς λύχνῳ φαίνοντι ἐν αὐχμηρῷ τόπῳ in 2 Pet. 1.19 is an allusion to common light imagery related to Scripture in texts such as Ps. 119.105, Wis. 18.4 and *4 Ezra* 12.42.[60] If this is so, then it would appear that the reference to Scripture here is reasonably developed. In contrast, 1 Pet. 1.10-12 gives no indication as to the textual nature of the message given through the Spirit of Christ, though Osborne rightly concludes that 1 Peter does indeed understand Scripture as written text.[61] It can be assumed that since this passage agrees with the use of scriptural texts elsewhere in the epistle, as is argued below, it does indeed refer to written texts, though it cannot be proven. This, of course, made possible Selwyn's argument that the Prophets referred to are not the authors of Israel's Scriptures but rather early Christian figures. As it noted above, there are a variety of convincing reasons to explain why the majority of scholars do not agree with this view. In the same way, factors such as the use of aorist verbs undermine the possibility that the prophets in 2 Pet. 1.19-21 are Christian prophets.[62]

Whilst 1 Pet. 1.10-12 attributes an eschatological orientation to the prophetic ministry, the nature of the eschatology in 2 Pet. 1.19, if indeed it can be regarded as eschatological, is hotly disputed. One area of debate is whether or not the prophetic witness here is to the first or the second coming of Christ. It has been argued that

---

58. Steven J. Kraftchick, *Jude, 2 Peter* (ANTC; Nashville: Abingdon, 2002), p. 115.

59. These terms are seen as synonymous by D. A. Carson, '2 Peter', in Beale and Carson, eds., *Commentary on the New Testament*, p. 1048, Bauckham, *2 Peter*, p. 224, and Kraftchick, *2 Peter*, p. 114, who suggests that the terms refer either to the whole of Scripture or to specific eschatological texts such as Num. 24.17; Ps. 2.9; and Dan. 7.13-14. Cf. *2 Clem.* 11.2, where προφητικὸς λόγος is used as part of a citation formula (λέγει γὰρ καὶ ὁ προφητικὸς λόγος).

60. Carson, '2 Peter', p. 1048.

61. Osborne, 'L'Utilisation de l'Ancient Testament', p. 74. Cf. Boring, 'Narrative Dynamics in First Peter', p. 26, and the use of the formulae διότι γέγραπται in 1.6 and διότι περιέχει ἐν γραφῇ in 2.6.

62. Cavallin, 'False Teachers', p. 265.

since the 'prophetic word' is 'made firm' (καὶ ἔχομεν βεβαιότερον τὸν προφητικὸν λόγον) in v. 19, seemingly because of the author's witness to the transfiguration of Jesus, that it is the first coming to which the word refers, given that the transfiguration is seen to relate to the resurrection of Christ rather than his return in the Synoptic Gospels. Likewise, it has been argued that if the Prophets spoke simply of an event yet to come, the author's claim to have personal experience of Christ's coming in v. 18 would be meaningless. However, Kelly argues strongly in favour of a future referent for the passage and hence the prophetic word.[63] He notes that the term παρουσία only begins to refer to the first coming of Christ in second-century documents such as Ign., *Phil.* 9.2 and Justin's *1 Apol.* 52.3 and *Dial.* 14.8, and that in 2 Pet. 3.4 and 12 it is used to refer to the last days as a period in the future. Kelly also argues that a future orientation for 2 Pet. 1.16-21 is consistent with the apparent 'heresy', in which the continuing power of Christ was doubted, that occasioned the writing of the epistle. Finally, Kelly notes that in Origen's *Commentary on Matthew* 12.31, the transfiguration is seen to refer to the second coming of Christ.[64] Because of this, the reference to the author's experience in vv. 16 and 18 may be to an experience of the transfiguration as an event which revealed something of the future.

Terrence Callan argues that the passage is indeed eschatological, suggesting that φωσφόρος refers not to the morning star or venus, but to Christ as the dawning sun, a figure of the parousia.[65] In addition to this, Callan argues that the phrase ἐν ταῖς καρδίαις ὑμῶν does not modify ἀνατείλῃ as is usually thought, but goes with γινώσκοντες in v. 20, making it more likely that the metaphor is eschatological rather than psychological.[66] Yet whilst it is clear that the understanding of the referent of prophecy is eschatological, a potential interest in the parousia is quite different from 1 Pet. 1.10-12, where the eschatological referent of prophecy is the sufferings of Christ and the glories after, even though, as Kelly points out, the 'parousia' is an

---

63. Kelly, *Peter*, pp. 317–18.

64. Cf. J. H. Neyrey, 'The Apologetic Use of the Transfiguration in 2 Peter 1.16-21', *CBQ* 42 (1980), pp. 504–19, who argues that the transfiguration is viewed here as a proof of the parousia.

65. Cf. Carson, '2 Peter', p. 1048, who notes the eschatological and primarily messianic use of 'star' terminology in *T. Levi.* 18.3; *T. Jud.* 24.1; CD A 8.18-20; 1QM 9.6-7; 4Q175.9-13, and Rev. 22.16.

66. Terrence Callan, 'A Note on 2 Peter 1.19-20', *JBL* 125 (2006), pp. 265–70. This is contested by Stanley E. Porter and Andrew W. Pitts, 'τοῦτο πρῶτον γινώσκοντες ὅτι in 2 Peter 1.20 and Hellenistic Epistolary Convention', *JBL* 127 (2008), pp. 165–71, who argue for the traditional interpretation on the basis of comparison with other uses of the 'disclosure formula'. Cf. John T. Curran, 'The Teaching of II Peter 1.20: On the Interpretation of Prophecy', *TS* 4 (1943), pp. 347–68 (348). J. Boehmer, 'Tag und Morgenstern? Zu II Petr i 19', *ZNW* 22 (1923), pp. 228–33, offers a detailed study of the background of the terms ἡμέρα, διαυγάζειν and φωσφόρος in v. 19, arguing that the importance of 'day' and 'light' imagery suggests that φωσφόρος ought to be understood as 'morning light'. Of particular value is Boehmer's analysis of the use of ἡμέρα in OG Scripture and the New Testament which expresses the primarily eschatological use of the term: further evidence, perhaps, that 2 Pet. 1.19 refers to the parousia.

important idea in 1 Peter. In addition to this, it is clear that the eschatology of these verses functions to explain something of the new insight into the prophetic revelation that the community addressed by the epistle possess: καὶ ἔχομεν βεβαιότερον τὸν προφητικὸν λόγον.[67] To some extent, possibly to a lesser degree than in 1 Pet. 1.10-12, the community have a privileged access into Scripture.

Some degree of similarity can also be seen in views of prophetic inspiration expressed in the text. In 1 Pet. 1.10-12 inspiration, or rather revelation, appears to be twofold. Verse 11 appears to address the initial revelation given to them at the time of prophetic utterance or writing through 'the Spirit of Christ', whilst v. 12 refers to a later revelation in which they came to understand the sought-after meaning of their prophecies. In contrast, 2 Pet. 1.21 simply addresses the inspiration of the original prophetic writings through the Holy Spirit, though it could be argued that 2 Pet. 1.20 implies that the interpretation of Scripture requires revelation or inspiration (see the discussion below). The comparable functions of both the Spirit of Christ and the Holy Spirit in 1 and 2 Peter respectively might offer support to the view, argued above, that the terms are synonymous as in Rom. 8.9.[68]

Block suggests that the description of prophetic inspiration in 2 Pet. 1.20-21 reflects the view of inspiration in the counsel of YHWH and the prophet's speech '*ex cathedra*' in Jer. 23.16-22:[69]

כה אמר יהוה צבאות
אל תשמעו על דברי הנבאים הנבאים לכם מהבלים המה אתכם חזון לבם ידברו
לא מפי יהוה: אמרים אמור למנאצי דבר יהוה שלום יהיה לכם וכל הלך בשררות
לבו אמרו לא תבוא עליכם רעה: כי מי עמד בסוד יהוה וירא וישמע את דברו מי
הקשיב דברי וישמע:
הנה סערת יהוה חמה יצאה וסער מתחולל על ראש רשעים יחול: לא ישוב אף
יהוה עד עשתו ועד הקימו מזמות לבו באחרית הימים תתבוננו בה בינה: לא
שלחתי את הנבאים והם רצו לא דברתי אליהם והם נבשו: ואם עמדו בסודי
וישמעו דברי את עמי וישבום מדרכם הרע ומרע מעלליהם:

This, perhaps, seems unlikely since Jeremiah does not posit a role for the Spirit, nor does he suggest that the true prophets are passive, in the sense of being 'borne along' as in 2 Peter. Instead, their inspiration seems to come from their attentiveness or proximity to YHWH.

Perhaps a greater degree of similarity can be seen in the two texts' vigorous assertion of determinate meaning. In 1 Pet. 1.10-12, Scripture is seen to have a single sphere of reference: the sufferings of Christ and the glories after. It is not seen

---

67. Assuming, first, that ἔχομεν here relates to the community as a whole rather than the more specific ἡμεῖς referring to the apostles in 1.18. D. Edmund Hiebert, 'The Prophetic Foundation for the Christian Life: An Exposition of 2 Peter 1.19-2', *BSac* 141 (1984), pp. 158–68 (159), notes that the remainder of v. 19 addresses the community in general.

68. See the pneumatological comparison in William Joseph Dalton, 'The Interpretation of 1 Peter 3.19 and 4.6: Light from 2 Peter', *Bib* 60 (1979), pp. 547–55 (549).

69. Block, 'View from the Top', p. 176.

to have meaning pertaining to the Prophets' own times, hence it was revealed to them that they served not themselves but the community born of the proclaimed Good News. Similarly, in 2 Pet. 1.20 the single meaning of Scripture is asserted, not as a means of elevating the eschatological significance of the communities to which the letter is written, but to argue against particular readings of Scripture which are perceived to be erroneous: Τοῦτο πρῶτον γινώσκοντες ὅτι πᾶσα προφητεία γραφῆς ἰδίας ἐπιλύσεως οὐ γίνεται. Yet, it must be noted that the referent of ἰδίας here is far from certain. Who is the interpreter referred to?[70] Is it the prophet himself as he transforms inspiration into Scripture, in which case v. 21 is an explanation of the fact that no human interpretation features in the production of Scripture? Or is it that ἰδίας refers to the hypothetical reader, in which case v. 21 explains that meaning is given by God and hence is determinate: as God intended through the Holy Spirit? John T. Curran explores the various options and argues that the verse is directed towards Christian interpretation of the prophetic scriptures, rather than any kind of interpretation offered by the Prophets themselves.[71] Curran argues that ἰδίας ἐπιλύσεως οὐ γίνεται is not to be understood as a genitive of origin[72] ('no prophecy of Scripture came through [a prophet's] own interpretation') but rather as possessive genitive ('no prophecy of Scripture is a matter of one's own interpretation', NRSV) as in Lk. 20.14, purely because the former is unusual. Furthermore, he points out that the singular ἰδίας is unlikely to be intended to correspond to the plural ἄνθρωποι, referring to the Prophets, in v. 21 and that if ἐπιλύσεως were intended as a genitive of origin it would probably be accompanied with a clarifying reference to 'signs' or 'visions'. Curran dismisses the reading of this verse offered in the Theophylact Commentary PG 125.1264 which supports the genitive of origin interpretation, suggesting that this is taken to support an anti-Montanist agenda. Instead, he draws attention to Rufinus' recension of Origen's *Homilies on the Book of Numbers* 18 c4, which provides evidence for the possessive interpretation. Additional support for Curran's argument is provided by Kelly, who argues that vv. 20 and 21 would express the same idea twice if they were both an expression of the divine origin of prophecy.[73] Furthermore, 2 Pet. 3.16 appears to support the possessive genitive interpretation as an attack on the scriptural interpretation of the author's opponents, writing of Paul's letters ἃ οἱ ἀμαθεῖς καὶ ἀστήρικτοι στρεβλοῦσιν ὡς καὶ τάς λοιπὰς γραφὰς πρὸς τήν ἰδίαν αὐτῶν ἀπώλειαν.

---

70. Kelly, *Peter*, p. 321, notes the diverse usage of ἐπίλυσις (*Vit. Cont.* 75; *Deipn.* 10.450e; *Ant.* 8.167; Mk 4.34, and *Sim.* 5.5.1. However, Bauckham, *2 Peter*, p. 231, and R. M. Spence, 'Private Interpretation', *ExpTim* 8 (1896–97), pp. 285–6 (285), suggest that the evidence for the translation of ἐπίλυσις as 'interpretation' is not very strong. Cf. E. P. Boys-Smith, '"Interpretation" or "Revelation": 2 Pet I. 20, Part II', *ExpTim* 8 (1896–97), pp. 331–2.

71. Curran, 'Teaching', pp. 348–59. Cf. Spence, 'Private Interpretation', pp. 285–6.

72. As argued by P. Thompson, '"Interpretation" or "Revelation": 2 Pet I. 20, Part I', *ExpTim* 8 (1896–97), p. 331, on the basis of the use of γίνεται.

73. Kelly, *Peter*, p. 321.

1. *1 Peter 1.10-12: A Hermeneutical Statement?*

Like Curran, Bauckham admits that there is little in the verse itself to decide either way, though he concludes that it most likely refers to the Prophets as interpreters.[74] Whilst agreeing that this reading is grammatically awkward since a prophet is not mentioned, Bauckham argues that ἰδίας had the status of a technical term in Hellenistic Jewish and early Christian literature that attempted to assert the divine origin of Scripture against the accusation that it simply reflected the view of its authors.[75] He suggests that the thought of 1.20 is perhaps closest to *Sim.* 5.3.1-2, 5.4.2-3 etc. in which visions and their interpretation are viewed as separate events of inspiration given to the Shepherd of Hermas. Yet Bauckham contends that, ultimately, the rhetorical purpose and context of the epistle decides the meaning of 1.20. Since 1.16-21 could be described as 'defensive' in tone, attempting to show the reliability of the author's message, it is unlikely that v. 20 is an attack upon the false interpretation alluded to in 3.16. However, it is quite plausible that 1.20 alludes to the same opponents as 3.16, albeit in a defensive manner, suggesting that whilst the author and his fellows do not interpret Scripture in their own way, others do. The common use of ἰδίας in each case makes a common referent likely.

Bauckham is right to note the defensive nature of the context from 1.16, yet this need not be a reason to reject the interpretation of v. 20 as directed towards Christian readers of Scripture. As Neyrey argues, v. 20 could easily function as a defence of the author's own interpretation of Scripture.[76] This raises the possibility of a certain parallelism between vv. 16-18 and 19-21. Verses 16-18 defend the certainty of the author's witness as not being 'wise myths' by pointing to the concrete nature of the revelation from which it proceeds. Likewise, vv. 19-21 assert the certainty of the author's interpretation on the basis of the nature of the revelation worked through the Prophets. The divine origin of the words of prophecy provides for the assertion that interpretation is not private, just as the author's interpretation of prophecy is not his own. As Kraftchick concludes,

> This yields the sense that legitimate interpretation of prophecy is not a matter of individual whim, but an objective statement outside the control of the individual, since it comes from God. Since it is from inspiration and not from human design, the interpretation bears divine authority. As a result, prophetic witness is the basis for human understanding, and therefore on a par with the transfiguration as verification for the truth of the apostolic teaching about the second coming.[77]

* * *

---

74. Bauckham, *2 Peter*, pp. 229–33.
75. Philo, *Spec. Leg.* 1.65; 4.49; *Quest. Gen.* 3.10; Hippolytus, *Antichr.* 2; Pseudo-Justin, *Cohortatio* 8; Methodius, *Convivium* 8.10; and Josephus, *Ant.* 4.121. Cf. Kraftchick, *2 Peter*, p. 117. Bauckham, *2 Peter*, p. 230, also notes that the use of ἰδίας in *Clem. Hom.* 2.22 supports the opposing view that it refers to the interpretation of prophetic Scriptures by later readers.
76. Neyrey, 'Apologetic use of the Transfiguration', pp. 516–19.
77. Kraftchick, *2 Peter*, p. 118.

4. Theological Narrative in 1 Peter 1.10-12

Much of the analysis of 1 Pet. 1.10-12 offered above is uncontroversial and where there are elements of uncertainty, such as regards the nature of Χριστὸν παθήματα, the analysis above has generally agreed with the position of the majority of scholars.[78] However, recent studies of the use of Scripture in 1 Peter which focus upon the role of theological narrative substructure rely upon 1 Pet. 1.10-12 in ways that disagree with much of this scholarship. Whilst it is clear that 1 Pet. 1.10-12 expresses something of the author's understanding of salvation history, albeit in a very compressed form, it is not clear that this narrative features the ideas of continuity emphasised by scholars such as Green and Joseph. Whether or not Peter viewed his communities as a continuation of the Israel of the Scriptures has significant implications for the scriptural hermeneutic apparently expressed in these verses.

An understanding that Peter views the events and people of the Gospel as representing a natural continuation of God's dealings with Israel has been a consistent feature of scholarship on 1 Peter.[79] Often, this sense of continuous *Heilsgeschichte* is linked specifically to 1 Pet. 1.10-12.[80] Goppelt, for example, maintains that 1.10-12 provides the theoretical basis for the extensive use of typology linking past and present. Because the Prophets are inspired by the Spirit of Christ, their writings refer also to the communities addressed by 1 Peter.[81] In contrast to Schutter, Goppelt rightly notes that the primary emphasis of scriptural interpretation in the epistle is not so much Christ, as it is the Church. Goppelt argues that 1 Peter displays a very broad typological understanding of the Church, not merely limited to its reference to particular biblical texts. For

---

78. Benjamin Sargent, 'The Narrative Substructure of 1 Peter', *ExpTim* 124 (2013), pp. 485–90.

79. Theophil Spörri, *Der Gemeindegedanke im ersten Petrusbrief* (Neutestamentliche Forschung 2/2; Gütersloh: Bertelsmann, 1925), p. 257, argues that 1 Peter views salvation history as representing ecclesiological continuity between Israel and the Christian communities. Cf. Bigg, *St Peter*, p. 6 who claims that Peter assumes an 'unbroken continuity between the law, the Prophets, and the Gospel' and Herzer, 'Alttestamentliche Prophetie', p. 18.

80. Douglas Harink, *1 & 2 Peter* (London: SCM, 2009), p. 50, suggests that 1 Pet. 1.10-12 betrays an understanding of the Prophets of Israel's past, discerning a '*pattern of messianic suffering and glorification* that is already *the divine secret of Israel's history*' (italics original). Cf. Achtemeier, *1 Peter*, p. 110, and Schlosser, 'Ancien Testament et Christologie', p. 95.

81. Goppelt, *Typos*, pp. 152–3. Cf. Paul J. Achtemeier, 'The Christology of First Peter', in *Who Do You Say That I Am? Essays on Christology* (ed. Mark A. Powell and David R. Bauer; Louisville: Westminster, 1999), pp. 140–54.

example, Goppelt argues that 1 Pet. 1.18 draws an implicit and typological comparison between the redemption of the communities from 'slavery' to a former pattern of life and the redemption of Israel from real slavery in Egypt.[82] In this respect, Goppelt anticipates later work on narrative substructure in the epistle. As noted in the introduction to this study, narrative continuity is an important feature in both Green's and Joseph's explanations of the use of Scripture in 1 Peter.[83]

However, as will be argued below, with the possible exceptions of 1 Pet. 3.6 and 21, typology does not appear to be that significant as an explanation of how Scripture is interpreted in 1 Peter. Whilst Peter is clearly keen to describe the communities to which he writes using the language of Israel, there is no indication that he understands this language to have the dual reference both to the past and the present that one would expect to see in the use of typology. Goppelt assumes that Peter is aware that this language refers to Israel in the past, but this is by no means an obvious conclusion to draw. It will be argued below that typological interpretation is too sophisticated a mode of scriptural interpretation in 1 Peter, a work which is primarily indebted to a primitive apocalyptic approach which views the past as having little status compared to the present. There is no evidence to suggest that the theological narrative of 1 Peter includes a concept of continuation and the essential similarity of past and present necessary for a typological reading of the past, of events in Scripture. Indeed, Boring concludes regarding the treatment of Sarah and Noah in 1 Pet. 3.6 and 3.19-21 (the two most plausible examples of typology in 1 Peter), 'nothing is made of the pre-Moses/covenant/Israel narrative location of these two segments'.[84]

---

82. Goppelt, *Typos*, p. 155, similarly argues that the phrase διὸ ἀναζωσάμενοι τὰς ὀσφύας τῆς διανοίας ὑμῶν in 1.13 is a reflection of the similar and common scriptural exhortation, often to Israel (2 Kgs 4.29; 9.1; Job 38.3; 40.7; Jer. 1.17; and Prov. 31.17). The most important use of a comparable phrase, as far as Goppelt's view of a broad typology is concerned, is Exod. 12.11. He suggests that Peter sees Israel's preparation to leave Egypt as typologically significant for the communities addressed by 1 Peter. However, the similarity with extant OG readings of Exod. 12.11 (οὕτως δὲ φάγεσθε αὐτό αἱ ὀσφύες ὑμῶν περιεζωσμέναι) is so weak as to suggest that this is unlikely to have been a deliberate scriptural allusion. Cf. Hanson, *Living Utterances*, p. 143, who agrees with this analysis.

83. Green, *1 Peter*, pp. 252–6; idem, 'Narrating the Gospel in 1 and 2 Peter', pp. 262–77, and Joseph, *Narratological Reading of 1 Peter*, pp. 23–31.

84. Boring, 'Narrative Dynamics in 1 Peter', p. 27, and Lutz Doering, 'Gottes Volk: Die Adressaten als "Israel" im Ersten Petrusbrief', in *Bedrängnis und Identität: Studien zu Situation, Kommunikation und Theologie des 1. Petrusbriefes* (ed. David S. du Toit; BZNW 200; Berlin: de Gruyter, 2013), pp. 106–9.

Moreover, it is not clear that the narrative hinted at in 1.10-12 is one of continuity at all. The present knowledge possessed by the communities is contrasted with the past ignorance of the Prophets. The communities are served whilst the Prophets are the servants. Even the angels, often seen to have a mediatory, and thus privileged, function in apocalyptic Judaism and the New Testament are seemingly excluded from something of which the communities have full knowledge.[85] The communities addressed by 1 Peter are more than simply the current expression of the Israel of the past, leaving aside the issue of supercessionism in the epistle for which there is too little evidence to draw firm conclusions.[86] What is beyond doubt is that 1 Pet. 1.10-12 draws attention to a radical disjuncture between the past and the present. This disjuncture makes Green's use of continuity as the basis for typological reading as an element in Peter's scriptural hermeneutic very difficult, quite apart from the fact that there is simply no evidence that Peter regarded Scripture in so sophisticated a way as to consider events to have more than one meaning.[87] For Peter, the whole of the scriptural witness is about the glorious eschatological age of which he and his audiences are a part.

Certainly, a salvation-historical narrative of discontinuity is suggested elsewhere in 1 Peter. 1 Peter 1.20 is interesting, in that it refers to Christ as προεγνωσμένου μὲν πρὸ καταβολῆς κόσμου φανερωθέντος δὲ ἐπ' ἐσχάτου τῶν χρόνων. Though Christ is in some sense understood to be eternal here, the 'last days' are significant as a time in which he is made known. The implication is that prior to these 'last days', Christ had not be revealed and hence was not known. This may, of course, explain the apparent ignorance of the Prophets suggested in 1.10. The relation of

85. See the privileged 'mediatory' function of angels in Acts 7.53; Gal. 3.19; Heb. 2.2; Josephus, *Ant.* 15.136; Hermas, *Sim.* 8.3.3, perhaps derived from, as Betz, *Galatians*, p. 169, suggests, traditions expressed in OG Deut. 33.2, OG Ps. 102.20; 103.4; *Jub.* 2.1-2 and *1 En.* 60.1-3. Cf. H. Strack and P. Billerbeck, *Kommentar zum Neuen Testament aus Talmud und Midrasch*, vol. 3 (Munich: Beck, 1922), pp. 554–56.

86. Judith Lieu, *Image and Reality: The Jews in the World of the Christians in the Second Century* (Edinburgh: T. & T. Clark, 1996), p. 4, and Betsy Bauman-Martin, 'Speaking Jewish: Postcolonial Aliens and Strangers in First Peter', in Webb and Bauman-Martin, eds., *Reading First Peter*, pp. 152–3, argue that the application of Jewish scriptural terms to the communities is clearly supercessionist. Cf. Mbuvi, *Temple, Exile and Identity*, p. 5, in relation to the cultic language of the temple applied to the communities of 1 Peter.

87. Sargent, 'Narrative Substructure of 1 Peter', pp. 485–90. Green, *1 Peter*, pp. 36–43, himself notes something of this disjuncture or contrast in his detailed analysis of the narrative implied in 1 Pet. 1.20, characterising the period prior to the 'revelation' of Christ as the period of 'ignorance'.

Christ to the people of God reflects an historical disjuncture between the past and the present. Though Christ is clearly understood to have existed in the past, it is not clear that he is understood to have been active in the past. Because of this, the narrative possesses a greater sense of discontinuity between past and present than, for example, the Epistle to the Hebrews in which the pre-incarnate Christ is understood to be the speaker of certain passages of Scripture.[88] Here, though, something of the sense in which the mission of Jesus stands at the climax of history is emphasised and indicates the disjuncture between past and present. Similarly, more than simply being Israel in the present (equivalent to God's chosen people led out of Egypt in the past) the communities addressed by Peter have a heightened significance due to their position at the climax of salvation history. The Prophets' concern was to speak of the grace that would come to these communities as they spoke of the sufferings of Christ and the glories after. They spoke, not for their own benefit, nor for the benefit of their initial hearers, but so as to serve the communities to which 1 Peter is addressed. These communities have received good news so precious that even the angels long to know it. The sense in which the communities have received things denied to others emphasises the sense of their eschatological significance. For Peter, Scripture is understood to relate directly to the needs of his audiences because the whole of God's plan for his creation is focused upon the time and circumstances of which they are a part as people who have responded to the proclamation of Jesus Christ. This is the conclusion Boring draws in his work on the theological narrative substructure of 1 Peter. Boring observes that the theological narrative projected by the epistle is comprised of two distinct sections: ποτέ and νῦν.[89] The past is seen as a poor relation to the present, as being of a quite different status to that enjoyed by the audiences of the epistle which begins with the work of Christ:

> From the era between creation and Christ, the author of 1 Peter draws only a couple of illustrations of Christian points from the Bible and traditions. Yet these points do not seem to be connected into a line. There is no direct sense that the Christian community is the continuation of the Old Testament story. The Christian community is described with a profusion of biblical phraseology...addressing the Christian readers as the people to and of whom the Scriptures speak. Yet there is no explicit history-of-salvation story line continued and fulfilled in the readers' experience.[90]

---

88. Heb. 2.11-13 and 10.5-9. Cf. Heb. 11.26.
89. Boring, 'Narrative Dynamics in 1 Peter', pp. 24–7.
90. Boring, 'Narrative Dynamics in 1 Peter', p. 27.

In a similar way, Mbuvi argues for a narrative of discontinuity, difference and change in which the expectations of a former period are shown to be far removed from the eschatological present. In particular, the expected temple restoration is seen to relate to a 'Temple-Community' as the house of God, rather than a sacred place.[91] Mbuvi suggests that the salvation historical narrative behind 1 Peter features three distinct periods: Exodus, Exile and Apocalyptic. Whilst this stress upon distinct and different periods is helpful, any attempt to define such periods is fraught with difficulty. Does 1 Peter refer to the Exodus as an historical event, or does it simply use the language of Exodus to refer to Christ and the Community? The latter seems most likely. Furthermore, to what extent is the exile seen as an historical event rather than simply a scriptural means of referring to the present condition of the communities to which 1 Peter is addressed? Unfortunately, Mbuvi's pattern, as does his argument as a whole, appears to depend upon the exile being understood by Peter as an historical event leaving an unresolved tension to be met by the fulfilment achieved by Christ and his temple people. Perhaps the most that can be suggested, certainly in relation to the period prior to Christ, is a single time period in which the Prophets looked forwards and in which events, such as the Flood, prefigured a greater age to come.

5. Paraenesis and Kerygma in 1 Peter 1.10-12

1 Peter 1.10-12 appears to make two important hermeneutical claims about the prophetic witness: it is oriented towards the suffering and glories of Christ (1.11) and it exists the serve those who would later have the Gospel proclaimed to them (1.12). It will be argued below that these two claims roughly equate to two principal ways of interpreting Scripture in 1 Peter: paraenesis and kerygma. As Bauckham observes:

> The lavish use of OT quotations and allusions falls into two main categories: prophetic interpretation and paraenetic application, although, as we shall see, these two categories are not wholly distinct.[92]

One of these aspects is related to teaching or proclamation of theological truths and may be described more generally as kerygmatic: the prophecy of the sufferings of Christ and the glories after. The other relates to the

---

91. Mbuvi, *Temple, Exile and Identity*, p. 133. Here Mbuvi draws upon Robert J. McKelvey, *The New Temple: The Church in the New Testament* (London: Oxford University Press, 1969), whose insights into the 'Temple-Community' in 1 Peter he explores and extends into a detailed treatment of the epistle.

92. Bauckham, 'James, 1 and 2 Peter, Jude', p. 309. Cf. Schlosser, 'Ancien Testament et Christologie', pp. 92–3.

fact that Scripture is seen to address the communities quite directly as paraenesis. These two uses or functions of Scripture in 1 Peter are laid out in 1.10-12. As is suggested by the analysis above, which broadly affirms many of the traditional positions in scholarship on this passage, the Prophets of the past spoke of the sufferings experienced by Christ and the glories that followed. These events in salvation history form the basis of the kerygma celebrated in 1 Peter and this passage reveals Peter's assumption that Scripture has a kerygmatic function: instructing the Church with knowledge of Christ.[93]

A substantial body of scholarship has developed relating to the paraenesis of 1 Peter. Eduard Lohse notes that paraenetic is a significant feature of 1 Peter and is integral to the purpose of the epistle, suggesting that it is often derived from earlier paraenetic material:

> Der Brief wendet sich an Christen, die in Leiden und Anfechtungen stehen. Sie darin zu stärken und zu trösten, ist die Absicht des Verfassers, der dieser Aufgabe das übernommene paränetische Gut dienstbar zu machen sucht und es dadurch einem einheitlichen Leitgedanken – der Bewährung des Christen im Leiden – unterordnet.[94]

Lohse notes that Scripture is often used directly as paraenetic, drawing attention particularly to the use of Lev. 19.2 in 1 Pet. 1.16 and the use of Prov. 3.4 in 1 Pet. 5.5.[95] Similarly, van Unnik argues that the ethics of 1 Peter are not distinctive but that the justification for them in the letter is distinctly Christian: this includes the use of Scripture as paraenesis,

---

93. Horrell, *Peter and Jude*, p. 28.

94. Eduard Lohse, 'Paränese und Kerygma im I. Petrusbrief', *ZNW* 45 (1954), pp. 68–89 (73). ET, 'Parenesis and Kerygma in 1 Peter', in Talbert, ed., *Perspectives on First Peter*, pp. 37–59. Cf. Kelly, *Peter*, p. 135, and Goppelt, *Erste Petrusbrief*, p. 224. John Piper, 'Hope as the Motivation of Love: 1 Peter 3.9-12', *NTS* 26 (1980), pp. 212–31, who argues particularly for an eschatological dimension to the paraenesis of 1 Peter, noting, for example, that in 1.14 ταῖς πρότερον ἐν τῇ ἀγνοίᾳ ὑμῶν ἐπιθυμίαις are condemned as the result of 'ignorance' because they show no awareness of the eschatological call in 1.15. Cf. Scot Snyder, 'Participles and Imperatives in 1 Peter: A Re-examination in the Light of Recent Scholarly Trends', *Filologia Neotestamentica* 8 (1995), pp. 187–98.

95. Lohse, 'Paränese und Kerygma', pp. 85–7. Lohse suggests that the placing of the paraenetic before the citation is characteristic of 1 Peter when compared with the Pauline practice of placing 'kerygma' first. Cf. Earl Richard, 'The Functional Christology of First Peter', in Talbert, ed., *Perspectives on First Peter*, p. 124, and Dennis L. Stamps, 'The Use of the Old Testament in the New Testament as a Rhetorical Device: A Methodological Proposal', in *Hearing the Old Testament in the New Testament* (ed. Stanley E. Porter; Grand Rapids: Eerdmans, 2006), pp. 26–30.

providing a positive and often eschatological motivation.⁹⁶ Troy W. Martin adds to this that the scriptural motivation for paraenesis includes christological assertion.⁹⁷

Lauri Thurén's in-depth study of paraenesis in 1 Peter suggests that all previous research is lacking because motivations behind the paraenesis are actually various: it is the rhetorical function of the epistle which provides unity. Whilst there are many specific motivations employed by Peter, including christological example and both certainty of salvation as well as the eschatological threat of judgement, all these features combine to assert a very general and wide-ranging demand for distinctive Christian identity.⁹⁸ This is both to be understood theologically by the audiences of the epistle as well as understood in terms of the practical demands Christian identity makes ethically. Thurén notes that Scripture is often a feature in articulating this identity as well as demanding it in paraenesis.⁹⁹ Similarly, J. de Waal Dryden's study demonstrates that many of the themes represented in 1 Pet. 1.10-12 are important features in the letter's paraenetic strategy. Dryden argues that many of the paraenetic features of 1 Peter can also be seen in Greco Roman paraenetic epistles, noting the common use of narrative worldviews, remembrance and antithesis, moral instruction and moral exemplars. According to Dryden, 1 Pet. 1.3-12 is a narrated worldview, akin to what is suggested in Seneca's *Epistulae morales ad Lucilium* 95, as in 95.4:

> Deinde etiam si recte faciunt, nesciunt facere se recte. Non potest enim quisquam nisi ab initio formatus et tota ratione compositus omnes exequi numeros, ut sciat, quando oporteat et in quantum et cum quo et quemadmodum et quare. Non potest toto animo honesta conari, ne constanter

---

96. W. C. van Unnik, 'The Teaching of Good Works in 1 Peter', *NTS* 1 (1954–55), pp. 92–110. Likewise, Wolfgang Nauck, 'Freude im Leiden: Zum Problem einer urchristlichen Verfolgungstradition', *ZNW* 46 (1955), pp. 68–80, argues that joy associated with scripturally defined status is the motivation behind the paraenesis. Cf. the opposing view in Herbert Preisker, *Das Ethos des Urchristentums* (Darmstadt: Wissenschaftliche Buchgesellschaft, 1949), p. 38.

97. Troy W. Martin, *Metaphor and Composition in 1 Peter* (SBLDS 131; Atlanta: Scholars Press, 1992).

98. Lauri Thurén, *Argument and Theology in 1 Peter: The Origins of Christian Paraenesis* (JSNTSup 114; Sheffield: Sheffield Academic, 1995), pp. 223–4. The motivation for 1 Peter's parenesis is distinctive insofar as it uses the theological status of the people of God to encourage aspiration. Cf. Lauri Thurén, 'Motivation as the Core of Paraenesis – Remarks on Peter and Paul as Persuaders', in *Early Christian Paraenesis in Context* (ed. James Starr and Troels Engberg-Pedersen; BZNW 125; Berlin: de Gruyter, 2004), pp. 370–71.

99. Thurén, *Argument and Theology*, p. 88.

quidem aut libenter, sed respiciet, sed haesitabit. 'Si honesta' inquit 'actio ex praeceptis venit, ad beatam vitam praecepta abunde sunt: atqui est illud, ergo et hoc'. His respondebimus actiones honestas et praeceptis fieri, non tantum praeceptis.[100]

The purpose of 1.3-12 as narrative worldview is to 'supply an ideational context for moral deliberation and education', an ideological foundation upon which to advance paraenesis.[101] In particular, 1.10-12 merges two distinct narratives concerning the salvation-historical plan of God and the particular experience of the communities so as to explain the significance of the communities as the recipients of foretold grace and the service of the Prophets. This claim to status, Dryden argues, is essential for the one important aspect of 1 Peter's paraenesis which lacks precedent in Greco-Roman paraenetic epistles: the creation of corporate identity. Dryden explains this lack of precedent as due to the focus upon the individuals in the genre, though he notes a possible similarity in the development of philosophical schools, such as the Epicureans and Pythagoreans, which encouraged communal identity as an aid to progress in virtue.[102] Corporate identity in 1 Peter functions to develop the character of the communities by enabling them to realise their own status and thus why they must appear distinctive amongst the rest of society. This corporate identity is developed in 1 Pet. 2.9, where scriptural language is applied to the communities, and in 2.11-12, where the practical significance of the term παρεπίδημοι, mentioned already in 1.1, is developed. 1 Peter 1.3-12 lays the foundation for this aspect of the paraenesis of the epistle by providing a theological framework in which the importance of the

---

100. Dryden, *Theology and Ethics*, pp. 58–1. Cf. Boring, 'Narrative Dynamics in 1 Peter', pp. 34–7 and Joel B. Green, 'Narrating the Gospel in 1 and 2 Peter', *Int* 60 (2006), pp. 262–77, who draws attention to the development of theological narrative in 1 Peter, noting various stages in salvation history in 1.13-21, beginning with the primordial pre-existence of Christ, describing the ignorance of the communities in the past, the revelation of Christ and subsequent alienation of the communities as his followers before promising a final revelation and vindication.

101. Dryden, *Theology and Ethics*, p. 194. According to Elliott, *Home for the Homeless*, p. 104, 'The function of such ideology is not only to interpret but to motivate. Sectarian ideology is designed to assure members of their contact with the ultimate power(s) of existence and thereby reinforce their motivation to act. Members "will gain courage from perceiving themselves as part of a cosmic scheme" and undertake actions that "now have the legitimacy which proximity to the sacred provides".' Reference is made here to Edward Shils, 'The Concept and Function of Ideology', in *The International Encyclopedia of the Social Sciences* (New York: Macmillan, 1968), p. 72.

102. Dryden, *Theology and Ethics*, pp. 117–18.

community can be expressed. One might add to Dryden's work that the paraenetic role of Scripture as a warrant for instruction is a feature of the corporate identity expressed in 1.10-12. The communities are those for whom the Prophets of Israel's past wrote as servants. This is the theological identity of the communities narrated by Peter which is foundational for his paraenesis. Because of this, Scripture ought to be heard as directly addressing the situation of the communities, just as Peter assumes in practice in the epistle.

Whilst 1 Pet. 1.10-12 anticipates the paraenetic use of Scripture in the epistle by defining the prophetic witness as something divinely intended to serve the Christian communities, it also anticipates a kerygmatic use of Scripture as oriented towards the suffering and glories of Christ. An understanding of 1 Peter's use of Scripture as 'christological' has dominated the limited amount of scholarship that exists in this area. As noted above, the dominant assumption prior to Schutter's *Hermeneutic and Composition* was that Peter reads Scripture christologically.[103] Schutter's study slightly nuances this christological focus but Christology still provides his dominant explanation of the use of Scripture in 1 Peter as oriented towards the sufferings and glory of Christ.[104] Similarly, Achtemeier argues that 1.10-12 offers a 'Christocentric' account of Scripture which explains the christological interpretation of Scripture in 1 Peter.[105] There can be little doubt that there is a strong christological element in 1 Peter's use of Scripture, an element which has its hermeneutical grounding in 1.10-11. This analysis of 1.10-11 certainly explains why the stone texts of 2.6-8 are understood to be about Jesus Christ who is both chosen by God and rejected by humankind, and why Isaiah 53 is understood to be about the sufferings of Christ in 2.21-25. Scripture functions here as kerygma: it is a proclamation of the suffering and glories of Christ, in advance, through the Prophets whose words had no meaning other than to refer to this future.

But to see this simply as christological interpretation is to miss the broader purpose for which these uses of Scripture are intended. As will be argued below, in each case, the kerygmatic function of Scripture is subordinated to its paraenetic function. Scripture proclaims Christ and his sufferings so that the communities might be encouraged to live good lives. The primary function of Scripture is to justify, or simply provide,

---

103. Selwyn, *St Peter*, p. 24; Beare, *Peter*, p. 46; Reicke, *James, Peter and Jude*, p. 70; Schlosser, 'Ancien Testament et Christologie', pp. 65–96, and Bénétreau, 'Évangile et Prophétie', p. 178.
104. Schutter, *Hermeneutic and Composition*, p. 171.
105. Achtemeier, 'Suffering Servant', pp. 176 and 183.

paraenesis since the Prophets spoke to serve the very communities to whom Peter writes. It will be argued that the use of Scripture in 1 Peter reflects 1.10-12 as a hermeneutical statement with two important elements: Scripture as kerygma and Scripture as paraenesis. However, whereas scholarship has tended to emphasise the kerygmatic and christological element, it is more appropriate to see the paraenetic or ecclesiological element as dominant.[106] For Peter, the Prophets served not themselves but those who have had the Gospel proclaimed to them.

---

106. There is a parallel here with the somewhat more revolutionary argument of Richard B. Hayes, *Echoes of Scripture in the Letters of Paul* (New Haven: Yale University Press, 1989), pp. 165–8, which challenged the traditional assessment of Paul's use of Scripture as christological by noting a much more significant application of Scripture to the 'eschatological community'. Similarly, this reassessment takes seriously possible hermeneutical statements, such as 1 Cor. 10.11 (ταῦτα δὲ τυπικῶς συνέβαινεν ἐκείνοις, ἐγράφη δὲ πρὸς νουθεσίαν ἡμῶν, εἰς οὓς τὰ τέλη τῶν αἰώνων κατήντηκεν), which appear to place the 'eschatological community' within the intentions of those who wrote Scripture, in a manner similar to 1 Pet. 1.12.

Chapter 2

FORMAL CITATION OF SCRIPTURE IN 1 PETER

At the end of the opening of 1 Peter, the communities are told where they stand in relation to the Prophets of Israel's past. They are told that Scripture is fundamentally oriented towards the reality they know as followers of Jesus Christ and that it was written by those whose purpose it was to serve them. This chapter will explore the extent to which this hermeneutic is reflected in the use of scriptural citations in 1 Peter, whilst the next chapter will focus upon scriptural allusions. There are obvious problems with considering allusions and quotations separately. Citations and allusions are not always identifiable, nor are they always distinguishable, as will be seen below in the debate concerning the number of citations in 1 Peter. Furthermore, citations and allusions are often closely related, as in the case of iterative allusions. However, citations are typically easier to identify as deliberate references to Scripture. This can be seen in the much closer agreement between scholars on the number of allusions in 1 Peter compared to the wide range of views concerning the number of allusions in the epistle. At the same time, an analysis of the scriptural hermeneutics involved in the citation of a text is often much easier than if a text is simply alluded to, since the references typically function quite differently. A citation is often supplied in support of an argument, in which case the reason for the reference can be readily apparent. This is not so straightforward when one investigates the use of an allusion which is typically incorporated into the author's own words and may not even have been intended to be heard as a reference to Scripture. Because of this, the following two chapters will discuss citations and allusions separately, insofar such as is possible.

In this chapter, each citation of Scripture will be examined in turn. The form of the cited text will be discussed in brief, since this type of analysis was performed in such detail by Schutter and need not be repeated. The function of each citation within the argument of the epistle will be examined in greater detail so as to enable a view of Peter's scriptural hermeneutic specific to each citation. Each particular interpretation

2. Formal Citation of Scripture in 1 Peter

of Scripture will then be discussed in the light of 1 Pet. 1.10-12 as a hermeneutical statement. In the case of the citations of Scripture, it will be shown that the univocal meaning of Scripture suggested by the theological narrative implied in 1.10-12 is witnessed in the straightforward application of Scripture directly to Christ as kerygma and, primarily, to the audiences as paraenesis. But before an analysis of these citations can be conducted, some reflection on the nature of citation is needed in order to determine the number of such citations in 1 Peter.

1. What Is a Citation and How Many Are There in 1 Peter?

For its size, 1 Peter contains a significant number of scriptural citations. To this extent, all scholars agree. However, it is often difficult to determine the exact number of citations or quotations due to the difficulty in defining the precise nature of biblical citation in general. The discussion of what constitutes a citation or quotation has been an important feature of recent research into the use of the Old Testament in the New Testament.

For many scholars, a citation is really only known to be present if it is introduced using a citation formula. The use of formulae such as forms of λέγων/λέγοντος/λέγει/εἴρηκεν[1] and καθὼς γέγραπται[2] are well attested in the New Testament, perhaps representing the typical way in which a significant excerpt from Scripture is introduced. Consequently, the use of a citation formula with a reference to Scripture is a determining feature of what constitutes a citation in 1 Peter for many scholars.[3] As noted above, Michaels identifies only four formal citations in 1 Peter: 1.16, 24-25; 2.6 and 3.10-12. All of these use some form of the citation formula διότι, except 3.10, which simply uses γάρ, and are identified by Schutter

---

1. These are typically used as part of a larger clause indicating the identity of the speaker. Heb. 1.6, 7, 13; 2.12; 3.7, 15; 4.3, 7; 5.5, 6; 6.14; 7.21; 8.8; 9.20; 10.5, 8, 9, 15; 11.18; 12.5, 26; 13.6. Such modes of introduction are popular in the Epistle to the Hebrews, which typically posits Scripture as actively spoken by God or the pre-incarnate Christ. See, e.g., Andrew Lincoln, *Hebrews: A Guide* (London: Continuum, 2006), p. 75. Cf. Acts 2.17, 25, 34; 3.22, 25; 4.25; 7.3, 6 etc.

2. These are especially prominent within the Pauline corpus. E.g. Rom. 1.17; 2.24; 3.4, 10; 4.17; 8.36; 9.13, 33; 10.15; 11.8, 26 etc. Cf. Mk 1.2; 7.6; 11.17 and 14.27. This is also a feature of Q, as in Mt. 4.4, 6, 7 and 10.

3. Such as Steve Moyise, 'Quotations', in *As It Is Written: Studying Paul's Use of Scripture* (ed. S. E. Porter and C. D. Stanley; Atlanta: Society of Biblical Literature, 2008), p. 15, and idem, *The Old Testament in the New: An Introduction* (London: Continuum, 2001), p. 5, though it is not clear that Moyise himself thinks a citation needs a formula.

as 1 Peter's only 'explicit citations'.[4] In addition to this, Schutter regards 1 Pet. 4.8, 18 and 5.5b as 'implicit citation' of a lesser degree of 'literary dependence', using ὅτι and καὶ to introduce the reference. Elliott also includes 1 Pet. 2.25 as an implicit citation because of its introduction with γὰρ as in 3.10.[5] The great difficulty with insisting on the use of a citation formula before a reference can be labelled as a citation is that it is not always clear what a formula is.[6] Is καὶ ever a citation formula? Is ὅτι a formula? These are important questions in the study of the use of Scripture in 1 Peter if quotations are always introduced with a formula. Other scholars look for verbal similarity between a scriptural reference and its source: the closer the agreement between the two, the more likely the New Testament text contains a citation.[7] The difficulty here is that an assessment of verbal similarity relies too much on whether the majority readings of extant OG Scripture, to which a possible citation might be compared, was really available the New Testament writer in question.[8] The requirement for verbal similarity ignores the plurality of Greek translations of Scripture in the New Testament period, assuming the normativity of the 'LXX' version. Other scholars define citations in relation to rhetorical and reader-response factors, asking primarily whether a phrase is heard as a quotation from Scripture by its audience.[9] This approach is perhaps the most helpful, though it raises a host of unanswerable questions associated with an audience's education and

---

4. Michaels, *1 Peter*, p. xl, Schutter, *Hermeneutic and Composition*, pp. 36–7. The formulae in 1 Peter are comparably minimal, justifying the observation by Feldmeier, *Letter of Peter*, p. 26, that the majority of citations in 1 Peter are 'merged' with the language of the letter.

5. Elliott, *Commentary*, p. 13.

6. Stamps, 'Rhetorical Device', pp. 12–13, and S. E. Porter, 'The Use of the Old Testament in the New: A Brief Comment on Method and Terminology', in *Early Christian Interpretation of the Scriptures of Israel* (ed. C. A. Evans and J. A. Saunders; JSNTSup 148; Sheffield: Sheffield Academic, 1997), pp. 79–96.

7. R. T. France, *Jesus and the Old Testament* (London: Tyndale, 1982), pp. 259–63; Robert G. Bratcher, *Old Testament Quotations in the New Testament* (London: UBS, 1961), p. vii, and L. P. Trudinger, 'Some Observations Concerning the Test of the Old Testament in the Book of Revelation', *JTS* 17 (1966), pp. 82–8. In research on the use of Scripture in 1 Peter, this approach is employed by Woan, 'Psalms in 1 Peter', p. 213.

8. McLay, *Use of the Septuagint*, p. 6.

9. R. H. Gundry, *The Use of the Old Testament in St Matthew's Gospel: With Special Reference to the Messianic Hope* (NovTSup 8; Leiden: Brill, 1975), p. 9, and Stanley, *Arguing with Scripture*, p. 62. Cf. idem, '"Pearls Before Swine": Did Paul's Audience Understand his Biblical Quotations?', *NovT* 41 (1999), pp. 124–44.

familiarity with Scripture. The rhetorical force of a citation depends upon the extent to which it stands out from the text as a citation: as a plea to a higher authority. A citation disrupts the author's discourse by introducing words which are in some way alien, either because of the sense of authority given to it or because it introduces elements which are not explained in the text in which it is cited.[10] The best example of this in 1 Peter is the reference to Isa. 8.12 in 1 Pet. 3.14. There is no citation formula to identify this as a citation, nor is there much verbal agreement with extant OG readings of Isa. 8.2, yet this is still clearly a citation because it appears as something which interrupts Peter's own discourse, introducing the word αὐτῶν, which bears no relation at all to the discourse. A citation need not require the use of a citation formula, simply enough disjuncture to make it clear to an audience that the speaker or writer is borrowing words from elsewhere. Verbal correspondence to a source also creates awareness of a citation amongst an audience if a text is familiar.[11] However, a lack of verbal correspondence between a potential extant source and a potential citation need not rule out the possibility that a citation is present. Such a citation could be a reference to a text now unknown. As Hayes notes, since forms of scriptural reference depend significantly upon their reception by readers, scholars face the difficulty that often the text thought to contain scriptural references is itself the only source of information about the readers for whom it was originally intended.[12]

So how many citations or quotations are there in 1 Peter? Schutter describes 1.16, 24-25a; 2.6-8 and 3.10-12 as explicit citations and 4.8, 18 and 5.5b as implicit citations.[13] Elliott accepts each of these but includes 2.5 as well on the basis of its introduction with γάρ, as with 3.10-12, whereas Jobes raises the number to 14.[14] The majority of scholars agree that the citation formula διότι περιέχει ἐν γραφῇ in 2.6 includes the references to Isaiah 28, Psalm 118 and Isaiah 8 that follow, enabling them to be defined as citations, though not each introduced with its own formula.

---

10. This sense of incongruity is a feature of Julia Kristeva's work on intertextuality. Reference in a text to another text introduces features of a cited text which cannot be easily reconciled by the reader to the final text. Intertextuality marks the end of an author's control over his or her text's meaning by introducing another hand. Julia Kristeva, *Desire in Language: A Semiotic Approach to Literature and Art* (New York: Columbia University Press, 1980).
11. Moyise, 'Quotations', pp. 15–16.
12. Hayes, *Echoes of Scripture*, pp. 28–9
13. Schutter, *Hermeneutic and Composition*, pp. 36–7.
14. Elliott, *Commentary*, p. 13, and Jobes, 'Textual Tradition in 1 Peter', p. 315.

This study differs by including 3.14 as a citation on the basis of its interruption of the discourse. Rather interestingly, Moyise suggests that the use of this formula introduces each reference up to and including the reference to Exod. 19.6, which is usually regarded as an allusion.[15] This raises interesting questions about the nature of a citation and whether an allusion might be introduced by a formula. Moyise raises this question again regarding the reference to Ps. 34.7 in 1 Pet. 2.3, which he regards as citation due to the explicit citation of a large part of that psalm in 3.10-12, though, interestingly, this long citation lacks a citation formula as such.[16]

2. Analysis of the Citations in 1 Peter

This chapter will analyse eleven citations which fulfil the definition of citation argued for above. It will be argued that the dominant use of the citations is to provide or support the paraenesis of the letter. At the same time, it will be seen that some of the citations also have a kerygmatic or proclamatory function, describing the significance of Jesus Christ and the communities addressed by the letter, though this function is always related to a broader paraenesis.

a. 1 Peter 1.16 and Leviticus 19.2

The precise form of the refrain from Leviticus cited here matches Lev. 19.2 in extant OG versions, whilst bearing a very close resemblance to its other occurrences in Lev. 11.44; 20.7 and 20.26.[17] The citation is paraphrased in the preceding verse, which gives some indication of how it is understood by Peter.[18] This verse interprets the citation before it is

---

15. Moyise, 'Isaiah in 1 Peter', p. 175. Cf. Elliott, *Commentary*, p. 13, who includes the allusion to Hosea in 2.10 as introduced by the formula in 2.6.

16. Moyise, 'Isaiah in 1 Peter', p. 175.

17. Achtemeier, *1 Peter*, p. 122. Lev. 11.44 follows a longer form: καὶ ἁγιασθήσεσθε καὶ ἅγιοι ἔσεσθε, ὅτι ἅγιός εἰμι ἐγὼ κύριος ὁ θεὸς ὑμῶν, which is mirrored in 20.7 without καὶ ἁγιασθήσεσθε, whereas 20.27 begins καὶ ἔσεσθε μοι ἅγιοι. In 20.7 and 27, εἰμι is also absent, as it is in many readings of 1 Pet. 1.16. NA²⁷ is rather indecisive here, but the evidence against inclusion is rather strong: ℵ, A* and B, but with 𝔓72 including the term.

18. Schutter, *Hermeneutic and Composition*, p. 40, defines 1 Pet 1.15 as an iterative allusion to the text explicitly cited in 1.16. This verse is not without its difficulties, such as whether τὸν καλέσαντα is substantive, making ἅγιον an predicative adjective, or vice versa ('as He who has called you is holy' or 'as the Holy One has called you'). Achtemeier, *1 Peter*, p. 121, advocates the former whilst Michaels, *1 Peter*, pp. 58–9, chooses the latter. Both substantives have significant precedent

given, as is also the case in 2.4-6, just before the catena of 'stone' texts.[19] The exhortation καὶ αὐτοὶ ἅγιοι ἐν πάσῃ ἀναστροφῇ γενήθητε makes it clear that holiness is understood primarily in practical or ethical terms, rather than being purely ontological.[20] This prepares the ground for the citation which likewise relates corporate holiness to the holiness of God. As Achtemeier notes, there is nothing in the etymology of the term 'holy' that implies moral action, yet the connection of vv. 15-16 to the paraenesis in v. 14 (which makes demands upon the communities' behaviour) with the adversative conjunction ἀλλά, as well as the separation (from a dominant culture regarded as depraved) demanded by holiness, makes it clear that the citation is meant to support a call to distinctive behaviour.[21] The agreement between the form of the text in 1.16 with extant OG versions of Lev. 19.2, as well as the use of the citation formula διότι γέγραπται, explain why this is universally regarded as a citation. This is the only example of this citation formula in 1 Peter, though others use διότι with other terms.

Selwyn argues that the use of the citation suggests that Peter understood the Christian communities to have a neo-levitical status, an idea enforced by the references to priesthood in 2.5 and 9.[22] Whilst Selwyn's claim depends upon the assumption that Peter understood this text to have had a cultic significance (an understanding not necessarily obvious if Peter's scriptural source was some sort of testimonia collection, or even a baptismal formula as Selwyn suggests), the original literary context of the citation is also important for those who reject Selwyn's view. Mbuvi argues that the context of the citation within Leviticus is significant for its use in 1 Peter. Against Selwyn, he suggests that the command is directed towards the nation whose holiness is seen in relation to the cult, rather than to the Levitical priesthood in particular.[23]

---

both in the OG Scriptures in the case of ἅγιον (Pss. 70.22; 77.41; 88.19; Isa. 1.4; 5.16; 14.27 etc., though neither Michaels nor Achtemeier are certain of 1 Jn 2.20) and the New Testament in the case of τὸν καλέσαντα (Rom. 9.12; Gal. 1.6; 5.8). As Achtemeier suggests, the presence of the substantive τὸν καλέσαντα in 1 Pet. 2.9 and 5.10 is decisive.

19. Michaels, *1 Peter*, p. 59. Cf. Heb. 8.7-8.

20. As Wayne A. Grudem, *The First Epistle of Peter: An Introduction and Commentary* (TNTC; Leicester: IVP, 1988), p. 79, notes, ἀναστροφη is used to refer to both ethical and depraved behaviour in 1 Pet. 1.18; 2.12; 3.1, 2 and 16. Cf. 2 Pet. 2.7 and 2 Pet. 3.11.

21. Achtemeier, *1 Peter*, pp. 120–2.

22. Selwyn, *1 Peter*, pp. 369–74, and Michaels, *1 Peter*, p. 60.

23. Mbuvi, *Temple, Exile and Identity*, pp. 75–8. Cf. Elliott, *The Elect and the Holy*, pp. 208–9, and idem, *Commentary*, p. 364.

This association of temple and people is exploited in 1 Peter, according to Mbuvi, as the communities are depicted as the 'Temple-Community': a people to whom the language of the temple can be applied. Mbuvi notes a similar understanding of community in 1QM 5.5; 12.7; 16.1; 1QSb 1.5, and suggests that the concept of תרומת שפתים in 1QS 9.3-6 and 26 is equivalent to πνευματικαὶ θυσίαι in 1 Pet. 2.5: the appropriate sacrifices to be offered in the 'Temple-Community'. Likewise, for Carson, the form of the citation, resembling most closely Lev. 19.2, is significant. He suggests that the citation in this form recalls the Holiness Code, from which the citation is taken, rather than the Passover or Exodus contexts in which the other instances of the refrain are to be found.[24] Carson, whilst noting that Peter does not associate the citation with the ritual of the Holiness Code (in contrast to Qumran), does not appear to explain the exegetical significance of his suggestion that Peter would have had the context of the citation in mind when he used it. The difficulty with exploring this suggestion is that, with such a familiar phrase as the citation, would such precise detail have mattered? Would Peter's audience have known the various forms of the refrain and known where they featured in Leviticus? Can one be sure that the OG text of Leviticus did not harmonise the various versions of the refrain along the lines of that cited by Peter?

Cranfield suggests that Peter's use of this refrain from the Holiness Code is consistent with its function in Leviticus, since both predicate conduct as the people of God upon the nature of God.[25] Likewise, Best notes the etymological sense of holiness as 'separation' evident within the Holiness Code and likens this to the 'separation' from paganism required of the communities in 1 Peter. This accords with Elliott's analysis of the use of the citation to enforce or consolidate the social alienation already experienced by the community.[26] Best's comparison is problematic due to the scholarly disagreement on the nature of the relationship between the communities and 'gentile' society in 1 Peter. Whilst the communities are urged both to regard themselves and live as having a unique theological status as the people of God, it is not clear

---

24. Carson, '1 Peter', pp. 1017–18.
25. Cranfield, *Peter*, p. 37. Cf. Joseph, *A Narratological Reading of 1 Peter*, p. 84, and Green, *1 Peter*, p. 44, who suggests that 1 Pet. 1.17 (καὶ εἰ πατέρα ἐπικαλεῖσθε τὸν ἀπροσωπολήμπτως...ἐν φόβῳ...) is a reflection of Lev. 19.3 (ἕκαστος πατέρα αὐτοῦ καὶ μητέρα αὐτοῦ φοβείσθω).
26. Best, *1 Peter*, pp. 86–7; Feldmeier, *Letter of Peter*, pp. 106–7, and Elliott, *Home for the Homeless*, p. 136.

that a separation from those who are not God's people, comparable to the separation from the surrounding nations encouraged in Leviticus, is evident.[27]

The use of Scripture here represents an example of the paraenetic type suggested in the previous chapter.[28] The future ἔσεσθε is clearly intended to function as an imperative as in Mt. 5.48: a direct equivalent of the Hebrew qal imperfect תהיו (Lev. 19.2) and qal consecutive perfect והייתם (Lev. 11.44).[29] Scripture, understood to be written for the benefit of Jesus' followers, addresses Peter's audience directly in paraenetic style. It is not that it describes the situation of those who have had good news proclaimed to them; rather, it is a text written to serve them as it exhorts them to holiness in the face of suffering and alienation. Achtemeier suggests that the application of the citation from the Holiness Code to the communities addressed by 1 Peter is 'further evidence of the way the author of 1 Peter has appropriated for the Christian community the specific commands to, and attributes of, Israel'.[30] As Jobes explains,

> By quoting from Leviticus, Peter immediately applies in verse 16 the principle he has explained in 1.10-12 – that the prophets knew they were ministering not to themselves but "for your sake." He claims that his readers must be holy in their whole way of life because God has said to his people "Be holy because I am holy." Peter assumes that the OT writings are authoritative and normative for his Christian readers, regardless of their previous ethnic origin. He makes no distinction between the Jewish and Gentile Christians in his application, nor does the span of time between Leviticus and his letter mitigate the relevance of God's ancient revelation of himself.[31]

However, there is no evidence, both in the use of this citation here as well as in the theological narrative of 1.10-12, that the citation is understood to refer both to Israel at the time of the exodus as well as the communities in the present. Whilst it is possible that Peter does understand Scripture to have a dual referent when it functions as paraenesis, the direct application to the communities as well as the conviction that the Prophets served not their own situation but that yet to come in 1.12

---

27. Yet, as Kelly, *Peter*, p. 70, notes, the Qumran community *was* able to articulate its separation from society in terms of its holiness (1QM 3.5; 12.7; 16.1; 1QSb 1.5).
28. Thurén, *Argument and Theology*, pp. 108–11.
29. Bigg, *St Peter*, p. 116.
30. Achtemeier, *1 Peter*, p. 122.
31. Jobes, *1 Peter*, pp. 113–14. Cf. Joseph, *Narratological Reading of 1 Peter*, pp. 84–5.

demonstrates that the present is what has importance for Peter. Again, this importance is related to the theological narrative of salvation history which positions the communities addressed by 1 Peter with Christ at the grand climax of God's plan from before the foundation of the world.

b. 1 Peter 1.24-25 and Isaiah 40.6b and 8

Just as the citation from Lev. 19.2 encourages Peter's audiences to be distinctive as they strive to be holy, so the next citation emphasises the extent to which these Christians are distinct from others in society by virtue of their spiritual birth.

The citation itself contains few significant variations from extant OG versions. Peter includes ὡς in the first clause of the citation, probably for stylistic reasons.[32] This is omitted in ℵ², A, Ψ and several uncials, perhaps representing attempts to 'correct' the citation. Αὐτῆς (αὐτοῦ in ℵ* and bo^ms) is also included in the second clause of the citation despite an absence in extant OG versions. This appears to be a substitute for ἀνθρώπος, referring instead back to σάρξ. It is hard to see why Peter might change the text in this way, hence many commentators consider such variants to be unimportant.[33] Furthermore, the form of the text cited in 1 Pet. 1.24-25a agrees with extant OG texts in its omission of the Hebrew יבש חציר נבל ציץ כי רוח יהוה נשבה בו אכן חציר העם from Isa. 40.7.[34] Perhaps the most substantial disagreement between the citation and extant OG versions is in the final clause of the citation where κυρίου appears to replace τοῦ θεοῦ ἡμῶν. This, if it is a change made by Peter rather than simply a witness to a variant OG reading, may be in order to emphasize the christological sense of the text, in which the citation is seen to relate to the good news about Jesus Christ proclaimed to Peter's audience.[35] There is some extant evidence of OG readings of Isa. 40.8

---

32. Bigg, *St Peter*, p. 24. Moyise, 'Isaiah in 1 Peter', p. 176, notes that ὡς is used 27 times in the epistle.

33. Hort, *St Peter*, p. 94; Bigg, *St Peter*, p. 24; Michaels, *1 Peter*, p. 77, and Selwyn, *Peter*, p. 152. Selwyn suggests here that variants are likely to reflect the source available to Peter or else represent a remembered version of Isa. 40.6.

34. Though, as Schutter, *Hermeneutic and Composition*, p. 124, notes, this verse is also absent in 1QIsa and may reflect a common reading in Hebrew also.

35. As argued by Bigg, *St Peter*, p. 25; Best, *1 Peter*, p. 96, and Elliott, *Commentary*, p. 391. Frederick W. Danker, '1 Peter 1 24–2 17 – A Consolatory Pericope', *ZNW* 58 (1967), pp. 93–102 (94), suggests that this is a deliberate change made by the author of 1 Peter to enable an easier transition to the use of Ps. 33.9 in 1 Pet. 2.3, which uses κύριος. Moyise, 'Isaiah in 1 Peter', p. 177, agrees that the use of κύριος here represents a deliberate change, perhaps drawing upon the use of the title in Isa. 40.5, the verse prior to the cited passage. However, Achtemeier, *1 Peter*, p. 141, draws the opposite conclusion from the presence of κύριος in Isa. 40.5,

which employ κυρίου, principally in L¹, 46, 233, 456 and Co Syp^a, though Moyise contends that these readings may have been influenced by 1 Pet. 1.25.³⁶

The citation and material immediately associated with it serve to support the paraenesis of 1.22 by defining the special status of the communities. The communities are told that they have experienced a new birth or begetting from imperishable seed through the word of God and hence have a quality of permanence which distinguishes them from their social setting.³⁷ In 1.23, Peter's audiences are described as having been born (ἀναγεγεννημένοι) through the living word of God. The word is described as imperishable in order to emphasise the certainty or the quality of the birth undergone by the audiences.³⁸ This 'new birth' is, as Peter proclaims in 1.3, achieved through the resurrection of Jesus Christ. In light of this, 1.23-25 probably represents the application of this new birth to the communities through their reception of the word about the Lord: the Gospel.³⁹ However, as E. A. LaVerdiere points out, the syntax of διὰ λόγου ζῶντος θεοῦ καὶ μένοντος in v. 23 is awkward and could mean 'through the word of the living and enduring God', rather than 'through the living and enduring word of God'.⁴⁰ Most scholars appear to

---

suggesting that it may have been a feature of the source of Isa. 40.8 upon which 1 Pet. 1.25 depends. Indeed, as Schutter, *Hermeneutic and Composition*, p. 126, observes, the addition of κύριος does not help Peter's application of the text to the Gospel as a message 'about the Lord' since the phrase continues to be a subjective genitive.

36. Moyise, 'Isaiah in 1 Peter', p. 176. Cf. Schutter, *Hermeneutic and Composition*, p. 124.

37. Many scholars have noted the similarity between this and other New Testament texts. Bigg, *St Peter*, p. 123, and Grudem, *1 Peter*, p. 90, suggest that the imperishable seed as ὁ λόγος τοῦ θεοῦ is indebted to Lk. 8.21. Cranfield, *Peter*, p. 42, and Best, *1 Peter*, p. 94, compare the divine birth with that in Jn 1.13 whereas Kelly, *Peter*, pp. 80–1, notes the similarity with Jas 1.18. Kelly also notes that λόγος is frequently employed to refer to the Gospel message rather than the speech of God or Scripture in the New Testament (1 Cor. 14.36; 2 Cor. 2.17; Col. 1.25; 1 Thess. 1.6; 2 Thess. 3.1) and suggests that the use of σπέρμα in 1 Jn 3.9 is similar to the use of σπορά in 1 Pet. 1.23 insofar as both are used to represent the Gospel received by members of the letters' audiences.

38. Carson, '1 Peter', p. 1019, suggests that the distinction drawn by v. 23 is in terms of the fragility of ordinary life compared with the life God offers. Cf. 1 Pet. 1.3-4.

39. Best, *1 Peter*, p. 95. Cf. Schutter, *Hermeneutic and Composition*, p. 126, and Feldmeier, *Letter of Peter*, p. 124.

40. E. A. LaVerdiere, 'A Grammatical Ambiguity in 1 Pet. 1.23', *CBQ* 36 (1974), pp. 89–94. This reading is taken by Michaels, *1 Peter*, p. 76, who notes that the description 'living God' is commonplace (Deut. 5.26; Josh. 3.10; 1 Sam. 17.26,

adopt the latter meaning in view of the dominant theme of the 'word' and because Isa. 40.6b and 8 seem to be cited in support of the word's imperishability.[41]

Michaels argues that σπορά is used rather than the perhaps more obvious σπέρμα because it implies the act of sowing and anticipates the grass simile in the citation.[42] Achtemeier disagrees, arguing that σπορά must be taken as a reference to human production since the grass imagery in the citation relates to durability rather than production.[43] Indeed, Best notes that the 'imperishable seed' is of relative unimportance and is not clearly identified; rather, it is the 'word' as the agent of birth which is important.[44] 'Birth' and 'seed' imagery in v. 23a is quite separate, then, from the citation which merely clarifies the nature of the 'word' as the agent of this birth. Because the 'word' is the sole agent in the spiritual birth of the communities, it is unlikely that any reference to baptism is meant here.[45]

Following the citation, in v. 25 Peter seeks to clarify the meaning of the citation as something which relates particularly to the experience of his audiences. Peter identifies the ῥῆμα of the citation with the good news proclaimed to them. This draws the comparison between 1.12 and 1.22-25 much closer: it is the proclamation of good news which features in each case. Likewise, the citation enhances the contrast between the audiences' present status as the people of God with their previous status before their transformation by the word of the Lord. As noted above, the rejection of a previous or inherited way of life is an important feature of the paraenesis in 1.13-21, as it is in Greco Roman paraenetic epistles.[46]

36; 2 Kgs 19.4, 16; Pss. 42.2; 84.2; Isa. 37.4, 17; Jer. 10.10; 23.36; Dan. 6.20, 26; Hos. 1.10; Mt. 16.16; 26.63; Acts 14.15; Rom. 9.26; 2 Cor. 3.3; 6.16; 1 Tim. 3.15; 4.10; Heb. 3.12; 9.14; 10.31; 12.22; and Rev. 7.2). The 'ambiguity' is eliminated in various texts, including Ψ.

41. This reading is supported by the suggestion of Schutter, *Hermeneutic and Composition*, p. 125, that the phrase is an iterative allusion to Isa. 40.8 (a clear reference to the 'word') featuring μένοντος and μένει.

42. Michaels, *1 Peter*, p. 76.

43. Achtemeier, *1 Peter*, p. 139. Cf. Green, *1 Peter*, p. 54.

44. Best, *1 Peter*, p. 94.

45. Goppelt, *Erste Petrusbrief*, p. 132, and Achtemeier, *1 Peter*, p. 139.

46. Dryden, *Theology and Ethics*, pp. 94–5, notes the similarity between the rejection of the past here and Stoic notions of προκοπή. As Dryden notes, the use of memory of the past state of those addressed by paraenesis as the antithesis of virtue functions to motivate those addressed by reminding them of their prior progress. This is demonstrated in Epictetus' *Discourses* 2.17.36-37, εἶτ' ἀλλήλοις ὀνείρους διηγησάμενοι πάλιν ἐπὶ ταὐτὰ ἐπανέρχεσθε ὡσαύτως ὀρέγεσθε, ὡσαύτως ἐκκλίνετε, ὁμοίως ὁρμᾶτε, ἐπιβάλλεσθε, προτίθεσθε, ταὐτὰ εὔχεσθε, περὶ ταὐτὰ σπουδάζετε.

This way of life is described in v. 14 as conformity to ταῖς πρότερον ἐν τῇ ἀγνοίᾳ ὑμῶν ἐπιθυμίαις and in v. 18 as τῆς ματαίας ὑμῶν ἀναστροφῆς πατροπαραδότου.⁴⁷ Moyise suggests that the citation of Isa. 40.6 and 8 is intended to relate to this previous way of life in its depiction of flesh as grass which withers in contrast to the word which remains.⁴⁸

As in 1 Pet. 1.16, the use of Scripture here also serves a paraenetic purpose.⁴⁹ On either side of the citation are exhortations to ἐκ [καθαρᾶς] καρδίας ἀλλήλους ἀγαπήσατε ἐκτενῶς (1.22) and ἀποθέμενοι...πᾶσαν κακίαν καὶ πάντα δόλον καὶ ὑποκρίσεις καὶ φθόνους καὶ πάσας καταλαλιάς (2.1), connected to the citation by means of οὖν. At the same time, the use of Scripture is kerygmatic, informing Peter's audiences of their status as people born of the imperishable word of the Gospel. This dual function of the citation (both paraenetic and kerygmatic) is an example of Thurén's assertion that 'gospel and paraenesis' serve the same purpose in 1 Peter.⁵⁰

An important hermeneutical question emerges from some scholarly assessment of this citation: Does Peter conceive of Isa. 40.6 and 8 as referring *exclusively* to his Christian audiences? A number of scholars follow Selwyn in suggesting that Peter knew of the exilic historical and literary context of the citation from Isaiah.⁵¹ The words of comfort Isaiah spoke to the exiles in Babylon were chosen by Peter because his audiences were similarly aliens and strangers. There is some suggestion that Peter did in fact know some of the literary context of the citation. For example, some suggest that the explanatory τοῦτο δέ ἐστιν τὸ ῥῆμα τὸ εὐαγγελισθὲν εἰς ὑμᾶς in v. 25b is a reflection of Isa. 40.9 (ἐπ'ὄρος ὑψηλὸν ἀνάβηθι, ὁ εὐαγγελιζόμενος Ζιων ὕψωσον τῇ ἰσχύι τὴν φωνήν σου, ὁ εὐαγγελιζόμενος Ιερουσαλημ), and so is a continuation of the scriptural reference.⁵² Likewise the presence of κύριος in Isa. 40.5 (καὶ ὀφθήσεται ἡ δόξα κυρίου, καὶ ὄψεται πᾶσα σὰρξ τὸ σωτήριον τοῦ θεοῦ ὅτι κύριος

---

47. On the significance of πατροπαράδοτος in 1 Peter's critique of the former way of life of its audiences, see W. C. van Unnik, 'The Critique of Paganism in 1 Peter 1.18', in *Neotestamentica et Semitica: Studies in Honour of Matthew Black* (ed. E. Earle Ellis and Max Wilcox; Edinburgh: T. & T. Clark, 1969), pp. 140–1. Van Unnik examines similar terminology in Epictetus' *Ench.* 31 and Porphyrius' *Ad Marcellam* 18, and notes the high value of tradition as guarantor of national culture and social order.
48. Moyise, 'Isaiah in 1 Peter', p. 177.
49. Thurén, *Argument and Theology*, pp. 116–19.
50. Thurén, *Argument and Theology*, p. 223.
51. Selwyn, *Peter*, p. 153; Green, *1 Peter*, p. 53, and Jobes, *1 Peter*, pp. 125–7.
52. Best, *1 Peter*, p. 95; Michaels, *1 Peter*, p. 79.

ἐλάλησεν) might explain the apparent change to Isa. 40.8 in 1 Pet. 1.25.[53] However, there is no clear indication that Peter has in mind the historical situation of his citation's first audiences.[54] Peter is interested in only one audience and he assumes that Scripture is the same.

The mode of citation and the concluding comment in 1.25 seem to suggest that in a rather straightforward way Isa. 40.6b-8 is directed towards the communities to whom he writes in particular: '*This* is the word that was proclaimed as good news to *you*'. The cited text is understood to be fundamentally oriented towards the experience of the communities.[55] This is perhaps unsurprising given Peter's view in 1.10-12 that the prophetic writings lacked meaning within the time they were written and referred to the future: specifically the future Christ and the glory after him. If this is the case, Carson's suggestion that Peter understood something of the exilic context in which his citation first had meaning (and that his use of it in his letter reflects his perception of a common discouragement shared by the exiles and his audiences) is difficult.[56] Given Peter's use of exilic language in 1.1 to describe his audiences, this interpretation seems plausible. But would Peter really have understood Isa. 40.6b-8 as originally addressing the exiles? Such awareness of the original historical context of Scripture is not uncommon in the New Testament. For example, the author of Hebrews is aware that Ps. 95.8-11 was written by David in the land of Israel, a fact which

---

53. Moyise, 'Isaiah in 1 Peter', p. 177. Perhaps the use of πᾶσα σάρξ in both Isa. 40.5 and the cited passage in 1 Pet. 1.24-25 serves to support this possible relationship. Cf. Achtemeier, *1 Peter*, p. 141.

54. As Kelly, *Peter*, p. 81, notes, 'our writer's interest is focused, not of course on the historical situation recalled by the passage [from Isaiah], but on the way it highlights the enduring reliability of the Lord's utterance'. Cf. Doering, 'Gottes Volk', pp. 106–9.

55. Selwyn, *Peter*, p. 153, suggests that τοῦτο δέ ἐστιν τὸ ῥῆμα τὸ εὐαγγελισθὲν εἰς ὑμᾶς simply brings the citation to 'events of the contemporary scene', yet it is more the case that this is the means of application of the text to the communities and hence the justification for citing the text. Because Peter understands the communities to be essentially defined by their privileged reception of the Gospel (understood as the 'word'), he employs a text which he understands to refer to this 'word' to proclaim the communities' identity as the basis of his paraenesis.

56. Carson, '1 Peter', pp. 1021–2. Carson's reading is certainly plausible since it is not absolutely clear that Peter views the citation as determinate. It could be that the citation merely functions as a description of the word of God, employed by Peter as a text thought to be principally about that word, rather than a prophecy of the birth through the word his readers are to have undergone.

conditions his application of that text to his audience.⁵⁷ However, it seems unlikely that Peter would have understood a passage such as Isa. 40.6b-8 to refer to two particular groups of people at different times given his description of prophetic ministry in 1.10-12. For Peter, Isa. 40.6b-8 is about the communities to which he writes and the proclamation they have received. Schutter also notes the relation of this use of Scripture to the 'hermeneutic' of 1 Pet. 1.10-12, which he understands to be primarily christological:

> Thus the relationship between the Isaianic quotation to 1.22-3 is more than simply that of a proof-text which ascribes the enduring nature of Christian existence to properties inherent in God's word, because it specially identifies that word with the message about the Lord Jesus. What seems to be involved is an eschatological disclosure of an oracle's hidden meaning on the order of I Pet. 1.10-2, the 'unriddling of a riddle' characteristic of a pesher-like hermeneutic.⁵⁸

Here Schutter's understanding of the 'hermeneutic' of 1 Pet. 1.10-12 as primarily related to the orientation of prophecy to the sufferings and glory of Christ limits his analysis of the hermeneutic employed in 1.22-25. Schutter has such difficulty with the subjective genitive in v. 25a because he needs to demonstrate that the Isaiah quotation is understood, in some way, to be about Christ and the message of the Gospel about him. Yet the analysis of 1.10-12 in the previous chapter of this study suggests that the primary focus of Peter's scriptural hermeneutic is the communities to which he writes: those served by the Prophets, including, presumably, Isaiah. Certainly, Scripture is understood to be about Christ, but its primary orientation is towards the communities for which it was spoken or written as an act of service. Hence, whether the 'word' in 1.25a is 'about the Lord' or not, this hermeneutic is expressed in the relation between that 'word' and the 'word' of the Gospel proclaimed to the communities. Elliott suggests that the aorist passive participle εὐαγγελισθὲν 'recalls' 1 Pet. 1.12 and demonstrates how the citation is applied to the communities because of their unique position described in 1.10-12:

> The phrase 'to you'..., located last for emphasis, once again illustrates the stress placed in this letter on the 'for-you-ness' of the good news... Their privileged reception of this good news marks the divinely conferred

---

57. R. T. France, *Jesus and the Old Testament: His Application of Old Testament Passages to Himself and His Mission* (Grand Rapids: Baker, 1971), p. 271 and Harold W. Attridge, '"Let Us Strive to Enter That Rest": The Logic of Hebrews 4.1-11', *HTR* 73 (1980), pp. 279-88 (280).

58. Schutter, *Hermeneutic and Composition*, pp. 126–7.

dignity of the believers in contrast to their public demeaning, and the enduring power of this good news provides the strength for their familial solidarity.[59]

This direct application of Isa. 40.6 and 8 to the communities is also possible because, as Jobes suggests, Peter understands the Spirit of Christ (1 Pet. 1.11) to be at work in Isaiah as a prophet.[60] Whilst it is not clear that Peter knew of this text as belonging to Isaiah (though this is certainly plausible given the naming of Isaiah in relation to citations from Isaiah in the New Testament – Mk 1.2; Lk. 3.4; 4.17; Acts 28.25; Rom. 9.27, 29), it is right to note the fundamental understanding of Scripture's inspiration through the Spirit of Christ which apparently gives the prophetic witness an essential orientation towards the needs of the communities.

c. 1 Peter 2.6-10: Stone *Stichwört* Catena and Associated Allusions

The next three citations all feature the word λίθος and have often been thought to have been associated with one another through a common source: a florilegium or catena. Whether these texts were available to Peter as a written source remains open to question. In any case, these texts are presented as a catena of clearly identified citations. 1 Peter 2.6-10 represents the most sophisticated and complex treatment of Scripture within 1 Peter and has offered scholars interested in the use of Scripture in 1 Peter much to consider. It will therefore be explored in some detail in terms of its possible sources, purpose and exegetical style before each cited text is considered in turn.

(1) *The Source of the Catena.* Stone and architecture provide a common source of christological and ecclesiological metaphor in the use of Scripture in the New Testament.[61] In Mk 12.10 and parallels, Jesus cites Ps. 118.22 (OG Ps. 117.22) to explain his significance in spite of his rejection by humankind. In Acts 4.11, the same scriptural passage is cited to define the exclusive significance of Jesus. In Eph. 2.19-22, the Church is described as a temple in the process of being built, held

---

59. Elliott, *Commentary*, p. 392.
60. Jobes, *1 Peter*, p. 127.
61. Of which Norman Hillyer, '"Rock-Stone" Imagery in 1 Peter', *TynBul* 22 (1971), pp. 58–60, provides a helpful overview. Of particular interest is Hillyer's observation that צור is often translated θεός in OG Scriptures and that in *Gen. Rab.* 70.9 the covering stone at the well in Gen. 29.2 is interpreted as referring to the Shekinah.

2. Formal Citation of Scripture in 1 Peter

together by Jesus as ἀκρογωνιαῖος.[62] What is interesting in 1 Peter is that these christological and ecclesiological elements are combined. Is this an indication that the catena texts employed here are taken from an existing collection of texts featuring this popular motif? Or does the catena represent a distinctive contribution to the tradition, using texts chosen by Peter?

Since the catena employs certain popular texts, appears to be formed on the basis of a *Stichwört* and bears a strong resemblance to Rom. 9.32-33 (both texts cite from Isa. 28.16 and 8.14 and depart from extant OG readings of 28.16 by using the phrase λίθον ἀκρογωνιαῖον), it has become commonplace since Dodd to regard it as employing an already existing source.[63] Various suggestions regarding the origins of the catena have been made.[64] Bigg argues that the catena originated as a midrash on Ps. 118.22, as a popular early Christian text, incorporating Isa. 28.16 and 8.14, and suggests that Rom. 9.32-33 is more likely to be dependent upon 1 Pet. 2.6-8 than vice versa since Romans conflates the two Isaiah texts and a later reader would be unlikely to separate them.[65] Selwyn

---

62. This is quite unlikely to be an allusion to Ps. 118.22 since ἀκρογωνιαῖος is not used in that text. Cf. John Muddiman, *The Epistle to the Ephesians* (London: Continuum, 2001), p. 142, who notes that ἀκρογωνιαῖος is used in OG Ps. 117.22 in some recensions, but that the imagery does not fit the context of Eph. 2.20 and J. Jeremias, 'Κεφαλὴ γωνίας – Ἀκρογωνιαῖας', *ZNW* 29 (1930), pp. 264–80. Interestingly, D*, with its tendency to 'correct' New Testament references to Scripture in line with OG versions, reads λίθου here, suggesting that Eph. 2.20 was viewed as a reference to Ps. 118.22, though one would still expect to read κεφαλοῦ γωναίου instead of λίθου. In fact, Ernest Best, *A Critical and Exegetical Commentary on Ephesians* (ICC; Edinburgh: T. & T. Clark, 1998), p. 284 n. 83, suggests that the use of λίθου represents an attempt to clarify the text because the meaning of ἀκρογωνιαῖος is uncertain. Cf. C. L. Mitton, 'The Relationship between Ephesians and 1 Peter', *JTS* 1 (1950), pp. 67–73, which argues for 1 Peter's dependence upon Ephesians through the common use of the architectural metaphor. Snodgrass, 'I Peter II. 1-10', p. 101, rejects Mitton's argument on the basis of important differences, such as the rejection of Christian status as πάροικοι in Eph. 2.19 whilst in 1 Peter it is an important motif.

63. C. H. Dodd, *According to the Scriptures* (London: Fontana, 1965), pp. 42–3.

64. Thomas D. Lea, 'How Peter Learned the Old Testament', *SwJT* 22 (1980), pp. 96–102, argues that Peter's use of 'stone' imagery is dependent upon his experience of Jesus' own use of such imagery and texts in Mk 12.10 and parallels. His evidence for this claim, other than the common use of Ps. 118.22, is the use of the same text again in Peter's speech in Acts 4.11. Cf. Hillyer, 'Rock-Stone', p. 61 and Goppelt, *Erste Petrusbrief*, p. 144.

65. Bigg, *St Peter*, p. 130. Cf. Barnabas Lindars, *New Testament Apologetic: The Doctrinal Significance of the Old Testament Quotation* (London: SCM, 1961), pp. 169–74. Bigg's suggestion is generally rejected on the grounds that it requires a very difficult early dating of 1 Peter. Cf. Michaels, *1 Peter*, p. 94, who also agrees that Peter would be unlikely to unpick the conflated text in Rom. 9.33.

argues that the citation formula in v. 6 suggests that the catena is cited as a pre-existing hymn from which both 1 Peter and Romans draw.⁶⁶ This has not attracted widespread support.⁶⁷

Snodgrass argues against Hort and Beare's suggestion that the use of the catena is dependent upon Rom. 9.32-33 by developing a compelling case for a testimonia collection featuring Isa. 28.16, Ps. 118.22 and Isa. 8.14.⁶⁸ Snodgrass maintains that a literary relationship between Isaiah 28 and Isaiah 8 might exist within the Hebrew texts themselves and that this might be one reason why they were brought together into a testimonia collection. The phrase שטף ועבר from Isa. 8.8 appears to be adapted in 28.15 and 18, whilst the phrase וכשלו בם רבים ובפלו ונשברו ונוקשו ונלכדו from 8.15 is adapted in 28.13. Likewise, Snodgrass argues that there is a deliberate interplay between the two texts in that in 8.14 the sanctuary is destined for destruction whereas in 28.16 it comes to represent security. Snodgrass also suggests that the interpretation of these texts in pre-Christian exegesis would make them attractive to early Christians. He notes that Isa. 28.16 is interpreted eschatologically in 1QS 5.5; 8.5; 1QH 6.25-27, and 7.8-9, and that *Tg. Isa.* 28.16 understands אבן as a powerful king. He then suggests that the eschatological and messianic reading of this passage in intertestamental literature may well have commended it to be included in a testimonia collection. Moyise supports the notion of a pre-Christian relationship between the catena texts, suggesting that the extant OG versions of Isa. 8.14, with their 'insertion' of καὶ ἐὰν ἐπ'αὐτῷ πεποιθὼς ᾖς, indicate an earlier relationship between this text and Isa. 28.16 on the basis of shared stone imagery and the absence of an equivalent phrase in the Masoretic Text.⁶⁹ Moyise also notes that this

---

66. Selwyn, *St Peter*, pp. 274–7, noting a number of such 'hymnic' texts composed largely of scriptural material, such as OG Ps. 13.3, the *Psalms of Solomon* and the Lukan Canticles. Cf. Windisch, *Die Katholischen Briefe*, p. 60.

67. This is rejected by Elliott, *The Elect and the Holy*, pp. 133–8; Schutter, *Hermeneutic and Composition*, p. 37 n. 64, and Michaels, *1 Peter*, p. 94, who regards Selwyn's proposition as purely speculative. Likewise, Ernest Best, '1 Peter II:4-10 – A Reconsideration', *NovT* 11 (1969), pp. 270–93, argues that the Catena is not traditional but that the texts were chosen by Peter. Carson, '1 Peter', p. 1024, similarly argues that the association of these texts may be oral rather than through a written source.

68. Snodgrass, '1 Peter II. 1-10', pp. 99–101. Cf Hort, *St Peter*, p. 116; Beare, *Peter*, p. 40; Achtemeier, *1 Peter*, p. 12, and Hillyer, 'Rock-Stone', p. 61.

69. Moyise, 'Isaiah in 1 Peter', p. 179. Cf. Schutter, *Hermeneutic and Composition*, p. 132, and Woan, 'Psalms in 1 Peter', p. 219. The OG versions of Isa. 28.16 may have been attractive to early Christian readers because of its use of ἐπ'αὐτῷ, which is certainly open to messianic interpretation. Schutter also draws attention to

tradition is supported by 1QS 8.4-5. According to Moyise, it is this relationship that is evidenced by the form of the citation in Rom. 9.33, which appears to be a conflation of the two passages.[70] However, Moyise also points out that the OG reading of Isa. 8.14 – καὶ οὐχ ὡς λίθου προσκόμματι συναντήσεσθε, οὐδὲ ὡς πέτρας πτώματι – in which the stone is promised *not* to be a cause of stumbling, is taken up by neither 1 Peter nor Rom. 9.33. This might suggest something of a disjuncture between 1 Peter and OG interpretation of this passage, though 1 Peter's use of the passage does not disagree substantially with its OG treatment. The OG version of Isa. 8.14 asserts that for those who trust in the Lord, he will not be a cause of stumbling or falling. The inverse of this is that those who do not trust in the Lord will indeed find him to be as a stone which causes stumbling. This, of course, is what Peter attempts to convey in his use of the citation by omitting the negatives οὐχ and οὐδὲ.

(2) *The Purpose of the Catena*. Peter's purpose in employing a catena of citations is apparently outlined in 2.4-5.[71] Having described how his audiences were begotten through the word of God and are now to desire spiritual milk, Peter describes the continued growth of God's people into a spiritual house and holy priesthood. This growth is something God's people engage in as passive objects: as living stones. Essential to Peter's use of the scriptural catena is his description of Jesus Christ as λίθος in 2.4, through which the stone texts are seen to refer to him. Yet what does it mean to regard the communities addressed by the epistle as a 'spiritual house' and 'holy priesthood'?

Selwyn, Schlosser and Achtemeier argue that the purpose of 1 Pet. 2.4-10 is to claim temple status for the communities to whom the epistle is addressed.[72] Likewise, Goppelt argues that the use of οἶκος πνευματικός relates temple language typologically to the communities, suggesting that the notion of judgment beginning at God's οἶκος (meaning the communities) in 1 Pet. 4.17 alludes to the judgement that begins with the Jerusalem Temple in Ezek. 9.6.[73] He describes the temple language applied to

---

the possible conflation of Isa. 28.16 and 8.14 in 1QS 8.4-10, though a reference to the former is more obvious than to the latter.

70. Cf. Hillyer, 'Rock-Stone', p. 62, who notes the apparent association between Ps. 118 and Isa. 8.14 in Lk. 20.17, which follows the citation with πᾶς ὁ πεσὼν ἐπ'ἐκεῖνον τὸν λίθον συνθλασθήσεται.

71. Bigg, *St Peter*, p. 130.

72. Selwyn, *St Peter*, pp. 274–7; Schlosser, 'Ancien Testament et Christologie', 65, and Achtemeier, *1 Peter*, pp. 164–5.

73. Goppelt, *Typos*, p. 153, who also draws the parallel between the use of οἶκος πνευματικός in 1 Peter and its clearer 'temple' meaning in Eph. 2.21.

the communities as a 'typological heightening' of that language, arguing that Peter asserts a conceptual similarity between the Temple and the communities:

> The Church of the crucified and resurrected one is now the place where God is present (1 Cor 14.25), and this is where he is worshipped in Spirit and in truth and is revered through true sacrifice (1 Pet 2.5b).[74]

However, though 1 Peter uses the term ἀντίτυπος in 3.21 and clearly understands the scriptural *event* of the Flood as prefiguring Christian baptism, it is by no means certain that scriptural *texts*, and indeed the institution of the Temple, are understood typologically. For Goppelt's analysis to be supported, one would need to see an understanding in 1 Peter that the Temple has its own historical value which is then applied to the new reality of the communities and their identity. Instead, 1 Peter is silent about the Temple within Israel's history and simply applies language which may or may not have Temple associations to the communities. Goppelt accounts for this apparent silence:

> The argument does not proceed from the old. It does not begin by asking how the temple, priesthood, and sacrifice are replaced. The new is the focus of attention, and the old serves to make the glory and the nature of the new shine forth: so one relationship shades into the other.[75]

Yet, whilst it is undoubtedly true that Peter's focus is almost exclusively on the present, there does not appear to be any evidence that Peter sees the Temple as prefiguring the Church. To argue that typological interpretation of the Temple is taking place in 1 Pet. 2.4-10 is to assume a much more sophisticated understanding of scriptural meaning than there is evidence for or is accounted for in the simple determinate hermeneutic of 1 Pet. 1.10-12.

Similarly, yet without recourse to typology, Best argues that the essential image of the catena is the communities as embodying the temple, reflecting a tradition of non-material understanding of sacrifice and the temple.[76] The 'temple' interpretation of 1 Pet. 2.6-10 has been most substantially articulated recently by Mbuvi.[77]

---

74. Goppelt, *Typos*, p. 154.
75. Goppelt, *Typos*, p. 154.
76. Best, *1 Peter*, pp. 99–103. Cf. idem, 'Spiritual Sacrifice: General Priesthood in the New Testament', *Int* 14 (1960), pp. 280–90. Best's examples of the tradition of non-material sacrifice are Isa. 1.11-17; Hos. 6.6; Mic. 6.6-8; Pss. 50.13, 14, 23; 51.17; 141.2; 1QS 8.9; 9.3 and 4QFlor 1.6.
77. Mbuvi, *Temple, Exile and Identity*, pp. 90–109.

Elliott argues that the Stone Catena is a midrash which draws upon traditional material and associations between the texts cited. Yet he suggests that the primary focus of the midrash is upon the audiences as the elect people of God, as a 'royal priesthood', a theme which he argues is also a feature of the cited texts within their original literary contexts.[78] To this end, the use of the Catena is Peter's own: quite distinct from previous use of the 'stone' texts. It is certainly clear that Peter develops the use of stone texts to apply them more directly to the communities by creating an association between Christ as the 'living stone' and the community members who are built up as 'living stones' as they come to him. As Green notes, this association leads to the communities sharing the status of Christ as both rejected yet elect and honoured.[79] Against Selwyn and others, Elliott also argues that the primary interest of 1 Pet. 2.4-10 is the elect status of the communities, rather than the characterisation of the communities as a spiritual temple in contrast to the Jerusalem temple.[80] In contrast, Mbuvi argues that the distinctive use of the stone texts resides in their application to the communities, not simply as the elect, but as the 'Temple-Community'.[81] Whatever the precise meaning intended by the Petrine use of the Stone Catena, the use of these stone texts provides a clear illustration of the hermeneutical principle suggested in 1.10-12, particularly the narrative emphasis upon Christ and the communities who have had the good news proclaimed to them. Because Christ and his people are identified by the prophetic witness as the climax of salvation history, it is no surprise that the scriptural texts of the Stone Catena are understood as relating to Christ and his people. This is, of course, the connection drawn in 2.4-5, πρὸς ὃν προσερχόμενοι λίθοι ζῶντα...καὶ αὐτοὶ ὡς λίθοι ζῶντες οἰκοδομεῖσθε.

---

78. Elliott, *The Elect and the Holy*, pp. 38 and 219.

79. Green, *1 Peter*, p. 60. Feldmeier, *Letter of Peter*, p. 131, characterised the 'Petrine' development of the stone text tradition as an expression of an Hellenised soteriology, drawing upon the language of rebirth and childhood as well as describing the communities as participating in the changeless status of Jesus through their association with Christ as the 'living stone'. Michaels, *1 Peter*, p. 95 argues nearly the opposite, that the catena is employed in opposition to Hellenistic paganism. Cf. Pierre Prigent, '1 Pierre 2, 4-10', *RHPhR* 72 (1992), pp. 53–60 (59).

80. Elliott, *Home for the Homeless*, pp. 158–9 and 168–70. Cf. Achtemeier, *1 Peter*, p. 152.

81. Mbuvi, *Temple, Exile and Identity*, p. 98.

An even more adventurous suggestion is provided by Frederick W. Danker, who argues that the whole of 1 Pet. 1.24–2.17 forms a single 'consolatory pericope' using careful selection of scriptural texts.[82] According to Danker, the pseudonymous author encourages his audiences in the face of persecution by noting the frailty of humankind (using Isa. 40.6 and 8) in contrast to the solidity of God, from whom spiritual milk must be received (alluding to Ps. 33.9). This will enable the audience to grow as God's people (using the various allusions to Exodus and Hosea in vv. 9-10) into the 'stone-like' status (employing the 'Stone' Catena) of Jesus Christ. With this status, the audiences may have the confidence to endure suffering, as encouraged in 1 Pet. 2.11-17. Danker argues that the author of 1 Peter has a firm grasp of the literary context of each of his citations, all of which are chosen because the same dynamic of suffering and divine deliverance is present within each text in its context. These contexts are thought to be evident in other features of the 'pericope'. For example, Isa. 28.16 is cited in 1 Pet. 2.7 partly because of what it evokes about the declining power of Ephraim from its own context within Isaiah 28, where v. 9 mentions 'milk', as used in 1 Pet. 2.2.[83] Danker rejects the possibility that the sources of the scriptural citations in 1 Peter are testimonia collections and assumes that the author has a detailed knowledge of such texts; indeed, this is why Danker rejects both Petrine authorship and the Silvanus amanuensis theory of Selwyn and others.[84] Whilst the suggestion of such literary sophistication is doubtful, Danker also draws significant and important parallels between the argument of his 'consolatory pericope' and 1QH, which are discussed in the penultimate chapter of this study. Also doubtful is Danker's designation of 1 Pet. 1.24–2.17 as a distinct pericope. Whereas Bauckham's suggestion offers a passage self-contained by its possible function explaining the christological and ecclesiological claim of 2.4-5, there is little to suggest that 1.24–2.17 is in any way self-contained. Why does Danker's pericope begin with a citation whose citation formula indicates that the citation is employed to demonstrate something from the previous verse? At the same time, the imperative to honour everyone,

---

82. Danker, 'Consolatory Pericope', pp. 93–102.

83. Danker, 'Consolatory Pericope', p. 95. The problem with this argument is that γάλακτος in Isa. 28.9 is something people must be weaned off, whereas in 1 Pet. 2.2 it is to be desired by the audiences.

84. Danker, 'Consolatory Pericope', p. 101. However, as Feldmeier, *Letter of Peter*, p. 37, notes, detailed knowledge of OG texts need not preclude Petrine authorship, just as Paul's use of such Greek texts does not preclude Pauline authorship of Romans.

including the 'Emperor' in 2.17 is not so different from the *Haustafel* that follows it.[85] Perhaps these problems reflect the great difficulty in attempting to divide texts dominated by an associative style of reasoning (even if sophisticated enough to employ a pre-existing catena of scriptural quotations) into neat sections or pericopae.

(3) *The Exegetical Style of the Catena*. There has been significant discussion of the way in which the catena functions and relates to the argument of its immediate context within the epistle. Questions have been raised as to whether the catena is a sophisticated *midrash* or a series of proof-texts. These often require a close examination of the structure of the catena and its broader setting in 2.4-10. Elliott has argued that the catena is simply a set of proof-texts to support the assertions in 2.4-5.[86] He offers a structural analysis to support this relationship:

Verses 4-5	**Verses 6-8, 9-10**
v. 4	vv. 6-8
Jesus Christ, the rejected-elect stone	belief/nonbelief in Jesus the stone
	believers (v. 7a) contrasted to
	nonbelievers (vv. 7b-8)
v. 5	vv. 9-10
believing community, elect and holy	people of God, elect and holy
house(hold) of the Spirit	royal residence
holy priestly community	priestly community
offer spiritual sacrifices	declare the praises of God
	believers (vv. 9-10) again contrasted
	to nonbelievers (vv. 7b-8)[87]

However, Best argues that the catena represents a new development in the argument of 2.4-10, grounding a new argument for the elect status of the communities.[88] Yet Bauckham regards the Stone Catena as simply the first part of a larger 'thematic' or midrashic pesher-style exposition of both Christ as the 'living stone' and the audiences as 'living stones' in 1 Pet. 2.4-10, reaching as far as the allusion to Hosea. His suggestion of how this passage is structured and fits together is worthy of consideration in some detail. The following is Bauckham's assessment of the structure of 2.4-10:

---

85. Elliott, *Commentary*, p. 512.
86. Elliott, *The Elect and the Holy*, pp. 16–49.
87. Elliott, *Commentary*, p. 408.
88. Best, 'Reconsideration', p. 278.

vv. 4-5	Introductory statement of theme		
v. 4		A	Jesus the elect stone
v. 5		B	Jesus the elect stone
vv. 6-10	Midrash		
v. 6a		Introductory formula	
vv. 6-8		A¹	The elect stone
vv. 6b+7a			Text 1 (Isa. 28.16) + interpretation
v. 7b+c			Interpretation + Text 2 (Ps. 118.22)
v. 8a+b			Text 3 (Isa. 8.14) + interpretation
vv. 9-10		B¹	The elect people
v. 9			Text 4 (Isa. 43.20-21) + Text 5 (Exod. 19.5-6) conflated, the expansion of Text 4
v. 10			Text 6 (Hos. 2.23) paraphrased (cf. Hos. 1.6, 9; 2.1).[89]

Bauckham attempts to respond to the debate between Elliott and Best regarding the relation of 2.4-5 to the catena of scriptural 'stone' texts in 2.6-8. Bauckham argues that 1 Pet. 2.4-5 should be understood as similar to Jude 4, an introductory verse stating themes which will be developed or supported by subsequent biblical references. Just as references to the wilderness generation, Sodom and Gomorrah, the Archangel Michael, Cain, Balaam, Enoch and the teaching of the Apostles, prove and explain the claims of Jude 4, so 1 Pet. 2.6-10 prove and explain the claims made in 2.4-5. The notion of Christ as the λίθον ζῶντα in v. 4 is supported by the λίθος texts cited in vv. 6-8 and the notion of God's people as λίθοι ζῶντες in v. 5 is supported by the scriptural allusions of vv. 9-10. Whilst it is not difficult to perceive the relation between v. 4 and the catena of stone texts, it is much harder to demonstrate the same for v. 5 and vv. 9-10 since none of the allusions in the latter employ λίθοι or similar terminology.

Bauckham's analysis of the catena is helpful in showing the complex relationships between its texts. However, it is probably more accurate to emphasise the *pesher* element of Bauckham's description, rather than describing it as midrashic. As Woan points out, the catena is not used for a midrashic purpose since it does not aim to explicate a text.[90] Rather

---

89. Bauckham, 'James, 1 and 2 Peter, Jude', p. 310. Cf. Cranfield, *Peter*, p. 43.

90. Woan, 'Psalms in 1 Peter', p. 219, and Elliott, *The Elect and the Holy*, pp. 16–49. Cf. Piper, 'Hope as the Motivation of Love', p. 223, also notes this too in relation to the use of Ps. 34.13-17 (OG 33.13-17) in 1 Pet. 3.9-12, which he regards, not as exegetical, but as related to proof of the paraenesis. 1 Peter does not appear to demonstrate much interest in self-consciously discussing or 'interpreting' Scripture, unlike rabbinic Midrash. Cf. E. Earle Ellis, 'Midrash, Targum and the New Testament Quotations', in Ellis and Wilcox, eds., *Neotestamentica et Semitica*, p. 68.

more like thematic *pesherim*, texts are cited here to supply scriptural evidence in support of the author's theological assertion: they do not have an exegetical purpose.

(4) *The Catena Texts*. *1 Peter 2.6 and Isaiah 28.16*. The form of the citation here varies significantly from extant OG versions, perhaps reflecting an apocopated form of such versions or, at the very least, a less periphrastic original translation. Instead of the phrase ἐγώ ἐμβαλῶ εἰς τὰ θεμέλια, 1 Pet. 1.6 simply reads τίθημι ἐν. This reading is also used in Rom. 9.33. Similarly, πολυτελῆ is absent and the order of ἐκλεκτὸν ἀκρογωνιαῖον ἔντιμον is different. Again, εἰς τὰ θεμέλια αὐτῆς is absent in 1 Pet. 1.6. The final clause of the citation matches the OG reading precisely. Jobes claims that these differences are of enough significance as to suggest the possibility of a different *Vorlage* behind the text cited by Peter.[91] The citation is introduced with the formula διότι περιέχει ἐν γραφῇ, a formula which, as noted above, is taken to introduce at least the next three citations.

Isaiah 28.16 is clearly the source of the language used in 2.4 to describe the living stone. Because the living stone is chosen and honoured by God, according to the citation from Isa. 28.16, and Peter's audiences are described as being 'as living stones', the implication is that they too are chosen and honoured by God, the speaker of the citation. Moyise notes that this allusion to the catena is essential in Peter's argument from Christology to Ecclesiology, which requires a basic similarity between Jesus the living stone and members of the communities as living stones, since the first citation (Isa. 28.16) employs the more exclusive λίθον ἀκρογωνιαῖον.[92] Bornemann notes that the phrase οὐ μὴ καταισχυνθῇ also appears in Ps. 34.6 (OG 33.6) and argues that this is also a reference to Psalm 34, as well as being a citation from Isaiah.[93]

The interpretation of Isa. 28.16 in 1QS 5.6 provides for an interesting comparison with the use of the Stone Catena in 1 Peter. The application of the text is similar to 1 Peter insofar as it is given an eschatological referent, in this case the Qumran community.[94] Whilst Peter apparently understands Isa. 28.16 to refer to Jesus Christ, the whole of the Catena is given a secondary function in proving the assertion in 2.5 that through Christ, the single stone, the communities may become stones. Hence the

---

91. Jobes, 'Textual Tradition in 1 Peter', p. 331.
92. Moyise, 'Isaiah in 1 Peter', p. 180.
93. Bornemann, 'Der erste Petrusbrief', p. 216. Cf. Woan, 'Psalms in 1 Peter', p. 216.
94. Michaels, *1 Peter*, p. 96.

use of the Catena is both christological and ecclesiological: kerygmatic and paraenetic. It is this 'ecclesiological' dimension that has some similarity to 1QS.

1 Peter 2.7 and Psalm 118.22 (OG 117.22). The form of the citation here is identical to the majority extant OG reading of Ps. 117.22, though there is some variation in relation to the terms ἀκρογωνιαῖον and κεφαλὴν γωνίας.[95] The manner in which Ps. 118.22 is cited here is interesting insofar as Peter employs it seemingly as part of his own sentence. Because of this it lacks any typical citation formula. Nevertheless, it should still be regarded as a citation since it follows the formula in v. 6 as part of a catena of citations.

The citation appears to offer an explanation of the adverse of the statement from Isa. 28.16 that ὁ πιστεύων ἐπ' αὐτῷ οὐ μὴ καταισχυνθῇ, since the introductory phrase in 1 Pet. 2.7 employs πιστεύουσιν and ἀπιστοῦσιν.[96] Whilst those who believe in the living stone will never be put to shame, perhaps despite the experience of shame felt by Peter's audiences of aliens and strangers, those who do not believe are fundamentally mistaken since the stone they reject is in fact of supreme importance.[97] In citing Ps. 118.22 as a christological text, Peter develops a clear New Testament tradition: that the rejected stone is Jesus Christ.[98] The psalm itself appears to have been well known in the earliest Christian communities. Dodd suggests that ἐκύκλωσαν με from Ps. 118.10 (OG 117.10) is alluded to in Jn 10.24 and that δεξιὰ κυρίου ὕψωσέν με from Ps. 118.16 (OG 117.16) is 'echoed' in Acts 2.33.[99] The first of these suggestions lacks any real evidence, whilst the second is quite unlikely since the presence of similar language in Acts 2.33 can be explained as a reference to Ps. 110.1, which is actually cited. However, a reference to

---

95. Cf. Michael Cahill, 'Not a Cornerstone! Translating Ps 118,22 in the Jewish and Christian Scriptures', *RB* 106 (1999), pp. 345–57, presents an overview of the options for translating κεφαλὴν γωνίας before arguing that the phrase refers to something akin to a battlement, or the 'capstone of the castle', as in the uses of פנה in Zeph. 1.16; 3.6 and 2 Chron. 26.15. In part, Cahill reaches his descision through an investigation of the 'proverb' of Ps. 118.22.

96. Bornemann, 'Der erste Petrusbrief', p. 19, and Woan, 'Psalms in 1 Peter', p. 216 argue for a closer relationship, suggesting that the final clause of the Isa. 28 citation is also a reference to Ps. 34.6 and claim that Ps. 118.22 may have been chosen for the catena due to its similarity to this verse.

97. Carson, '1 Peter', p. 1027.

98. As Goppelt, *Erste Petrusbrief*, p. 140, notes, this psalm does not appear to have had any real significance to the Qumran community as part of its theological assertion of its identity, unlike the two other catena texts in 1 Pet. 2.6-8.

99. Dodd, *According to the Scriptures*, p. 99.

Ps. 118.25-26 in Mk 11.9 is more likely since the psalm's εὐλογημένος ὁ ἐρχόμενος ἐν ὀνόματι κυρίου matches the text in Mark, though Dodd's suggestion that ὦ κύριε σῶσον δή ὦ κύριε εὐόδωσον δή from the psalm is represented by ὡσαννά in Mark is somewhat doubtful. The use of Ps. 118.22 in Mt. 21.42-44 and parallels as well as Acts 4.11 is beyond any doubt and agrees significantly with the treatment of this text in 1 Peter. As Dodd notes,

> The importance of this psalm as a source of *testimonia* is manifest. The Stone rejected, the Stone of stumbling, the Foundation-stone of Zion, appear to have been associated at a very early stage as symbolic of the coming of Christ and its effects, in various related aspects. The whole psalm was evidently interpreted with reference to the sufferings and rejection of Christ, succeeded by his glorious resurrection and exaltation, all of which is 'the Lord's doing, marvellous in our eyes' (23) – to which the psalmist immediately adds (24) 'this is the Day which the Lord has made', which would naturally be understood as indicating that the day of Christ's coming is the prophetic 'Day of the Lord'.[100]

The interpretation here is perhaps less christological than it is Ecclesiological. It is not made clear that the stone is Christ. Jesus' exegetical conclusion in v. 43, as well as the response of the religious authorities in v. 45, suggests that the primary function of the citation is to support Jesus' supercessionism.

Assuming that Peter understood this excerpt to belong to a psalm, its use here suggests that the description of the prophetic role in 1.10-12 pertains to more than simply texts attributed to the Prophets. Of course, the interpretation of psalms as prophetic is well attested in the New Testament. In Acts 2.29-35, this tendency receives its fullest expression as David is defined by Peter as a prophet.[101] Susan Gillingham offers a very helpful analysis of the development of the practice of interpreting the Psalter, or at least certain psalms, as prophetic.[102] She notes that

---

100. Dodd, *According to the Scriptures*, p. 100. Cf. Norman Hillyer, 'First Peter and the Feast of Tabernacles', *TynBul* 21 (1970), pp. 39–70 (47), who notes that the use of Ps. 118 during the Feast of Tabernacles is attested in *Sukkah* 3.9.

101. Fitzmyer, 'David "Being Therefore a Prophet"'. Cf. Flint, 'David at Qumran'. The *Davidssohnfrage* in Mk 12.35-37 and parallels sees Ps. 110.1 (OG 109.1) explained on the basis of an assumed Davidic authorship as well as an assumption that the text refers to the Messiah, i.e. is eschatological. See Vincent Taylor, *The Gospel according to St Mark: The Greek Text with Introduction, Notes and Indexes* (London: Macmillan, 1952), p. 491.

102. Susan Gillingham, 'From Liturgy to Prophecy: The Use of Psalmody in Second Temple Judaism', *CBQ* 64 (2002), pp. 470–89.

certain passages in the pre-exilic Prophets adopt psalm forms, such as Amos 2.3 which resembles Ps. 2.10. This is the first phase in the prophetic reading of the Psalter. The second represents a transition from literary similarity to explicit interpretation as prophecy. Gillingham notes that early Second Temple worship featured a significant liturgical role for the Psalter. Since many of the psalms are royal psalms, it is likely that these were assumed to have an orientation towards the future and the hope of restoration witnessed in Zech. 2.12. This transitional stage is also seen in the OG translation of the superscriptions of the Psalter, especially in the translation of the liturgical term למנצח as the eschatological εἰς τὸ τέλος. In the final stage of this development, the Psalter is explicitly interpreted as prophecy of events to come, as in 11QPs^a. The use of Ps. 118.22 in the Stone Catena here, along with other New Testament examples, represents this final stage.

1 Peter 2.9 and Isaiah 8.14. The form of the citation here appears to differ significantly from extant OG versions of Isa. 8.14, which typically read καὶ οὐχ ὡς λίθου προσκόμματι συναντήσεσθε αὐτῷ οὐδὲ ὡς πέτρας πτώματι. Perhaps the most significant difference is the absence of the negatives οὐχ and οὐδὲ. Peter's version of the citation says the opposite of the OG versions, which render the verse as a part of an exhortation rather than a predictive threat. It must be said, however, that in reading Isa. 8.14 as describing a stone which *will* cause stumbling, the citation in 1 Peter is closer to the Hebrew text of Isa. 8.14. In this respect it is similar to the version of Isa. 8.14 in Rom. 9.32 (both of which agree in reading σκανδάλον instead of πτώματι) and seems likely to represent a common variant OG tradition of translation for that text. Again, Jobes claims that these differences are of enough significance as to suggest the possibility of a different *Vorlage* behind the text cited by Peter.[103] There is some evidence to suggest that this text was well known to New Testament authors and is alluded to on several occasions.[104] Yet, Brox argues that this is not a citation at all since it does not agree with any extant version.[105] However, Brox's argument assumes the non-existence

---

103. Jobes, 'Textual Tradition in 1 Peter', p. 331.

104. Some of the evidence for these allusions is scant. In Lk. 2.34, the participle πτῶσις is considered by NA[27], I. Howard Marshall, *The Gospel of Luke: A Commentary on the Greek Text* (NIGNT; Carlisle: Paternoster; Grand Rapids: Eerdmans, 1978), p. 122, and David W. Pao and Eckhard J. Schnabel, 'Luke', in Beale and Carson, eds., *Commentary on the New Testament*, p. 273, as a reference to Isa. 8.14 probably on conceptual grounds.

105. Norbert Brox, *Der Erste Petrusbrief* (EKKNT; Zurich: Benziger, 1979), p. 79.

of an OG version matching that of 1 Pet. 2.9, which simply cannot be proved. Too little is known about the Scriptural sources available to the earliest Christians for this claim to be decisive.

Just as Ps. 118.22 was cited as an explanation of the significance of not believing in Jesus Christ the living stone, so is the citation of Isa. 8.14, connected to the previous citation by a simple καί.[106] Not only have those who do not believe come to the wrong conclusion about the significance of Jesus, they will also find him to be a πέτρα σκανδάλου. This stone of stumbling is expounded by Peter as causing stumbling because of the disobedience of those who reject it. Just as in 1 Pet. 2.4, at the beginning of the Stone Catena passage, Peter's audiences are said to be chosen by God, so too are those who stumble in a negative sense. Achtemeier argues that this citation is directed specifically against the unbelieving neighbours of members of the community, perhaps particularly those who are the cause of the sufferings and persecutions Peter mentions.[107]

(5) *The Hermeneutic of the Catena*. The Stone Catena provides a very clear illustration of Peter's 'hermeneutic' from 1.10-12.[108] This much seems to have gained a significant degree of scholarly support. However, since there is no consensus as to the precise nature of the 'hermeneutic' implied by 1.10-12, analysis of the Stone Catena in relation to 1.10-12 varies. The Prophets are said to have spoken of the sufferings of Christ and the glory after, through the Spirit of Christ. For Peter, it was obvious that Isa. 28.16, Ps. 118.22 and Isa. 8.14 would refer in some way to Jesus, since that is what Scripture does. Scripture, here, has an essentially descriptive function. It serves those who have had good news proclaimed to them by telling them more about what Jesus offers them and the consequences facing those who do not believe the message which they have believed. As Jobes contends, the use of catena texts is 'consistent with [Peter's] view that the OT prophets serve Christians'.[109] Yet, at the same time, a paraenetic purpose behind the citations is observable: the issue of Christian identity with which Peter's use of the Stone Catena is ultimately concerned is never purely abstract in 1 Peter.[110] It must be

---

106. This is a common feature of citation as part of a catena, as seen in Heb. 1.10. See also the formula καὶ πάλιν in Rom. 15.10, 11, 12; Heb. 1.6 and 2.13 (twice).
107. Achtemeier, *1 Peter*, p. 161.
108. Hines, 'Peter and the Prophetic Word', p. 235.
109. Jobes, *1 Peter*, p. 142.
110. Thurén, *Argument and Theology*, pp. 127–31.

remembered that the Stone Catena closely follows the exhortation in 2.4: πρὸς ὃν προσερχόμενοι λίθον ζῶντα.

Similarly, Schutter argues that 1 Pet. 1.10-12 is reflected in the treatment of the catena texts. He argues that the orientation of Scripture towards the 'suffering and glories' of Christ functions as an 'organising principle' in 2.4-8.[111] Yet, as is often the case, Schutter exaggerates the scope of 'suffering and glories'. In 1.11, as noted in Chapter 1 of this study, the Χριστὸν παθήματα is more likely to refer to the quite specific suffering endured by Christ, rather than the general suffering experienced on behalf of Christ by the communities. The seeming extension of suffering to the communities in the catena by association with Christ is quite different, then, from that about which the Prophets are said to have spoken in 1.10-12. Moyise rejects the relation between 1.10-12 and the Stone Catena altogether because of perceived failure in Schutter's analysis. He argues that because the catena does not betray a belief that Scripture is fundamentally concerned with 'suffering and glory', 1.10-12 is unlikely to be a 'theory of prophecy' which determines Peter's interpretation of Scripture.[112]

Kelly, like Bauckham, regards the catena as midrashic, being 'rabbinic in method but Christian in application'. Because of this, he considers it to be an example of 'learned exegesis' rather than the citation of a pre-existing collection of texts.[113] There is some evidence to support this characterisation. One could argue that the use of texts employing a common term is an example of *gezerah shewah*, yet the catena is not self-consciously exegetical in the sense that rabbinic exegesis typically is: there is no indication that Peter understands the catena as an interpretation of Scripture intended to disclose meaning. For Peter, the meaning is self-evident. Schutter's characterisation of the catena as containing many of the familiar features of *pesharim* is surely more appropriate. He notes the presence of multiple *Stichwörten*, the near conflation of Ps. 118.22 and Isa. 8.14 and the supposed grammatical adaptation of terms.[114]

d. 1 Peter 3.10-12 and Psalm 34.12-16 (OG 33.13-17)

The form of the citation differs significantly from extant OG versions of Ps. 33.13-17, which are themselves quite accurate renditions of the

---

111. Schutter, *Hermeneutic and Composition*, p. 123.
112. Moyise, *Evoking Scripture*, pp. 78–95.
113. Kelly, *Peter*, pp. 82–3.
114. Schutter, *Hermeneutic and Composition*, p. 137. Cf. Achtemeier, *1 Peter*, p. 151.

Hebrew versions.¹¹⁵ The differences, however, are consistent and are mainly grammatical, due to the incorporation of the citation into the argument of 1 Peter.¹¹⁶ The version of the psalm cited by Peter does not see these verses as directed to the τέκνα of Ps. 33.12. Instead, they are interpreted as a general moral statement rather than didactic instruction to particular people. To this end, σου is omitted from Ps. 33.14. So the first clause (Ps. 33.13) is no longer the question it is in the extant OG versions, but is an indicative statement. Therefore, the question τίς ἐστιν ἄνθρωπος; is not present in Peter's version. After this, the imperative verbs (παῦσον, ἔκκλινον, ποίησον, ζήτησον and δίωξον) directed to the τέκνα in the extant OG version are read as subjunctives. In addition to this a few particles appear in Peter's version: γὰρ (the citation formula),¹¹⁷ καὶ, δὲ and ὅτι. The only other significant difference is that the OG text reads (in OG Ps. 33.13) ὁ θέλων ζωὴν ἀγαπῶν ἡμέρας ἰδεῖν ἀγαθάς, whereas Peter's version reads, not the participle ἀγαπῶν, but the infinitive ἀγαπᾶν, suggesting that both the 'to love life' and 'see good days' are the object of ὁ θέλων. This part of the citation in 1 Pet. 3.12 is identical to the extant OG of Ps. 33.16-17a, perhaps because this is a general statement in keeping with the style of the rest of the citation as it appears in 1 Pet. 3.10-11. Some scholars have argued that the possible changes to the cited text represent a deliberate attempt to enable the citation to support the argument of the paraenetic.¹¹⁸ For example, John Piper suggests that the changes made to the psalm offer the only convincing explanation

---

115. Perhaps the only significant difference is that translation of מגורות as τῶν παροικιῶν. It is probable that this represents a mistaken identification of the root גור. Jobes, 'Textual Tradition in 1 Peter', p. 331, suggests that the differences between extant OG versions of Ps. 33 and the citation in 1 Peter are of enough significance to postulate a separate textual tradition behind the latter.

116. Michaels, *1 Peter*, p. 179; Achtemeier, *1 Peter*, p. 224, and Woan, 'Psalms in 1 Peter', p. 220. Michaels notes that the use of the psalm in *1 Clem.* 22.2 agrees much more closely with extant OG versions.

117. For the introductory function of γὰρ, see Bigg, *St Peter*, p. 156; Elliott, *Commentary*, p. 611; and Feldmeier, *Letter of Peter*, p. 187. Larsolov Eriksson, *'Come, Children, Listen to Me!' Psalm 34 in the Hebrew Bible and in Early Christian Writings* (CBOTS 32; Stockholm: Almqvist & Wiksell, 1991), p. 117, notes that a single term functions in this way in 1 Pet. 1.24 (διότι) and in 5.5 (ὅτι).

118. E.g. Selwyn, *St Peter*, p. 190, who argues that the phrase θέλων ζωὴν ἀγαπᾶν is meant to indicate something quite different from θέλων ζωήν in OG Ps. 33.13. Rather than simply 'life', Selwyn claims that Peter/Silvanus has in mind a Christian understanding of 'eternal life', similar to that in 1 Jn 5.12 and 16. Likewise, Cranfield, *Peter*, p. 79, claims that the 'changes' to the text of the psalm give it a 'Christian turn'.

of the phrase ὅτι εἰς τοῦτο ἐκλήθητε ἵνα εὐλογίαν κληρονομήσητε in 3.9b. The debate here is whether τοῦτο refers to the preceding paraenesis or the inheritance of the blessing mentioned at the end of the verse: whether the blessing is a consequence of fulfilling the paraenesis or whether it is something already received which ought to motivate obedience to the paraenesis.[119] According to Piper, the changes made to the text of the quotation render the psalm more open to eschatological interpretation, so placing eschatologically oriented hope as a motivation to do good.[120] Principally, this change is achieved by the replacement of the participle ἀγαπῶν with the infinitive ἀγαπᾶν, rendering 'life' and 'good days' as parallel concepts pertaining to the future. Piper rightly notes that both 'life' and the promise of 'inheritance' (3.9b) are understood eschatologically in 1 Peter, in 3.7 and 1.4 respectively.[121] However, apart from the fact that the notion of New Testament 'changes' to texts depend upon an unwarranted assumption of the normativity of extant OG texts, how likely is it that this particular 'change' is not merely a scribal error, made either by the writer of 1 Peter or his source? Others argue that the 'changes' to the psalm represent a simple attempt at stylistic improvement, either on the part of Peter or the author of the version of the psalm he used as a source. For example, Elliott suggests that the version of the psalm cited in the epistle is a deliberate improvement of the extant OG versions which employ a confusing combination of second and third person verbs.[122]

Goppelt and Carson, however, note that the context of the citation is utterly concerned with the audiences' way of life within their present context of suffering.[123] This is certainly the sense of ζωήν and ἡμέρας ἀγαθάς when they appear in OG intertestamental literature.[124] Indeed, as

---

119. Kelly, *Peter*, p. 137, argues for the latter view suggesting that ὅτι εἰς τοῦτο ἐκλήθητε becomes an awkward parenthesis if it is taken to refer to the paraenesis, that in 1 Pet. 4.6 τοῦτο refers to something mentioned later and that an understanding of ethical action in order to merit blessing is quite alien to the paraenetic tradition to which 1 Peter relates. Cf. Piper, 'Hope as the Motivation of Love', p. 225 and Goppelt, *Erste Petrusbrief*, p. 228 n. 15.

120. Piper, 'Hope as the Motivation of Love', pp. 226–7. Cf. Jobes, *1 Peter*, p. 219.

121. Cf. Schelkle, *Petrusbriefe*, p. 95.

122. Elliott, *Commentary*, p. 612. However, as Selwyn, *St Peter*, p. 190, suggests, the use of the third person παυσάτω is probably simply due to the possible elimination of the interrogative in OG Ps. 33. Cf. Bigg, *St Peter*, p. 157, who claims that the epistle generally demonstrates a better style of Greek than the 'LXX'.

123. Carson, '1 Peter', p. 1037.

124. E.g. Tob. 4.5; Sir. 14.14; 41.13; and 1 Macc. 10.55.

Lars Olov Eriksson notes in his detailed study of Psalm 34 and its early reception, it is precisely the psalm's depiction of the righteous individual and his or her relation to evil and suffering which gave it appeal both to Peter and to other early Christian writers.[125]

Psalm 34.13-17 is cited in support of the paraenetic sentence in 1 Pet. 3.8-9.[126] This sentence does not appear to introduce any of the language of the citation, unlike the commentary on the citations in 1.15-16, 23-24 and 2.4-8. This is unusual in 1 Peter and perhaps suggests that the primary orientation of the citation is towards the argument of 3.13-17, rather than 3.8-9.[127] The terms important in 3.8-9, such as ὁμόφρονες and λοιδορίας, and the promise of blessing, do not feature in the citation. The relation between the paraenetic and the citation, then, is more general: the citation shows how God favours those who turn from κακός, the only term from the citation to be picked up in vv. 8-9.[128] It is not clear whether the use of ἀγαθός in v. 13 is intended as a reference back to the citation, which features ἡμέρας ἀγαθὰς, but not ἀγαθός as a general moral concept. Certainly the suggestion that good action will not provoke opposition might be regarded as in keeping with the idea in the citation that God upholds the righteous.

The citation of Ps. 34.13-17 provides another example of Scripture being taken to address directly the needs of the Church. Psalm 34.13-17 can be taken as an exhortation to shun evil and practise good because Scripture is understood by Peter to be fundamentally oriented towards those who have had good news proclaimed to them (1 Pet. 1.12). Carson suggests that this direct mode of application of the text to the situation of the audience is achieved by means of its supposedly original meaning as David's expression of God's desire to bless the righteous during his

---

125. Eriksson, *'Come, Children, Listen to Me!'*, pp. 125, 161.

126. Piper, 'Hope as the Motivation of Love', pp. 220–2, details something of the paraenetic tradition behind 1 Pet. 3.9. He notes that the phrase μὴ ἀποδιδόντες κακὸν ἀντὶ κακοῦ has parallels in Prov. 17.13 and in *Jos. Asen.* 28.4, whilst ἡ λοιδορίαν ἀντὶ λοιδορίας, τοὐναντίον δὲ εὐλογοῦντες (with much in common with Epictetus' *Discourses* 3.12.10 and *Encheiridion* 10 and 42) reflects a paraenetic tradition also seen in 1 Cor. 4.12, λοιδορούμενοι εὐλογοῦμεν. Cf. Snyder, 'Participles and Imperatives in 1 Peter', p. 195.

127. Selwyn, *St Peter*, p. 191. This is by no means a popular view. Bigg, *St Peter*, p. 156; Cranfield, *Peter*, p. 79; Kelly, *Peter*, pp. 128–9; Grudem, *1 Peter*, p. 148; and Elliott, *Commentary*, p. 601, all argue that Ps. 34.13-17 functions as a proof-text to support vv. 8-9, rather than introducing the more extensive discourse on 'suffering for doing good' beginning at 3.13.

128. See the discussion of Woan, 'Psalms in 1 Peter', pp. 222–4, and Snodgrass, '1 Peter II 1-10', pp. 102–3, below.

time spent among the pagan Philistines.[129] The similarity between David's context and that of Peter's audiences thus provides the basis for the direct application of Ps. 33.13-17 to Peter's audiences. Just as David was able to speak of God's love of the righteous during his time as an alien and a stranger, so his psalm is able to exhort Peter's audiences who now find themselves to be aliens and strangers within a pagan culture. However, there appears to be little evidence to suggest that Peter believed that Psalm 34 was originally written or uttered within the context of his sojourn among the Philistines. Indeed, even the OG superscription does not necessarily present this connection to the Philistines.[130]

Green characteristically suggests that the fabula or narrative substructure of righteous suffering is a feature in the use of Psalm 34:

> …like other NT theologians, Peter interprets Israel's Scriptures by drawing on their significance within the Scriptures, even while drawing his audience into those Scriptures so as to reappropriate their meaning. The storyline of Psalm 34 is a familiar one, known to us through the story of Joseph, the psalms of the suffering righteous, the stories of Daniel and his friends, Isaiah's Servant Songs, any number of Jewish texts from the Second Temple period, and pre-eminently in the career of Jesus Christ. This plotline runs through 1 Peter, tying together these three narratives – the narrative of Israel, the narrative of Christ (his life, death, and resurrection), and the narrative of Peter's audience.[131]

Whilst these are narratives evoked by Psalm 34, it is not clear that they are all evident behind 1 Peter in the way Green assumes. Notably absent is a narrative of Israel that expresses the 'storyline' of the psalm. Indeed, Peter collapses the history of Israel into something to be contrasted negatively with the glories of the present age.[132]

The use of Psalm 34 is not descriptive, or kerygmatic, in the way that the Stone Catena was, telling the audiences of 1 Peter about the significance of Christ in accordance with Peter's understanding that the meaning of the Prophets' writing was known by them to be the sufferings of the Christ and the glories after. Rather, Ps. 34.13-17 testifies to the Prophets' function of serving the Christian community by offering them direction and encouragement.

---

129. Carson, '1 Peter', p. 1037.
130. OG Ps. 33.1, Τῷ Δαυιδ, ὁπότε ἠλλοίωσεν τὸ πρόσωπον αὐτοῦ ἐναντίον Αβιμελεχ, καὶ ἀπέλυσεν αὐτόν, καὶ ἀπῆλθεν. Though papyrus Londiniensis Musei Britannici 37 reads Αχιμελεχ instead, this probably represents a further mistake rather than an attempt to correct Αβιμελεχ.
131. Green, *1 Peter*, p. 107.
132. Sargent, 'Narrative Substructure of 1 Peter', pp. 1–6.

(1) *The Scope of Psalm 34 in 1 Peter*. For several scholars, Psalm 34 is much more prominent in 1 Peter than simply providing material for this citation as well as a probable allusion in 2.3. Bornemann argues that Psalm 34 is of immense importance to Peter, who refers to it throughout the epistle which he regards as a baptismal homily based on that text.[133] Bornemann is supported by Snodgrass, who states that

> while [Bornemann's] suggestion is extreme, particularly with its emphasis on baptism, Ps. xxxiv does play a formative role in the composition of I Peter and especially of ii. 10. I would go so far as to say that the author of I Peter attempted to convey the consolation and exhortation of the righteous sufferer in Ps. xxxiv to his readers and that he used explicit quotations, allusions, and themes from Ps. xxxiv to do so.[134]

Schutter argues that, whilst Bornemann is correct to observe the importance of Psalm 34 in 1 Peter, his case is overstated. Schutter notes that only three of the commonly agreed 46 or so scriptural quotations and allusions are references to Psalm 34 and he disputes 33 of Bornemann's 51 proposed instances of dependence on Psalm 34.[135] For example, Schutter argues that εὐλογητὸς ὁ θεός in 1 Pet. 1.3 is unlikely to be

---

133. Bornemann, 'Der erste Petrusbrief', p. 147, and idem, 'Taufrede'. Cf. Dryden, *Theology and Ethics*, p. 193, who suggests that the language derived from the Ps. 34 citation is the most prominent feature of the letter's paraenesis. The argument that Ps. 34 is taken from a catechetical source is not without its more recent supporters. Notably, Selwyn, *St Peter*, p. 413; Kelly, *Peter*, p. 135; and Michaels, *1 Peter*, p. 175 (who suggests that this possible catechetical source is behind Rom. 12.9-21). Elliott, *Commentary*, p. 600, argues that the use of Ps. 34 here reflects early Christian paraenetic tradition but notes that it quite distinctive, with either four or five New Testament *hapax legomena* in 3.8. Dodd, *According to the Scriptures*, p. 108, suggests that Ps. 34 is one of the 'primary sources of testimonia' for the New Testament, though this may be an exaggerated claim. Eriksson, *'Come, Children, Listen to Me!'*, p. 110, identifies only possible references to the psalm in the New Testament, of which only three (1 Pet. 2.3; 3.10-12; Jn 19.36) are to be accorded any significance.

134. Snodgrass, 'I Peter II 1-10', p. 102. Examples of literary similarity noted by Snodgrass here include the use of παροικία from Ps. 34.5 in 1 Pet. 1.17, the use of ἅγιοι and φοβέω/φόβος from Ps. 34.10 in 1 Pet. 1.15 and 17, the 'partial quotation' of Ps. 34.9 in 1 Pet. 2.3 and the use of προσέρχεσθαι and φωτίζειν from Ps. 34.6 in 1 Pet. 2.4 and 9. Cf. Woan, 'Psalms in 1 Peter', pp. 222-4.

135. Schutter, *Hermeneutic and Composition*, pp. 44-9. If a criticism could be made of Schutter's arguments against Bornemann's proposed evidence of literary dependence it would be that they appear to be more directed against the possibility of conscious allusion to elements of Ps. 34 rather than mere literary influence, which might still be regarded as plausible in a number of cases despite Schutter's rigorous critique. Cf. Eriksson, *'Come, Children, Listen to Me!'*, p. 111.

dependent upon εὐλογήσω τὸν κύριον from Ps. 34.2, as argued by Bornemann, since this formula is a conventional element in early Christian thanksgiving periods, as seen in Eph. 1.3. In any case, the literary similarity extends here to a single word, used quite differently in 1 Peter and Psalm 34. Likewise, Schutter rejects Bornemann's proposal that ἰδόντες in 1 Pet. 1.8 is dependent upon the phrase γεύσασθε καὶ ἴδετε χρηστὸς ὁ κύριος from Ps. 34.8. To some extent, this proposal is more plausible than some others since Ps. 34.8 is clearly alluded to in 1 Pet. 2.3, yet, as Schutter points out, the meaning of the verb in 1 Peter and Psalm 34 is too different for any dependence to be likely: the former uses the verb literally to refer to something that cannot be seen at the time of writing, whereas the latter use is 'metaphorical'. In addition to this, Schutter disputes Bornemann's claim that 1 Pet. 5.5b-6 is dependent upon ἐγγὺς κύριος τοῖς συντετριμμένοις τὴν καρδίαν καὶ τοὺς ταπεινοὺς τῷ πνεύματι σώσει in Ps. 34.18. Whilst Schutter recognises the real conceptual similarity between the two passages, he notes that literary dependence is unlikely since Peter employs, not Ps. 34.18, but Prov. 3.34 in 5.5b as a citation to support the paraenesis.

Perhaps the most significant piece of research in support of Bornemann's thesis is Woan's study of the use of the Psalms in 1 Peter. Woan does not recognise as many references to Psalm 34 as Bornemann but develops his argument, claiming that Psalm 32 is not only important in 1 Peter but that the citation in 1 Pet. 3.10-12 determines the structure of the whole epistle.[136] She argues that the citation exhibits 'Janus behaviour' in relation to the structure of 1 Peter: it summarises and draws together elements of the argument prior to the citation and it sets out elements of the paraenesis to follow it. Examining material prior to the citation, Woan argues that the use of ἐλπίδα ζῶσαν in 1.3 reflects ζωήν in the citation, ἰδόντες in 1.8 reflects ἰδεῖν, κακίαν and δόλον in 2.1 reflect κακοῦ, κακὰ and δολόν, κακοποιῶν in 2.12 and 2.14 and κακίας in 2.16 reflect κακοῦ, ἀγαθοποιοῦντες in 2.20 reflects ποιησάτω ἀγαθόν, δόλος in 2.22 reflects δολόν, δικαίως in 2.23 reflects δικαίους and κακὸν ἀυτὶ κακοῦ in 3.9 reflects κακοῦ and κακὰ. After the citation, κακώσων in 3.13 reflects κακὰ in the citation, δικαιοσύνην in 3.14 reflects δικαίους, ἀγαθοποιοῦντας in 3.17 reflects ποιησάτω ἀγαθόν and κακοποιοῦντας in 3.17 reflects κακοῦ. However, is this enough to demonstrate that Peter consciously shaped 1 Peter around the citation in 3.10-12, or is it more likely that he simply borrowed language from the psalm? Perhaps the

---

136. Woan, 'Psalms in 1 Peter', pp. 222-4. Cf. Snodgrass, '1 Peter II 1-10', pp. 102-3.

psalm was chosen simply because it reflects the language of 'doing good' which Peter was keen to use. Against Woan's argument, it must be noted that ἀγαθοποιοῦντος and κακοποιῶν (in differing forms) are used on either side of the citation, suggesting that there is not such a clear distinction between what the citation is supposed to summarise and what it is supposed to point forward to.

e. 1 Peter 3.14-15 and Isaiah 8.12 and 13

These verses appear to contain both a citation and an allusion. Whilst the reference in 1 Pet. 3.14b lacks a citation formula, it may still be regarded as a citation.[137] For a citation from Scripture to function rhetorically, it must be heard as a deliberate appeal to something outside of the author's own discourse. The awareness of such a reference is usually created by the citation formula which interrupts the author's own language, indicating that a different, *scriptural* voice is about to speak. This sense of interruption is created by the citation itself in this case through the sheer incongruity of the language of the citation.[138] In particular, the use of αὐτῶν cannot be understood as part of a continuation of Peter's own words.[139] To what might it refer? Who are these people and what do they fear? Or, if one understands these words as meaning simply 'do not fear them', who are the 'them' to which the citation refers? Peter makes no mention of any group in 3.13-14 with whom his audience is compared in such a way. Several scholars note that the inclusion of αὐτῶν represents a deliberate change in the text to enable it to relate to its new context

---

137. Whilst δέ is almost certainly a feature of the source text, it is not outside the realms of possibility that it may function here as a citation 'formula' or other identifier (as in Acts 2.34; 7.6, 33; Rom. 10.20, 21; Heb. 7.4, 21). Similarly, ἀλλ' is attested within the New Testament as a means of introducing a citation (Rom. 9.7). Furthermore, it is clear that 1 Peter is not averse to employing a particle to introduce a citation.1 Pet. 4.18 uses καί to introduce an isolated citation whereas 2.9 uses the same term to introduce another as part of a sequence of references. In 3.10, γάρ is 'inserted' into the text of a citation, perhaps in a similar manner to 3.14, to introduce the reference (cf. Rom. 2.24).

138. As Selwyn, *St Peter*, p. 192, notes, 'had St Peter not been quoting, he would have written [the more natural] μή φοβηθῆτε αὐτούς'.

139. This term is, of course, a variant from extant OG readings of the text. It would be difficult to attribute it to Peter's own hand since there is no obvious group in Peter's discourse to which it might refer. Moyise, 'Isaiah in 1 Peter', p. 185, takes this to be an objective genitive meaning 'fear them', or more literally 'do not fear the fear of them'. Michaels, *1 Peter*, pp. 186–7, suggests that the OG reading αὐτῶν is a reference to the King of Assyria.

better, but it is far from clear that is effective.[140] Αὐτῶν creates a disjuncture between Peter's words and those of Isa. 8.13 and 14 which would enable 1 Pet. 3.14b to be heard as a citation from Scripture. A similar disjuncture indicating a quotation can be found in Mk 9.47-48:

Καὶ ἐὰν ὁ ὀφθαλμός σου σκανδαλίζῃ σε, ἔκβαλε αὐτόν καλόν σέ ἐστιν μονόφθαλμον εἰσελθεῖν εἰς τὴν βασιλείαν τοῦ θεοῦ ἢ δύο ὀφθαλμοὺς ἔχοντα βληθῆναι εἰς τὴν γέενναν, ὅπου *ὁ σκώληξ αὐτῶν οὐ τελευτᾷ καὶ τὸ πῦρ οὐ σβέννυται*.[141]

Again, it is the sudden and unexplained use of αὐτῶν which indicates that these words are something other than the author or speaker's own words. Again, there is a break in the natural flow of the discourse, alerting the reader to a scriptural reference which can only be heard as a quotation. The reference to Isa. 66.24 must, similarly, be more than an allusion since allusions demonstrate a greater grammatical conformity to the discourse in which they occur.[142] Even so, the quotation of Isa. 8.12 in 1 Pet. 3.14 represents an apocopated form of extant OG versions of Isa. 8.12, the result of either Peter's own hand or the character of his source. Moyise also regards the reference to Isa. 8.12 here as a citation, though he does so on the basis of its similarity to extant versions of the text, noting that the phrase τὸν δὲ φόβον is extremely rare, occurring in Prov. 1.29 as well as Isa. 8.12.[143] This apocopation is only slight. Peter's version omits the unnecessary οὐ, seen in the extant OG versions, and shortens οὐδὲ μὴ to μηδὲ. In addition to this, as mentioned above, the

---

140. Bigg, *St Peter*, p. 158, and Jobes, *1 Peter*, p. 229. P. Benedict Schwank, 'L'Epître (1 P 3,8-15)', *AsSeign* 59 (1966), pp. 16–32 (26), argues that αὐτῶν is intended to universalise the citation. Yet even if this is the case, it is not clear who 'them' might be from the argument it follows. Elliott, *Commentary*, p. 625, suggests that αὐτῶν refers to 'abusive neighours', yet, again, these 'neighbours' are not anticipated in the preceding verses. Furthermore, the interoggative τίς in 3.13 seems to imply that there will be no-one of whom the communities are likely to be afraid if they do good.

141. The reference to Isa. 66.24 is italicised in NA[27]. The reference is very close to extant OG readings of Isa. 66.24 (σκώληξ αὐτῶν οὐ τελευτήσει, καὶ τὸ πῦρ αὐτῶν οὐ σβεβθήσεται) with only some minor changes to the tense of the verbs and the omission of the second αὐτῶν. As Rikk E. Watts, 'Mark', in Beale and Carson, eds., *Commentary on the New Testament*, pp. 111–250 (193), points out, the association of Isa. 66.24 with Gehenna reflects a common rabbinic association (*Midr. Ps.* 12.5; m. *'Abot* 5.20; b. *Sanh.* 100b; *Lev. Rab.* 32.1; *Num. Rab.* 23.5; *Lam. Rab.* 1.40; and *Eccles. Rab.* 7.23).

142. Cf. Adela Yarbro Collins, *Mark: A Commentary* (Minneapolis: Fortress, 2007), p. 454, who describes the reference as an allusion.

143. Moyise, 'Isaiah in 1 Peter', p. 185.

plural αὐτῶν is used in Peter's version in place of the singular αὐτοῦ in the extant OG versions, which refer to the collective λαός mentioned at the beginning of Isa. 8.12.[144]

After the citation, in 1 Pet. 3.15, Peter appears to allude to or rewrite the verse which immediately follows the text he cites from Isa. 8.12.[145] The terms κύριον and ἁγιάσατε, used in 1 Pet. 3.15, are also found in Isa. 8.13. This is more than a coincidence and suggests a christological rendering of Isa. 8.13, utterly in keeping with Peter's belief that the true referent of scriptural prophecy is Jesus Christ. Such a clear reference to the literary context of a citation is interesting since it suggests something that is very important in the work of scholars such as Carson: that Peter was aware of the literary contexts of his biblical references.

Schutter considers the reference here (along with every other reference between the use of Ps. 34 in 1 Pet. 3.10-12 and the end of the main body of the epistle in 4.11) to be so closely woven into Peter's own words that it is impossible to identify the hermeneutical significance of the reference.[146] This is perhaps a little too dismissive. The use of Isa. 8.12 here represents Peter's second, exhortative and paraenetic use of Scripture as the reference to Scripture is incorporated directly into the paraenesis. Isaiah 8.12 serves those who have had good news proclaimed to them by encouraging them not to fear. Though Peter does not explain the referent of αὐτῶν in the citation, Isa. 8.12 is clearly understood as a text oriented towards his audiences, written to serve them according to their needs. It is perhaps astonishing that even though the quotation is incongruous and this incongruity might imply to readers that it does not refer precisely to their situation (after all, who are 'them'?), Peter nevertheless relates it directly to the communities as paraenesis. This is yet another example of the paraenetic use of Scripture, written by Prophets who served not themselves but the communities who stand at the climax of salvation history.

---

144. This extant OG reading is in fact closer to the Hebrew מוראו, with its masculine singular pronominal suffix, than Peter's version. In contrast, the next citation (the use of Prov. 10.12 in 1 Pet. 4.8) is much closer to extant Hebrew readings than other Greek readings.

145. Schutter, *Hermeneutic and Composition*, pp. 148–51; Feldmeier, *Letter of Peter*, p. 195, and Achtemeier, *1 Peter*, p. 232. Others describe it more as a continuation of the quotation in the previous verse, albeit 'christianised' (Michaels, *1 Peter*, p. 184, and Grudem, *1 Peter*, p. 152), whilst others simply describe it as a quotation, perhaps representing the imprecise terminology of an earlier period of scholarship (Bigg, *St Peter*, p. 158; Selwyn, *St Peter*, p. 192, and Kelly, *Peter*, pp. 142–3).

146. Schutter, *Hermeneutic and Composition*, p. 152.

f. 1 Peter 4.8 and Proverbs 10.12

The use of ἀγάπη καλύπτει πλῆθος ἁμαρτιῶν in 1 Pet. 4.8 is a probable citation from Prov. 10.12, identified as a citation by the use of ὅτι as a citation formula.[147] The similarity of Peter's citation with extant OG versions of Prov. 10.12 is conceptual, rather than verbal. This is perhaps because the OG phrase πάντας δὲ τοὺς μὴ φιλονεικοῦντας καλύπτει [καλύψει in Alexandrinus] φιλία is a rather periphrastic translation of the Hebrew ועל כל־פשעים תכסה אהבה.[148] Here one might realistically posit the existence of an OG version of Prov. 10.12 as cited by Peter since the text more closely resembles extant Hebrew versions and, as will be noted below, the form of words in 1 Pet. 4.8 is well attested in other early Christian literature.[149] The notion of 'covering' sin is not uncommon (Pss. 32.1; 85.2; Dan. 4.24; Sir. 5.6; Tob. 4.10;[150] and Rom. 4.7) and refers simply to the forgiveness of sin.[151] Similarly, the idea of the 'multitude of sins' is seen in Pss. 5.10/OG 5.11 (τὸ πλῆθος τῶν ἀσεβειῶν); 85.3/ OG 84.3 (כסית כל־חטאתם/ἐκάλυψας πάσας τὰς ἁμαρτίας αὐτῶν); Ezek. 28.18 (πλῆθος τῶν ἁμαρτιῶν); Sir. 5.6; and 1QH^a 12.19 (וכרוב פשעיהם).

Aside from the significant difference between Peter's version and extant OG versions, the idea that 1 Pet. 4.8 employs a citation from Prov. 10.12 has not attracted universal support. Various scholars argue that ἀγάπη καλύπτει πλῆθος ἁμαρτιῶν could, instead, be based on a common early Christian tradition, perhaps derived from Prov. 10.12, rather than being an explicit citation of that text.[152] The phrase is certainly popular in early Christian literature.

---

147. ὅτι is often employed to introduce direct discourse (Mt. 26.72; 27.43; Mk 13.7; 2.16 etc.). Because of this, it is also employed relatively frequently to mark a scriptural citation: Mt. 2.23; 21.16; Mk 12.19; Lk. 2.23; Jn 10.34; Rom. 8.36; 1 Cor. 14.21; and Heb. 11.18.

148. Though it must be noted that πάντας is a better translation of כל than πλῆθος.

149. Jobes, 'Textual Tradition in 1 Peter', p. 315.

150. The particularities of these latter two suggested to Friedrich Spitta, 'Der Brief des Jakobus', in *Zur Geschichte und Litteratur des Urchristentums*, vol. 2 (Göttingen: Vandenhoeck & Ruprecht, 1896), p. 152, that the use of this concept in early Christian paraenesis relates to the idea of a heavenly record of sin which might be erased or 'covered over'.

151. Though Jobes, *1 Peter*, p. 279, argues that the sense of 'covering' has more to do with it being ignored by members of the community in a spirit of love.

152. Goppelt, *Erste Petrusbrief*, pp. 284–5; Achtemeier, *1 Peter*, p. 295; Green, *1 Peter*, p. 140; Elliott, *Commentary*, p. 751; and Jobes, *1 Peter*, p. 278. Carson, '1 Peter', p. 1040, regards this approach as problematic, describing the potential early Christian sources as 'meagre'.

2. Formal Citation of Scripture in 1 Peter

Clement of Rome's interpretation of the phrase (ἀγάπη καλύπτει πλῆθος ἁμαρτιῶν) in *1 Clem.* 49.5 bears little comparison with that of 1 Pet. 4.8. Whilst both feature the citation as part of an exhortation to love, the former is within the immediate context of a definition of love bearing a greater deal of similarity to 1 Cor. 13.4-7. *1 Clement* 49.4-5 reads:

> Τὸ ὕψος εἰς ὃ ἀνάγει ἡ ἀγάπη ἀνεκδιήγητόν ἐστιν. ἀγάπη κολλᾷ ἡμᾶς τῷ θεῷ ἀγάπη καλύπτει πλῆθος ἁμαρτιῶν ἀγάπη πάντα ἀνέχεται, πάντα μακροθυμεῖ οὐδὲν βάναυσον ἐν ἀγάπῃ, οὐδὲν ὑπερήφανον ἀγάπη σχίσμα οὐκ ἔχει, ἀγάπη οὐ στασιάζει, ἀγάπη πάντα ποιεῖ ἐν ὁμονοίᾳ ἐν τῇ ἀγάπῃ ἐτελειώθησαν πάντες οἱ ἐκλεκτοὶ τοῦ θεοῦ δίχα ἀγάπης οὐδὲν εὐάρεστόν ἐστιν τῷ θεῷ.[153]

Because of this, ἀγάπη καλύπτει πλῆθος ἁμαρτιῶν provides more of a definition of love, rather than a direct motivation to love. Importantly, the phrase is not identified as a citation, nor indeed is it seen to stand out in any way from Clement's own words. However, the form of the phrase is exactly the same in both 1 Peter and 1 Clement which may be significant given the considerable variance of the text from other extant OG readings. Yet as Beare and Kelly have noted, 1 Pet. 4.8 cannot be dependent on *1 Clem.* 49.5 as this requires too late a date for 1 Peter.[154]

Of course, 1 Pet. 4.8 is not the only possible reference to Prov. 10.12 in the New Testament and comparison can also be made with Jas 5.20 – γινωσκέτω ὅτι ὁ ἐπιστρέψας ἁμαρτωλὸν ἐκ πλάνης ὁδοῦ αὐτοῦ σώσει ψυχὴν αὐτοῦ ἐκ θανάτου καὶ καλύψει πλῆθος ἁμαρτιῶν. The form of the reference (except for the omission of ἀγάπη) is identical to the reading of 1 Pet. 4.8 in Codex Alexandrinus. The omission of ἀγάπη is quite a crucial difference since it alters the meaning of the reference to Prov. 10.12 significantly. Instead of love covering a multitude of sins, in James it is rather the act of turning a sinner away from an erroneous way that covers a multitude of sins.[155] Because of this conceptual difference, it is more likely that Jas 5.20 simply *echoes* the language of Prov. 10.12. Indeed, many commentators do not suspect any form of deliberate scriptural reference here.[156] It is certainly not a quotation since the reference,

---

153. Interestingly, little comparison can be made between this passage and the pseudonymous *2 Clem.* 16.4, which also uses the phrase ἀγάπη καλύπτει πλῆθος ἁμαρτιῶν in exactly the same form as *1 Clement* and 1 Peter.

154. Kelly, *Peter*, p. 12, and Beare, *Peter*, p. 29.

155. Although it is not clear whose sin is covered: the sinner's or the one who turns them away from sin. Cf. Ralph P. Martin, *James* (WBC 48; Waco: Word, 1988), p. 220.

156. Martin, *James*, p. 200; Peter H. Davids, *The Epistle of James: A Commentary on the Greek Text* (NIGTC; Grand Rapids: Eerdmans, 1982), pp. 200–201;

if one is intended, is presented as James' own words of exhortation. It could be an allusion, but only if one assumed that the act of turning a sinner was being presented as the act of love which hearers of Jas 5.20 would recognise in Prov. 10.12.[157]

Clement of Alexandria's *Paed.* 3.91.3 (ναὶ μὴν καὶ περὶ ἀγάπης, ἀγάπης φησίν καλύπτει πλῆθος ἁμαρτιῶν) and the *Didascalia Apostolorum* 4.3 (which claims that the phrase is spoken by 'the Lord') probably regard this as a dominical saying. At very least, there is a good case to be made that ἀγάπη καλύπτει πλῆθος ἁμαρτιῶν was simply a very popular early Christian saying, whether dominical or not. The fact that the phrase bears such a close resemblance to extant Hebrew readings of Prov. 10.12 weights the evidence further in the direction of its status as a scriptural reference. The difficulty with dating 1 Peter in relation to James, and the 'omission' of ἀγάπη, means that it is not possible to posit a pre-Petrine use of the phrase employed in 1 Pet. 4.8. All other uses of the phrase are most certainly later and are probably dependent upon 1 Pet. 4.8. Whilst ἀγάπη καλύπτει πλῆθος ἁμαρτιῶν may have the status of an early Christian proverb in *1* and *2 Clement* and for Clement of Alexandria, one simply cannot say whether it is understood by Peter to be from Scripture. As Carson argues, there is simply not enough evidence to posit the existence of ἀγάπη καλύπτει πλῆθος ἁμαρτιῶν as an early Christian saying prior to 1 Peter.[158] The use of ὅτι to introduce the phrase in 1 Pet. 4.8 suggests that it is at least a reference to something other than Peter's own words.

Whether it is a reference to Prov. 10.12 or an early Christian proverb, ἀγάπη καλύπτει πλῆθος ἁμαρτιῶν functions to support Peter's exhortation at the beginning of v. 8 (πρὸ πάντων τὴν εἰς ἑαυτούς ἀγάπην ἐκτενῆ ἔχοντες) by giving a reason for his audiences to see love as particularly valuable.[159] The exhortation has an eschatological dimension, being

---

Martin Dibelius and Heinrich Greeven, *James: A Commentary on the Epistle of James* (trans. Michael A. Williams; Hermeneia; Philadelphia: Fortress, 1976), pp. 258–60. Luke Timothy Johnson, *The Letter of James: A New Translation with Introduction and Commentary* (AB; New York: Doubleday, 1995), p. 338 argues instead that a 'faint allusion' to Lev. 19.17b (ἐλεγμῷ ἐλέγξεις τὸν πλησίον σου, καὶ λήψῃ δι'αὐτὸν ἁμαρτίαν) is intended here.

157. This is the view taken by D. A. Carson, 'James', in Beale and Carson, eds., *Commentary on the New Testament*, p. 1012. Cf. Douglas J. Moo, *The Letter of James* (Grand Rapids: Eerdmans; Leicester: Apollos, 2000), p. 250.

158. Carson, '1 Peter', p. 1040.

159. On the imperatival nature of the participles ἔχοντες and διακονοῦντες, see Snyder, 'Participles and Imperatives in 1 Peter', pp. 195–6.

prefaced in v. 7 by Peter's claim that πάντων δὲ τὸ τέλος ἤγγικεν. The use of Scripture here resembles the exhortative function derived from the notion that Scripture was written to serve the very people to whom Peter writes. This, the first of three citations from Proverbs, witnesses to the unusual prominence of wisdom literature in 1 Peter. Feldmeier suggests that the prominence of wisdom literature in 1 Peter may be due to the general paraenetic function of the epistle.[160]

g. 1 Peter 4.14 and Isaiah 11.2

Elliott regards the reference to Isa. 11.2 in this verse as a citation on the basis of his definition of ὅτι as a citation formula.[161] However, there is little here to identify the phrase τὸ τοῦ θεοῦ πνεῦμα ἐφ' ὑμᾶς ἀναπαύεται as a citation, though it bears some similarity to Isa. 11.2 (καὶ ἀναπαύσεται ἐπ'αὐτὸν πνεῦμα τοῦ θεοῦ, πνεῦμα σοφίας καὶ συνέσεως, πνεῦμα βουλῆς καὶ ἰσχύος, πνεῦμα γνώσεως καὶ εὐσεβείας). But must it be a reference to Scripture? As Moyise notes, Isa. 11.2 is the only OG text to employ πνεῦμα, θεός and ἀναπαύω in the same sentence, suggesting that if 1 Pet. 4.14 contains a reference it is most likely to be a reference to this text.[162] Certainly, Schutter regards the verse as containing a reference to Isa. 11.2, albeit with a substantially modified text. Schutter argues that these changes allow the scriptural reference to serve Peter's paraenetic purpose here: the use of the second person plural instead of the original third person singular enables the text to refer to a broader group, whilst the change of the tense of the verb (ἀναπαύσεται to ἀναπαύεται) enables the text to be seen as a promise that has found fulfilment.[163] In addition to this, Schutter argues, along with Goppelt, that the phrase τὸ τῆς δόξης is a supplement to the reference to Isa. 11.2, evoking an association of suffering and glory.[164] An alternative to Isa.

---

160. Feldmeier, *Letter of Peter*, p. 26.
161. Elliott, *Commentary*, n.p.
162. Moyise, 'Isaiah in 1 Peter', p. 185. Though Moyise also notes that 1 Pet. 4.14 does employ anything from the long list of attributes in Isa. 11.2, using instead τὸ τῆς δόξης, which does not appear in Isa. 11.2. Moyise also suggests OG Isa. 61.2 as a possible text to which 1 Pet. 4.14 alludes, since this speaks of 'glory' in close proximity to 'the Spirit of the Lord'. Schutter, *Hermeneutic and Composition*, p. 154, is sure that that phrase itself must be an allusion, noting that it appears in Judg. 9.8; Pss. 72.19; 79.9; Neh. 9.5; Dan. 3.52; 1 Macc. 14.10; and *3 Macc.* 2.9, but does not suggest a particular textIt could be that this is simply scriptural language.
163. Schutter, *Hermeneutic and Composition*, p. 153; Michaels, *1 Peter*, p. 265, and Achtemeier, *1 Peter*, p. 308.
164. Goppelt, *Erste Petrusbrief*, p. 305 n. 29, and Schutter, *Hermeneutic and Composition*, p. 154.

11.2 as the principal text referred to in 1 Pet. 4.14 is suggested by Dennis E. Johnson. Johnson argues that 1 Pet. 4.12-19 is loosely based on Mal. 3.2 and its notion of the eschatological purification of the temple, understood by Peter as relating to the Christian community as the embodiment of the temple.[165] In Johnson's view, πυρώσει in 4.12 refers to the refining fire promised in Malachi 3 and, consequently, the notion of glory remaining in 4.14 alludes to the presence of God returning to the temple.[166] However, like many claims of possible allusions, it is not possible to substantiate the presence of an allusion to Malachi 3. Furthermore, since Malachi 3 does not itself promise the return of God's glory to the temple, it is somewhat difficult to relate 4.14 to 4.12, especially since Johnson does not deny the presence of a reference to Isa. 11.2 in the former.

Part of the difficulty in regarding the phrase in 4.14 as a reference is that it is quite unexceptional insofar as the notion of the Spirit being upon someone is commonplace in the New Testament literature.[167] Another difficulty is that, from Peter's point of view, Isa. 11.2 is full of christological potential as a description of Jesus Christ, to whom the Prophets testified. It is somewhat unlikely that Peter would have consciously undermined the christological value of this text by interpreting it as he does, relating it as a promise to his audiences.[168] Isaiah 11.1 is interpreted messianically in the Targum Isa. 11.1 – ויפוק מלכא מבנוהי דישי ומשיחא מבני בנוהי יתרבי. Ephesians 1.17; Mt. 3.16; Jn 1.32; 4QpIsa[a], and *Pss. Sol.* 17.39-44 also offer messianic interpretations of Isa. 11.2. The transformation of this popular interpretation in 1 Peter would certainly demonstrate Peter's commitment to applying Scripture primarily to the community. Indeed, if a reference to Scripture is intended here, the use agrees with the essential function of Scripture as oriented directly towards the community, in this case as a kerygmatic explanation of the nature of suffering as a Christian. Yet this is also a promise justifying the paraenesis in the subsequent verse: μὴ γάρ τις ὑμῶν πασχέτω ὡς φονεὺς ἢ

---

165. Dennis E. Johnson, 'Fire in God's House: Imagery from Malachi 3 in Peter's Theology of Suffering', *JETS* 29 (1986), pp. 285–94. Cf. OG Mal. 3.2.

166. Johnson, 'Fire in God's House', p. 289. Cf. Bigg, *St Peter*, p. 177, and Jobes, *1 Peter*, pp. 291–2.

167. Schutter, *Hermeneutic and Composition*, p. 153, notes the association of glory, suffering and the presence of God in Mk 13.9, Acts 6.15 and 7.56.

168. Carson, '1 Peter', p. 1041, does not think this corporate interpretation of a text read by early Christians as christological is not unusual. He notes that ordinary Christians are often identified with Christ in the New Testament, particularly in the Pauline theology of 'union with Christ'. Furthermore, he suggests that Isa. 11.2 is interpreted as relating to ordinary Christians in Eph. 1.17, which uses the words δώῃ ὑμῖν πνεῦμα σοφίας.

κλέπτης ἢ κακοποιὸς ἢ ὡς ἀλλοτριεπίσκοπος.[169] Green argues that one would expect Isa. 11.2 to be applied to the Messiah. Considering the christological orientation of the prophetic witness suggested in 1 Pet. 1.10-12, it is somewhat surprising that it is instead applied to the 'messianic community'.[170] Maintaining his belief in a primarily christological hermeneutic in 1 Peter, Green argues that this application to the communities exploits a communal aspect of Isa. 11.1-2 related to the apparent promise of the Messiah: the root of Jesse from which a fruitful branch will emerge. However, such a detailed understanding of Isaiah 11 may not be necessary to explain the application of this text to the communities addressed by 1 Peter. The application of Isa. 11.2 to these communities is another example of Peter's hermeneutic which views the Prophets as speaking to serve the very people to whom he now writes. In the light of 1 Pet. 1.12, it is not surprising that the promise of Isa. 11.2 is applied to the communities as a promise in support of paraenesis.

h. 1 Peter 4.18 and Proverbs 11.31

The use of the question εἰ ὁ δίκαιος μόλις σῴζεται, ὁ ἀσεβὴς καὶ ἁμαρτωλὸς ποῦ φανεῖται; in 1 Pet. 4.18 is likely to be a citation of Prov. 11.31 due to real verbal similarity between the two texts. The only difference between Peter's citation and the extant OG versions of Prov. 11.31 is the absence of μὲν from Peter's version. It is perhaps not surprising that this is missing, as the second clause lacks the δὲ one might expect. Either Peter or his OG source might have deliberately omitted μὲν. In any case, the difference is not significant. This is in marked contrast to the previous citation from Prov. 10.12 which, as was suggested, seems to bear a closer resemblance to extant Hebrew versions than OG versions.[171] This is not the case regarding Peter's version of Prov. 11.31, which follows extant OG versions even in the rather odd rendering of בארץ ישלם simply as σῴζεται and the use of μόλις, which is

---

169. On the meaning of this final term, see Jeannine K. Brown, 'Just a Busybody? A Look at the Greco-Roman Topos of Meddling for Defining ἀλλοτριεπίσκοπος in 1 Peter 4.15', *JBL* 125 (2006), pp. 549–68.

170. Green, *1 Peter*, p. 152. Cf. Jobes, *1 Peter*, p. 288.

171. On the relation of the Greek text of Proverbs to extant Hebrew versions, see Johann Cook, 'The Greek of Proverbs – Evidence of a Recensionally Deviating Hebrew Text?', in *Emanuel: Studies in Hebrew Bible, Septuagint and Dead Sea Scrolls in Honor of Emanuel Tov* (ed. Shalom M. Paul, Robert A. Kraft, Lawrence H. Schiffman and Weston W. Fields; VTSup 94; Leiden: Brill, 2003), pp. 605–18, who concludes that the widespread differences are to be accounted for in terms of the Greek as a free translation, without recourse to the possibility of a different recension of the Hebrew text.

unwarranted due to the lack of an equivalent term in extant Hebrew and Aramaic readings.[172] If the question really is intended to be heard as a citation, it might be possible to regard the καὶ at the beginning of 1 Pet. 4.18 as a citation formula. Καὶ certainly is used to introduce a citation in 1 Pet. 2.9, though the text it introduces is part of a catena initially introduced with the more formal διότι περιέχει ἐν γραφῇ. It is likely that καὶ in 1 Pet. 2.9 represents the author's own interjection into the catena, one serving to signify that another text is about to be used. If this is the case, Schutter may be incorrect to suggest that the use of καὶ in 4.18 is primarily a means of integrating the reference into the 'natural flow of the author's discourse' since the citation formula is always, to some extent, an interruption of this, introducing an alien element into the discourse.[173]

Peter uses the citation from Prov. 11.31 to support the distinction made in his question in 1 Pet. 4.17 between the present suffering of his audiences and the much greater suffering to come for those who do not obey the message of good news. Indeed, the rhetorical question in v. 17 appears to be based on the logic and structure of the reference to Prov. 11.31.[174] Peter perhaps reminds his audiences that their suffering for obedience to the Gospel has a divine origin, as in 1.7. Their suffering at the present time represents God's judgement, perhaps, if 1.7 speaks of the same thing, God's refining of the audiences' faith.[175] This 'hard' way

---

172. James Barr, 'בארץ – ΜΟΛΙΣ: PROV. XI. 31, 1 PET. IV. 18', *JSS* 20 (1975), pp. 149–64, notes that it is difficult to explain the inclusion of μόλις in OG versions of Prov. 11.31 since most other ancient language versions, such as the Vulgate and the Peshitta, agree with the Hebrew of the Masoretic Text. He argues that the attempt by S. R. Driver, 'Problems in the Hebrew Text of Proverbs', *Bib* 32 (1951), pp. 173–97 (180), to identify a derivation from ארץ in the Aramaic *Sam. Targ. Num.* 22.26 meaning 'to coerce or compel' (thus explaining the Greek translation) fails because the root of this ארץ is actually רצם. Likewise, Barr dismisses the possible relation of ארץ to the Arabic *raṣīn* ('weight' or 'pressure') as too late to have influenced the 'LXX'. Instead, Barr suggests that terms indicating 'scarcity' belong to a later development than the Hebrew represented in the Masoretic Text and notes that μόλις is used as a translation of בהזק in Sir. 25/22.7. 'Strength' may have evolved into the meaning 'only be strength', represented by μόλις. So why then does the OG read μόλις here? Barr suggests that the Greek translator recognised something of a כל והמר argument in Prov. 11.31 and simply attempted to replicate something of this in translation.

173. Schutter, *Hermeneutic and Composition*, p. 37.

174. Michaels, *1 Peter*, p. 272.

175. However, James A. Kelhoffer, *Persecution, Persuasion and Power: Readiness to Withstand Hardship as a Corroboration of Legitimacy in the New Testament* (WUNT 270; Tübingen: Mohr Siebeck, 2012), p. 121, does not see this

of salvation, in which God's judgement is felt through the suffering that refines faith, corresponds to the first clause of the citation.[176] The second clause, which raises the question of the fate of those who are not righteous, supports Peter's own similar question about those who have not obeyed the good news which his audiences have obeyed. Both Peter's question in v. 17 and the citation in v. 18 resemble the form of reasoning characteristic of *qal wahomer*. It is unlikely that this reflects a conscious exegetical choice by Peter since the condition of the first clause in v. 17 is not specifically drawn from Scripture.[177] The resemblance is more likely to be due to the citation, the form of which Peter appears to follow closely in v. 17.

Again, Scripture is used here to exhort and encourage Peter's audiences, reflecting the prophetic vocation of its writers to serve those who have had good news proclaimed to them, as Peter's audiences are described again by implication in 4.17, prior to the citation. Yet the interpretation of Prov. 11.31 by Peter is undoubtedly eschatological.[178] It is significant that in 1 Peter's narrative of salvation history, the communities addressed by the letter occupy an eschatological climax to be contrasted with Israel's past.[179] Because of this view of the eschatological

---

suffering as characterized in a positive or 'optimistic' manner: it will not refine faith nor witness to the pagan world as suffering does in 2.12; 3.1-2 and 13-16. Yet Jobes, *1 Peter*, p. 293 (and those who see reference to the purification of an eschatological temple community here, such as Green, *1 Peter*, p. 153; Schutter, *Hermeneutic and Composition*, p. 154; and Johnson, 'Fire in God's House', pp. 285–94), does see this as purification: certainly as an act of judgement. Cf. Carson, '1 Peter', p. 1042.

176. It also reflects, as Michaels, *1 Peter*, p. 272, and Jobes, *1 Peter*, p. 294 note, a well-attested early Christian tradition linking salvation with suffering (Mk 8.35; 13.20; and Lk. 13.23-24).

177. Though Carson, '1 Peter', p. 1041, notes that the phase τοῦ οἴκου τοῦ θεοῦ has scriptural roots in Ezek. 9.5-6; Zech. 13.9, and Mal. 3.1-3. Cf. Jobes, *1 Peter*, p. 293, who links this back to 1 Pet. 2.4-5.

178. Jobes, *1 Peter*, p. 293; Green, *1 Peter*, p. 153, and Achtemeier, *1 Peter*, p. 317. Goppelt, *Erste Petrusbrief*, p. 311, suggests that the use of καιρός in 4.17 indicates that the expected judgement is eschatological. Feldmeier, *Letter of Peter*, p. 299, argues that this eschatological interpretation is a result of the OG gloss μόλις σῳζεται. Likewise, the possible allusion to Ezek. 9.6 also frames the argument eschatologically, relating it to the tradition of eschatological judgement upon the temple. See Schutter, *Hermeneutic and Composition*, p. 154, and Green, *1 Peter*, p. 153. At the same time, Mark Dubis, *Messianic Woes in First Peter: Suffering and Eschatology in 1 Peter 4.12-19* (SBLSBL 33; New York: Lang, 2002), pp. 163–7, argues that Prov. 11.31 is used to support an expectation of the Messianic Woes.

179. Sargent, 'Narrative Substructure of 1 Peter', pp. 1–6.

significance of the communities served by the Prophets, it is not surprising that Prov. 11.31 is seen to relate to a situation of great importance to the community in support of Peter's paraenesis.

Schutter argues that in the discourse on suffering following 1 Pet. 4.12, scriptural texts are related to the communities via their primary orientation towards the suffering and glories of Christ: because of the communities' association with the Christ who suffered, these texts apply to them too.[180] Whilst there is simply not enough evidence either to prove or disprove that the application of Isa. 11.2 to the communities in 4.14 is secondary to a belief that it is principally about the suffering and glories of Christ, the use of Prov. 11.31 in relation to the eschatological suffering cannot be understood to have a prior reference to the suffering of Christ. Here Schutter's suffering and glories hermeneutic does not provide an adequate explanation of the use of Scripture. The communal and paraenetic approach to interpretation, grounded in the hermeneutic of 1 Pet. 1.12, is quite clearly witnessed here.

i. 1 Peter 5.5 and Proverbs 3.34

Here ὅτι functions as a formula introducing the citation ὁ θεὸς ὑπερηφάνοις ἀντιτάσσεται, ταπεινοῖς δὲ δίδωσιν χάριν from Prov. 3.34.[181] When compared to extant OG versions of Prov. 3.4, the only difference is Peter's use of ὁ θεὸς in the place of κύριος. In contrast, extant Hebrew versions lack a divine name entirely in Prov. 3.34, referring back to יהוה in v. 33 by means of הוא. It could be argued that the omission of κύριος in 1 Pet. 5.5 is due to the christological use Peter typically makes of the term, as in 1.3 εὐλογητὸς ὁ θεὸς καὶ πατὴρ τοῦ κυρίου ἡμῶν Ἰησοῦ Χριστοῦ, where the term refers to Jesus as distinct from God his Father. However, it is generally thought that this difference is of little significance.[182] Indeed, the use of θεὸς is also seen in the use of Prov. 3.34 in Jas 4.6 (μείζονα δὲ δίδωσιν χάριν; διὸ λέγει ὁ θεός ὑπερηφάνοις ἀντιτάσσεται, ταπεινοῖς δὲ δίδωσιν χάριν) and *1 Clem.* 30.2. The apparently widespread use of Prov. 3.34 in this form suggests that it may have been common in early Christian paraenesis: indeed the connection of the citation to the paraenesis in 1 Pet. 5.4 is similar to the connection in

---

180. Schutter, *Hermeneutic and Composition*, p. 165.
181. Elliott, *Commentary*, pp. 848–9; Achtemeier, *1 Peter*, p. 333, and Michaels, *1 Peter*, p. 290, who notes a parallel with the use of ὅτι in 1 Pet. 4.8. Cf. John H. Elliott, 'Ministry and Church Order in the New Testament: A Traditio-Historical Analysis (1 Pt 5,1-5 & plls.)', *CBQ* 32 (1970), pp. 367–91 (370).
182. Schutter, *Hermeneutic and Composition*, p. 166, notes that there is 'no special advantage' to the 'change'. Cf. Elliott, *Commentary*, p. 148, and Carson, '1 Peter', p. 1043.

1 Clem. 30.2.¹⁸³ However, as Selwyn notes, the use of the citation in 1 Pet. 5.4 is quite different from that in Jas 4.6, where it is used as an illustration of God's grace, rather than an exhortation to humility.¹⁸⁴

A significant interpretative question here has been whether the paraenesis of 5.1-5 is directed towards Church life and πρεσβύτεροι who are the leaders of the community, or more simply to family life in which they are simply 'older men'.¹⁸⁵ Sadly, this rather complex question has little to contribute to a discussion of the interpretation of Prov. 3.34 here. At the same time, there is also an interesting debate regarding the extent to which the paraenesis agrees with Greco-Roman ethics.¹⁸⁶ A more important discussion in relation to this study is the structural issue of which elements of the paraenesis of 1 Pet. 5.1-6 the citation is intended to support. Elliott argues that the citation is primarily the basis for the exhortation in 5.6.¹⁸⁷ This is hard to deny, given that the exhortation begins with οὖν and repeats an important term from the citation. However, Green suggests that v. 6 represents a new exhortation.¹⁸⁸ Feldmeier is probably right to argue that there is no clear change in the paraenesis between vv. 5 and 6, and that the citation is part of an associative and smooth transition from one exhortation to another.¹⁸⁹ What is clear from this discussion is the obvious paraenetic use of Prov. 3.54.

---

183. Elliott, *Commentary*, p. 848 and Achtemeier, *1 Peter*, p. 333.
184. Selwyn, *St Peter*, p. 418.
185. Marie-Émile Boismard, *Quatre Hymnes Baptismales dans la Premiere Epître de Pierre* (Lectio Divina 30; Paris: Cerf, 1961), pp. 133–63, suggests that πρεσβύτεροι in v. 5 relates to the family situation because of the use of πάντες δὲ. However, Nauck, 'Freude im Leiden', p. 66, regards the passage as part of a primitive instruction on Christian office looking particularly at a Qumranic background, especially the concept of the מבקר as a prototype for the Christian overseer. Cf. Chloe Lynch, 'Who Are the πρεσβύτεροι and What Is Said about their Role?', *ExpTim* 123 (2012), pp. 529–40.
186. Green, *1 Peter*, p. 171, notes that the appeal to humility reflects Sir. 10.7 but would be deeply troubling to a Greco-Roman audience. Cf. Jobes, *1 Peter*, p. 309. However, Goppelt, *Erste Petrusbrief*, p. 354, argues that the rejection of 'arrogance' would appeal to a common suspicion of hubris. Yet, as Michaels, *1 Peter*, p. 290, notes, ὑπερηφάνοις is probably not meant to be taken as a reference to those with a general moral characteristic, but to specific people who reject the Christian message.
187. Elliott, *Commentary*, pp. 846–50, though Elliott also notes the similarity of 1 Pet. 5.5 with 1.16, 24; 3.10-12; 4.8 and 18 which introduced scriptural references following exhortation.
188. Green, *1 Peter*, p. 171. Cf. Schutter, *Hermeneutic and Composition*, p. 166, who relates the citation to 5.1-5a.
189. Feldmeier, *Letter of Peter*, p. 243.

The citation from Prov. 3.34 serves to support Peter's exhortation to young men to submission to elders and humility in v. 5, as well as the more general exhortation to humility in v. 6. Again, this is another example of Peter's primarily paraenetic hermeneutic: Scripture written to serve the Christian communities. Jobes suggests that the grounding of Peter's paraenesis in Scripture here represents his belief in the continuous role of Scripture in challenging the people of God 'wherever they have lived'.[190] She suggests that this use of Scripture is evidence of a belief that Prov. 3.31 offers the same challenge to the communities as it did to Israel in the past: a demonstration of the continuity between Israel and the Christian communities. Whilst this conclusion is certainly plausible, there is simply no evidence that Peter has any interest in what a scriptural text may have done in the past. As far as 1 Peter is concerned, the present is the only context of any significance: 'we are the people Scripture is meant for', he might say. As will be seen in the next chapter, even the waters of the Flood are seen to be essentially related to the reality experienced by the communities in the present.

3. Conclusion

There are many aspects of the use of scriptural citations in 1 Peter that cannot be established with any certainty. There is unlikely to be agreement on what constitutes a citation or an allusion, or indeed whether these terms have any meaning at all. However, a good case can be made for the definition of all of the scriptural references discussed in this chapter as 'citations', though Isa. 40.6 and 8 in 1 Pet. 1.24-25, for example, is much clearer than Isa. 11.2 in 4.14.

What is somewhat clearer is the predominantly paraenetic use made of scriptural texts. The analysis of the citations in 1 Peter has suggested that Schutter and others are right to conclude that 1.10-12 describes something of the scriptural hermeneutic employed in the epistle. However, the conclusion that the principal hermeneutical idea of this sentence is a christological one is inadequate as an explanation of how Scripture is interpreted. Whilst it is clear that both 1.10-12 and the use of Scripture in 1 Peter have a christological or kerygmatic interest, if 1.10-12 is understood to be primarily kerygmatic and christological it does not offer a very good explanation of how Scripture is used in the letter. For this reason, Schutter struggles to relate every use of Scripture to the suffering and glories paradigm he sees in 1.10-12.[191] Yet, if the hermeneutical

---

190. Jobes, *1 Peter*, p. 309.
191. Moyise, *Evoking Scripture*, p. 93.

significance of 1.10-12 is that it establishes an understanding of Scripture both as kerygmatic and paraenetic, it offers a much better explanation of the use of Scripture in 1 Peter. The dominant hermeneutical idea in 1.10-12 is the notion in v. 12 that the prophetic witness was offered in service to an eschatological people standing at the climax of God's redemptive plan: the Christian communities addressed by 1 Peter. Because Scripture was written as an act of service to these communities, it is interpreted as though it addresses their needs directly: as though it comforts them where they need comforting and challenges them where they need challenging. As will be argued below, this hermeneutic, with its assumption of the importance of the community in and for which Scripture is interpreted, can best be described as 'primitive' and 'sectarian' and is typical of an apocalyptic Jewish context.

Chapter 3

ALLUSION TO SCRIPTURE IN 1 PETER

This chapter explores possible allusions to Scripture in 1 Peter. Whereas the previous chapter explored each quotation of Scripture in some depth, the nature of allusions makes them generally more hypothetical and often purely speculative.[1] Because of this, some possible allusions will be discussed briefly, whilst others will be treated in greater depth.

There are at least three reasons to treat allusions separately in a study such as this. First, allusions are typically more tentative than quotations: there may only be one or two scholars who detect an allusion in a certain text. Secondly, and very significantly, allusions are typically harder to discuss in terms of hermeneutics than quotations. It is often very difficult to know why an allusion has been made and it may be that an author is simply borrowing language (in our case Biblicisms) from another text, rather than making a claim about the meaning of another text. Finally, it will be argued here that there is a distinction between the use of allusions and the use of quotations in 1 Peter. Whereas allusions to texts are often similar in function to the use of quotations (they are incorporated into paraenesis and are used to make claims about the status of the communities addressed by Peter), two of the most prominent allusions in 1 Peter are not to texts but to events. Peter's application of texts to his audiences reflects the determinate meaning derived from the theological narrative behind 1.10-12. Hence, Peter has no concerns relating to what texts may have meant to Israel in the past: they are exclusively oriented towards the suffering and glories of Christ and the service of the communities. However, allusions to events (such as the allusions to Sarah's obedience and to the Flood) function quite differently. These events typologically prefigure something to happen later.

---

1. Richard Garner, *From Homer to Tragedy: The Art of Allusion in Greek Poetry* (London: Routledge, 1990), p. 1.

This chapter will not discuss iterative allusions associated with formal citations: these were treated in relation to their citations in the previous chapter. In addition to this, the chapter will not discuss every possible allusion suggested in the secondary literature on 1 Peter: there are simply too many possibilities. After a discussion of the nature and number of allusions, seventeen of the most widely supported allusions will be discussed with a view to furthering an understanding of the scriptural hermeneutic of 1 Peter.

1. What Is an Allusion and How Many Are There in 1 Peter?

The identification of biblical allusions in 1 Peter is even more complex than the identification of citations. There are many factors which make assessment of allusions difficult. Certain scholars might well be able to perceive allusions and echoes in every verse of 1 Peter and there is often too little evidence to affirm or deny the proposals on a clear basis. It may be that an author has adopted a deliberately 'scriptural' style, as Jacob Jervell suggests is the case regarding Luke–Acts,[2] in which case it is difficult to distinguish between the use of scriptural language (Biblicisms) and the reference to biblical texts (allusions). Allusions depend on verbal similarity and knowledge of what texts might be known to the author and his audience. When we know so little about the textual traditions of the first century, how can we be sure that allusions based on perhaps one or two words really are references to a particular text? Given that we cannot be sure of how much access first-century Christians had to scriptural texts, how can we be sure that the possible allusions detected by scholars today really were read or heard as such in the first century? After all, scholars of the contemporary academy may have a much more detailed acquaintance with both the Old Testament text potentially referred to (as well as the New Testament text in which the possible allusion occurs) than the latter's first readers and hearers.

Michael Thompson, in his study of possible allusions to Jesus traditions in Rom. 12.1–15.13, offers a helpful distinction between scriptural allusions and Biblicisms as well as some criteria for discerning a possible allusion. According to Thompson, the difference is one of authorial intent: an allusion is deliberate whereas an echo is coincidental. Thompson states:

---

2. Jervell, 'The Future of the Past', p. 110. Cf. Daryl Schmidt, 'The Historiography of Acts: Deuteronomistic or Hellenistic?', *SBLSP* 24 (1985), pp. 417–26.

> In order for the allusion to be successful, the audience must *recognise* the sign, *realise* that the [similarity] is deliberate, *remember* aspects of the original text to which the author is alluding, and *connect* one or more of these aspects with the alluding text in order to get the author's point.[3]

The great difficulty here is that an audience may never be aware of an allusion if they are not acquainted with the texts alluded to, perhaps because they have no long-standing acquaintance with the Scriptures of Israel.[4] Several of Thompson's criteria relate particularly to the problem of detecting allusion to the quite elusive teaching of the historical Jesus, yet the majority are helpful for detecting allusion to Scripture. Some degree of verbal similarity is important. How many terms do the potential source and receiving text have in common? How significant are the terms that are shared? Is an unusual combination of terms evident in both texts? Thompson argues that conceptual similarity is important. Is the meaning of both texts similar? Do both texts share an unusual combination of ideas? He also suggests that structural similarity might be evident. In addition to these questions, Thompson asks whether a potential source is plausible in light of its precise form and dating.

Schutter suggests a definition of the allusions in 1 Peter using four categories based on literary similarity between 1 Peter and possible sources: explicit, implicit, incipient and iterative.[5] Explicit allusions are those which are relatively undeniable, probably because they employ a significant amount of material from the scriptural text to which they refer. In this category, Schutter includes 1 Pet. 2.3 (Ps. 34.8), 2.9 (various texts featuring election and the people of God), 2.10 (a large portion of Hosea), 2.22 (Isa. 53.9), 2.24 (Isa. 53.9), 2.25 (Isa. 53.6), 3.6 (Gen. 18.12), 3.14 (Isa. 8.12), 3.20 (Gen. 7.13), 3.22 (Pss. 8.6-7; 110.1) and 4.14 (Isa. 11.2). In addition to this, he also includes 1 Pet. 2.12 (Isa. 10.3) and 4.17 (Ezek. 9.6) though neither of these employ a significant number of terms from the texts to which they allude, or at least, one should say, from extant versions of those texts. However, as Schutter points out, not all of these feature an excerpt of Scripture. The likely allusion to Gen. 18.12 in 1 Pet. 3.6 is certainly an allusion of the most explicit kind since Sarah is mentioned by name, even though Peter does

---

3. Michael Thompson, *Clothed with Christ: The Example and Teaching of Jesus in Romans 12.1–15.13* (JSNTSup 59; Sheffield: JSOT, 1991), p. 29. Cf. Hayes, *Echoes of Scripture*, p. 29.
4. Stanley, *Arguing with Scripture*, pp. 38–61.
5. Schutter, *Hermeneutic and Composition*, p. 36. Cf. Woan, 'Psalms in 1 Peter', p. 215, who understands allusions as references to Scripture which lack a citation formula, occur in the middle of a sentence and are a less accurate replication of their source text than quotations.

not employ terminology from that passage of Scripture. Likewise, the similarly unclear allusion to Noah and the Flood in 1 Pet. 3.20 is clearly an explicit allusion though it does not employ any scriptural terms from the passage to which it alludes. Schutter also notes that allusions may be to conflated texts (as in 1 Pet. 2.9) or 'telescoped' texts (as in 2.10). In the latter, a long piece of text, the opening chapters of Hosea, is compressed into a single verse which employs some terms from the passage alluded to. Schutter also suggests that there may be as many as twenty implicit allusions in 1 Peter: 1.18 (Isa. 52.3), 1.19 (Isa. 53.7; Exod. 12.5 or 29.38), 1.21 (Isa. 52.13), 1.25b (Isa. 40.9), 2.4 (Ps. 34.5), 2.9 (Isa. 42.12; Mal. 3.17 or Hag. 2.9), 2.17 (Prov. 24.21), 2.23 (Isa. 53.7 or 53.12), 2.24 (Isa. 53.4 or 53.12), 3.6 (Prov. 3.25), 3.13 (Isa. 50.9), 3.18 (OG Isa. 53.11), 4.19 (Ps. 31.5), 5.7 (Ps. 55.22) and 5.8 (Ps. 22.14 or Job 1.7). Carson adds 1.1 (Isa. 11.11-12 or Jer. 31.8-14) and 1.2 (Exod. 24.7) as allusions worthy of consideration. Though he does not draw a distinction between explicit and implicit types, these are clearly of the latter sort. Schutter regards seven of his list as most plausible allusions on the basis of the amount of text they contain. In addition to this, a further nine allusions are considered plausible on the basis of the proximity to clearer references to the same text. Some of these iterative allusions are more plausible than others and some depend simply upon a single word. For example, the use of εὐαγγελισθὲν in 1 Pet. 1.25b is thought by Schutter to be a further reference to Isaiah 40, albeit Isa. 40.9 which is not part of the citation in 1.24-25a.[6] The difficulty with this type of allusion is that it often offers scholars a licence to find interesting allusions to Scripture in perhaps the most unlikely of places, creating the possibility of novel (but not entirely plausible) readings of New Testament texts. Hence, it will not be possible to give each of the suggested allusions of this type much attention in the analysis below. Many of these suggestions are indeed interesting but are still largely speculative.

6. Schutter, *Hermeneutic and Composition*, p. 38. Isa. 40.9 reads, ἐπ' ὄρος ὑψηλὸν ἀνάβηθι ὁ εὐαγγελιζόμενος Σιων ὕψωσον τῇ ἰσχύι τὴν φωνήν σου ὁ εὐαγγελιζόμενος Ιερουσαλημ ὑψώσατε μὴ φοβεῖσθε εἰπὸν ταῖς πόλεσιν Ιουδα ἰδοὺ ὁ θεὸς ὑμῶν. The transposition of εὐαγγελισθὲν εἰς ὑμᾶς in 1 Pet. 1.25b in $\mathfrak{P}^{72}$ is of no real significance to Schutter's proposal, nor is the possible allusion recognised in NA[27]. Of course, if this is a deliberate allusion to Isa. 40.9 and Isaiah's proclamation to Zion becomes a proclamation the communities of 1 Peter, this would be another example of 1 Peter's 'supercessionist' use of scriptural language. However, some iterative allusions are more plausible than others. The use of παρεδίδου in 1 Pet. 2.23 may well be a reference to the use of παρεδόθη in Isa. 53.12 due to the sheer density of indisputable explicit allusions in 1 Pet. 2.21-25. See Lohse, 'Paränese und Kerygma', p. 88 n. 109.

As noted above, related to Schutter's analysis of biblical allusion in 1 Peter is the question of Biblicisms.[7] As Achtemeier notes, 'virtually all of the imagery of 1 Peter is drawn from [Biblical] writings' and it is possible to see apparent Biblicisms in practically every verse of 1 Peter.[8] However, as Schutter notes, Biblicisms display such a limited 'literary dependence' to a particular scriptural text, to the extent that it is impossible to establish their relation to a particular source with any confidence that the study of them is of little value. For this reason, Schutter limits his discussion to possible examples of quotation and allusion. As noted above, this chapter will limit discussion to just seventeen of the most plausible (or interesting) allusions.

It will be argued here that there is an important distinction between allusion to scriptural text and allusion to scriptural event in 1 Peter. Whilst allusions to scriptural texts appropriate texts to the needs of the communities in precisely the same manner as is the case with citations in the epistle, scriptural events have a more complex relation to the communities. Whilst there is no sense in which 1 Peter uses texts as though they have a prior context, the allusions to events of the past which have no clear verbal similarity to extant scriptural texts imply that those events are real in their own right as well as bearing a typological relation to the present. This is seen in the manner in which Sarah's submission, in 3.6, is seen as exemplary to the women of the communities, whose children they can become. This is also seen in the way in which the waters of the Flood in 3.21 are taken as an 'antitype' of the baptism which now saves the communities. In this way, history itself is seen to have an orientation towards the great and glorious events of which the communities are now a part. Just as Scripture is understood to exist to serve the communities by witnessing to the sufferings of Christ and the glories which follow them, so too are the events of history understood as bearing witness in some way to the climax of God's plan.

---

7. Schutter, *Hermeneutic and Composition*, pp. 41–3, discusses the following possible biblicisms; 1 Pet. 1.2 (Dan. 4.1 or 6.26 in Θ), 1.3 (Sir. 16.12), 1.7 (Prov. 17.3; 27.21; Zech. 13.9; Mal. 3.2-3; Sir. 2.5), 1.10 (1 Macc. 9.26), 1.12 (Pss. 14.12; 85.11; Lam. 3.50; *1 En.* 9.1; Jas 1.25; Gen. 28.12), 1.13 (Exod. 12.11; Jer. 1.17; 2 Kgs 4.29; 9.1; Prov. 31.17), 1.17 (Jer. 3.19; Pss. 62.12; 89.27; Prov. 24.12), 1.23 (Dan. 6.27 in Θ), 2.9 (Isa. 9.2), 2.11 (Gen. 23.4; Ps. 39.13), 2.23 (Jer. 11.20), 2.25 (Ezek. 34.5, 16; Job 10.12; Wis. 1.6), 3.3-4 (Isa. 3.18-24), 3.19 (Ps. 88.4, 6), 4.12 (Prov. 17.3 and the same possible sources as 1 Pet. 1.7) 4.14 (Pss. 72.19; 79.9), 4.19 (2 Macc. 1.24), 5.4 (Isa. 28.5), 5.6 (Gen. 16.9; Exod. 3.19; 6.1; Deut. 9.26; Job 30.21) and 5.7 (Wis. 12.13). On 1 Pet. 5.4, see Hillyer, 'Feast of Tabernacles', p. 60, for a rather tenuous suggestion that τῆς δόξης στέφανον may allude to the festal tradition witnessed to in *Sim.* 8.2.

8. Achtemeier, *1 Peter*, p. 12.

a. 1 Peter 1.1 and διασπορᾶς

Carson suggests that the use of διασπορᾶς in this verse is an allusion to exilic language in Old Testament texts such as Isa. 11.11-12 and Jer. 31.8-14.[9] However, διασπορά does not appear to be a common term in OG or Septuagintal texts. Jeremiah 31.10 (OG 38.10), which appears similar conceptually, actually uses the substantive participle λικμήσας to describe the God who scatters his people. Διασπορά is used of Israelites living in foreign lands in Deut. 28.25 and 30.4, though these are two different Hebrew terms: זעוה and נדח respectively. The term is, however, used of the Assyrian or Babylonian exiles in Ps. 147.2 (OG 146.2), Isa. 49.6 and 2 Macc. 1.27. Whilst it is by no means commonplace, the presence of the term in the Psalter and in Second Isaiah makes the suggestion that διασπορᾶς in 1 Pet. 1.1 is an allusion plausible, since such texts appear to be as popular in 1 Peter as they are in the New Testament generally. What is clear is that the term had a common usage in Judaism by the first century A.D. and here, as Cranfield notes, it is adopted to refer to the communities to whom the epistle is addressed, possibly as an expression of a supercessionist understanding of that community.[10]

The use of παρεπιδήμοις in 1 Pet. 1.1 is interesting. The term is also used Heb. 11.13 as part of a description of the patriarchs' trust in God's promises. Here the term forms part of what is probably an allusion to Gen. 23.4 where the term is used in the singular by Abraham to describe his status among the Hittites. This allusion has been widely recognised.[11]

---

9. Carson, '1 Peter', pp. 1015–16. Cf. Torrey Seland, *Strangers in the Light: Philonic Perspectives on Christian Identity in 1 Peter* (BIS 76; Leiden: Brill, 2005), p. 2, who also suggests that this language is connected to the use of παροίκους καὶ παρεπιδήμους in 1 Pet. 2.12, which he argues evokes particular descriptions of Jewish proselytes, seen in OG translations of גר as well as Philonic use of this terminology.

10. Cranfield, *Peter*, p. 14. However, Michaels, *1 Peter*, p. xlix, rightly notes that there is no suggestion of supercessionism in 1 Peter, since an unbelieving Jewish community is never mentioned. Whilst other uses of Ps. 118.22 in the New Testament (as in Mt. 21.42-44) employ the text to proclaim the rejection of fruitless Israel, 1 Pet. 2.7 does not.

11. See, e.g., August Strobel, *Der Brief an die Hebräer* (Göttingen: Vandenhoeck & Ruprecht, 1991), p. 330, who also notes the Philonic parallels in *Quest. Gen.* 3.45, *de Cher.* 120 and *de Som.* 1.65, and Harold W. Attridge, *Hebrews* (Philadelphia: Fortress, 1989), p. 330. Attridge identifies the use of παρεπιδήμοι with a more widespread 'confession', beginning with Gen. 23.4, but also including Gen. 47.4, 9; Lev. 25.23; Ps. 39.13 (OG 38.13) and 1 Chron. 29.15. However, only two of these verses (including Gen. 23.4) use παρεπιδήμοι or derivatives. The rest use forms of the more common παροικεῖν/πάροικοι, a fact which appears to have influenced the 'correction' of Heb. 11.13 in D*. In addition to this, 1 Chron. 29.15 barely stands

However, given the much more general setting of παρεπιδήμοι in 1 Pet. 1.1, where it is related to exilic language, rather than a particular scriptural context (as in Heb. 11.13), it is quite unlikely to be an allusion to Gen. 23.4. Given that the term is not common in the Old Testament, being used only in Ps. 39.13 (OG 38.13) in addition to Gen. 23.4, it is unlikely that its use in 1 Pet. 1.1 is intended to evoke a particular scriptural concept or image. Indeed, for Elliott, the term is primarily a reference to the actual social status of the communities.[12] However, Moses Chin rejects Elliott's argument that πάροικοι, οἶκος τοῦ θεοῦ and παρεπίδημοι refer to the *social* status of the communities to whom 1 Peter is addressed, whilst affirming with Elliott the importance of these terms in the epistle.[13] Firstly, Chin argues that in the OG Scriptures, πάροικοι and παρεπίδημοι are synonymous, since they appear to be used interchangeably as translations of Hebrew terms such as גור. Secondly, Chin suggests that these terms are consistently used to refer to the spiritual status of the people of God. For example, Leviticus 25–26 uses the terms to express the status of Israel *after* they have occupied the land of Canaan whilst in 1 Chron. 29.14-15 David describes himself and his subjects as πάροικοι. As Chin argues, this spiritual rather than legal understanding of the terms is consistent with their use by Philo as well as in early Christian texts such as salutation of *1 Clement*: ἡ ἐκκλησια τοῦ θεοῦ ἡ παροικοῦσα Ῥώμην τῇ ἐκκλησίᾳ τοῦ θεοῦ τῇ παροικούσῃ Κόρινθον, κλητοῖς, ἡγιασμένοις ἐν θελήματι θεοῦ διὰ τοῦ κυρίον ἡμῶν Ἰησοῦ Χριστοῦ. The similarity of this salutation to that of 1 Peter is startling both in its use of 'sojourning' language and its terminology of election and sanctification, as well as its use of the rare optative πληθυνθείη. As Chin points out, a text such as this provides an illuminating comment upon how the 'sojourning' language of 1 Peter was received.

If it is possible to detect the use of a particular hermeneutic here, it could be argued that the application of 'diaspora' to the communities addressed by 1 Peter is equivalent to the exclusive application of the Exodus badges of Israel discussed below. It may be that Peter sees the communities as the true dispersed people of God, to whom the Scriptures refer.

---

within the 'confession' tradition, referring to the people as aliens towards God rather than aliens in the land. The use of the unusual παρεπιδήμοι just after a discussion of Abraham makes it most likely that Heb. 11.13 alludes to Gen. 23.4. Cf. Walter Grundemann, 'παρεπιδήμος', *TDNT*, vol. 2, pp. 64–5.

   12. Elliott, *Home for the Homeless*, pp. 21–49.

   13. Moses Chin, 'A Heavenly Home for the Homeless: Aliens and Strangers in 1 Peter', *TynBul* 42 (1991), pp. 96–112. Cf. Elliott, *Home of the Homeless*, pp. 21–100.

b. 1 Peter 1.2 and ῥαντισμὸν αἵματος

In this verse, the words καὶ ῥαντισμὸν αἵματος are thought to allude to either Exod. 12.7, 22; 24.3-8; Lev. 8.10-30; 16.15; or Numbers 19,[14] all of which feature this sacrificial imagery. Though Exod. 12.7 and 22 might be considered due to the paschal and Exodus themes often noted in 1 Peter, the lack of verbal similarity ought to rule these texts out.[15] Mbuvi is doubtless correct to conclude that a variety of texts, or rather a textual tradition, is alluded to here and the application of sprinkling to both the temple and the people in these texts provides some interesting evidence in favour of his argument that the communities addressed by 1 Peter are viewed as having been sanctified as the 'Temple-Community'.[16]

Whilst there is some agreement that a scriptural allusion is to be found here, there is very little certainty as to what καὶ ῥαντισμὸν αἵματος refers within the context of the phrase εἰς ὑπακοὴν καὶ ῥαντισμὸν αἵματος Ἰησοῦ Χριστοῦ. Some commentators take the genitive Ἰησοῦ Χριστοῦ to qualify both 'obedience' and 'blood'. In which case, the genitive is both objective in relation to 'obedience' ('for obedience') and possessive in relation to 'blood' ('the blood of Christ').[17] Carson, however, argues that Ἰησοῦ Χριστοῦ is unlikely to be both an objective and possessive genitive at the same time, a very difficult concept to grasp syntactically.[18] Instead, he follows Beare in taking ὑπακοὴν καὶ ῥαντισμὸν as a hendiadys.[19] He does this by suggesting that Peter is aware of the literary context of his allusion to Exod. 24.3-8, in which obedience and sacrifice are two aspects of a single covenantal ritual.[20] The combination of these two ideas in both the text alluded to and 1 Pet. 1.2 is striking and suggests that the allusion is to the broader concept of the covenant – but was Peter aware of this?

---

14. Num. 19 is the source preferred by Michaels, *1 Peter*, p. 12, though this view has not gained much support. The most important argument in favour of this source is the christological interpretation of the sacrifice of the red heifer and the use of its ashes (mixed with water and sprinkled) to remove sin in *Ep. Barn.* 8.1-2.

15. An interesting parallel to this verse is 2 Thess. 2.13, which similarly equates 'election' with 'sanctification': ὅτι εἵλατο ὑμᾶς ὁ θεὸς ἀπαρχὴν εἰς σωτηρίαν ἐν ἁγιασμῷ πνεύματος καὶ πίστει ἀληθείας. Sargent, 'Chosen through Sanctification', pp. 117–20.

16. Mbuvi, *Temple, Exile and Identity*, pp. 71–3.

17. E.g. Best, *1 Peter*, p. 71.

18. Carson, '1 Peter', pp. 1016–17. Cf. Achtemeier, *1 Peter*, p. 87, describes this as a 'grammatical monstrosity' that would be 'confusing to the reader/listener.'

19. Cf. Beare, *Peter*, pp. 76–7.

20. Carson, '1 Peter', pp. 1016–17. Jobes, *1 Peter*, p. 72, also suggests that 'obedience' and 'blood sprinkling' are parallel aspects of a reference to Exod. 24.7. She also suggests that the use of the exilic term διασπορᾶς in 1.1 raises the possibility that 1.2 alludes to the combined 'obedience' and 'sprinkling' in Ezek. 36.24-28.

Carson notes that other scholars have not identified the depth of the allusion in 1.2 to the same extent that he has. A principal problem with his suggestion is that, though it is impossible to know the precise form of the Greek Scripture available to Peter, extant versions do not use the term ὑπακούειν in Exod. 24.7, which one would perhaps expect. Instead, the OG simply employs the etymologically related, but still different, verb ἀκούειν. Both terms are typically translations of the Hebrew שמע, so an OG text employing ὑπακούειν is plausible.

Another possibility is that Ἰησοῦ Χριστοῦ is to be understood as a subjective genitive for both ὑπακοὴν and ῥαντισμὸν αἵματος, and εἰς is understood to be causal. Proposing this approach, Francis H. Agnew translates the verse as follows: '*because* of the obedience and the sprinkling of the blood of Jesus Christ'.[21] In this reading, 'obedience' is taken to be the obedience shown by Jesus Christ, rather than the obedience of the elect communities.[22] Behind this rendering of the translation is an observation that the imitation of Christ is an important feature of New Testament Christology in general and 1 Peter in particular. However, it is not clear that the obedience of Jesus is recognised as especially significant in 1 Peter. The only exemplar of obedience in 1 Peter is Sarah in 3.6. This suggests that the personal obedience of Christ is not an important concept in 1 Peter, and certainly not important enough to feature in the salutation of the letter.[23]

Perhaps the most persuasive interpretation of εἰς ὑπακοὴν καὶ ῥαντισμὸν αἵματος Ἰησοῦ Χριστοῦ is that taken by Achtemeier and Feldmeier.[24] They both suggest that the genitive Ἰησοῦ Χριστοῦ relates just to αἵματος and that 'obedience' is absolute. If this is correct, the reference to Exod. 24.3-8 is simply to 'sprinkling', rather than to the covenantal combination of obedience and sprinkling suggested by Beare, Jobes and Carson. Whatever the precise source of the allusion in 1.2, it is clear that a sacrificial image and language is applied to Jesus Christ. Whether or not

21. Francis H. Agnew, '1 Peter 1.2 – An Alternative Translation', *CBQ* 4 (1983), p. 70. The italics in the quotation are original. This interpretation is also taken by Green, *1 Peter*, p. 20.

22. Goppelt, *Erste Petrusbrief*, p. 86, also takes the genitive as subjective, but reading εἰς as telic, suggesting that the phrase reflects a baptism formula comparable to the initiation rite in 1QS 3.6-8. However, Goppelt's view is rejected by Elliott, *Commentary*, p. 320; Achtemeier, *1 Peter*, p. 87, and Jobes, *1 Peter*, p. 72, who note that the primary interest of the salutation is election, rather than initiation.

23. See the rhetorical and introductory function of 1 Pet. 1.1-2 in Philip I. Tite, 'The Compositional Function of the Petrine Prescript: A Look at 1 Pet 1.1-3', *JETS* 39 (1996), pp. 47–56.

24. Achtemeier, *1 Peter*, pp. 87–8 and Feldmeier, *Letter of Peter*, p. 49.

the genitive Ἰησοῦ Χριστοῦ implies that Christ is the one who sprinkles the blood, it is beyond doubt that the blood originated in the body of Christ and that this is a reference to his suffering and death. This may reflect the orientation of Scripture towards the sufferings and glories of Christ suggested in 1.10-11. Yet, at the same time, it must be noted that this christological application of scriptural language serves a broader purpose of defining the identity of the communities to whom Peter writes: the scattered elect. Again, it seems likely that the 'ecclesiological' element of the hermeneutic indicated in 1.10-12 is dominant, though it is not expressed here in paraenesis.

c. 1 Peter 1.6-7 and Zechariah 13.9

Mbuvi argues that 1.6-7 (ὀλίγον ἄρτι εἰ δέον ἐστὶν λυπηθέντες ἐν ποικίλοις πειρασμοῖς, ἵνα τὸ δοκίμιον ὑμῶν τῆς πίστεως πολυτιμότερον χρυσίου τοῦ ἀπολλυμένου διὰ πυρὸς δὲ δοκιμαζομένοι, εὑρεθῇ εἰς ἔπαινον καὶ δόξαν καὶ τιμὴν ἐν ἀποκαλύψει Ἰησου Χριστοῦ) is an allusion to scriptural tradition predicting the purification of the renewed Temple. This tradition is witnessed in Isa. 48.10, Zech. 13.9 and Mal. 3.3, each of which feature the term πῦρός, though Zech. 13.9 has the closest verbal correspondence to 1 Peter, featuring δοκιμάζω and χρυσίον also.[25] The tradition of reference to spiritual testing and refinement is also seen in Ps. 66.10, Prov. 17.3, Sir. 2.1-6 and 1QS 8.4, though these texts do not feature eschatological, cultic renewal or restoration following the exile. Mbuvi considers the context of Zech. 13.9 to bear a close enough resemblance to 1 Pet. 1.6-7 as to suggest that this is the passage being alluded to, arguing that the 'covenant formula' in Zech. 13.9b is also echoed in the use of Hos. 2.23 in 1 Pet. 2.10. Mbuvi also notes that the context of Isa. 48.10 relates to the restoration of Israel after the exile.

The principal difficulty with Mbuvi's argument here (aside from the fact that it depends upon Peter's detailed knowledge of the context of the scriptural texts to which he refers) is that 1 Pet. 1.6-7 is not about the refinement of the people, but of their faith. It is faith itself that is compared to gold in 1 Pet. 1.6-7.[26] Yet the notion of faith being refined is absent from the exilic restoration texts Mbuvi suggests may be alluded to here, though it could be said to relate conceptually to the broader

---

25. Mbuvi, *Temple, Exile and Identity*, pp. 134–5. Cf. Elliott, *Commentary*, p. 343.

26. Goppelt, *Erste Petrusbrief*, p. 101, notes the similar concepts in Jas 1.2–3; 1 Pet. 4.12 and 1 Cor. 3.13, suggesting the existence of an early Christian tradition. Cf. Feldmeier, *Letter of Peter*, p. 224; Bigg, *St Peter*, pp. 103–4 (on the relation of 1 Pet. 1.6-7 and Jas 1.2-3), and Johnson, 'Fire in God's House', p. 288.

tradition of spiritual refinement noted above. In addition to these problems with Mbuvi's emphasis on Zech. 13.9, it must be noted that the majority of scholars either do not recognise the scriptural background to the language of refinement here, or else see it as a general Biblicism, rather than an allusion to a specific text.[27] However, if Mbuvi is right and the eschatological purification of Zech. 13.9 is being claimed for the communities addressed by 1 Peter, this would be another example of the 'ecclesiological' focus of the use of Scripture in 1 Peter.

d. 1 Peter 1.10-12 and the Prophets

Whilst 1 Pet. 1.10-12 clearly alludes to a certain understanding of biblical history as regards the ministry of the Prophets, it is not clear that any particular scriptural texts are alluded to here. The idea that the prophetic writings find their meaning in events which lie in the future, from the perspective of the prophet, is widely attested in the Old Testament.[28] Yet it is unlikely that any of these are intentionally alluded to in 1.10-12 since no significant verbal similarity is witnessed. Importantly, the implication of the Prophets' ignorance in 1 Pet. 1.12 (that they served, not themselves but those of a later age) is not a feature of these texts, nor is it a feature of 1QpHab 7.1-8.

Possibly the closest verbal similarity to a specific scriptural text here is the use of ἐξεζήτησαν καὶ ἐξηραύνησαν in 1.10 as well as in 1 Macc. 9.26 – καὶ ἐξεζήτουν καὶ ἠρεύνων τοὺς φίλους Ιουδου καὶ ἦγον αὐτοὺς πρὸς Βακχίδην, καὶ ἐξεδίκα αὐτοὺς καὶ ἐνέπαιζεν αὐτοῖς. As Schutter notes, this is unlikely to be intended as an allusion since the context of 1 Macc. 9.26 is so different from the way in which these verbs are used in 1.10, to the extent that it is impossible to identify what such an allusion would be intended to convey to the audiences of the epistle.[29] If this were an allusion, it would not be possible to determine exactly what was intended by its use. As discussed above, there are several plausible influences upon the angelic inquiry of 1 Pet. 1.12, such as Gen. 28.12; Ps. 85.11;

---

27. Those who see the phrase as a general Biblicism reflecting a range of texts including Zech. 13.9: Kelly, *Peter*, p. 55; Elliott, *Commentary*, pp. 15 and 341; Jobes, *1 Peter*, p. 94; Achtemeier, *1 Peter*, p. 102 and Schutter, *Hermeneutic and Composition*, p. 41 who claims that this is 'nothing other than a stock expression'. However, Bigg, *St Peter*, p. 104; Best, *1 Peter*, p. 78, and Michaels, *1 Peter*, pp. 30–1 make no reference to Zech. 13.9 at all.

28. Dan. 9.2, 23-27; 12.6-13; *4 Ezra* 4.33–5.13. Cf. Mt. 26.56; Lk. 1.70; 18.31; Rom. 1.2; Heb. 1.1, and Rev. 10.7.

29. Schutter, *Hermeneutic and Composition*, p. 41. Cf. Achtemeier, *1 Peter*, p. 108; Beare, *Peter*, p. 90, and Schelkle, *Petrusbrief*, p. 39 n. 2.

Lam. 3.50; *1 En.* 9.1; 16.3. Schutter rightly rejects the possibility of an allusion to any of these texts in 1.12 since the background of the concept of angelic inquiry is too complex for any one text to be clearly alluded to.³⁰

e. 1 Peter 1.19 and ὡς ἀμνοῦ ἀμώμου καὶ ἀσπίλου

The use of the phrase ὡς ἀμνοῦ ἀμώμου καὶ ἀσπίλου is a clear reference to scriptural language of sacrifice, though, as Carson suggests, it is unlikely to allude to a particular scriptural text.³¹ Indeed, many scholars see this as an allusion to the Passover lamb and the general sacrificial tradition associated with it.³² However, Schutter regards this reference as an incipient allusion reflecting a pre-Petrine tradition of interpreting Isaiah 52–53, even though it has a closer verbal similarity to Exod. 29.38: καὶ ταῦτά ἐστιν ἃ ποιήσεις ἐπὶ τοῦ θυσιαστηρίου ἀμνοὺς ἐνιαυσίους ἀμώμους.³³ However, this is problematic since 1 Peter does not appear to bear comparison with the only other extant early Christian traditions of interpreting Isaiah 53. The only other indisputable reference to Isaiah 52–53 in relation to the death of Christ in the New Testament is in Acts 8.32-33, which cites Isa. 53.7 and 8.³⁴ This reference appears to emphasise the injustice of the Servant's suffering, rather than its soteriological or ethical value. It is often noted that the treatment of this passage in 1 Peter represents one of the epistle's principal distinctive contributions to early Christian theology.³⁵ Again, if Schutter is correct, the hermeneutic of Christ's 'suffering and glories' he discerns in 1.10-12 is evident here, though ultimately the allusion is made to support the paraenesis in 1.17 – ἐν φόβῳ τὸν τῆς παροικίας ὑμῶν χρόνον ἀναστράφητε.

---

30. Schutter, *Hermeneutic and Composition*, p. 41. Cf. Achtemeier, *1 Peter*, p. 112.

31. Carson, '1 Peter', p. 1019.

32. Kelly, *Peter*, p. 74; Feldmeier, *Letter of Peter*, p. 118; Green, *1 Peter*, p. 41, and Achtemeier, *1 Peter*, p. 129.

33. Schutter, *Hermeneutic and Composition*, p. 39. Schutter is well supported in this position by Michaels, *1 Peter*, p. 65. Best, *1 Peter*, p. 90, agrees that Isa. 53.7 is alluded to but thinks that the primary influence on the phrase is the Passover. He notes, in support of an allusion to Isa. 53.7, that Isa. 52.3 is alluded to in 1 Pet. 1.18.

34. For other New Testament uses of Isa. 52–53, see Mt. 8.17; Lk. 22.37; Jn 12.38; Rom. 10.16; 15.21.

35. Best, *1 Peter*, p. 120; Feldmeier, *Letter of Peter*, pp. 174–5, and Jobes, *1 Peter*, pp. 191–2, who also notes that 1 Peter is the only New Testament author to incorporate Christ's sufferings (using Isa. 53) to household code material. However, Green, *1 Peter*, p. 83, suggests that the unusual claims premised upon Peter's use of Isaiah suggest that this use of Isaiah in 2.21-25 reflects a popular tradition.

f. 1 Peter 2.1 and Psalm 34.14 (OG Psalm 33.14)

Bornemann and Woan both regard the terms κακίαν and δόλον as a reference to OG Ps. 33.14 (παῦσον τὴν γλῶσσάν σου ἀπὸ κακοῦ καὶ χείλη σου τοῦ μὴ λαλῆσαι δόλον) as part of their arguments for the importance of Ps. 33/34 in 1 Peter.[36] Eriksson agrees that there is a reference to Ps. 34.14 here and suggests that the psalm allusion confirms the admonition, giving it the authority of Scripture.[37] If there is an allusion to Ps. 34.14 here, it would serve a paraenetic function, as Eriksson suggests.

However, are κακίαν and δόλον used here to allude to Ps. 34.14, or are they simply important terms to Peter which explain why he later chooses to allude to and quote from Psalm 34? These terms could simply be a reflection of important themes in 1 Peter that led Peter to an interest in Psalm 34, rather than that Peter's argument is influenced by Psalm 34.[38]

g. 1 Peter 2.3 and Psalm 34.8 (OG Psalm 33.9)

The short phrase εἰ ἐγεύσασθε ὅτι χρηστὸς ὁ κύριος here is quite clearly a reference to Ps. 34.8 (OG 33.9).[39] Despite its brevity, this is made certain by the long citation from Ps. 34.12-16 (OG 33.13-17) in 1 Pet. 3.10-12. Indeed, the idea that Peter was very familiar with this psalm has gained widespread support.[40] Whereas many suggested references to Psalm 34 lack substance, as shown by Schutter in the discussion above, the allusion in 2.3 is relatively indisputable, despite some verbal dissimilarity to its source.

---

36. Bornemann, 'Taufrede', p. 147, and Woan, 'Psalms in 1 Peter', p. 222. This does have much scholarly support. Michaels, *1 Peter*, p. 86, comes close by noting that the other uses of κακίαν and δόλον in 1 Peter are in references to Scripture.

37. Eriksson, *'Come, Children, Listen to Me!'*, pp. 111–12.

38. Schutter, *Hermeneutic and Composition*, pp. 44–9 and Elliott, *Commentary*, p. 396. Yet Jobes, *1 Peter*, p. 131, notes that these terms are popular in lists of vices contemporary to 1 Peter, such as Rom. 13.13; Eph. 4.25-32; Col. 3.5; and 1QS 4.9-11. *Did.* 5.1 also makes use of κακία, δόλος and ὑπόκρισις, suggesting that the use of such terms in 1 Pet. 2.1 is of little significance.

39. This reference is clearly identified by Thomas of Harkel (syh), who develops this verse into a clearer citation. At the same time, other early witnesses such as 𝔓[72], miss the reference entirely, substituting χρηστὸς with χριστὸς. It is recognized by the majority of scholars, even those who do not see the influence of Ps. 34 as widespread, such as Schutter, *Hermeneutic and Composition*, p. 44; Feldmeier, *Letter of Peter*, p. 131; Bigg, *St Peter*, p. 127; Elliott, *Commentary*, p. 403, and Achtemeier, *1 Peter*, p. 148.

40. Bornemann, 'Taufrede'; Snodgrass, 'I Peter II.1-10'; Carson, '1 Peter', pp. 1022–3; Woan, 'Psalms in 1 Peter', p. 222; Kelly, *Peter*, p. 87, and Jobes, *1 Peter*, pp. 137–8.

The reference adds a condition to the paraenesis of 2.2: a reference to tasting to support the charge to 'crave pure, spiritual milk, in order that you might grow into salvation'.[41] This paraenesis, as J. Francis argues, is also related to the citation from Isa. 40.6 and 8 in the previous chapter and the claim which precedes it that members of the communities to which Peter writes have been 'born again' διὰ λόγου ζῶντος θεοῦ καὶ μένοντος.[42] Francis argues that this is not baptismal imagery because ὡς is stronger than the rabbinic metaphor of proselytes as children in *b. Yeb.* 22a, 48b, 62a and ἀρτιγέννητα refers to divine regeneration, which exceeds typical rabbinic notions of God's agency, usually limited to creation.[43] He also argues, though, that it relates to descriptions in Scripture of Israel as a child (Jer. 31.20; Hos. 11.1; Ps. 103.13; Isa. 1.2; 30.1; 66.10-13). This is consistent with depiction of the dispersed communities addressed by 1 Peter as Israel. Yet, as Tite argues, the conceptual background to the nursling metaphor used here is much broader than purely scriptural or Jewish traditions.[44] The child image serves to encourage communities in their new family status, given by God through the word, whilst encouraging them to keep receiving the word which they have tasted and know to be good.[45]

Dryden argues that the allusion to Psalm 34 is part of Peter's use of remembrance and antithesis in his paraenesis, drawing a distinction between the status of community members in the past and the change which ought to have taken place at their conversion.[46] The 'act of tasting', having taken place in the past, refers to the conversion and provides the basis for the challenge in 2.2. The allusion to Psalm 34 here provides the paraenetic antithesis to this former way of life. Characteristically,

---

41. Cf. 1QH 9.35-36 and *Odes Sol.* 8.13-14.

42. J. Francis, '"Like Newborn Babies" – The Image of the Child in 1 Peter 2.2-3', in *Studia Biblica 1978*. Vol. 3, *Papers on Paul and Other New Testament Authors* (ed. E. A. Livingstone; JSNTSup 3; Sheffield: Sheffield Academic, 1980), p. 113.

43. Francis, 'Like Newborn Babies', pp. 112 and 114. Cross, *Paschal Liturgy*, p. 33, supports the liturgical view of the use of Ps, 34 here, though this is also rejected by Michaels, *1 Peter*, p. 88, and Best, *1 Peter*, p. 99.

44. Philip L. Tite, 'Nursing, Milk and Moral Development in the Greco-Roman Context: A Reappriasal of the Paraenetic Utilisation of Metaphor in 1 Peter 2.1-3', *JSNT* 31 (2009), pp. 378–86, who argues that the metaphor is not one related to motherhood, but rather implies the use of a wet-nurse.

45. Though Hort, *St Peter*, p. 101; Michaels, *1 Peter*, p. 89, and Jobes, *1 Peter*, p. 137, reject the association of 'milk' with the 'word'.

46. Dryden, *Theology and Ethics*, pp. 110–13. Cf. Tite, 'Nursing, Milk and Moral Development', pp. 394–5.

Schutter argues the difficult case that the allusion demonstrates the christological 'suffering and glories' hermeneutic he discerns in 1.10-12. He claims that as Psalm 34 describes the 'righteous sufferer', it relates well to the sufferings of Christ. Since the allusion identifies the 'tasting' of Christ with the word in 1.25, Schutter suggests that this demonstrates a christological orientation in Peter's use of the psalm. Finally, the χρηστός of the Lord 'tasted' by the communities must relate to all that is theirs through Christ: the glories that accompany the sufferings of Christ in 1 Pet. 1.11.[47]

h. 1 Peter 2.5 and οἶκος πνευματικὸς

There has been some debate as to whether or not the phrase οἶκος πνευματικὸς is an allusion to scriptural language used to describe the Jerusalem Temple, here applied to the communities as a spiritual representation of the Temple. This debate occurs in spite of the fact that the phrase cannot be found anywhere in the extant OG Scriptures. Selwyn suggests that the meaning of the phrase is 'religious and sacerdotal', noting the use of οἶκος to refer to temples and, indeed, the Jerusalem Temple (Euripides, *Phoen.* 1372 f., OG Pss. 69.10; 116.19; 118.26, as well as Jn 2.17). Furthermore, Selwyn notes that the reference to Isa. 56.7 (ὁ οἶκός μου οἶκος προσευχῆς κληθήσεται πᾶσιν τοῖς ἔθνεσιν) in relation to Jer. 7.11 in the cleansing of the Temple by Jesus in the Mk 11.17 identifies the Temple as a 'spiritual house': a place of prayer for all the nations.[48] Indeed, the association of οἶκος πνευματικὸς with the parallel concept of the communities as ἱεράτευμα ἅγιον ἀνενέγκαι πνευματικὰς θυσίας in 2.5 suggests a sacerdotal understanding of the former. Yet Kelly drives a sharp distinction between the two concepts, arguing that οἶκος πνευματικὸς refers to the spiritual 'house' whilst ἱεράτευμα ἅγιον is the sacerdotal image; in his view Peter is not claiming the communities are both temple and priests.[49]

---

47. Schutter, *Hermeneutic and Composition*, p. 129, and Elliott, *Commentary*, p. 403. Furthermore, Clement of Alexandria's *Paed.* 1.6 enhances the χρηστός/Χριστός relationship from an aural similarity to an explicit word change.

48. Selwyn, *St Peter*, p. 160. Likewise, Bigg, *St Peter*, p. 128, suggests that οἶκος πνευματικὸς is equivalent to the ecclesiological ναός ἅγιος in Eph. 2.21-22.

49. Kelly, *Peter*, pp. 90–1. It is this distinction between images used to describe the communities both before and after the Stone Catena that Grudem, *1 Peter*, p. 99, does not take account of. He suggests that the presence of clearly sacerdotal phrases here gives weight to the understanding of οἶκος πνευματικὸς as Temple language. However, Kelly and, particularly Elliott, demonstrate that these phrases are not directly interrelated.

The designation οἶκος πνευματικὸς is crucial to Elliott's argument in *The Elect and the Holy*. Οἶκος is a term with a complex background in the OG Scriptures and Elliott notes that its use here is related to the stone imagery of the catena. Elliott suggests that the meaning of οἶκος in 1 Pet. 2.5 is reminiscent of Num. 12.7, where it is used to refer to the chosen people of God. He argues that the concept is related to the designation βασίλειον from Exod. 19.6, used after the catena. Elliott argues that βασίλειον is a substantive in its OG source, as reflected in the texts dependent upon OG Exod. 19.6: 2 Macc. 2.17, *De Sobr.* 66 and *De Abr.* 56.[50] Since the latter are roughly contemporary with 1 Peter, 1 Pet. 2.9 is seen to employ the term in the same way. Because of this, and because *De Sobr.* 66 interprets βασίλειον in Exod. 19.6 as a royal dwelling place, Elliott claims that οἶκος πνευματικὸς and βασίλειον ἱεράτευμα are related. Elliott maintains that πνευματικὸς is meant in a 'non-metaphorical' sense of being created and inhabited by the Holy Spirit, rather than implying that the house is immaterial, noting the role of the 'Spirit' in proclaiming the Gospel and sanctifying the elect people of God in 1 Pet. 1.11 and 1.2.[51] Furthermore, Elliott notes that οἶκος is never used to refer to the temple in the New Testament, except through the use of a scriptural quotation (as in Jn 2.17 and Mk 11.17 and parallels) or else qualified in some way (as in Jn 2.16: τὸν οἶκον τοῦ πατρός μου).[52] He argues, following Phillip Veilhauer, that the emphasis provided by the stone texts is upon the growth of the communities established through Christ the stone, and that therefore the use of οἶκος is a symbol of such growth. Therefore, Elliott suggests that the term does not represent an attempt to apply temple language to the communities, arguing that ναὸς πνευματικὸς would provide a better phrase for this purpose. Instead, he claims that the purpose of the designation is to affirm the elect status of the communities as the people of God, and prefers the meaning 'household'. Elliott notes the use of the phrase τοῦ οἴκου τοῦ θεοῦ in 4.17 as a reference to the

---

50. Elliott, *The Elect and the Holy*, pp. 149–54. Cf. Selwyn, *Peter*, pp. 165–7.
51. See Elliott, *The Elect and the Holy*, pp. 153–6, and idem, *Commentary*, p. 414, in which Elliott translates 'a house(hold) of the Spirit'. Cf. Kelly, *Peter*, p. 90; Achtemeier, *1 Peter*, p. 157, and Feldmeier, *Peter*, p. 136 who take the same view. Jobes, *1 Peter*, p. 149, suggests, similarly yet contrary to Elliott, that πνευματικὸς denotes the sanctifying presence of the Holy Spirit, as in the Temple. The opposite 'metaphorical' view is argued by Bigg, *St Peter*, pp. 128–9, who compares the use of πνευματικὸς here with its use in *Mundi Op* 22.1.15. In support of this, Michaels, *1 Peter*, p. 100, claims that there is no indication that πνευματικὸς is a reference to the Holy Spirit.
52. Elliott, *The Elect and the Holy*, p. 157 n. 2.

communities as a 'household' and draws attention to the use of the term οἰκονόμοι in close connection to the *Haustafel* in 4.10.[53]

However, Mbuvi disagrees, noting the extent of cultic use of οἶκος and that it is often applied to people in this cultic sense. Mbuvi notes that in OG Scripture οἶκος has the dual function of בית, which may refer to a physical building or a human structure, such as a dynasty, and that this dual function forms the basis of it suitability both as a reference to the temple as well as the 'Temple-Community'.[54] Because of this Mbuvi argues that the application of this phrase to the communities is a sign that 1 Peter is, in part, a polemic against first-century Judaism. The similarity of the application of 'Jewish' institutional titles to people in both 1 Peter and certain Qumran texts could be evidence for a common attitude towards a mainstream religious culture from which both communities have separated themselves.[55] Mbuvi notes that 1QS 5.6 and 8.5 apply temple language to the community, CD 7.1, 20.10 and 13 apply 'house' to the community and 1QH 6.25-29 even speak of the community as 'city'. Whilst this argument has some appeal, it does depend entirely upon the possibility of temple reference in 1 Peter, a reading which has not attracted scholarly consensus. In addition to this, there is also the problem which complicates the broader discussion of supercessionism in the epistle: 1 Peter does not mention any rival religious group. To this extent, it differs significantly from polemical literature at Qumran, which

---

53. Elliott, *The Elect and the Holy*, pp. 157–9. See also Phillip Veilhauer, 'OIKODOME: das Bild vom Bau in der christliche Literatur vom Neuen Testament bis Clemens Alexandrinus' (Heidelberg Karlsruhe, Ph.D. dissertation, 1940), pp. 60–2 and 145–50. Jobes, *1 Peter*, p. 150, supports Elliott here by noting that the phrase τῷ οἴκῳ Ιακωβ is used in Exod. 19.1-6, an important text for the fringes of the Stone Catena.

54. Mbuvi, *Temple, Exile and Identity*, pp. 90–1. Cf. Selwyn, *Peter*, p. 285; Best, *1 Peter*, p. 102; and Achtemeier, *1 Peter*, p. 159, who also see the phrase as a reference to the temple, though Achtemeier agrees in sympathy with Elliott that 1 Peter's primary interest is the 'household': the community of believers. J. Goetzmann, 'οἶκος', *NIDNTT* 2, p. 247 notes that like בית, οἶκος serves two functions.

55. Mbuvi, *Temple, Exile and Identity*, pp. 91–2. Best, *1 Peter*, p. 102, makes the same comparison with the 'Temple-Community' of Qumran, noting too 4QFlor 1.1-7, 1QpHab 12.1 and 4QpIsa[d] frag. 1, where members of the community are described as stones. Cf. Kelly, *Peter*, p. 91, who also draws attention to the 'spiritual reinterpretation' of Temple sacrifice at Qumran in 1QS 9.3-5, though he sees this as more closely related to ἱεράτευμα ἅγιον in 2.5 (as with Rom. 12.1; Eph. 5.2; Phil. 4.18) since he does not regard οἶκος as Temple language. As Green, *1 Peter*, p. 61, notes, the arrival of a new Temple to surpass the old is an event anticipated in Hag. 2.9. Hence, Green concludes that οἶκος in 2.5 refers to the Communities as the Temple.

often makes quite detailed reference to the institutions and people against which the community is defined. Furthermore, whilst οἶκος does refer to the temple (as in Pss. 23.6; 26.8; 27.4; 52.9; 84.4; 92.13; 122.1), there is also an important tradition in which the very concept of a house for God is rejected as anathema (2 Sam. 7.5; 1 Kgs 8.27; Isa. 66.1). This is the tradition witnessed in Stephen's speech in Acts 7.48-50.[56] Given the ambiguity created by this tradition, it is not so easy to assume that οἶκος refers to the temple. Feldmeier's view reflects both 'temple' and 'house/household' perspectives. He suggests that the primary metaphor is of the communities being built together and that this metaphor alludes to the concept of the communities as a temple.[57]

Whilst it is difficult to determine the intended significance of οἶκος πνευματικός, the 'hermeneutical' perspective offered in 1.10-12 might help to explain the meaning of the phrase. According to 1 Pet. 1.11, the sufferings of Christ and the glories after are the focus of the scriptural revelation of the Prophets. This event and its implications represent the decisive moment of God's plan from the foundation of the world. This decisive moment is described in 1 Peter in cultic terms: the communities are those who have been sprinkled with the blood of Jesus Christ (1.2), the spotless sacrificial lamb prepared for the present climactic last times (1.19-20). Given the christological focus of this narrative and the christological appropriation of temple sacrifice language, Elliott is surely right both to regard οἶκος πνευματικός as a token of election, rather than cultic status, as well as to regard the priestly description of the communities in 2.5 and 2.9 as general and not Levitical, reflecting Exod. 19.6.

Yet it must be remembered that the communities also stand at the climax of the salvation-historical narrative of 1 Pet. 1.10-12, as well as Christ. Could they not be regarded as the prophetic fulfilment of the Temple? Again, given the christological focus of temple sacrifice

---

56. D. D. Sylva, 'The Meaning and Function of Acts 7.46-50', *JBL* 106 (1989), pp. 261–75, and Richard I. Pervo, *Acts: A Commentary* (Philadelphia: Fortress, 2009), pp. 191–3. The latter views the use of this tradition as a Lukan reflection back upon the destroyed temple, explaining why its loss is not problematic. The use of οἶκος here is somewhat problematic textually, insofar as the strongest texts (P74, ℵ*, B, D, H, etc.) read τῷ οἴκῳ Ἰακώβ in 7.46 (instead of τῷ θεῷ Ἰακώβ in ℵc, A, C, E, Ψ, etc.), an awkward contrast to the οἶκος belonging God mentioned in vv. 47 and 49, though the reading does illustrate the dual use of the term. Cf. Marion L. Soards, *The Speeches in Acts: Their Content, Context, and Concerns* (Louisville: Westminster John Knox, 1994), pp. 149–54 who draws attention to the particular thematic and linguistic similarity between Stephen's speech and 2 Esd. 19.6–20.1.

57. Feldmeier, *Peter*, pp. 135–6. Cf. Joseph, *Narratological Reading of 1 Peter*, p. 90 and Jobes, *1 Peter*, p. 149 who also appear to combine the two rival meanings.

language, this seems unlikely, despite the Qumranic precedent for the appropriation of such language to a community. Elliott and Joseph both attempt to understand οἶκος πνευματικὸς in relation to the broader context of the narrative of election of the communities within 1 Peter.[58] This is helpful given the hermeneutic function of the theological narrative substructure of the epistle. Whilst the election of the community is clearly an important theme in this narrative which accounts for the use of Scripture in 1 Peter, the temple is not clearly a feature of this narrative. There is no suggestion that the Temple, or the Tabernacle which preceded it, is considered either to have played a significant part in the history of Israel (as in Stephen's speech) or served as an antitype of the work of Christ (as in the Epistle to the Hebrews). Because of this, it might be more obvious to read οἶκος πνευματικὸς as a description of the communities' elect status, rather than their status as a 'Temple-Community' in anything other than a Levitical sense.

i. 1 Peter 2.5 and εἰς ἱεράτευμα ἅγιον ἀνενέγκαι πνευματικὰς θυσίας

The debate concerning the meaning of οἶκος πνευματικὸς in 1 Pet. 2.5 is closely connected to that regarding πνευματικὰς θυσίας, since the latter can be seen as something of a definition of the former: οἰκοδομεῖσθε οἶκος πνευματικὸς εἰς ἱεράτευμα ἅγιον ἀνενέγκαι πνευματικὰς θυσίας. Indeed, Michaels' understanding of οἶκος πνευματικὸς is derived from his closer study of ἱεράτευμα ἅγιον ἀνενέγκαι πνευματικὰς θυσίας.[59] Whilst agreeing with Elliott that οἶκος most probably means 'house' or 'household' (perhaps alluding to Exod. 19.6),[60] Michaels argues that the purpose of that house as pertaining to the work of a 'holy priesthood' suggests that some sort of temple is in mind, though not necessarily the Temple, now understood as the Christian communities.[61] He likens πνευματικὰς θυσίας to the concept λογικὴ θυσία in *Corp. Herm.* 1.31, 13.18 and 21, suggesting that these sacrifices are 'first of all something offered up to God as

---

58. Joseph, *Narratological Reading of 1 Peter*, pp. 90–1.
59. Michaels, *1 Peter*, pp. 100–101. Cf. Selwyn, *St Peter*, p. 160, and Achtemeier, *1 Peter*, p. 156.
60. Elliott, *The Elect and the Holy*, pp. 50–128; Bigg, *St Peter*, p. 129; Kelly, *Peter*, p. 91, and Best, *1 Peter*, p. 102, who also notes the importance of OG Exod. 23.22; Isa. 61.6; 2 Macc. 2.17; *Jub.* 16.18 and *De Sobr.* 66, which are dependent upon Exod. 19.6. Cf. Torrey Seland, 'The "Common Priesthood" of Philo and 1 Peter: A Philonic Reading of 1 Peter 2.5, 9', *JSNT* 17 (1995), pp. 87–119.
61. Cf. Green, *1 Peter*, p. 61, who notes that the corporate nature of the priestly task reflects 1 Sam. 15.22-23 and Jer. 7.21-23.

worship (ἀνενέγκαι) and, second, a pattern of social conduct'.[62] Michaels notes the metaphorical understanding of sacrifice as a description of prayer in Pss. 50.13-14, 23, 51.17 and 141.2, as well as within the Qumran community, implying that 1 Peter relates to this tradition of understanding sacrifice as non-literal.[63] Again, as with the designation οἶκος πνευματικὸς, a description of Israel's status is applied directly to the communities addressed by 1 Peter, reflecting the theological narrative that places these communities at the pinnacle of salvation history, exalted above prophets and angels.[64]

j. 1 Peter 2.9 and Isaiah 43.20b-21, Malachi 3.17 or Exodus 19.5-6
Whilst there is no certainty about which text or texts are alluded to in 1 Pet. 2.9, all commentators agree that some sort of reference to Scripture, whether direct or indirect, is intended. The words περιποίησιν and τὰς ἀρετάς, and the concept of a γένος ἐκλεκτόν, suggest a possible allusion to Isa. 43.20b-21: …ὅτι ἔδωκα ἐν τῇ ἐρήμῳ ὕδωρ καὶ ποταμοὺς ἐν τῇ ἀνύδρῳ ποτίσαι τὸ γένος μου τὸ ἐκλεκτόν, λαόν μου, ὃν περιεποιησάμην τὰς ἀρετάς μου διηγεῖσθαι. The combination of these three elements make it extremely likely that 1 Pet. 2.9 is an allusion to this verse, despite the apparent change from the verb περιεποιησάμην to the noun περποίησις[65] and the use of the unusual verb ἐξαγγείλητε instead of διηγεῖσθαι.[66] Yet,

---

62. Michaels, *1 Peter*, p. 101. Cf. Jobes, *1 Peter*, p. 150, who agrees that some understanding of the communities as a 'temple' is unavoidable. However, Michaels' understanding of 'spiritual sacrifices' is by no means clear as Jobes' concise overview of interpretative options suggests.

63. Best, *1 Peter*, p. 103, however, notes that the concept of a communal priesthood is utterly alien to the Qumran community.

64. Cf. David Hill, '"To Offer Spiritual Sacrifices…" (1 Peter 2.5): Liturgical Formulations and Christian Paraenesis in 1 Peter', *JSNT* 5 (1982), pp. 58–9.

65. Moyise, 'Isaiah in 1 Peter', p. 182, notes that the use of this noun is unusual in that it typically appears with another qualifying noun in the New Testament, as in 1 Thess. 5.9 (with σωτηρίας) and 2 Thess. 2.14 (with δόξης). The use of the noun in the Thessalonian correspondence as well as 1 Peter is no doubt significant to those who argue for Selwyn's Silvanus amanuensis theory of Petrine authorship.

66. There has been some discussion of this apparent variant from extant OG readings of the text. Schutter, *Hermeneutic and Composition*, p. 40, suggests that the change is due to the influence of Isa. 42.12, τὰς ἀρετὰς αὐτοῦ ἐν ταῖς νήσοις ἀναγγελοῦσι. However, Moyise, 'Isaiah in 1 Peter', p. 182, points out that this is unlikely since it does not explain the use of ἐξαγγέλω. Cf. Achtemeier, *1 Peter*, p. 166 n. 214. Michaels, *1 Peter*, p. 110, proposes the influence of OG Ps. 8.14, ὅπως ἂν ἐξαγγείλω πάσας τὰς αἰνέσεις σου ἐν ταῖς πύλαις τῆς θυγατρὸς Σιών, which also uses ὅπως with the subjunctive as in 1 Pet. 2.9. Whilst this is certainly plausible, one wonders if it is always right to attempt to identify one particular scriptural text to

at the same time, the passage bears a remarkable resemblance to the OG versions of Exod. 19.5-6, thought to be important in 2.5. There, one finds the use of βασίλειον ἱεράτευμα and ἔθνος ἅγιον in the same order as in 1 Pet. 2.9, and the phrase ἔσεσθέ μοι λαὸς περιούσιος ἀπὸ πάντων τῶν ἐθνῶν which is conceptually similar to Peter's λαὸς εἰς περιποίησιν and γένος ἐκλεκτόν. In addition to this, Jobes suggests that the use of εἰς περιποίησιν is an allusion to OG Mal. 3.17, also noted in NA[27].[67] Whilst Jobes recognises that that the latter term is also to be found in the OG versions of 2 Chron. 14.12 and Hag. 2.9, she argues that the context of Mal. 3.17 within an encouragement to continued faithfulness is closer to its use in 1 Pet. 2.9. The similarity 1 Pet. 2.9 bears with each of these passages may suggest that Peter was more interested in evoking scriptural language, or alluding quite generally to a variety of texts, rather than to a particular text. One might expect a deliberate allusion to refer to one particular piece of Scripture and be less ambiguous. However, some scholars go further, arguing that Isa. 43.20b-21 is actually *quoted* here.[68] Of course, there will always be the possibility that Peter had access to an OG text of Isaiah 43 which bore a much closer resemblance to 1 Pet. 2.9 than any extant versions. But the fact remains that there is nothing in 1 Pet. 2.9 to indicate the presence of a citation: the language appears to function as Peter's own, without any sense of incongruity, and there is no citation formula.

Elliott's detailed analysis notes the similarity of Isa. 43.20b-21 and Mal. 3.19 to Exod. 19.6 but does not consider them to offer rival explanations of the allusion in 1 Pet. 2.9.[69] Elliott considers this allusion to be of great significance to the catena in 2.6-8, which he views as explaining the means by which the communities became the elect people of God, the βασίλειον ἱεράτευμα of Exod. 19.6. Elliott points out that this text in its original context, its reception history in apocalyptic and rabbinic Judaism, as well as its use in 1 Peter, relates to a distinctly different

---

explain every divergence from extant versions. It may be that Peter's source, if indeed he had one (this could be a case of free composition inspired by scriptural language), contained the variant reading witnessed in 1 Peter. Cf. Elliott, *Commentary*, p. 439.

67. Jobes, 'Minor Prophets', p. 143. Albert Vanhoye, 'L'Epître (1 P 2,1-10): La maison spirituelle', *AsSeign* 43 (1964), p. 27, also suggests that γένος ἐκλεκτὸν alludes to Exod. 19.5; Deut. 7.6 and 14.2.

68. Moyise, *Evoking Scripture*, p. 88 (though at p. 82 n. 10 he lists 1 Pet. 2.9 as an allusion). But Achtemeier, *1 Peter*, p. 163, appears to agree that Isa. 43.20-21 is interpolated into Exod. 19.6.

69. Elliott, *The Elect and the Holy*, p. 40 n. 2.

tradition from the Levitical priesthood.[70] The principal understanding of the phrase βασίλειον ἱεράτευμα pertains to an outward 'priestly' witness to the world, not to a sacrificial Levitical priesthood. Because of this, Elliott suggests that 1 Pet. 2.5 and 9 are not to be regarded as representative of a polemic against Levitical priesthood. Elliott's analysis of the theology of 1 Pet. 2.4-10 is helpful even if he may be wrong in regarding βασίλειον ἱεράτευμα as an allusion to Exod. 19.6, especially because Elliott relates the passage to the theological narrative of 1 Peter:

> The formation, election, and sanctification of this community is an eschatological salvific event. This act of salvation and 're-creation', according to I P, involves the consummation of all that God had planned for His Israel. The focal point of this event is Jesus Christ. People become participants in the event of salvation and rebirth in that they hear His word and confess Him to be the κύριος. They who believe in Jesus and the Elect and Precious One are gathered together as the elect and precious people.[71]

Carson suggests that 1 Pet. 2.9 bears a somewhat closer resemblance to Isa. 43.20b-21 than Exod. 19.5-6, yet still suggests that an exodus typology is employed by Peter.[72] It is difficult to see what evidence there might be for this within the context of 1 Pet. 2.9, except, perhaps the phrase τοῦ ἐκ σκότους ὑμᾶς καλέσαντος εἰς τὸ θαυμαστὸν αὐτοῦ φῶς[73] and the assumption that Peter would have known Exod. 19.5-6 to be about God's people recently rescued from Egypt (hence the application of its language to Christians indicates a typological reading). Whether a typological interpretation is evident here or not, what is clear is that Peter is keen to apply scriptural definitions of God's people of the past to his audiences: God's people in the present. This is consistent with Peter's tendency to see Scripture as relating directly and perhaps exclusively to Christ and the people who have had his message of good news proclaimed to them. It is not at all obvious that Peter understood the scriptural terms he employs in 2.9 to refer initially to people at particular instances in the past and now, in a secondary manner, to people in the present.[74] If 2.9 is in fact an allusion to Isa. 43.20b-21, there is good evidence to suggest that Peter may have understood this text to be

---

70. Elliott, *The Elect and the Holy*, pp. 50–128. This view is widely supported. Achtemeier, *1 Peter*, 163–7; Michaels, *1 Peter*, pp. 108–9, and Jobes, *1 Peter*, pp. 160–1.
71. Elliott, *The Elect and the Holy*, pp. 221–2.
72. Carson, '1 Peter', p. 1030.
73. Green, *1 Peter*, p. 65; Achtemeier, *1 Peter*, p. 69, and Joseph, *Narratological Reading of 1 Peter*, pp. 64–5.
74. Michaels, *1 Peter*, p. 107.

straightforwardly predictive, referring exclusively to the present reality of the Church. Peter's use of Isaiah elsewhere implies an assumption that this Scripture is determinate, following his view of the meaning of the Prophets' speech or writing described in 1.10-12. In any case, the application of scriptural designations of the people of God to the communities addressed by the epistle is of substantial paraenetic significance. As Dryden argues, 1 Pet. 2.9, as with 2.10, functions to develop the corporate identity of the communities as the basis for paraenesis that urges distinctive behaviour, as in 2.11-12.[75] As is often the case, the distinction between kerygma and paraenesis is blurred, as the essentially descriptive and kerygmatic use of scriptural texts here provides the theological foundation for subsequent paraenesis.

k. 1 Peter 2.10 and Hosea 1.6, 9; 2.23 (OG 2.25)

1 Peter 2.10 presents a fairly unambiguous allusion to the 'name' motif in Hosea, employing οὐ λαὸς and οὐκ ἠλεημένοι. In Hosea, these names are used for the prophet's symbolic children and the nation they represent in 1.6 and 9, and are referred back to in 2.23 (OG 2.25). The only significant difference between 1 Pet. 2.10 and the names used in Hosea is the absence of a possessive genitive to accompany λαὸς. This gives the impression that Peter contrasts, not rejection by God with belonging to God, but lack of status with enjoying status as God's people.[76] Yet Jobes asks whether this verse really does allude to Hosea. She notes that the affirmation of being God's people from Hosea is often associated with the texts of the Stone Catena, as in Rom. 9.25-33 and *Ep. Barn.* 6.2-4, and suggests that 1 Pet. 1.10 might simply reflect just such a traditional association.[77] However, Jobes concludes that an allusion to Hosea really is intended.[78]

---

75. Dryden, *Theology and Ethics*, p. 195. Indeed, as Elliott, *Home for the Homeless*, p. 119, suggests, these allusions imply social contrast and distinctiveness.

76. Elliott, *Home for the Homeless*, p. 122.

77. Jobes, 'Minor Prophets', p. 143. However, Jobes' suggestion is a little unclear. She writes about a 'my people' reference in 1 Pet. 2.10 (as in Rom. 9.25) which is clearly absent, whilst acknowledging that οὐ λαὸς and οὐκ ἠλεημένοι can only be references to Hosea. Cf. Achtemeier, *1 Peter*, p. 167.

78. Jobes, 'Minor Prophets', pp. 143–4, uses this reference to Hosea and her view that 1 Pet. 2.9 includes a reference to Mal. 3.17 to claim that Peter refers to these texts so as to suggest that all of the minor Prophets witness to Christ, since Hosea and Malachi begin and end the books of the Twelve. Whilst this suggestion seems to agree theologically with the description of the Prophets in 1 Pet. 1.10-12, it rather depends upon audiences noticing an allusion to Malachi with, essentially, just one word in 1 Pet. 2.9.

The purpose of the allusion to Hosea is to support the scriptural claims made about Peter's audiences in 2.9, perhaps in particular the phrase τοῦ ἐκ σκότους ὑμᾶς καλέσαντος εἰς τὸ θαυμαστὸν αὐτοῦ φῶς. God has made the audiences his people through their reception of his mercy; his people who are to declare his praises in contrast to those who have rejected the message of good news, who have stumbled on the stone of Christ (2.9). This sense of distinctive identity is important justification for the paraenetic which follows in 2.11-12, in which the audiences' status as παροίκους καὶ παρεπιδήμους becomes something to be nurtured.

Carson argues that in order to understand Peter's use of Hosea, one needs to know something of his allusion's literary context: the plan of Hosea 1–2.[79] Carson points out that the people who have been addressed as those who are not God's people, in Hos. 1.10, are the people of Israel. He suggests that Peter understood this and so used an allusion to this text to emphasise that those in his audiences who were of Jewish origin had the same status as those of Gentile origin. Both groups were once neither God's people, nor recipients of his mercy, but are now both God's people and recipients of his mercy. However, the ethnic composition of the audience of 1 Peter has been notoriously difficult to define.[80]

Again, Peter employs Scripture as referring directly to his audience whom the Prophets sought to serve as they spoke or wrote. As Schutter notes, the allusion to Hosea is seen to be fulfilled through the creation of the eschatological community.[81] The hermeneutic here is one of fulfilment: the true referent of Hosea 1–2 is seen to be the communities addressed by Peter. There is no indication that Peter reasons that, just as Israel were deemed 'not my people' and then became 'my people', so too the Christian communities were once 'not a people' but now are 'the people of God'.[82] Peter shows no interest in Hosea's relation to Israel in the past. As far as he is concerned, this is a text written to serve those who have had the Gospel proclaimed to them.

---

79. Carson, '1 Peter', pp. 1031–2. Cf. Windisch, *Katholischen Briefe*, p. 61.
80. Feldmeier, *Letter of Peter*, p. 142; Jobes, *1 Peter*, p. 164, and Michaels, *1 Peter*, p. 112, all take the primary significance of this allusion to be in relation to the inclusion of a predominantly Gentile Christian group of communities.
81. Schutter, *Hermeneutic and Composition*, p. 137.
82. Contra Green, *1 Peter*, p. 63: 'Peter collapses the historical distinctives between ancient Israel and contemporary Christians in favor of theological unity, but not in order to deny the importance of history. Rather, in a world where history is honored, he roots this "elect clan" in the antiquity of the relationship between God and Israel.' Yet, the theological narrative of 1 Peter places greater emphasis on the present, as the great climax of history, and is only derogatory about the past as a time of relative ignorance, subservient to the present.

1. 1 Peter 2.12 and Isaiah 10.3

1 Peter 2.12 contains a possible allusion to Isa. 10.3 with the use of the phrase ἐν ἡμέρᾳ ἐπισκοπῆς. Peter's version of the phrase lacks the two definite articles used in extant OG version, though this need not be seen to undermine the possibility of a specific reference to Isa. 10.3. Whilst Peter is clearly familiar with a great deal of material from Isaiah, as Schutter shows that Isa. 10.3 is a more probable text that could be alluded to than Wis. 3.7 or Malachi 17,[83] there is little to suggest that Isa. 10.3 is being referred to here.[84] As Grudem notes, the phrase does not appear in this precise form in any text to which Peter might allude.[85] At the same time, the language of 'visitation' is so common in Scripture and early Christian and Jewish literature that ἐν ἡμέρᾳ ἐπισκοπῆς is unlikely to allude to one particular text.[86] An important element in the possible Isa. 10.3 source text is that the phrase ἐν τῇ ἡμέρᾳ τῆς ἐπισκοπῆς occurs as part of a question. One might expect this to have featured in Peter's use of Isa. 10.3 if he intended his readers to detect an allusion to a particular scriptural text. As it stands, it is more likely that the scriptural language used in 1 Pet. 2.12 is a Biblicism rather than an allusion to a specific text. By using this language, Peter identifies with scriptural eschatology, whether Isaianic or not. His use of the phrase may have sounded familiar and scriptural, without evoking a particular text.[87]

However, not all commentators agree that ἐν ἡμέρᾳ ἐπισκοπῆς is eschatological.[88] Moffatt suggests that ἐν τῇ ἡμέρᾳ τῆς ἐπισκοπῆς refers to legal proceedings taken against Christians.[89] Indeed, there is nothing in the phrase, other than the traditional associations of the concept of 'visitation', to suggest particularly that a day of *divine* visitation is meant.

---

83. Schutter, *Hermeneutic and Composition*, p. 37. Cf. Danker, 'Consolatory Pericope', p. 98.

84. No one other than Schutter appears to argue that 1 Pet. 2.12 is an allusion to any specific verse, though Bigg, *St Peter*, p. 138, and Elliott, *Commentary*, p. 470, note that the phrase appears in Isa. 10.3.

85. Grudem, *1 Peter*, p. 117.

86. Isa. 13.6-9; 34.8-12; Jer. 46.9-12; Ezek. 30.1-9; Obad. 15-18; Zeph. 2.1-15; Mal. 3.22; Sir. 18.21; Wis. 3.7; 1QS 3.18; 4.6-8; CD-A 7.9; Lk. 19.44; Acts 2.20; 1 Cor 1.8; 2 Pet. 3.10; *Ep. Barn.* 15.4; *1 Clem.* 50.3.

87. Carson, '1 Peter', p. 1033

88. Those that do include, Bigg, *St Peter*, p. 138; Van Unnik, 'Teaching of Good Works', p. 98; Kelly, *Peter*, p. 106; Best, *1 Peter*, p. 112; Goppelt, *Erste Petrusbrief*, p. 160; Michaels, *1 Peter*, pp. 119–20; Feldmeier, *Letter of Peter*, p. 150, and Green, *1 Peter*, p. 69.

89. James Moffatt, *The General Epistles: James, Peter, and Judas* (New York: Doubleday, 1928), p. 121.

Selwyn and Elliott also reject an eschatological interpretation of the phrase, noting that the imminent eschatological destruction of unbelievers indicated in 1 Pet. 4.17-18 does not agree with the possibility in 2.11-12 that unbelievers might turn and glorify God on the last day.[90] Instead, they argue that the phrase refers to God's visitation of individual non-believers who, because of the example they have witnessed in believers, give glory to God on that day. However, as Green argues, the eschatological orientation of 1 Peter is simply too significant for the use of common eschatological imagery, such as that in 2.12, to refer to some other form of visitation, divine or human.[91]

As Kelly notes, the phrase ἐν τῇ ἡμέρᾳ τῆς ἐπισκοπῆς is connected to the paraenesis of 2.11-12 in such a way as to reflect Peter's 'preoccupation with practical Christianity'.[92] If this phrase is an allusion to Isa. 10.3 (which is unlikely), then this is another example of Peter using Scripture as though its purpose was to serve the communities to which he writes by encouraging them to choose to lead lives that exemplify goodness.

* * *

Excursus: The Definition of 1 Peter 2.22-25 as Allusion

Why is the long and undeniable reference to Isaiah 53 in 1 Pet. 2.22-25 not discussed as a citation? One verse, 2.22, is very similar to its source, Isa. 53.9, such that if verbal similarity alone was determined the difference between an allusion and a citation, this would be the latter. Using the more rhetorical understanding of citation outlined in Chapter 2 of this study, 1 Pet. 2.22-25 cannot be defined as a citation. There is nothing in 2.22-25 to alert a reader or hearer to the fact that these are anything other than Peter's own words.[93] There is no citation formula.[94] The only

---

90. Selwyn, *St Peter*, 171, and Elliott, *Commentary*, p. 471. Cf. Exod. 3.16; 1 Sam. 2.21, and Job 10.12 which feature God's visitation in a non-eschatological sense.

91. Green, *1 Peter*, p. 69, noting the eschatological immanence indicated in 1 Pet. 1.5, 7, 13; 4.7, 14, 17; and 5.1.

92. Kelly, *Peter*, p. 106.

93. Though, as Rudolph Bultmann, 'Bekenntnis und Lied-fragmente im erste Petrusbrief', in *Exegetica: Aufsatze zur Erforschung des Neuen Testaments* (ed. E. Dinkler; Tübingen: Mohr, 1967), p. 14, points out, there is some disjuncture between the second person speech used by Peter in v. 21 and the first person used in the rest of the hymn. However, the second person is also used at the close of the hymn in v. 25, which still draws on the imagery from Isaiah.

94. Though ὅτι in 2.21 could be regarded as introductory. Cf. Achtemeier, *1 Peter*, p. 192.

clue that a reference is taking place, like other allusions, is verbal similarity to the source text. Yet, even granted this verbal similarity, there are so many differences and interpolations in 2.22-25 that a reader who might be informed enough to recognise similarity would probably conclude that Isaiah 53 was in Peter's mind but not being quoted. Could 2.22 be a citation if vv. 23-25 are an allusion? This depends on whether one takes 2.21-25 as a unit: a pre-existing hymn or other liturgical text. There is a strong tradition of seeing this long reference to Isaiah 53 in this way.[95]

The 'hymn' uses short excerpts from Isaiah 53 combined with other material describing the significance of the sufferings of Christ and thereby interprets the Isaiah references as relating to these sufferings.[96] Schutter argues that the hymn displays some sophistication in its reference to Isaiah 53, which might suggest its existence prior to the composition of 1 Peter. Schutter notes that references in the hymn prior to 2.24 come from the latter part of the servant song, whereas those after 2.24 come from the first part of the song.[97] The change occurs in 2.24, where the phrase ὃς τὰς ἁμαρτίας ἡμῶν αὐτὸς ἀνήνεγκεν conflates Isa. 53.4 and 12. However, Achtemeier argues against the notion of 2.21-25 as a hymn, suggesting that its treatment of Isaiah 53 is the author of 1 Peter's own.[98] Achtemeier notes, as above, that there is nothing in the 'hymn' to distinguish it from the author's own words. In addition to this, he draws attention to the very particular use of Isaiah 53 which contrasts with other early Christian uses, suggesting that 1 Peter is unlikely to be drawing upon an established source.

* * *

m. 1 Peter 2.21-25 and Isaiah 53.4, 5, 6, 9 and 12

The 'hymn' of 1 Pet. 2.21-25 contains four short excerpts from Isaiah 53 which show a significant degree of similarity to extant OG versions. These excerpts vary in length from three to nine or, perhaps, eleven words, none of which have a citation formula or anything other than their verbal similarity to extant texts to announce them as references to Isaiah 53. The first excerpt occurs in v. 22: ὃς ἁμαρτίαν οὐκ ἐποίησεν οὐδὲ εὑρέθη δόλος ἐν τῷ στόματι αὐτοῦ. Ὅς ἁμαρτίαν does not occur in extant

---

95. Windisch, *Katholischen Briefe*, p. 64; Bultmann, 'Bekenntnis und Liedfragmente', pp. 1–14; Hill, 'Spiritual Sacrifices', p. 46; Goppelt, *Erste Petrusbrief*, p. 190; Schlosser, 'Ancien Testament', p. 88 n. 86; Richard, 'Functional Christology', p. 127; Selwyn, St Peter, pp. 17–18, and Schutter, *Hermeneutic and Composition*, p. 143.

96. Feldmeier, *Letter of Peter*, p. 93.

97. Schutter, *Hermeneutic and Composition*, p. 143.

98. Achtemeier, *1 Peter*, pp. 192–3. Cf. Thomas P. Osborne, 'Guide Lines for Christian Suffering: A Source-Critical and Theological Study of 1 Peter 2, 21-25', *Bib* 64 (1983), pp. 381–408.

OG versions of Isa. 53.9, which instead read ὅτι ἀνομίαν. The significance of this difference is, of course, unclear. Peter's description of the death of Christ as relating to ἁμαρτία in 2.24 (a scriptural excerpt), 3.18 and 4.1 (in which the relation of Jesus' death to human sin is probably implied rather than stated) may suggest that Peter adapted the citation to suit his theology of the atonement. However, this is unlikely since the primary purpose of 1 Pet. 2.21-25 is to display Jesus' death as a model for Christian suffering, rather than to proclaim a theology of the atonement.[99] Since ἁμαρτία appears in Isa. 53.4, 5 (as a synonymous parallel to ἀνομία), 6, 10, 11 and 12, because it translates not only חטאת but עון as well, it may be that Peter's source text here featured the reading of Isa. 53.9 he employs. What is most likely, though, is that since the hymn as a whole is a developed allusion to Isaiah 53 with some employment of phrases from that passage, rather than a strict attempt to offer a single and recognisable citation, the precise replication of a source text is not Peter's priority. This is clear when one considers the degree to which the excerpts differ in the order they are used by Peter when compared to extant OG versions.[100] As the use of Ps. 34.12-16 (OG 33.13-17) in 1 Pet. 3.10-12 suggests, Peter was quite able to cite a text with a greater degree of accuracy than in 2.21-25 if he intended something to be heard as a citation.

The use of ὃς τὰς ἁμαρτίας ἡμῶν αὐτὸς ἀνήνεγκεν in 1 Pet. 2.24 may be a reference to either Isa. 53.4 or 12, though it matches the extant versions of neither and is probably a conflation of the two.[101] If Peter's phrase is based on οὗτος τὰς ἁμαρτίας ἡμῶν φέρει in Isa. 53.4, then the difference in the form of the verb may simply be due to Peter's incorporation of that text into a hymn dominated by aorist verbs. This does not explain the difference in word order, however. It is even less likely that Peter's phrase is based entirely upon αὐτὸς ἁμαρτίας πολλῶν ἀνήνεγκεν in Isa. 53.12 so as to be heard as a citation, since the important πολλῶν is missing. It is most likely that Peter intended to allude to both of these verses, rather than cite one in particular. The even shorter possible reference to Isaiah 53 in 1 Pet. 2.24 with significant verbal similarity is the phrase τῷ μώλωπι ἰάθητε. This is quite clearly a reference to τῷ μώλωπι αὐτοῦ ἡμεῖς ἰάθημεν in extant versions of Isa. 53.5, despite the absence of ἡμεῖς and

---

99. Cf. Selwyn, *St Peter*, pp. 90–101.
100. Cf. Schutter, *Hermeneutic and Composition*, p. 143.
101. 𝔓[72] and B read ὑμῶν in the place of ἡμῶν. This might suggest that these sources read 1 Pet. 2.24, not as a citation, but as Peter's own words, reflecting the use of ὑμῶν in v. 21 and tried to enhance a sense of the hymn's consistency.

the verb's change of person to reflect the frequent second-person reference of Peter's hymn, and despite the absence of αὐτοῦ, replaced by the relative pronoun οὗ. Again, unless Peter's source for Isa. 53.5 was markedly different from extant OG versions, it is likely that the phrase τῷ μώλωπι ἰάθητε is an allusion to Isa. 53.5 rather than an attempt to replicate it as a citation.[102]

The final reference in the hymn which includes a significant degree of verbal similarity with Isaiah 53 is the use of the phrase ὡς πρόβατα πλανώμενοι in 1 Pet. 2.25. Again, this is simply too short to be a formal citation, yet it does resemble ὡς πρόβατα ἐπλανήθημεν from Isa. 53.5 very closely. Elliott does, however, regard this reference as a citation due to its introduction with γάρ. Yet Moyise is correct in rejecting this as a citation on the basis of a lack of verbal similarity, instead regarding 2.22 as the only true citation in the hymn, even though it lacks any kind of citation formula.[103] Interestingly, Peter follows this reference with an allusion to its 'sheep' language: ἀλλὰ ἐπεστράφητε νῦν ἐπὶ τὸν ποιμένα καὶ ἐπίσκοπον τῶν ψυχῶν ὑμῶν. This allusion turns the corporate 'repentance' of Isa. 53.6 around by suggesting that the audiences' 'straying' is at an end.

It is unclear as to whom ποιμένα καὶ ἐπίσκοπον refers.[104] Carson suggests that Christ is the 'shepherd and overseer', which is certainly coherent with the notion at the beginning of 1 Pet. 2.25 that the audiences were like sheep having strayed, who, as the rest of the 'hymn' claims, have been served by Christ suffering on their behalf, and to whom they have 'come' (2.4). The relation of Christ to the audiences up to v. 25 certainly makes the identification of him as the 'shepherd and overseer' plausible.[105] Against this interpretation, it must be noted that the

---

102. It is important to note that א*, 81*, vgmss, Ambrose and several other witness 'correct' the reference to Isa. 53.5, either by inserting αὐτοῦ or by changing the person of the verb to match the OG versions. However, these variants lack any significant authority.

103. Elliott, *Commentary*, p. 537, and Moyise, 'Isaiah in 1 Peter', p. 184.

104. Kelly D. Liebengood, '1 Peter's Fiery Trials and Zechariah 9–14's Pierced Shepherd-King' (unpublished SBL 2008 conference paper) argues that this is a reference to the depiction of God as a shepherd in Zech. 9.16; 10.3 etc. Jobes, 'Minor Prophets', pp. 144–5, also takes this view.

105. Goppelt, *Erste Petrusbrief*, p. 211, suggests that the phrase ἀλλὰ ἐπεστράφητε νῦν ἐπὶ τὸν ποιμένα may be due to an association between ἰάομαι and ἐπιστρέφω in Isa. 6.10. Yet Elliott, *Commentary*, p. 538, suggests that the imagery of the phrase may be an allusion to another text entirely, Ezek. 34.4 and 16. Yet, again, does every aspect of 1 Peter's composition need to be explained in terms of associations with scriptural texts?

previous use of ἐπισκοπή/ἐπίσκοπος in 1 Pet. 2.12 clearly refers to God's eschatological visitation.[106]

In addition to the four possible miniature citations discussed above, the 'hymn' also contains four probable echoes of Isaiah 53. These all occur in 1 Pet. 2.23. First, οὐκ ἀντελοιδόρει resembles the image of the passive sufferer in Isa. 53.7, though the phrase οὐκ ἀντελοιδόρει is not itself used in Isaiah 53. Secondly, the same can be said of Peter's phrase οὐκ ἠπείλει, perhaps related to ὡς ἀμνὸς ἐναντίον τοῦ κείροντος αὐτὸν ἄφωνος οὕτως οὐκ ἀνοίγει τὸ στόμα αὐτοῦ in Isa. 53.7. Thirdly, Carson suggests that παρεδίδου refers to Isa. 53.4 and 12.[107] This does not seem quite as likely as the two previous possible allusions in this verse, since Peter's understanding of the suffering servant entrusting himself is absent from Isa. 53.4 (except possibly as the ironic and unstated truth behind ἡμεῖς ἐλογισάμεθα αὐτὸν εἶναι ἐν πόνῳ καὶ ἐν πληγῇ καὶ ἐν κακώσει) and does not appear to feature in the same active sense used by Peter in Isa. 53.4. Finally, Peter's reference to divine justice (τῷ κρίνοντι δικαίως) in 2.23 may be an allusion to Isa. 53.8, though it is not clear as to whether this judgement is God's or simply that of those who condemned the suffering servant. In this final possibility, it must be noted that there is a much greater verbal similarity between Peter's τῷ κρίνοντι δικαίως and ἡ κρίσις αὐτοῦ from extant versions of Isa. 53.8. In addition to this, Moyise notes that the use of ἐπὶ τὸ ξύλον in 2.24 could be a reference to Deut. 21.23, either directly or as a reflection of early Christian tradition as witnessed in Gal. 3.13.[108]

These references to Isaiah 53 offer an illustration of the requirements for Christians who are slaves in the household code material of 1 Pet. 3.18-20. As is often pointed out, by considering slaves to be not only morally responsible to a social order, but to God, Peter departs from the

---

106. Feldmeier, *Letter of Peter*, p. 27, thinks that there is an allusion to Wis. 1.6 (ὅτι τῶν νεφρῶν αὐτοῦ μάρτυς ὁ θεὸς καὶ τῆς καρδίας αὐτοῦ ἐπίσκοπος ἀληθής) in 2.25. However, apart from the common use of the unusual title ἐπίσκοπος for God, there is little to support this idea.

107. Carson, '1 Peter', p. 1034. Best, *1 Peter*, p. 121, suggests that the use of Isa. 53 goes beyond the simple provision of an christological example. He claims that the use of παρεδίδου in 2.23 is a reference to the passive παρεδόθη in Isa. 53.12 and hence is a reference to Christ's sufferings as offering redemption. Cf. Achtemeier, *1 Peter*, p. 200, who disagrees, claiming that Isa. 53.12 is used to make the opposite point in 2.24, though this is far from clear.

108. Moyise, 'Isaiah in 1 Peter', p. 183. Schutter, *Hermeneutic and Composition*, p. 39, considers this to be quite plausible as an incipient allusion, referring indirectly to the text via an exegetical tradition.

broad traditions of the pagan *Haustafeln*.[109] The purpose of the 'hymn' is to provide an example (v. 21) of enduring suffering on account of doing good (v. 20): a form of suffering which is a characteristic feature of the life of discipleship to which Peter's audiences are called.[110] This understanding of suffering as a natural consequence of obedience to the Gospel of Christ is an important element in the theology of 1 Peter seen in 1.6, 4.12 and 5.9, though, in the older scholarship these texts have been seen to relate to quite different types of suffering. The connection between allegiance to Christ and suffering may be drawn from Peter's observation, expressed in 1 Pet. 2.20-21, that Christ himself led a life of suffering, culminating in a violent death.[111] Perhaps then, the use of Isaiah 53 here provides what is perhaps the clearest example of the christological element of the hermeneutic displayed in 1 Pet. 1.10-11. In fact, as Best suggests, it may be that this hymn and Isaiah 53 were in Peter's mind when he described the ministry of the Prophets (τὸ ἐν αὐτοῖς πνεῦμα Χριστοῦ προμαρτυρόμενον τὰ εἰς Χριστὸν παθήματα).[112] This is likely to be due to the hymn's emphasis upon the suffering of Christ (Χριστὸς ἔπαθεν ὑπὲρ ὑμῶν in 2.21 – cf. Χριστὸς ἅπαξ περὶ ἁμαρτιῶν ἔπαθεν in 3.18 and Χριστοῦ οὖν παθόντος σαρκί in 4.1) with its heavy dependence on, and allusion to, Isaiah 53.

Whilst the principal use of Scripture here is kerygmatic, proclaiming to the communities a vision of the suffering of Christ which represents the climax of salvation history by which the communities receive their identity as the people of God (as in 1 Pet. 1.2), it is also paraenetic. Indeed, one could argue that it is primarily paraenetic. As is often noted,

---

109. Carson, '1 Peter', p. 1035.

110. Karl Olav Sandnes, 'Revised Conventions in Early Christian Paraenesis – "Working Good" in 1 Peter as an Example', in Starr and Engberg-Pedersen, eds., *Early Christian Paraenesis in Context*, pp. 373–403 (400–401), argues that the ethical notion of 'doing good' in difficult situations is quite distinctive in 1 Peter. This principle leads to a process of 'borrowing, adaptation and acculturation or morality' from the dominant culture, a necessity given the theological claim to elevated status the audiences of 1 Peter have as the people of God. Cf. Dryden, *Theology and Ethics*, pp. 163–91 who notes the importance of the moral παράδειγμα in Greco Roman paraenesis, including in Philo, *Abr.* 1.4-5.

111. Green, *1 Peter*, p. 87: 'Peter refers his audience to Christ's "suffering" (rather than "death") in order to underscore the commonality of their suffering with his (2.19, 20, 23; 3.14, 17, 18; 4.1 [2×], 15, 19; 5.10)'.

112. Best, *1 Peter*, p. 81; Feldmeier, *Letter of Peter*, p. 93, and Schutter, *Hermeneutic and Composition*, pp. 139–44. Cf. Joseph, *Narratological Reading of 1 Peter*, pp. 103–4.

the use of Isaiah 53 here does not function simply to assert the soteriological value of Christ's vicarious suffering, though that may by abstracted from what is maintained about his suffering. The principal purpose of this use of Scripture is to offer an example to the communities of goodness in the face of suffering. Indeed, the 'hymn' is employed within an extended paraenetic section of the epistle and is introduced in 2.21 on the basis that the sufferings of Christ serve as an example to the communities. As Dryden notes, the paraenetic use of a moral exemplar is an important feature of the epistle's concern for the development of Christian character.[113] Once again, Peter displays his view that the communities to which he writes have an elevated status revealed in the way that Scripture, the work of the Prophets, is written to serve them in some way. According to 2.21, Christ suffered ὑμῖν ὑπολιμπάνων ὑπογραμμὸν ἵνα ἐπακολουθήσητε τοῖς ἴχνεσιν αὐτοῦ. The subsequent allusion to scriptural texts thought to describe the suffering of Christ suggests that Peter's conviction (expressed in 1.12, that the Prophets served not themselves but the communities) is reflected here.

n. 1 Peter 3.5-6 and the ἅγιαι γυναῖκες of Israel's History

This allusion to 'holy women', and the behaviour of Sarah in particular, alongside the allusion to the waters of the Flood in 1 Pet. 3.21, represents something of a departure from the exegetical norms of 1 Peter. The use of Scripture in these two instances might properly be regarded as typological, since the relation of past to present exceeds the predictive and exhortative interpretations used hereto by Peter. Instead, the past is seen to have an integrity of its own, from which an application for the present is drawn. This is seen both in the manner in which a tradition (or rather, a family) from the past may be entered into by those of the present, and the manner in which a certain feature of the past is a symbolic precursor of things to come. At the same time, the references to both Sarah and Noah are somewhat easier to identify as allusions than some other instances in 1 Peter. The use of personal names and scriptural events cannot but provoke awareness that an allusion to Scripture is taking place here – though, as the analysis of 3.6 below will make clear, the allusion is to be understood as a reference to an event rather than a clearly identifiable text.

---

113. Dryden, *Theology and Ethics*, p. 194. However, Dryden seems to limit his discussion of this feature to the Christology of 1 Peter. Another appropriate instance of an exemplar might be the description of Sarah in 1 Pet. 3.6.

Peter argues, in 3.1-4, that the wives (or women) in his audiences ought to consider their beauty to reside in a spiritual quality of submission to their husbands, rather than cosmetic appearance.[114] To support this exhortation, Peter alludes to certain ἅγιαι γυναῖκες of the past who ἐλπίζουσαι εἰς θεὸν, and who made themselves beautiful (ἐκόσμουν ἑαυτάς) by submitting to their husbands (v. 5). At this point, it is not clear to whom Peter is referring with the use of ἅγιαι γυναῖκες, since this allusion does not refer directly to any particular scriptural texts. As an example of a 'holy woman', Peter alludes in v. 6 to the example of Sarah, and perhaps, in particular, to Sarah's use of ὁ κύριος μου, in extant OG versions of Gen. 18.12, to refer to her husband, Abraham – ὡς Σάρρα ὑπήκουσεν τῷ Ἀβραάμ κύριον αὐτὸν καλοῦσα. A closer reference could have been achieved if Peter had used κύριον αὐτῆς (which is also closer to the extant Hebrew אדני used in Gen. 18.12). However, it is most likely that Peter intended to refer to Gen. 18.12 due to the absence of alternative passages in which Sarah calls Abraham κύριος. Since the context of the text alluded to is Sarah's laughter at the Oaks of Mamre due to the implausibility of her bearing children as promised by the three visitors, the second half of 1 Pet. 3.6 is extremely interesting. Peter challenges his female readers and hearers to do good and not give in to fear of the basis of their status as Sarah's children (ἧς ἐγενήθητε τέκνα ἀγαθοποιοῦσαι καὶ μὴ φοβούμεναι μηδεμίαν πτόησιν).[115] Yet it is unclear

114. See Alicia J. Batten, 'Neither Gold nor Braided Hair (1 Timothy 2.9; 1 Peter 3.3): Adornment, Gender and Honour in Antiquity', *NTS* 55 (2009), pp. 484–501, for a recent sociological critique. David L. Balch, 'Hellenization/Acculturation in 1 Peter', in Talbert, ed., *Perspectives on First Peter*, pp. 81–2, analyses the history of the *Haustafeln*, setting 1 Pet. 3.6 within this context. He suggests that Aristotle (*Politics* 1.1253b1-14) argues that harmony between people can be created when hierarchical relationships are fostered. Likewise, Polybius (*History* 6.2.9-10) and Dionysius of Halicarnassus (*Roman Antiquities* 2.3.5) claim that peace within the Roman Empire is dependent upon the proper observation of such domestic hierarchies (cf. Dio Cassius, *Roman History* 50.25.3). Such was the acceptance of these views and the relation of hierarchy to peace and order that the early Christians featured them in their apologetics, so as to avoid the accusation that Christianity was a cause of strife. Likewise, Josephus employs *Haustafeln* ideology in *Contra Apion* to counter such an accusation made against Judaism.

115. Greg Forbes, 'Children of Sarah: Interpreting 1 Peter 3.6b', *BBR* 15 (2005), pp. 105–9, notes that the conditional interpretation of this clause is rejected by the majority of commentators yet taken up by the majority of popular translations. He argues that the participles here have a resultive force, serving as imperatives, as is common in the *Haustafeln*. He also argues that a conditional understanding of the clause is inconsistent with the theological style of 1 Peter, which typically posits ethical instruction after establishing the theological status of the communities to whom the epistle is addressed. Cf. Thurén, *Argument and Theology*, pp. 12–13.

as to whether Peter intended to evoke Sarah's infertility here. It is, however, probable that the notion of becoming a child of Sarah reflects a covenantal prospect of belonging to the people of God. As Forbes argues, there is a significant precedent of relating covenant identity with descent from Abraham and Sarah in texts such as Isa. 51.2, *b. Shab.* 33b and *Gen. Rab.* 48.8.[116] Perhaps the closest parallel to the non-biological understanding of descent from Sarah in particular in 1 Pet. 3.6 is Gal. 4.21-31, in which those who are God's people through his promise are regarded as being like Isaac (Gal. 4.28, ὑμεῖς δὲ, ἀδελφοί, κατὰ Ἰσαὰκ ἐπαγγελίας τέκνα ἐστέ). As Forbes notes, the description of women in the communities to which 1 Peter is addressed as descended from Sarah is consistent with a dominant feature of the epistle's ecclesiology:

> Peter then, in conformity with his previous teaching regarding identity and status of believers in 2.9-10, links the faithful of both covenant eras under the one umbrella, here using the familial metaphor of mother and children. The people of God in the new covenant era (specifically here Christian wives) are designated ἧς ἐγενήθητε τέκνα ('whose children you have become'), with the antecedent of the relative pronoun clearly being Sarah.[117]

The communities to which 1 Peter is addressed are regarded as the true people of God: those who stand in continuity with God's people in the past. This is the necessary condition upon which rests Peter's claim that the communities are especially significant, standing at the climax of salvation history and served by the Prophets who were before them. As Achtemeier notes on 1 Pet. 1.11, as he discusses the relation of the verse to the rest of the epistle,

> The phrase points...to the continuity between prophets and gospel: both have the same inspirer and ultimately the same content. Underlying such continuity is the unity of the one people of God, unity that justified the author's appropriation for the Christian community of the history of, and language for, Israel found in the OT.[118]

Whilst the majority of commentators consider the allusion in 3.6 to be to Gen. 18.12 since it is the only scriptural text in which Sarah calls Abraham 'Lord', it is often noted that she does not actually use the term in the vocative (as suggested by Peter) by speaking indirectly about 'my Lord'. In addition to this, it has been noted that there is not a single extant instance of the verb ὑποτάσσειν being used to describe Sarah's

---

116. Forbes, 'Children of Sarah', p. 107.
117. Forbes, 'Children of Sarah', p. 106.
118. Achtemeier, *1 Peter*, p. 110.

relation to Abraham in Genesis.[119] This has led Troy W. Martin to argue very persuasively that Peter draws upon material from the *Testament of Abraham*, following the earlier suggestion by F. Manns.[120] Firstly, Martin notes that Sarah frequently refers to Abraham as 'Lord' in the *Testament of Abraham* (A 5.12-13; 6.2, 4, 5 and 8 etc.). Secondly, he notes that *Test. Abr.* infers that Sarah is the 'mother of the elect'.[121] Thirdly, *Test. Abr.* A 16.4-5, and several other passages, make a connection between a resistance to fear and the pursuit of good, as is probably the case in 1 Pet. 3.6b.[122] Another suggestion is offered by Mark Kiley, who argues that the verse refers not primarily to Gen. 18.12 but the narratives of Genesis 12 and 20, in which Sarah is subject to unjust treatment as she is passed off as Abraham's sister.[123] Kiley suggests that Gen. 18.12 is being referred to obliquely here, though it is unlikely to be the primary text alluded to since it does not appear to offer much support for the notion of submission. However, Kiley argues, the submission of Sarah to Abraham's plan to disown her as his wife is more appropriate, especially since in Genesis 12 and 20 the couple are 'sojourners' like the communities to which 1 Peter is addressed, Sarah's suffering in these texts is unjust (whilst the bearing of unjust suffering is commended in 1 Peter) and the interest in Sarah's beauty in Genesis 12 and 20 parallels 1 Pet. 3.3-5. Kiley anticipates the obvious objection that neither Genesis 12 nor 20 are 'quoted' in any sense in 1 Pet. 3.6 (since neither use the term 'Lord') and argues that this does not deny the possibility of a reference since Isaiah 53 is referred to without a quotation in 1 Pet. 2.21-25.[124] However, as is noted above, there is a significant degree of verbal correspondence between Isaiah 53 and 1 Pet. 2.21-25, even if one admits that it is not a quotation, which not

---

119. Carson, '1 Peter', p. 1036.

120. Martin, 'Background of 1 Pet 3,6', pp. 139–46. Cf. F. Manns, 'Sara, Modèle de la obéissante: Étude de l'arrière-plan juif de 1 Pierre 3,5-6', *BeO* 26 (1984), pp. 65–73 (73). Mann proposes a rabbinic background for 1 Pet. 3.6 on the basis of texts which, with the exception of *Testament of Abraham*, are rightly rejected by Martin as too recent.

121. This point is less persuasive. The examples Martin refers to (*Test. Abr.* A 3.6; 6.4-5; 7.2-7; 8.5-7 and B 7.5-18) simply highlight Sarah's status as mother of Isaac, rather than the whole people of God, though this may be implied.

122. *Test. Abr.* A 16.4-5.

123. Mark Kiley, 'Like Sara: The Tale of Terror behind 1 Peter 3.6', *JBL* 106 (1987), pp. 689–92. Cf. Balch, *Let Wives Be Submissive*, pp. 103–5, and Troy W. Martin, 'The TestAbr and the Background of 1 Pet 3,6', *ZNW* 90 (1999), p. 139. Cf. Joseph, *Narratalogical Reading of 1 Peter*, p. 146.

124. Cf. Chin, 'Heavenly Home', p. 101, and Martin, 'Background of 1 Pet 3,6', p. 140.

all scholars do. Yet any verbal correspondence is lacking here, suggesting that the allusion is not to a specific text of Scripture. Furthermore, Kiley's argument depends upon Peter and his audiences having knowledge of a significant amount of the narrative of Genesis, which may not have been the case. At the same time, neither the submission of Sarah nor the injustice of Abraham's plans are emphasized in Genesis 12 and 20, suggesting that the audiences of 1 Peter would be unlikely to detect a reference to these passages with specific verbal agreement between the passages and 1 Pet. 3.6.

Aída Besançon Spencer also argues, independently, that 1 Pet. 3.6 alludes to Gen. 12.11-20, rather than 18.12, noting that in the latter Sarah does not actually call Abraham 'Lord' using a vocative as suggested in 1 Pet. 3.6, but refers to him in the third person as such.[125] Instead of reading the reference to Sarah as an example of appropriate submission, as Kiley does, Spencer argues that Sarah is an exemplar of 'doing good'. Spencer understands the reference to Sarah as related to the paraenesis of the household material for wives with unbelieving husbands just prior to the allusion, suggesting that in Gen. 12.11-20 Abraham in portrayed as the unbelieving husband of a faithful wife. Yet Spencer also suggests that the allusion relates to material to follow, in particular 1 Pet. 3.18. She argues that just as Christ's suffering in the place of others is offered initially as an example to Christian slaves, so too Sarah's suffering in Gen. 12.11-20 is in the place of Abraham and is seen to anticipate the sufferings of Christ in some way.[126] However, this suggestion can claim little more evidence in its support than Kiley's or the traditional view that 3.6 alludes to Gen. 18.12.[127]

---

125. Aída Besançon Spencer, 'Peter's Pedagogical Method in 1 Peter 3.6', *BBR* 10 (2000), pp. 107–19 (113). Spencer also notes the contextual similarity between Gen. 12 and 1 Pet. 3.6, relating to themes of sojourning, beauty and obedience which Kiley considers to be of decisive importance. The fact that it is so difficult to determine which text is alluded to here is interesting. Jennifer G. Bird, *Abuse, Power and Fearful Obedience: Reconsidering 1 Peter's Commands to Wives* (LNTS 442; London: T&T Clark International, 2011), p. 32, suggests that the fact that Peter has chosen an episode in the life of Sarah marked by an uncharacteristic submission, such that it is difficult to determine the text to which he refers, indicates the extent to which he is keen to promote the subordination of women. Bird views the *Haustafel* in 1 Peter as an 'irruption' or contradiction of the exalted imagery and language applied to the community which is a 'royal priesthood' and a 'holy nation', which the *Haustafel* implies that women are excluded from.

126. Spencer, 'Peter's Pedagogical Method', pp. 114 and 117.

127. Achtemeier, *1 Peter*, p. 216.

Because it is so difficult to establish a single text to which 1 Pet. 3.6 alludes, it is more appropriate to view it as an allusion to a scriptural character, rather than a text. This character bears a typological relation to Christian wives, not in the sense that Sarah prefigures their existence,[128] but because she offers to Christian wives a means of participation in the people of God.[129] Joseph agrees with Kiley and Spencer in viewing 1 Pet. 3.6 as an allusion to Genesis 12 and 20:

> The author of 1 Peter sees in Sarah's attitude the kind of dependence on God that should be characteristic of the audience, and especially of the wives who could potentially face the dangers associated with being a believing spouse in a worldly environment; or even from being the believing wife of a believing husband who has to deal with the pressures of living in a hostile environment. They are Sarah's children, through emulating her example. They are not to fear anything because, since God did deliver Sarah from her dangerous situation, they too have the assurance that God will deliver them from their predicament.[130]

However, Sarah is more than simply an example taken from Israel's history: for the Christian woman, she can become a mother. This familial relation enables the character Sarah to transcend the distinction between past and present in a manner comparable with a type.[131] Sarah has significant status in 1 Pet. 3.6 despite belonging to the past in which Christ had not been revealed (1.20) and in which the Prophets spoke in messages destined exclusively for a later generation (1.10-11). Whilst Sarah, like other allusions, is employed to support Peter's paraenesis, her status as a figure of the past is not dissolved into whatever has significance for the eschatological community, as happens with scriptural citations. This may be because she is understood to be a person, relating very concretely to events in Israel's history (whatever they might be) rather than a text oriented exclusively towards a particular moment in the present.

o. 1 Peter 3.19-21 and Noah and the Spirits in Prison

The clear allusion to Noah, his family, the Flood and its victims has been the focus of significant scholarly discussion. Much of this is no doubt due the association of this passage with traditionally contested doctrines of Christ's descent to the dead and the 'harrowing of Hell'. In addition to

---

128. Kelly, *Peter*, p. 130.
129. This is not to ignore the debate surrounding the possible gnomic aorist ἐγενήθητε. Cf. Beare, *Peter*, p. 156; J. Schlosser, '1 Pierre 3, 5b-6', *Bib* 64 (1983), pp. 409–10, and Achtemeier, *1 Peter*, p. 216.
130. Joseph, *Narratological Reading of 1 Peter*, p. 146.
131. Goppelt, *Typos*, p. 157.

this, the allusion is one of the most interesting examples of the use of the Old Testament in the New Testament, both in terms of what it appears to add to the scriptural tradition to which it relates, and in terms of its clearly typological mode of interpretation – ὃ καὶ ὑμᾶς ἀντίτυπον νῦν σῴζει βάπτισμα.

One might properly regard Peter's reasoning here as associative, moving from the audiences' need to live lives which are distinct from a pagan world because of their goodness (vv. 15-16), through to the importance of suffering because of that goodness (v. 17), to Christ as the example of suffering for goodness by his death (v. 18) and on to the consequences of his death for the Flood generation (vv. 19-20) before describing baptism in relation to the Flood (v. 21).[132] Verse 18 is quite clearly connected to the preceding argument by means of ὅτι καὶ. Likewise the use of ἐν ᾧ καὶ in v. 19 refers back to the Spirit in v. 18. The allusion to the Genesis Flood narrative ought to be understood in relation to this associative reasoning. It is likely that the allusion functions as an aid to the continuation of the example of Christ as the paradigmatic good sufferer whose suffering results in good.[133] This is demonstrated ultimately by the vindication and glorification of Christ in v. 22.[134]

Bo Reicke, whose study of 1 Pet. 3.19 was, prior to Dalton, perhaps the most significant scholarly work on the Flood allusion, considers τοῖς ἐν φυλακῇ πνεύμασιν to refer to the 'angels' or 'sons of God' in Gen. 6.1-4.[135] Reicke argues that πνεῦμα is not normally used to refer to 'an ordinary person in the realm of the shadows' in the good Greek of which he sees 1 Peter as an example. This is indicated by the use of πνεύματι in 3.18 as a dative of agency referring to the power by which Christ was raised to life after suffering for sins. However, this term is used to refer to the 'sons of God' of Gen. 6.1-4 on many occasions in *1 Enoch* 6–36. An allusion to this text is extremely plausible since Jude 6, 14-15, 2 Pet. 2.4 and 9-10 almost certainly allude to it, Reicke argues. At the same

---

132. Achtemeier, *1 Peter*, pp. 243–4.
133. Richard, 'Functional Christology', pp. 130–3, suggests that the material in 3.18-22 shares a common christological hymn tradition with 1.18-21. According to Richard, there appear to be certain features which are common to each 'hymn', principally themes of the coming of Christ, the cosmic subjection of elements to Christ and the heavenly exaltation of Christ.
134. Carson, '1 Peter', p. 1039.
135. Bo Reicke, *The Disobedient Spirits and Christian Baptism: A Study of 1 Pet. III. 19 and its Context* (ASNU, 13; Copenhagen: Ejnar Munksgaard, 1946), p. 53.

time, these other New Testament references to Enoch also suggest that a Greek version was perhaps widely available at the time of the composition of 1 Peter.

Reicke offers an interesting suggestion as to how Peter is able to associate the death of Christ in 3.18 with preaching to the spirits in prison. In the Psalter, suffering is often described in terms of drowning. Examples include Pss. 42.7; 69.1-4, 13-15; 88.7, 17; and 128.1. Reicke notes that in the Synoptic Gospels the language of suffering used in the psalter is employed by Jesus in his final moments of suffering. For Reicke, this is particularly significant in Mt. 26.38 and parallels, which feature a quite plausible use of Ps. 42.6 in the garden of Gethsemane, a reference which, if used in such a way as implies its context (the use of drowning language in Ps. 42.7), might indicate the association made in 1 Pet. 3.18-19.[136] In addition to this, Reicke notes the use of Jonah typology in Mt. 12.40 in association with Jesus' suffering. This suggests to Reicke that imagery of drowning Flood waters was something Peter associated with Jesus' suffering and which provided the possibility of linking this suffering with his preaching to the condemned sons of God from *1 Enoch* 6–36. However, the evidence that Peter thought of Jesus' suffering in this way is hard to find.[137] The allusion, if that is what it is, is provided on the basis of an implied comparison between the Ninevites and the Jesus' γενεὰ πονηρὰ καὶ μοιχαλίς. In addition to this, the period of three days, rather than the location of the suffering, seems to be most significant. Jesus predicts that he will be in the heart of the earth: a reference to burial.

Dalton notes that in *2 En.* 7.1-4 the spirits of the dead who disobeyed God at the time of the Flood are understood as residing in the second heaven.[138] He uses this as the basis for arguing that Christ's preaching to the spirits in prison takes place as part of his ascension.[139] In addition to

---

136. Reicke, *Disobedient Spirits*, pp. 142–7.
137. Nolland, *Matthew*, pp. 510–11, details several of the many options provided to explain τὸ σημεῖον Ἰωνᾶ τοῦ προφήτου without mentioning the possibility that water symbolism is implied. Nolland suggests that in the Lukan version of this saying Jonah himself is the sign as a figure of judgement, whereas Matthew, he argues, views the incarceration of Jonah as a sign of the prophet's authenticity just as Jesus' death and resurrection will be a sign of his. Cf. Craig L. Blomberg, 'Matthew', in Beale and Carson, eds., *Commentary on the New Testament*, pp. 1–110 (44–5), who argues for the same view.
138. William Joseph Dalton, *Christ's Proclamation to the Spirits: A Study of 1 Peter 3.18–4.6* (Analecta Biblica 23; Rome: Pontifical Biblical Institute, 1965), p. 176.
139. Dalton, *Proclamation to the Spirits*, p. 167.

this, Dalton regards 3.18-22 as quite distinct from the reference to proclamation to the dead in 4.6. The latter is not to be understood as a scriptural reference of any sort, but a reference to the primitive eschatological anxiety concerning the fate of those who have received the Gospel but have died before the parousia seen in 1 Thess. 4.13-18. According to Dalton, 4.6 assures the communities that those who have died will not fail to see God's ultimate salvation and vindication.[140] But perhaps of greater interest to this study are not so much the sources behind Peter's treatment of the Flood, but his use of the Flood in relation to Baptism and the Christian communities to which he writes.

The majority of scholars contend that the use of water to save Noah and his family (v. 20) typologically foreshadows[141] the saving waters of baptism as an act of Christian initiation, understood οὐ σαρκὸς ἀπόθεσις ῥύπου ἀλλὰ συνειδήσεως ἀγαθῆς ἐπερώτημα εἰς θεόν.[142] However, R. E. Nixon argues that βάπτισμα refers not to a rite but to the refining

---

140. This interpretation of 4.6 as quite independent of 3.18-22 has gained a significant degree of scholarly support, as noted by David G. Horrell, 'Who Are "The Dead" and When Was the Gospel Preached to Them? The Interpretation of 1 Pet 4.6', *NTS* 49 (2003), pp. 70–89. Horrell objects to this interpretation arguing that there is no evidence of concern regarding Christians who have died in 1 Peter, that the dating of 1 Peter is too late for it to be compared with the anxiety expressed in 1 Thess. 4.13-18; that 1 Peter gives no indication that the vindication of the dead is in any doubt and that the reference should naturally be understood in relation to 3.18-22. In addition to this, the preaching mentioned in 4.6 is closely related to future judgement, implying that it offers the opportunity to prepare for this judgement. Likewise, the verse maintains that the dead have faced judgement already, which may not suit the possible purpose of comforting those who are anxious about the status of the dead.

141. Cf. Heb. 9.24: οὐ γὰρ εἰς χειροποίητα εἰσῆλθεν ἅγια Χριστός, ἀντίτυπα τῶν ἀληθινῶν, ἀλλ' εἰς αὐτὸν τὸν οὐρανόν, νῦν ἐμφανισθῆναι τῷ προσώπῳ τοῦ θεοῦ ὑπὲρ ἡμῶν. See also 1 Cor. 1.6, 11 and Rom. 5.14. Ἀντίτυπος, in its actual use, bears a much closer resemblance to the verb τύπτω ('to strike/to beat an image') than τύπος itself which has quite a variety of uses. The closest use of τύπος in the OG Scripture is in *4 Macc.* 6.11. In Philo, τύπος is used of both a model of something as well as a copy. H. Müller, 'Type, Pattern', *NIDNTT* 3, p. 903, and Ceslas Spicq, 'τύπος', *TLNT* 3, pp. 384–7.

142. Achtemeier, *1 Peter*, pp. 266–7; Michaels, *1 Peter*, p. 214; Feldmeier, *Letter of Peter*, p. 207, and Carson, '1 Peter', p. 1039. Carson's suggestion that the audiences are to find encouragement to persevere in the face of overwhelming adversity from the small numbers of those saved from the Flood appears to lack significant evidence from the passage itself. In addition to this, the size of the churches to which Peter writes does not receive any attention in 1 Peter, suggesting that it was not an issue of any particular concern.

experience of suffering, as seen in 1 Pet. 1.6-7.[143] This interpretation is supported by Hillyer, who notes the similarity of the purgative and salvific concept of suffering in 1 Peter with Mk 13.13, as well as the function of the Flood waters as an expression of God's judgement.[144] In addition to this, Hillyer notes the complete absence of reference to the Holy Spirit in 1 Pet. 3.21, which is certainly unusual given the common early Christian association of the rite of Baptism with the work of the Holy Spirit. However, Goppelt rejects attempts to distance 1 Pet. 3.21 from initiatory baptism.[145] He argues that Peter's interpretation of the Flood in relation to baptism is influenced by *Gen. Rab.* 7.7, which draws attention to Noah walking through the shallow waters of the Flood to the ark. He then argues that the relative pronoun in 1 Pet. 3.21 refers not simply to the Flood, but to Noah and his family walking through the water as an element in their eventual salvation. That is how water (and hence the ritual of Baptism, typologically prefigured) may be regarded as salvific.

In many ways, there is little that is surprising in the use of Scripture here, given some of the hermeneutical ideas expressed in 1 Pet. 1.10-12. The allusion to the Flood is clearly related to the suffering (3.18a) and glories (3.18b, 21-22) of Christ. In addition to this, the whole associative discourse begins with the paraenesis directed towards Christian slaves in 3.17. Characteristically, the allusion is seen to relate directly to the experience of the Christian communities: it is about the Baptism they have undergone. Yet, whereas the prophetic witness is seen to be exclusively oriented towards Christ and the eschatological communities, typological interpretation as in 3.21 recognises some inherent meaning for the antitype apart from its relation to the thing it foreshadows. The Flood is still the Flood, even though it also has additional meaning as the antitype of baptism. This is unusual in 1 Peter, where the author has no interest at all in the original historical uses or setting of scriptural texts. For example, he does not appear to have any interest in the relation of the titles in 2.5 and 9 to Israel in the past. There is some suggestion here, then, that Peter's hermeneutic recognises a distinction between texts

---

143. R. E. Nixon, 'The Meaning of "Baptism" in 1 Peter 3.21', in *Studia Evangelica*. Vol. 4, *Papers Presented to the Third International Congress on New Testament Studies Held at Christ Church, Oxford* (ed. F. L. Cross; Oxford: Oxford University Press, 1968), pp. 437–41.

144. Hillyer, 'Feast of Tabernacles', pp. 56–7.

145. Goppelt, *Typos*, p. 157. Cf. the discussion in Achtemeier, *1 Peter*, pp. 266–7, on the relative pronoun in v. 21.

alluded to or cited and events. It is possible that where historical narrative events are referred to they may also be understood to have significance for the communities that exceeds their value simply as events of the past. Whereas scriptural texts appear to be applied directly to the communities without any sense that they might have had meaning in another context, historical events cannot be treated in this way since they very obviously have a prior meaning in relation to the past. Yet since the narrative substructure of 1 Peter emphasises the present setting of the communities, events of the past are seen to have an additional significance for the present.

p. 1 Peter 3.22 and Psalms 110.1 (OG 109.1) and 8.6-7

The absence of Ps. 110.1 in 1 Peter is notable given its importance in early Christianity.[146] Yet Schutter defines the phrase ὅς ἐστιν ἐν δεξιᾷ [τοῦ][147] θεοῦ in 1 Pet. 3.22 as an explicit citation of Ps. 110.1 (κάθου ἐκ δεξιῶν μου).[148] This is unlikely to be a direct allusion to Ps. 110.1, but rather a reference to the popular early Christian tradition of Christ's *sessio ad dexteram*. As Hay argues in relation to 1 Pet. 3.22,

> As for early Christian allusions to the psalm, a considerable number apparently derive not directly from the psalm but from primitive church confessions or hymns in which were embedded phrases or ideas ultimately drawn from Ps 110.[149]

There is too little literary similarity between the possible allusion and the source text for an allusion to the psalm (rather than the tradition) to have been intended. If 1 Pet. 3.22 really was an allusion to Ps. 110.1, its

---

146. The importance of Ps. 110 is difficult to overstate. The use of Ps. 110 in Hebrews has been seen by George Wesley Buchanan, *To the Hebrews: Translation, Comment and Conclusions* (AB 36; New York: Doubleday, 1972), p. xix, to have a status similar to that argued for Ps. 34 in 1 Peter by Bornemann and Woan. Ps. 110.1 features in the *Davidssohnfrage* of Mk 12.35-37 par. as a messianic proof-text and is the principal source for the important *sessio ad dexteram* tradition alluded to here. Uses of Ps. 110.1 in the New Testament include Mk 12.36 par.; 14.62; 16.19; Lk. 22.69; Acts 2.34; Rom. 8.34; 1 Cor. 15.25; Eph. 1.20; Col. 3.1; Heb. 1.3, 13; 8.1; and 10.12. The principal study of the use of psalm is David M. Hay, *Glory at the Right Hand: Psalm 110 in Early Christianity* (SBLMS 18; Atlanta: Society of Biblical Literature, 1989).
147. A probable 'correction' in ℵ*, B and Ψ.
148. Schutter, *Hermeneutic and Composition*, p. 37.
149. Hay, *Glory at the Right Hand*, p. 39. Cf. Goppelt, *Erste Petrusbrief*, pp. 247–450; Jobes, *1 Peter*, p. 257, and Elliott, *Commentary*, pp. 682–3. The latter is significant, given his tendency to follow Schutter's analysis of scriptural references.

christological interpretation would not require any special Petrine scriptural hermeneutic since this interpretation has such an overwhelming precedent.

q. 1 Peter 5.8 and Psalm 22.14 (OG 21.14)

The possible reference to Scripture here might properly be regarded as an 'echo' employing the image of a lion representing Israel's enemies, since there is no extant scriptural witness to the notion of the devil as a lion.[150] Indeed, as Troy W. Martin makes clear, the lion metaphor has a widespread and diverse background, including impressions both of majesty and of terror.[151] The specific idea of the λέων ὠρυόμενος is found only in Ps. 22.14 (OG 21.14), a text which appears to have been well-known by the earliest Christians, and Schutter considers the phrase to be a reference to this scriptural text, as well as to Job 1.7 (ὁ διάβολος τῷ κυρίῳ εἶπεν περιελθὼν τὴν γῆν καὶ ἐμπεριπατήσας τὴν ὑπ' οὐρανὸν πάρειμι).[152] The second half of Ps. 22.14 reads ὡς λέων ὁ ἁρπάζων καὶ ὠρυόμενος.[153] Other OG scriptural uses of λέων to describe Israel's enemies employ the plural, as in OG Jer. 27.17, 28.38 and Ezek. 22.25 (which reads λέοντες ὠρυόμενοι), despite the use of the singular ארי שאג in extant Hebrew versions of Ezek. 22.25. As Kelly points out, ἀντίδικος is not used in the OG Scriptures to denote the devil, though διάβολος is a common OG translation of 'Satan'.[154] All of this casts doubt on the possibility of an

---

150. The image of the lion representing Israel's enemies is well attested: Jer. 27.17; 28.38; Ezek. 22.25; *Tg. Isa.* 35.9; *Tg. Jer.* 4.7; 5.6; *Tg. Ezek.* 19.6; 1QH 5.9; 13; 19.4; 4QpNah 1.5; and 4QpHos 1. However, as Feldmeier, *Letter of Peter*, p. 249, points out, the devil is described as a lion in *Jos. Asen.* 12.9-11.

151. Troy W. Martin, 'Roaring Lions among Diaspora Metaphors: First Peter 5.8 in Its Metaphorical Context', in du Toit, ed., *Bedrängnis und Identität*, pp. 167-79. Cf. David G. Horrell, Bradley Arnold and Travis B. Williams, 'Visuality, Vivid Description, and the Message of 1 Peter: The Significance of the Roaring Lion (1 Pet 5.8)', *JBL* 132 (2013), pp. 697-716, which also notes this variety but argues for a principal evocation of *ad bestias* execution.

152. Schutter, *Hermeneutic and Composition*, p. 38. Elliott, *Commentary*, p. 857, supports the view that the allusion is to Ps. 22.14. Jobes, *1 Peter*, p. 314, argues for similarity with Job, though she does not describe it as an allusion. It must be noted that the similarity to Job 1.7, other than the use of διάβολος, is merely conceptual.

153. The absence of ὁ ἁρπάζων καὶ in 1 Pet. 5.8 need not undermine the plausibility of the reference to the psalm since one simply cannot know the forms of the psalm text available in the first century.

154. Kelly, *Peter*, 209. Cf. 1 Chron. 21.1; Job 1.7, 9 (etc.); and Zech. 3.1. However, Elliott, *Commentary*, p. 857, notes an association in LXX 1 Sam. 2.10; Sir. 36.6; Ignatius, *Rom* 5.3; *Mart. Pol.* 2.4; 2 Tim. 4.7; and Rev. 13.1-2.

allusion here, though Ps. 22.14 provides the most likely source text if an allusion was intended by Peter.

Equally unclear is the nature of the threat alluded to in the devil's activity. Boris A. Paschke argues that the phrase actually refers to the threat of being thrown to the lions.[155] However, this assumes a more developed, and perhaps official, persecution as the setting for 1 Peter than has recently been thought. The same could perhaps not be said of the more traditional view that the phrase refers to persecution from specific local people,[156] though Jobes' view that it represents a widespread popular hostility arising from a contrasting pagan worldview is most appropriate.[157]

The reference to Ps. 22.14 (OG 21.14) may not have been intended to evoke that particular text. Instead, it may simply reflect a desire to use scriptural language to describe the devil.[158] It is important for Peter that his audiences have a heightened sense of the dangers that face them as Christians. To this end, he employs a vibrant image of the devil as a roaring lion by which the members of the communities to which Peter writes are seen as prey. The sense of danger evoked by the description of the devil serves to support Peter's exhortation at the beginning of 5.8. If an allusion is intended, it serves to support Peter's paraenesis at the close of the letter.

2. Conclusion

It is appropriate to characterise the interpretation of Scripture in 1 Peter as 'primitive and sectarian'. This is in no way intended to be a derogatory description. As will be argued in the next chapter, the use of Scripture in 1 Peter is similar to Qumranic exegesis. It is primitive in the sense that it employs no self-consciously exegetical argument: the meaning of a text of Scripture is never in doubt, nor is there any sense that the audience of the epistle may understand a text differently and therefore need to be persuaded. In this sense, the use of Scripture in 1 Peter is quite different from the more sophisticated approaches witnessed in some of

---

155. Boris A. Paschke, 'The Roman *ad bestias* Execution as a Possible Historical Background for 1 Peter 5.8', *JSNT* 28 (2006), pp. 489–500. Cf. Horrell, Arnold and Williams, 'Visuality'.
156. Kelly, *Peter*, pp. 209–10, and Best, *1 Peter*, p. 174.
157. Jobes, *1 Peter*, p. 314.
158. Carson, '1 Peter', p. 1044: 'This usage merely picks up a colourful metaphor from the OT and applies it to the devil. It is not obvious that Peter is attempting any other associative transfer'.

the speeches in Acts and in the Epistle to the Hebrews, for example. At the same time, the use of Scripture in 1 Peter is sectarian insofar as it considers the community in which it originates to receive special interest from Scripture. 1 Peter, like many Qumran texts, reads Scripture as addressing its community in particular as an exclusive group. Both of these primitive and sectarian characteristics are witnessed in the 'definition of Scripture' in 1 Pet. 1.10-12. The Scriptures of Israel are explained there as referring predicatively and exclusively to Jesus Christ: his sufferings and the glories which came after. This is a primitive and straightforward assertion of the scriptural text's determinate meaning. At the same time, 1 Pet. 1.12 asserts that the focus of those who uttered the words of scriptural prophecy did so with Peter's audience in mind: 'it was revealed to them that they were serving not themselves but us'. The Petrine community, like the Qumran community, was seen as the group to be a part of, an eschatologically significant community. However, the description of the use of Scripture in 1 Peter as 'primitive' does not ignore the very real sophistication of, for example, the Stone Catena which has some literary sophistication both in the way it draws appropriate 'stone' texts together as well as in the way that it clearly develops an existing exegetical tradition of using texts such as Psalm 118 christologically.

* * *

Excursus: Sectarian Exegesis in 1 Peter and the New Testament

It could be argued that the use of Scripture in the New Testament is generally 'sectarian'. Scripture is always interpreted to relate to the needs of a particular community or group of communities by someone who probably has some role within that community. Yet the degree to which scriptural interpretation in the New Testament is sectarian varies. There are probably three distinct degrees of sectarianism in New Testament interpretation of Scripture.

1. *Engaging Sectarianism*. Certain New Testament passages feature biblical interpretations which show a conscious awareness and engagement with other interpretations of a scriptural text, even though the purpose of such an engagement is refutation. This type of interpretation is most evident in the Synoptic Gospels, Acts and the Epistle to the Hebrews. The *Davidssohnfrage*, which occurs in each of the Synoptic Gospels, is a good example of interpretation which shows an awareness of (or interest in engaging with) other interpretations of a text. Here, whatever one regards as the theological assertion being made by Jesus about the Christ, it is clear that a certain popular interpretation of the Christ as the Son of David is being undermined using Ps. 110.1. What is interesting is that Ps. 110.1 is related to this debate, though it may not have been thought of in these terms

before, by interpreting it on the basis of assumptions about its Davidic authorship. Because David is understood to have called the Christ 'my Lord' he must be more than David's son. Likewise, the interpretation of Psalm 16 in Acts 2 represents an attempt to undermine a particular interpretation of that text. Psalm 16 is read here as a proof of Jesus' resurrection from the dead, but it is highly probably that the psalm was understood by many others to be about David and his incorruptibility. This is the interpretation offered in *Ps. Midr.* 16 and is indicated by Peter's reference to Davidic authorship here. Peter refutes this interpretation by arguing from the assumption of Davidic authorship that since David was a prophet his psalm must be prophetic, pointing forward in time to a later person, who unlike David, would not see decay.

The interpretation of Psalm 95 in Hebrews 3–4 is another example of engaging sectarian reading. The author of Hebrews it keen to show, through a variety of arguments, that κατάπαυσίν μου in the psalm does not refer to rest in a geographical promised land, but to an eschatological reality.[159] The author argues against another interpretation of his chosen passage, indicating an awareness of the fact that he is not the only interpreter of that text.

2. *Assumed Sectarianism.* Perhaps the majority of uses of Scripture in the New Testament are essentially sectarian, reading Scripture as unambiguously addressing the needs and interests of the community. However, few operate on the basis of articulated views of the communities' exclusive status; rather, it is simply assumed that Scripture relates naturally to the context of the community in and for which it is read. There is no attempt made to define why Scripture relates so perfectly to this context, nor is there any attempt to exclude other communities from having this same access.

3. *Enforced Sectarianism.* Some sectarian interpretation in the New Testament proceeds from an understanding that the community has a unique status and therefore a unique relation to Scripture. This type of sectarian reading can be seen in Paul, though not universally in the Pauline corpus. It is evident particularly in Romans 3 and in 2 Cor. 3.12-18. In the former, the Scriptures are said to have been for the benefit of Christian communities, though this does not clearly preclude the Scriptures having been understood by previous Jewish readers. Yet in 2 Cor. 3.12-18, the Christian communities are seen to have exclusive access to the meaning of Scripture which was and is unavailable to those who attempt to read it with 'hardened' minds. This can also be seen in Jn 8.39-47. Though this passage is not clearly about the interpretation of Scripture, understanding or reception of the word of God is seen to be possible only for those who are from God. Those who do not understand it are seen to be the offspring of the Devil, whose native tongue is falsehood. Yet enforced sectarian

---

159. On each of these examples of interpretation, see Benjamin Sargent, *David Being a Prophet: The Contingency of Scripture upon History in the New Testament* (BNZW 207; Berlin: de Gruyter, 2014), pp. 6–128.

exegesis receives its clearest expression in 1 Pet. 1.10-12, which both claims the communities as having paramount eschatological significance and explains the role of the prophets in terms of their service to the communities. Exegesis of this sort still involves a certain interaction with, or consciousness of, other communities or a broader social context. As Elliott argues, the theological status of the communities addressed by 1 Peter is not simply 'theology' in an abstract sense, but something conditioned as a response to social setting.[160] This sense of awareness is common to the literature of Qumran, in which the broader context of Palestinian society is important as perhaps a motivation for eschatological understandings of the Qumran community.[161]

---

160. Elliott, *Home for the Homeless*, pp. 106–12.
161. Though it must be noted that not all examples of 'exegetical' literature display sectarian theology. 4Q390 and 4Q375 as examples of parabiblical literature, for example, could belong to a variety of ancient Jewish settings.

Chapter 4

THE EXEGETICAL BACKGROUND TO THE USE OF SCRIPTURE IN 1 PETER

The use of the Old Testament in 1 Peter is determined by the author's view of prophecy in 1 Pet. 1.10-12. Peter views Scripture as principally concerned with one particular set of events relating to the sufferings of Christ and the glories after. In addition to this, Peter views Scripture as relating particularly and even exclusively to the communities to which he writes: after all, he considers the Prophets themselves to have written in order to serve the people who have had the Gospel proclaimed to them. This combination of regarding Scripture as having an eschatological focus upon one particular set of events and one particular community, or rather, group of communities, is remarkably similar to the interpretation of Scripture at Qumran. This chapter will argue that the use of the Old Testament in 1 Peter is best understood as belonging to the cultural milieu of sectarian Jewish apocalyptic. It will be argued that the use of the Old Testament is much more 'primitive' than typically thought, a suggestion which has some bearing upon the discussion of the authorship of 1 Peter in which the relative sophistication of the letter often features.

1. 1 Peter and Apocalyptic Judaism

That 1 Peter belongs to a general Apocalyptic Jewish milieu is beyond doubt, despite studies seeking to explain various aspects of the epistle in terms of Hellenistic background.[1] A number of scholars have noted a

---

1. Examples discussed in this study include van Unnik, 'Critique of Paganism'; Brown, 'Just a Busybody?'; Tite, 'Nursing, Milk and Moral Development'; Dryden, *Theology and Ethics*, pp. 163–91, and Michaels, *1 Peter*, p. 95. As John J. Collins, *The Apocalyptic Imagination: An Introduction to Jewish Apocalyptic Literature* (2d ed.; Grand Rapids: Eerdmans, 1998), pp. 33–7, notes, Hellenistic and Jewish ideas are not mutually exclusive in apocalyptic literature. Cf. Jane Heath, 'Homer or Moses? A Hellenistic Perspective on Moses' Throne Vision in Ezekiel Tragicus', *JJS* 43 (2007), pp. 1–18.

relationship between the letter and apocalyptic Judaism.[2] As discussed above, Apocalyptic Jewish texts or traditions are likely sources behind the allusions to Sarah (*Test. Abr.* A 16.4-5) and the Flood (*1 En.* 1.2) in 1 Pet. 3.6 and 4.20. Certain common features of Apocalyptic are observable in 1 Peter. Christopher Rowland concludes that 'Apocalyptic seems essentially to be about the revelation of the divine mysteries through visions or some other form of immediate disclosure of heavenly truths'.[3] Whilst 1 Peter does not feature visions or dreams, the disclosure of the unknown is an important element in Peter's understanding of history in 1.10-12 and 20-22, as well as his expectation of the imminent future in 1.7 and 1.13. Similarly, the tension between imminent deliverance and imminent evil, identified by Bauckham as a feature of Jewish and Christian Apocalyptic, is evident in 1.6-7; 2.11-12; 4.7-8, 12-13, 17-19, and 5.8.[4] Similarly, Jane Schaberg argues that 1 Pet. 3.22 reflects Merkabah imagery and Dan. 7.27.[5]

2. 1 Peter and Biblical Exegesis at Qumran

Since the discovery of the first Qumran scrolls, scholarship on 1 Peter has made extensive use of the literature. Because of 1 Peter's sectarian approach and its relation to apocalyptic Judaism, such comparison is extremely appropriate. As will be seen from the discussion of scholarship on 1 Peter which makes this comparison, a close cultural and ideological similarity is observable. Much of this similarity relates to the use of scriptural texts. After an analysis of biblical hermeneutics in the Dead Sea Scrolls, it will be argued that there is a significant degree of hermeneutical similarity between aspects of them and 1 Peter, particularly in the degree to which an assumption of determinate meaning is evident. In both, determinate meaning is grounded in theological claims about the status of the community in and for which Scripture is interpreted.

---

2. Selwyn, *Peter*, p. 25; Achtemeier, *1 Peter*, p. 108; Dautzenberg, 'Σωτηρία ψυχῶν', pp. 266–7, and Schutter, *Hermeneutic and Composition*, p. 102.
3. Christopher Rowland, *The Open Heaven: A Study of Apocalyptic in Judaism and Early Christianity* (London: SPCK, 1982), p. 70.
4. Richard J. Bauckham, 'The Delay of the Parousia', *TynBul* 31 (1980), pp. 3–36. Cf. Kelhoffer, *Persecution, Persuasion and Power*.
5. Jane Schaberg, 'Mark 14.62: Early Christian Merkabah Imagery?', in *Apocalyptic and the New Testament: Essays on Honor of J. Louis Martyn* (ed. Joel Marcus and Marion L. Soards; JSNTSup 24; Sheffield: Sheffield Academic, 1989), pp. 69–94 (73). One might also note that pseudonymity is also a common feature of Jewish Apocalyptic. Collins, *Apocalyptic Imagination*, p. 39.

a. Qumran in Scholarship on 1 Peter

As will be seen, Boring's analysis of the intellectual background of 1 Peter is largely accurate:

> There is no indication that the author had imbibed the kind of Jewish traditions cultivated in the rabbinic academies that later received written deposit in the Mishnah, Midrashim, and the Talmud. While there is no direct literary contact between 1 Peter and the Dead Sea Scrolls, the combination of thematic similarities such as election, purification by a water ritual, the community as the eschatological house of God, eschatological interpretation of Scripture, the identification of the community itself as the people of God, and the call to holiness may well point to the earliest stage of the tradition now found in 1 Peter as having originated in the same thought world as that of Qumran, namely on the margins of Palestinian Judaism, in tension with the dominant religious authorities.[6]

Achtemeier draws attention to numerous points of comparison between 1 Peter and Qumranic literature, first noting 'a general agreement between the thought-world of Qumran and the early Christianity in which 1 Peter shared, seen in terms of such general ideas as election, baptism, spiritual temple, the fulfilment of prophecy, the eschatological punishment of the unrighteous and the deliverance of the chosen'.[7] Whilst this similarity could be claimed for a number of New Testament texts, Achtemeier notes particular similarity in the use of scriptural catenae and the definition of the community as estranged from society in general, even though the Qumran community emphasised this estrangement by practical disengagement and withdrawal, in contrast to the communities represented by 1 Peter.[8] Elliott, in his sociological work on 1 Peter, makes significant comparisons between the epistle and the culture of the Qumran community, arguing for common exclusive sense of sectarian identity, defined by an 'apocalyptic dualism' which distinguishes the communities from wider society.[9] However, Balch suggests that Elliott overstates the similarity

---

6. Boring, *1 Peter*, p. 40. Cf. Kelly, *Peter*, p. 27, and Lohse, 'Päranese und Kerygma', p. 80: 'Diese Berührungen zwischen dem Abschnitt 1 Ptr 13 - 210 und den Palästinatexten, von denen wir hier einige Beispiele genannt haben, sind nun gewiß nicht auf eine direkte Übernahme durch den I Ptr zurückzuführen, sondern der I Ptr bezieht sich – wie der Vergleich mit zahlreichen Parallelen zu anderen neutestamenntlichen Schriften, insbesondere dem Jakobusbrief, zeigen kann – auf Traditionsgut das in bereits verchristlicher Gestalt aufgenommen wird.'

7. Achtemeier, *1 Peter*, p. 12.

8. Cf. Seland, 'Resident Aliens in Mission', p. 575, who notes that the focus of much of 1 Peter's paraenesis towards communal identity, even that which urges the importance of intramural love, has an outward focus upon the rest of society to whom good behaviour is a witness.

9. Elliott, *Home for the Homeless*, pp. 119–20 and 123–4.

between 1 Peter and Qumranic understandings of community because the sense of 'apocalyptic dualism' is not nearly as clear in 1 Peter as Elliott claims. For example, there is no suggestion in 1 Peter that Christians are to separate themselves from unbelievers: they are not spatially withdrawn in the sense that the Qumran community is.[10] In addition to this, Schutter claims that Elliott fails to take seriously certain texts (*1 Clem.* 1.1; Polycarp's *2 Phil.* 1.1; *Ep. Diog.* 5.5) in which language of alienation and sojourning is understood spiritually, rather than a literal expression of social identity.[11]

Lohse also makes a comparison between the identity of the Petrine and Qumran communities. In particular, he argues that the identity of the people of God as in some way set apart, chosen and holy (which is especially prominent in 1 Peter and is, as has been argued here, a feature of the way in which Scripture is interpreted in the epistle) resonates with similar ideas in the Qumran scrolls (1QpHab 10.13; 1QH 3.22; 4.25; 1QS 8.5-8).[12] Likewise, Lohse notes that the ethical use of light and darkness imagery in 1 Pet. 2.9 is similar to that in CD 6.20-21.[13]

Geza Vermes regards the exhortation of CD 1.1–8.21 as similar to use of paraenesis in 1 Peter.[14] The exhortation features paraenetic material combined with 'a theological interpretation of the history of Israel'. The use of history here is interesting in that it is primarily a source of examples demonstrating God's judgement against apostasy which functions to encourage the community in the choice they have made to be faithful in contrast to the apostate majority from whom they have disassociated themselves. To a certain extent, this is less of an eschatological view of history than one encounters elsewhere in the Qumran texts and in

10. Balch, 'Hellenization/Acculturation', pp. 83–4.
11. Schutter, *Hermeneutic and Composition*, p. 10.
12. Lohse, 'Päranese und Kerygma', pp. 78–9.
13. Lohse, 'Päranese und Kerygma', p. 79.
14. Geza Vermes, *Dead Sea Scrolls: Qumran in Perspective* (London: Collins, 1977), p. 50. Schutter, *Hermeneutic and Composition*, pp. 86–7, seems to suggest that Vermes associates the exhortation of CD with 1 Pet. 1.3–2.10 in particular, though, in fact, Vermes' suggestion is undeveloped, referring simply to the epistle in general alongside Hebrews, the Testaments of the Twelve Patriarchs and *4 Maccabees*. Whilst Schutter's criticisms are still valid, a comparison between CD and 1 Peter in general suggests a greater degree of similarity, especially in the generalised use of history to provide examples of enduring theological and paraenetic assertions, as seen in the allusions to Sarah and Noah in 1 Peter. As Schutter notes, Vermes (*The Dead Sea Scrolls in English* [Harmondsworth: Penguin, 1962], pp. 71–2) also draws attention to the similarities between 1QS and the 'Church Orders' in the *Didache*, to which 1 Peter might be compared.

1 Peter. The historical interest in CD stresses continuity, rather than climax and discontinuity.

Much of the scholarship comparing Qumran and 1 Peter focuses upon the use of Scripture. Whilst he by no means argues for literary dependence of 1 Peter upon Qumran material, Danker argues for a significant degree of similarity between the use of Scripture in 1 Pet. 1.24–2.17 and the theology of 1QH. For example, in 1QH 9.27 the בני האדם are described as characterised by עמודת העוון ומעשי הרמיה and in 1QH 4.25-27 the speaker laments his frail flesh (כי רוח בשר עבדך) and thanks God for רוח קודשך which elevated him to a position from which he can judge the treaties of frail humankind.[15] Likewise, in 1QH 18.22 the speaker tells of the divine fashioning of his spirit which has given him stability (כי אתה יצרה רוח עבדכה וכרצונכה הכיותני). According to Danker, these texts reflect the use of Isa. 40.6 and 8 in 1 Pet. 1.24-25, which is used to emphasise humankind's frailty in contrast to God's stability and, consequently, the stability his people possess.[16] Danker draws attention to similar 'stone' imagery to 1 Pet. 2.4-8 in 1QH 17.28, in which God is described as סלע עוזי, and suggests that the use of this description in contrast to frail humankind may be a similar conceptual association as that of 1 Pet. 2.2-4 which moves from 'milk' for the weak to the 'stone' of God's chosen king.[17] At the same time, the image of nurture implied in 1 Pet. 2.2 resonates with the language of 1QH 15.21, according to Danker, though in the case of the latter, it is the speaker of the *hodayah* who describes himself as the אומן of the community. Danker also relates the causal relationship between God's salvation and the purpose of his people to offer praise indicated in 1 Pet. 2.9 (ὅπως τὰς ἀρετὰς ἐξαγγείλητε τοῦ ἐκ σκότους ὑμᾶς καλέσαντος εἰς τὸ θαυμαστὸν αὐτοῦ φῶς) with 1QH 14.11.[18] However, in the latter, it is not clear that there is any sense of contingency: the 'men of God's council' do praise God but this is not

---

15. See also 1QH 5.20-21: [ומה אף ה]וא רוח בשר להבין בכול אלה ולהשכיל בסו[ד] פלאך ה[גדול ומה ילוד אשה בכול מעשיך הנוראים והוא מבנה עפר ומגבל מים א]שר עוון חטא[ה סודו ערות קלון ומ]קור [נדה ורוח נעוה משלה בו...רק בטובך יצדק איש.

16. Danker, 'Consolatory Pericope', p. 93. It must be noted that the references Danker uses are no longer those of most critical editions of 1QH. Instead, they follow the version in E. L. Sukenik, *Study of the Dead Sea Scrolls* (Jerusalem: Mosad Bialik/The Hebrew University, 1951 [Hebrew]), pp. 35–58.

17. Danker, 'Consolatory Pericope', p. 94. Cf. 1QH 5.18-19, which expresses the same sentiment without the 'stone' imagery and 11.37, אודכה אדוני כיה הייתה לי לחומת עוז. This latter image of fortification is developed wonderfully in 1QH 14.25-27: ואש[ען]באמתכה אלי כי אתה תשים סוד על סלע וכפיס על קו משפט ומשקלת א.[מת]לו[נ]טות אבני בחן לבנות עוז ללוא תתזעזע.

18. Danker, 'Consolatory Pericope', p. 98.

described as necessary feature of being one of God's people. Likewise, in 1QH 4.17 the speaker of the *hodayah* expresses his desire to praise God for his deeds but there is no sense here that God has intended the speaker for praise.[19] Finally, Danker notes a common description of suffering as a feature of God's plan for humankind in both 1 Pet. 2.9 and 1QH 7.17-18.[20] Danker's analysis of 1 Pet. 1.24–2.10 suggests a significant degree of similarity to 1QH. Whilst one might ask whether such similarity could be found with a whole range of texts from the same period, and indeed many from the Hebrew Bible itself, there is a clear affinity between the perceptions of God and of humankind in each. Whilst Danker rightly admits the implausibility of literary dependence, it might be correct to understand 1 Peter as belonging to a similar cultural milieu to 1QH.

Several scholars have noted the great similarity between the use of temple and building terminology in 1 Pet. 2.5 and 9 and certain Qumran texts. Many note the use of 'cornerstone' imagery in 1QS 8.7, whilst Gärtner draws comparison with 1QH 4, CD 3-4 and 4QpIsa[a], and Best notes the use of 'non-material' sacrifice in 4QFlor 1.6.[21]

Joseph argues that the similarity between the use of Scripture in 1 Peter and in Qumran pesharim resides in a common use of narrative.[22] Both interpret Scripture in relation to a narrative of communal identity: a narrative vision of what the community once was, what it is and shall be, and its relationship to those outside it. This certainly is a similarity between their uses of Scripture, though it is certainly not an exclusive one. Joseph also considers the narrative similarity to include a common

---

19. Something much closer to what Danker wishes to find in 1QH 14.11 is expressed in 1QH 9.28-31, a beautiful passage describing God's creation of and purpose for human language: אתה בראתה רוח בלשון ותדע דבריה ותכן פרי שפתים בטרם היותם ותשם דברים על קו ומבע רוח שפתים במדה ותוצא קוים לרזיהם ומבעי רוחות לחשבונם להודיע כבודכה ולספר נפלאותיכה בכול מעשי אצתכה ומ[שפטי צ]דקכה ולהלל שמכה בפה כול.

20. Danker, 'Consolatory Pericope', p. 96. Cf. 1QH 12.12-13.

21. Best, '1 Peter II:4-10', pp. 283–5; Bertil Gärtner, *The Temple and the Community in Qumran and the New Testament* (SNTSMS 1; Cambridge: Cambridge University Press, 1965), pp. 72–88; Georg Klinzing, *Die Umdentung die Kultus in des Qumrangemeinde und im Neuen Testament* (SUNT 7; Gottingen: Vandenhoeck & Ruprecht, 1971), p. 210; Richard Longenecker, *Biblical Exegesis in the Apostolic Period* (Grand Rapids: Eerdmans, 1975), pp. 200–204; Mbuvi, *Temple, Exile and Identity*, pp. 75–8, and Elizabeth Schüssler Fiorenza, 'Cultic Language in Qumran and the NT', *CBQ* 38 (1976), pp. 173–5. However, Fiorenza (p. 164) notes that the general membership of the Qumran community are not designated 'priests' or part of a 'priesthood'.

22. Joseph, *Narratological Reading of 1 Peter*, pp. 55–9.

narrative of salvation-historical continuity, governing both groups' relationship to Israel in the past. However, this sense of continuity is hard to establish in the case of 1 Peter, as was seen above.[23]

Osborne argues that 1 Peter understands Scripture to be written, rather than spoken.[24] Because of this, he argues that it bears a closer degree of similarity to the Qumranic use of כתב than the rabbinic אמר of the Mishnah.[25] Elliott also argues for a significant degree of similarity between the interpretation of Scripture at Qumran and its interpretation in 1 Peter, focusing particularly on the motivation, or theological hermeneutic, behind interpretation:

> The author of 1 Peter, like the early Church in general, read the prophets and the Sacred Scriptures in their entirety with the conviction that the things announced beforehand had now in these last days come to pass. This conviction the messianic sect shared with their contemporaries, the community of Qumran... The fundamental difference between these two groups, however, is that, for the Christians, Jesus as suffering and exalted Messiah constituted both the focal object of their interpretation and the prism through which the Sacred Scriptures were read. Accordingly, the Petrine author can claim that as ancient prophets inquired as to the future agent and time of salvation they were informed by 'the Spirit of Christ' who 'bore witness to the sufferings and glories destined for the Christ', none of which is stated in the OT.[26]

By far the most detailed comparison of biblical interpretation in 1 Peter and the Dead Sea Scrolls is Schutter's. Of the whole body opening of 1 Peter, Schutter writes:

> While there is thematic [similarity] there is nothing comparable to the fashion in which the OT has been used to provide [1 Pet. 1.13–2.10] with its framework, repeatedly bringing its theme to full literary expression and making explicit its indebtedness to Scripture...It is appropriate to note, however, that [1.13–2.10] does contain two literary types also

---

23. Cf. Sargent, 'Narrative Substructure of 1 Peter', pp. 1–6.
24. Osborne, 'L'Utilisation de l'Ancient Testament', p. 74.
25. In matters of exegetical style, comparison may also be drawn between the treatment of Isa. 53 in 1 Pet. 1.21-25 and the practice of redacting scriptural sources in certain Qumran texts. D. Dimant and J. Strugnell, 'The Merkabah Vision in Second Ezekiel', *RevQ* 14 (1990), pp. 331–48 (346), note that the interpretation of Ezek. 1 in 4Q385 4 features the omission of scriptural terms and their substitution with non-scriptural terms, the rewriting of the source text, interpretative additions and the interpolation of similar biblical texts. Cf. Monica Brady, 'Biblical Interpretation in the "Pseudo-Ezekiel" Fragments (4Q383-391) from Cave Four', in Henze, ed., *Biblical Interpretation at Qumran*, p. 97.
26. Elliott, *Commentary*, p. 352.

known at Qumran in which the OT figures prominently, the catena in 2.6-8 (4QTestimonia), and the florilegium of 2.3-10 (4QFlorilegium, 11QMelchizedek).[27]

Schutter argues for the thematic and exegetical similarity between some Qumran texts and 1 Pet. 1.13–2.10 but regards the closest affinity as being with the Proem form of midrashic homily.[28] Whilst this passage also bears some resemblance to 'missionary proclamation' (for which Schutter notes that there are no extant pre-Christian sources), 1QS and CD and the Philonic diatribe (*Leg. All.* 3.65-75a; *de Mut.* 253-263; *de Somn.* 2.17-30), only homiletic Midrash 'is flexible enough to accommodate the kinds of situations and materials they do' whilst featuring a more prominent structural role for scriptural citations.[29] In Schutter's analysis, the citation from Lev. 19.2 etc. in 1 Pet. 1.16 is the principal or *seder* text for the homily. The treatment of this text is expanded with the use of the secondary text from the Prophets, Isa. 40.6 and 8 in 1 Pet. 1.24-25. The principal text is echoed throughout the homily and is the subject of an iterative allusion in 1.15.[30] The holiness theme from the *seder* text is reiterated in 2.9 at the close of the 'homily'. However, it is not clear how the Stone Catena functions if the whole of 1.13–2.10 is understood as an exposition of Lev. 19.2. Where is the evidence that a

---

27. Schutter, *Hermeneutic and Composition*, p. 87.
28. Schutter, *Hermeneutic and Composition*, pp. 85–100. Cf. J. W. Bowker, 'Speeches in Acts: A Study in Proem and Yelammedenu Form', *NTS* 14 (1967), pp. 96–111, who argues that the Proem form may have influenced the form of, for example, the Pentecost Speech in Acts 2.14-36. This is a difficult argument to maintain since many of the Speeches in Acts employ barely any scriptural texts at all. Even in the case of the Pentecost Speech, Bowker is compelled to argue that the first text cited (Joel 3.1-5) is not the principal lectionary reading in contravention of the apparent norms of the Proem form. Cf. also the major study of Proem form in W. Bacher, *Die Exegetische Terminologie der jüdischen Traditionsliteratur* (Leipzig: J. C. Hinrichs, 1905).
29. Schutter, *Hermeneutic and Composition*, pp. 92–3.
30. Schutter, *Hermeneutic and Composition*, p. 93. The examples are as follows: ἀμώμου καὶ ἀσπίλου (1.19), καθαρᾶς (A, B, vg. 1.22), ἀφθάρτου (1.23), ἄδολον (2.2) which are thematic, and ἡγνικότες (1.22) and ἅγιον (2.5 and 2.9) which are regarded as *Stichwörten*. The classification of 1.15 as an iterative allusion is somewhat doubtful since it may be that the citation in the following verse is chosen in response to the paraenetic theme, rather than that 1.15 is framed to anticipate the citation. Likewise, the strategic placing of terms provides for a variety of structural suggestions. For example, Paul J. Achtemeier, '1 Peter 1.13-21', *Int* 60 (2006), pp. 306–8 (307), suggests that ἐλπίσατε and ἐλπίδα in 1.13 and 20, respectively, function as an *inclusio*. This is equally plausible, yet not compatible with Schutter's analysis, which views 1.13 simply as an introduction to the homiletic midrash.

catena of texts may inhabit the place of what is usually a third scriptural text in the proem form? In addition to this, the relationship between seder and haftarah texts is usually a literary one, constructed upon the basis of verbal similarity, yet the relationship between Lev. 19.2 and Isa. 40.6 and 8 is, at best, purely conceptual. Crucially, ἅγιον, the potential *Stichwört* identified by Schutter is absent from the secondary text. As Moyise suggests, Schutter's attempt to identify 1 Peter so closely with rabbinic exegesis can be seen as somewhat overambitious.[31] More generally, there are several significant problems with Schutter's association of 1 Peter with rabbinic homiletical Midrash. Firstly, as many have noted since Schutter's time of writing, there can be very little certainty about the nature of rabbinic teaching in the first century. For example, Gruden Holtz, in his general discussion of contemporary research on early rabbinic literature and tradition, notes that 'die Frage der Datierung rabbinischer Quellen veil von ihrer einstigen Brisanz verloren'.[32] Secondly, whilst polysemy is well-known as a feature of rabbinic scriptural interpretation,[33] 1 Peter appears to assume that scriptural texts have a single meaning related to the eschatological reality of Christ and his people. Yet, as was suggested above, scriptural determinacy is not simply assumed in 1 Peter, as it is elsewhere in the New Testament, but is asserted in 1.10-12. Determinacy is a prominent characteristic of the use of Scripture in 1 Peter and yet it is apparently unattested in extant rabbinic literature. Yet the same cannot be said of scriptural interpretation at Qumran. As will be seen below, there is some real similarity between scriptural determinacy in 1 Peter and a range of Qumran texts. Thirdly (as Woan notes in relation to midrashic assessments of the Stone Catena), in contrast to midrashic interpretation, 1 Peter displays no interest in the meaning of texts as an object of inquiry.[34] Scriptural texts are simply proofs employed in support of paraenesis and kerygma. This feature of scriptural interpretation is closely associated with Peter's assumption of scriptural determinacy. The meaning of citations is not discussed because there is no sense in which meaning is, or can be, contested.

---

31. Moyise, 'Isaiah in 1 Peter', p. 180.
32. Gruden Holtz, 'Rabbinische Literatur und Neues Testament: Alte Schwierigkeiten und neue Möglishkeiten', *ZNW* 100 (2009), pp. 173–98 (197).
33. See, e.g., the study by David Stern, 'Midrash and Indeterminacy', *CI* 15 (1988), pp. 120–39.
34. Woan, 'Psalms in 1 Peter', p. 219. Cf. Moyise, 'Isaiah in 1 Peter', p. 187.

The use of a hermeneutic of determinate meaning founded upon theological claims about the community for which interpretation is offered constitutes a significant area of similarity between the use of Scripture at Qumran and in 1 Peter. However, before this can be properly asserted as an important similarity, the nature of biblical hermeneutics at Qumran must be explored.

b. Biblical Hermeneutics in the Dead Sea Scrolls

Scholarly attention in the study of the use of Scripture at Qumran has typically focused upon the forms and styles of interpretation. These demonstrate a great deal of variety that far exceeds the quite well-known techniques of the *pesharim*.[35] However, comparatively little attention has been given to the actual hermeneutics which lead to the forms and styles of interpretation at Qumran. This is not the place to attempt to rectify that imbalance. Assessments of the biblical hermeneutics employed at Qumran suggest a strong tendency towards an eschatological and sectarian approach to biblical meaning which assumes the univocity of biblical texts.

Several recent attempts in *Dead Sea Discoveries* to define what is distinctive about the pesharim have isolated hermeneutical assumptions as the most prominent defining characteristic of the 'genre'. According to Paul Mandel,

> The particular stance of the pesher, in which current (or future) events are seen to be presaged in the biblical account, is conspicuously absent from early (Tannaitic) rabbinic exegesis, which rarely connects current or future events to biblical passages.[36]

Likewise, attempting to offer a clear definition of the pesharim that can accommodate the huge variety in exegetical techniques displayed, Robert Williamson argues that the pesharim is distinguished by an assumption that biblical texts contain mysteries 'whose secrets are revealed by God to a specially endowed interpreter within the community of interpretation through a promise related to dream interpretation'.[37] Williamson notes

---

35. George J. Brooke, *Exegesis at Qumran: 4QFlorilegium in its Jewish Context* (Sheffield: JSOT, 1985), p. 356. For a detailed study of the various exegetical 'methods' at Qumran, see Bilhah Nitzan, 'Approaches to Biblical Exegesis in Qumran Literature', in Paul et al., eds., *Emanuel*, pp. 347–65

36. Paul Mandel, 'Midrashic Exegesis and its Precedents in the Dead Sea Scrolls', *DSD* 8 (2001), pp. 149–68 (157).

37. Robert Williamson, 'Pesher: A Cognitive Model of the Genre', *DSD* 17 (2010), pp. 336–60.

4. *The Exegetical Background*

the exclusivity of the pesher hermeneutic which relates to a very elevated sense of communal identity. Similarly, A. P. Jassen defines the pesharim in relation to a common biblical hermeneutic:

> The ideological basis of the pesharim is the assumption that the ancient prophetic words do not refer to the specific points in time in which they were uttered. Rather, the words of the prophets are hidden ciphers that allude to the historical circumstances and eschatological expectations of the community of the Dead Sea Scrolls.[38]

George J. Brooke also concludes that the use of Scripture in the pesharim is sectarian. This is seen particularly in the direct application of Scripture to the community with the assumption that its meaning is obvious, perhaps because it relates back to the use of the same text in some event or debate within the community.[39]

Yet, even outside the *pesharim*, assumptions of determinate meaning and the exclusive eschatological significance of the Qumran community are clearly observable. As Geza Vermes argues, sectarian exegesis is displayed in CD 7.9-21 and 19.5-13 as scriptural texts are employed as proofs for the community's rules.[40] Similarly, the harmonisation of biblical texts in 11QT displays an assumption of interpretive authority, derived from the importance of the community for which they are interpreted.[41] The common eschatological and exegetical phrase אחרית הימים implies a future already participated in by the community and therefore

---

38. A. P. Jassen, 'The Pesharim and the Rise of Commentary in Early Jewish Scriptural Interpretation', *DSD* 19 (2012), pp. 363–98 (364). Cf. Maurya P. Horgan, *Pesharim: Qumran Interpretations of Biblical Books* (CBQMS 8; Washington: Catholic Biblical Association of America, 1979), p. 248, and Brooke, *Exegesis at Qumran*, p. 176.

39. George J. Brooke, *The Dead Sea Scrolls and the New Testament: Essays in Mutual Illumination* (London: SPCK, 2005), p. 63. Cf. David J. Chalcraft, 'The Development of Weber's Sociology of Sects: Encouraging a New Fascination', in *Sectarianism in Early Judaism: Sociological Advances* (ed. David J. Chalcraft; London: Equinox, 2007), pp. 52–73 (56–7), who notes the likelihood that individual community members feel the need to prove their conformity with the ideals of the sect, demonstrating their elect status. This may extend to accepting communal interpretations of Scripture.

40. Geza Vermes, 'Biblical Proof-Texts in Qumran Literature', *JSS* 34 (1989), pp. 493–508 (499). Cf. idem, 'Bible Interpretation at Qumran', *ErIsr* 20 (1989), pp. 184–91 (188), where Vermes argues that Qumranic biblical interpretation is characterized by an aggressive association of biblical texts with contemporary events.

41. Jacob Milgrom, 'Qumran's Biblical Hermeneutics: The Case of the Wood Offering', *RevQ* 16 (1994), pp. 449–56.

witnesses to a direct application of scriptural texts to events which are contemporary to the Qumran community at the point when interpretation takes place.[42] Likewise, the application of the status of 'temple' to the community in 1QH 4 and CD A 4 is 'rooted in the community's apocalyptic understanding of salvation history'.[43]

Whilst several of the exegetical middoth employed in early rabbinic biblical interpretation are employed in legal texts from Qumran and a variety of interpretations are acknowledged, legal texts such as 4QHalakha A differ significantly from interpretation in the Talmud.[44] Rather than presenting a variety of possible interpretations, legal material at Qumran attempts to identify an authoritative correct interpretation. Because of this, polysemy is admitted as a possibility, but not a necessary feature of biblical meaning, nor is it affirmed. It is never the intention in Qumranic legal material to allow members of the community to choose from a range of interpretive possibilities held by notable named interpreters. A determinate and sectarian focus for interpretation can also be seen in 1QapGen. Craig A. Evans notes that the interpretation of Abraham in 1QapGen casts the character purely as an exemplar (aimed at the community) of the qualities the community values.[45] Evans draws attention to the apologetic lengths to which the author of 1QapGen goes in order to ensure that Abraham serves this function despite his obvious flaws within the biblical narrative.

James C. VanderKam examines the apparent purposes for which Scripture is interpreted in Qumran texts and divides the use of Scripture into the following categories:

a. To inform/instruct
   1. About the meaning of a word or words
   2. About proper teachings

---

42. Annette Steudal, 'אחרית הימים in the Texts from Qumran', *RevQ* 16 (1993), pp. 225–8. Cf. Brooke, *Exegesis at Qumran*, p. 176.

43. Fiorenza, 'Cultic Language', p. 163.

44. Moshe J. Bernstein and Shlomo A. Koyfman, 'The Interpretation of Biblical Law in the Dead Sea Scrolls: Forms and Method', in Henze, ed., *Biblical Interpretation at Qumran*, pp. 75–87. In 4QHalakha A, for example, a variety of possible interpretations are not discussed but legal material is interpreted as though possessing a single meaning, presented as a natural extension of the law. Cf. J. M. Baumgarten, '4QHalakaha, the Law of Hadash, and the Pentecontad Calendar', *JJS* 27 (1976), pp. 36–46.

45. Craig A. Evans, 'Abraham in the Dead Sea Scrolls: A Man of Faith and Failure', in *The Bible at Qumran: Text, Shape, and Interpretation* (ed. Peter W. Flint; SDSSRL; Grand Rapids: Eerdmans, 2001), pp. 149–57.

b. To encourage by noting predictions
      1. Of the community and its leaders
      2. Of their opponents
      3. Of the triumph of the righteous at the end
   c. To warn
      1. Of the consequences for disobedience
      2. Of judgment on their opponents.[46]

Each of these purposes for interpretation displays a hermeneutic which views Scripture as referring directly to the communities either as prediction or instruction/warning. This is not a hermeneutic exclusive to the *pesharim*. However, whilst biblical interpretation at Qumran is characterised by a hermeneutic of determinate meaning, does biblical interpretation always display this hermeneutic? Several scholars suggest that some degree of polysemy or multivalent meaning is occasionally indicated at Qumran. For example, Shani Berrin argues that 4Q252 (4QcommGen A) interprets material from Genesis both by offering it as a rewritten narrative of persons and events in the past, as well as by interpreting it eschatologically in Colossians 5.[47] She suggests that this indicates an assumption of two types of meaning, comparable to the amoraic *petira*:

> Qumran *pesher* and the amoraic *petira* share another significant feature: a sense of the multivalence of biblical text. Whereas the Tannaitic עליו מפרש sought to provide the literal meaning of a univalent biblical text, and early Christian contemporizing exegesis provided allegorical interpretations of a biblical text that was viewed as devoid of literal meaning, Qumran *pesher* and the amoraic *petira* would have operated on the assumption of a multivalent biblical text possessing both literal and non-literal meanings.
>
> This understanding of pesher would be consistent with what is known about the Qumran community's approach to halakic exegesis. At Qumran, halakah is seen as twofold, with the *nigleh* and the *nistar* both firmly rooted in the Hebrew Bible, each in its own way.[48]

---

46. James C. VanderKam, 'To What End? Functions of Scriptural Interpretation in Qumran Writings', in *Studies in the Hebrew Bible, Qumran, and the Septuagint Presented to Eugene Ulrich* (ed. Peter W. Flint, Emanuel Tov and James C. VanderKam; Leiden: Brill, 2006), pp. 302–20 (311).

47. Shani Berrin, 'Qumran Pesharim', in *Biblical Interpretation at Qumran* (ed. Matthias Henze; SDSSRL; Grand Rapids: Eerdmans, 2005), pp. 110–33 (130).

48. Berrin, 'Qumran Pesharim', p. 132. Cf. L. H. Silberman, 'Unriddling the Riddle: A Study in the Structure and Language of the Habakkuk Pesher', *RevQ* 3 (1961–62), pp. 323–64; Collins, *Apocalyptic Imagination*, pp. 51–2; A. Finkel, 'The Pesher of Dreams and Scriptures', *RevQ* 4 (1963–64), pp. 364–70, and Isaac Rabinowitz, 'Pesher/Pittaron: Its Biblical Meaning and Significance in the Qumran

However, just as it is difficult to classify much scriptural interpretation in the New Testament as 'allegorical' (with the notable exception of Gal. 4.21-26), it is not at all clear that the authors of the *pesharim* would have conceived of their interpretations as 'non-literal'. As far as they were concerned, much of biblical literature was *actually* about the situations in which they, the Qumran community, found themselves. Whilst modern readers of biblical literature might be able to discern this type of meaning as non-literal, in that it could not represent the historical intentions of, for example, the author of Habakkuk, it does not appear to be likely that exegetes at Qumran would have made this distinction.

c. Determinate Meaning at Qumran and in 1 Peter

The use of Scripture in 1 Peter and at Qumran reflects a common sectarian matrix.[49] Longenecker argues that 1 Pet. 1.10-12 betrays a hermeneutic typical of the *pesherim*.[50] He claims that 1 Peter witnesses to biblical interpretation of this sort more than any other book of the New Testament and that 1.10-12 reflects the important notions of 'mystery' and 'interpretation' as it depicts the prophetic search for the meaning of their words and the subsequent revelation of the Holy Spirit. He argues that this hermeneutic is employed in the interpretation of Isa. 40.6 and 8 in 1 Pet. 1.25 with the simple and unambiguous interpretative statement, 'this is the word that was proclaimed to you'.

Another possible hermeneutic similarity between 1 Peter and Qumran is the use of internal interpretation: where Scripture is explained from the perspective of someone who inhabits the text and speaks with its voice. This can be clearly seen in legal examples of 'rewritten Bible', such as 11QT 48.7-11, argue Moshe J. Bernstein and Shlomo A. Koyfman.[51]

Literature', *RevQ* 8 (1973), pp. 213–32. Mandel, 'Midrashic Exegesis', pp. 163–68, suggests that the Tannaitic עליו מפרש is a reaction to the eschatological interpretation of Qumran and the New Testament.

49. Timothy H. Lim, *Pesharim* (CQS 3; London: Sheffield Academic, 2002), pp. 83–5, argues that whilst the formal similarity between the *pesharim* and the use of Scripture in the New Testament is not significant, both sets of texts belong to a 'common sectarian matrix' which distinguishes them from the mainstream of Second Temple Judaism. This common sectarian approach to Scripture is seen in the use of some of the same scriptural texts in both the *pesharim* and the New Testament (Isa. 54.11-12; Deut. 21.22-23; and Hab. 2.1-4). Cf. George J. Brooke, 'Thematic Commentaries on Prophetic Scriptures', in Henze, ed., *Biblical Interpretation at Qumran*, p. 138, and the use of the sectarian Samaritan Pentateuch in 4QTest and 4QpaleoExod^m.

50. Longenecker, *Biblical Exegesis*, p. 201.

51. Bernstein and Koyfman, 'Interpretation of Biblical Law', p. 68.

4. The Exegetical Background 161

Here, a quotation from Deut. 14.1 is supplemented with Lev. 19.28 before reference to Deut. 14.2 is resumed. The integration of sources, such as this, which do not display an obvious verbal or conceptual relation to each other, demonstrates a perspective of assumed insight in which the author does not claim to be interpreting Scripture at all. One can see this form of internal interpretation in the use of Isaiah 53 in 1 Pet. 2.21-25 which features source integration and interpolation of the author's own words.

However, it is the relation between biblical material and the communities for which it is interpreted that reveals the greatest area of similarity. Brooke, in his analysis of 4QTestimonia, argues that each biblical reference is taken to be prophetic, whether they were written to be so or not.[52] He notes that the 'Song of Moses is to be understood as an unfulfilled blessing of eschatological significance' and that each text is oriented towards an eschatological struggle. He suggests that the fourth excerpt, taken from the Apocryphon of Joshua (4Q378 and 4Q379) is regarded as an unfulfilled curse on 'a man of Belial': 'In all likelihood the person who put the extracts together in this single column understood the texts as belonging to the latter days, the period running up to the eschaton, a period which had already begun in the experiences of the community'.[53] This assumption that more texts than simply the biblical Prophets are 'prophetic' (that, in a sense, all of Scripture is oriented towards the eschatological community), resembles the use of the titles for Israel in 1 Pet. 2.5 and 9.

Perhaps the most striking similarity, which has been noted by the majority of scholars commenting on 1 Pet. 1.10-12, is the 'theory of prophecy' in 1 Peter and in 1QpHab 7.1-10. The assumption made in 1QpHab is that Habakkuk is a prophecy as yet unfulfilled, directed towards the experience of the community.[54] It is apocalyptic in style and assumes that the prophetic witness only has significance as a referent to the time of the eschatological community.[55] Both 1 Peter and 1QpHab

---

52. Brooke, 'Thematic Commentaries', pp. 139–40.
53. Cf. Brooke, *Exegesis at Qumran*, p. 309.
54. J. G. Harris, *The Qumran Commentary on Habakkuk* (London: Mowbray, 1966), pp. 47-8.
55. One possible difference between the scriptural hermeneutics at work in the Qumran scrolls and in 1 Peter is the conception of the Prophets of Israel's past. In 1 Pet. 1.10-12 the Prophets are given an apparently subordinate status to the communities addressed by the epistle since they are seen as both ignorant of the precise meaning of the utterances and the servants of the communities of the eschatological age. Alex P. Jassen, 'The Presentation of the Ancient Prophets as Lawgivers at

demonstrate a hermeneutic which functions upon a theological assumption concerning the importance of their communities in salvation history.[56]

3. Conclusion

Again, there is no indication that 1 Peter is dependent upon Qumran literature in any way. Indeed, other than the use of a *Stichwört* in the Stone Catena and the rewriting of Isaiah 53 in 2.21-25, there is very little formal similarity. The real similarity between biblical interpretation in 1 Peter and Qumran is hermeneutical. Both witness explicitly (in 1QpHab 7.1-10 and 1 Pet. 1.10-12) and implicitly (in their treatment of Scripture) to a conception of scriptural prophecy as mystery with a single eschatological referent related to events of significance to their communities. Both demonstrate an elevated and exclusivist view of their communities within salvation history, because of which the eschatological hermeneutic is not only justified, but becomes obvious: given the presumed importance of the communities and the events unfolding around them, how could prophecy refer to anything else? Of course, this eschatological 'ecclesiology' is more pronounced in 1 Peter. Whereas Qumran teaching typically regards the community as the contemporary expression of faithful Israel over and against the faithless majority, 1 Peter places its communities in a position of eschatological superiority over Israel in the past. It is, after all, the eschatological community whose baptism is anticipated in the Flood, whom the Prophets wrote to serve and who have known the message of Christ – once hidden but now revealed – into which the angels long to look.

Qumran', *JBL* 127 (2008), pp. 307–37, notes that whilst the sense in which contemporary communities exist at a climactic high point in salvation history is common in the scrolls, this elevation does not necessarily imply a diminished status for those in Israel's past, such as the Prophets. In contrast to 1 Peter, the Prophets are often regarded as having a significant status as lawgivers. For example, in 1QS 1.2-3 and 4QMMT C 31 the Prophets are seen to have a status similar to that of Moses. In addition to this, their message is understood to have as much meaning in the past as it does for the contemporary community as in 4QpHos[a] 2.1-6

56. Travis B. Williams, 'Ancient Prophets and Inspired Exegetes: Interpreting Prophetic Scripture in 1QpHab and 1 Peter', in du Toit, ed., *Bedrängnis und Identität*, pp. 223–46, extends this apparent similarity by arguing that both 1 Pet. 1.10-12 and 1QpHab share a common 'charismatic' understanding of the interpreter of Scripture. However, it is not at all clear that 1 Peter asserts a conscious notion of its own author's identity or role in scriptural interpretation.

The use of Scripture in 1 Peter can best be described as 'sectarian' because, not only does it interpret Scripture as though it plainly refers to the community (which is certainly not an unusual approach), but because a theological rationale is provided to justify the exclusive reference of Scripture to the community. Determinate meaning, premised on a claim to the eschatological significance of the community, is a feature of scriptural hermeneutics both in 1 Peter and at Qumran and must be regarded as a well-defined sectarian approach to Scripture.

Because determinate meaning in 1 Peter is grounded upon a theological narrative explaining the communities' eschatological significance (which must have been held by both author and audiences, since it is expressed purely as substructure), Scripture is interpreted as though its meaning is straightforward and unambiguous. When considering the development of early Christian biblical interpretation, the hermeneutic employed in 1 Peter must be regarded as primitive, as representing a very early stage in this development.

In many ways, the approach to Scripture in 1 Peter bears much closer comparison with the treatment of Scripture within the Pauline Corpus, as understood by Richard B. Hayes.[57] According to Hayes' analysis, Paul's hermeneutic focuses Scripture upon the eschatological community. In a manner similar to 1 Peter, Paul offers little or no explanation of how scriptural texts mean what he says they mean. Whilst Paul uses typological and allegorical interpretation (once), his general use of Scripture assumes determinate meaning. However, unlike Hayes' assessment of Paul, the use of Scripture in 1 Peter does not appear to display a sophisticated understanding of the context of a scriptural reference, nor is there a suggestion that such context influences the way Peter interprets his references.[58] In this sense, Peter is more 'primitive' than Paul.

* * *

Excursus: The Use of Scripture in 1 Peter and the Letter's Historical Setting

An understanding of the use of Scripture in 1 Peter as primitive and sectarian may help to shed some light on some of the more difficult historical issues relating to the study of the epistle: historical setting and authorship. As Michaels argues, there can never be any certainty about the authorship of 1 Peter since too little is known about

---

57. Hayes, *Echoes of Scripture*, pp. 165–8.
58. Cf. Danker, 'Consolatory Pericope', p. 101, who argues that because 1 Peter appears to know the contexts of its biblical citations and does not use testimonia collections, it cannot be Petrine.

the time and circumstances of the apostle Peter's death and the situation in which the epistle was written.[59] Similarly, there is no clear agreement on the time of writing and historical situation, though some suggestions have been more persuasive than others. The only significant evidence upon which to decide these issues is internal to 1 Peter, though how such internal characteristics relate to what is known about the probable historical period in and for which 1 Peter was composed is open to question.

Often the relative sophistication (or lack of sophistication) of the epistle is seen to provide evidence in favour of certain theses regarding authorship and setting. In early critical work on 1 Peter, the Greek style of the epistle was regarded as relatively sophisticated. Bigg wrote that

> The writer of the Epistle was probably unable to produce such work as we see in the highly finished preface to St. Luke's Gospel. Nevertheless he was quite awake to the difference between good Greek and bad, and used the language with freedom and a not inconsiderable degree of correctness.[60]

A perception of 1 Peter's style as sophisticated is a significant factor in the rejection of Petrine authorship by many scholars.[61] The assumption here is that the historical Peter, as a former Galilean fisherman, would be incapable of producing Greek of such high quality. Selwyn also claims that the Greek style of 1 Peter is relatively sophisticated:

> Its style is not only natural and unforced, indicating that it belongs to one who not only wrote, but also thought, in Greek; but it exhibits a felicity of phrase, a suppleness of expression, and a wealth of vocabulary which betoken a mind nourished in the best Greek thought and tradition.[62]

---

59. Michaels, *1 Peter*, pp. lxvi–lxvii. Michaels concludes that there are no entirely robust reasons, in particular, for rejecting Petrine authorship. Hillyer, *1 and 2 Peter*, pp. 1–3, shares this view.

60. Bigg, *St. Peter and St. Jude*, p. 5. Bigg's evidence for this claim (pp. 4–5) is the refined Greek style in 1.19, 2.16 and 3.7, seen in the use of the comparative ὡς. Whilst the construction ὡς ἀμνοῦ ἀμώμου καὶ ἀσπίλου Χριστοῦ in 1.19 is unusual in place of Χριστοῦ at the end of the clause, as it is the subject of the comparison, Bigg notes that this form is used in Plato, *Laws* 905B, Josephus, *Ant.* 18.9.5 and Heb. 7.7 and should not necessarily be thought of as bad style. He also notes that the use of the article in 1 Peter is rather more classical than other New Testament texts (drawing a comparison with Thucydides) even though it is often omitted entirely. This is especially the case when a noun is used with another as an attributive genitive as in 1.2, 3, 7 etc. In addition to this, Bigg notes that 1 Peter follows the New Testament habit of employing μή where οὐ is expected, though the use of οὐκ ἰδόντες in 1.8 is correct.

61. Including, Schutter, *Hermeneutic and Composition*, pp. 5–6, and Boring, *1 Peter*, pp. 30–1, who both regard the presence of citations from the LXX to distance the letter from an historical apostle Peter.

62. Selwyn, *Peter*, p. 25.

4. The Exegetical Background

As evidence of this, Selwyn notes Peter's use of compound words such as ἀνεκλάλητος, the 'massing of phrases' in 2.4-10, the use of balanced cadences such as ὑμῶν τὴν ἀγαθὴν ἐν Χριστῷ ἀναστροφήν, the use of metaphor and simple phrases.[63] Though Selwyn possibly overstates his case, it is clear that the Greek of 1 Peter is sophisticated in comparison with other New Testament literature, particularly that which is widely thought to be the work of authors whose primary language was not Greek. However, this analysis is contradicted by the important study by L. Radermacher which documents many of the grammatical and stylistic weaknesses of 1 Peter.[64] Likewise, Jobes assesses the Greek syntax of 1 Peter using R. A. Martin's seventeen syntactical criteria and suggests that 1 Peter exhibits a strong degree of Semitic 'bilingual interference' when compared with Polybius and, more surprisingly, Josephus.[65] This analysis makes authorship by an individual who originally, like the historical Peter, spoke or wrote in a Semitic language plausible.

Of course, the language of 1 Peter provides less of an obstacle to Petrine authorship of the letter if one ascribes, as Selwyn does, a significant creative role to Silvanus as an amanuensis.[66] Selwyn argues that Silvanus may have possessed a significant ability to communicate well in Greek and may have played the dominant role in composing 1 Peter, noting the use of διὰ λόγου πολλοῦ in Acts 15.27 and the similarly extensive use of παρακαλεῖν and στηρίζειν in both this passage and 1 Peter and the Thessalonian correspondence with which Silvanus is associated.[67] However, the current view is that, if Silvanus was involved at all, his most likely role is that of a courier.[68] Brox argues that the reference to Silvanus should be understood as equivalent to the similar references to the carriers in the letters of Ignatius.[69] However, as Seland points out, the use of διὰ...ἔγραψα in Ignatius is far from clear and does not necessarily relate simply to the carrying of a letter.[70]

Beare maintains the earlier critical position that the epistle is pseudonymous with a significant literary dependence upon Pauline material.[71] However, Elliott notes that

---

63. Selwyn, *Peter*, p. 26.
64. L. Radermacher, 'Der 1 Petrusbrief und Silvanus', *ZNW* 25 (1926), pp. 287–95.
65. Achtemeier, *1 Peter*, p. 4; Jobes, *1 Peter*, p. 325.
66. Selwyn, *Peter*, p. 12. Cf. Reicke, *Peter*, p. 70; Cranfield, *Peter*, p. 7, and Kelly, *Peter*, pp. 214–15, who regards Silvanus as too prominent a figure to have merely been a courier, as argued by Michaels, *1 Peter*, p. 307. Sargent, 'Chosen through Sanctification', pp. 117–20, argues that Silvanus' own diction is displayed in the phrase ἐν ἁγιασμῷ πνεύματος in relation to election in 1 Pet. 1.2. The only other New Testament example of this phrase is found in 2 Thess. 2.13, also in relation to election and also thought to have been composed with Silvanus as amanuensis.
67. Cf. Kelly, *Peter*, p. 33.
68. E. Randolph Richards, 'Silvanus Was Not Peter's Secretary: Theological Bias in Interpreting διὰ Σιλουανοῦ...ἔγραψα in 1 Peter 5.12', *JETS* 43 (2000), pp. 417–32, and Earl, 'Functional Christology', p. 122.
69. Brox, *Petrusbrief*, pp. 240–3.
70. Seland, *Strangers in the Light*, pp. 24–5.
71. Beare, *Peter*, p. 44, makes a great deal of the apparent animosity between the historical Peter and Paul, suggesting that Peter would not have wanted to indicate

much of what Beare regards as demonstrating literary dependence may suggest instead a literary affinity, which implies quite a different relationship between 1 Peter and the Pauline corpus:

> Literary affinity must be distinguished from literary dependence. Beare has noted the former but has not proved the latter. Furthermore, the close relationship between 1 Peter, Ephesians and Romans, in particular, requires a totally fresh assessment. If literary dependence between 1 Peter and Ephesians is conceivable, then a stronger case could be made for the priority of 1 Peter than vice versa. In the case of Romans the question must be asked whether the author of 1 Peter was dependent less on a letter of *Paul* than on a cherished document of the *Roman community* from which he wrote. The influence, then, would be more Roman than Pauline.[72]

It may be accurate to describe early critical work on the authorship of 1 Peter as being too ambitious, claiming a knowledge or familiarity with early Christianity, as well as with the historical Peter, which scholars in the twentieth and twenty-first centuries do not have. For instance, such scholars were too ready to draw relationships between 1 Peter and known events and texts of the early Christian period, as if such events and texts were as significant then as they are perceived to be now. This can be seen both in the readiness of scholars to suggest close literary relationships between extant texts (whilst ignoring the possible role of texts which are no longer available) and can be seen in the association of the text with well-known possible historical contexts (ignoring the possibility that 1 Peter may have originated in a now-obscure context). Best, Brown, Spicq, Gundry and Elliott moved the discussion away from direct literary dependence upon a known New Testament author to the possibility of early traditions which may have been a common influence upon both 1 Peter and other extant early Christian literature.[73] Within this context, the issue of

---

literary dependence on Paul. Furthermore, Beare suggests that the historical Peter's teaching would reflect more of Jesus' own language and teaching than 1 Peter apparently does.

72. Elliott, 'Exegetical Step-Child', pp. 7–8. Cf. Lohse, 'Päranese und Kerygma', pp. 70–1. Michaels, *1 Peter*, pp. xliii–xliv presents a very clear case for dismissing any attempt to claim the literary dependence of 1 Peter upon any extant material. Likewise, Snodgrass, 'I Peter II. 1-10', pp. 100–101, notes that in the case of the Stone Catena, Peter could only be said to be dependent upon Rom. 9 if it could be believed that he disentangled the conflated form of texts used and that, in many ways, the catena could just as easily be dependent upon Eph. 2.14-22. Cf. Dodd, *According to the Scriptures*, p. 43, and Hillyer, 'Rock-Stone', p. 62.

73. Cf. Best, *1 Peter*, pp. 36–45, and Achtemeier, '1 Peter 1.13-21', p. 306, who refers to popular persecution from a 'radically conformist society'. This is one of the great reversals of scholarly opinion so common in New Testament studies. In suggesting our relative ignorance of persecutions of early Christians, Elliott and others were simply repeating the cautionary line taken by Hort, *St Peter*, p. 1: 'Now what persecution can this have been? Here we have to bear in mind the extreme slenderness and incompleteness of all our knowledge about early persecutions. It is quite possible, nay one may even say probable, that we have no other record of those

authorship assumed a secondary importance, supplanted by the desire to identify traditions.[74]

At the same time, Elliot notes that scholars such as Beare attributed a great degree of significance to the term πυρώσις in 1 Pet. 4.12 as a means of establishing the historical setting of 1 Peter.[75] According to Elliott, attempts to relate 1 Peter to a context such as the imperial persecution of the Emperors Nero, Vespasian, Domitian or Trajan,[76] ignore the more likely possibility that the term reflects a more commonplace, local hostility, rather than a known and widespread persecution.[77]

particular troubles which called forth our Epistle.' Hort goes on (p. 4) to note that the positive way in which 1 Peter refers to the ruling authorities makes it quite unlikely that the epistle could have originated at a time of state-sponsored persecution, particular during one associated with a Roman Emperor such as Trajan, Nero or Domitian.

74. Lohse, 'Päranese und Kerygma', p. 83.

75. Elliott, *Commentary*, pp. 98–101, and Schelkle, *Petrusbriefe*, p. 9. Cf. Beare, *Peter*, p. 33 who also compares 1 Pet. 4.15 with the accusations against Christians in Pliny, *Ep.* 96.7 (Adfirmabant autem hanc fuisse summam vel culpae suae vel erroris, quod essent soliti stato die ante lucem convenire, catmenque Christo quasi deo dicere secum invicem seque sacramento non in scelus aliquod obstringere, sed ne furta ne latrociania ne adulteria committerent). Beare, *Peter*, pp. 26–8, follows Perdelwitz and Windisch in seeing 4.12 as originating with a different hand due to its apparently simpler Greek style and apparently greater specificity regarding persecution. Like them, he argues that the earlier material in 1.3–4.11 was 'published' when the need arose which is indicated in 4.12-19. Priesker, writing in the third edition of Windisch's commentary, adds to this view by asserting that 1.3–4.11 is the baptismal liturgy in which future suffering is warned of as a consequence of the profession taking place during the rite and 4.12-19 is addressed to those who, having been baptised, are now facing the reality of persecution. Cf. C. F. D. Moule, 'The Nature and Purpose of 1 Peter', *NTS* 3 (1956), pp. 1–11 (7), who, arguing that 1 Peter is a genuine letter, suggests that the two parts of the epistle are addressed to different audiences within the same community.

76. For Neronic persecution, see Cranfield, *Peter*, 17, and John A. T. Robinson, *Redating the New Testament* (Philadelphia: Westminster, 1976), p. 157. For a setting during the reign of Vespasian, see William M. Ramsey, *The Church in the Roman Empire Before A.D. 170* (London: Hodder & Stoughton, 1893), p. 282 who, whilst maintaining Petrine authorship, attempts to evade the suggestion of Peter's martyrdom in the Neronic persecution in Tertullian, *Scorpiace* 15, by noting the tradition, attested in Tertullian, *De Praescr. Haer.* 32, that Clement was ordained by Peter later than this persecution. Hence, Peter's martyrdom and the composition of 1 Peter must have taken place during the continued Neronic policy of persecution under Vespasian. For persecution during the reign of Trajan, see Beare, *Peter*, pp. 32–3.

77. Elliott, 'Exegetical Step-Child', pp. 13–14; Achtemeier, *1 Peter*, pp. 28–36, and Hillyer, *1 and 2 Peter*, p. 5. At the same time, Richard, 'Functional Christology', p. 126, rejects the common Trajanic persecution background theory as dependent on too late a date for 1 Peter. He suggests that one would expect to see some indication of structured and organised ministry (akin to that of Ignatius of Antioch's letters) or

This view is taken by Moule, Kelly and Best.[78] Schutter similarly rejects the association of 1 Peter with an 'official' persecution, but argues instead that persecution may have come in the form of criminal proceedings instigated by members of the public hostile to the communities, noting the possibly forensic meaning of ἀπολογίαν in 1 Pet. 3.15.[79] However, Lohse suggests that attempts to relate 1 Peter to unknown events or traditions must be undertaken with caution since such attempts require a significant degree of speculation.[80]

So what might be the implications of this study of the use of Scripture in 1 Peter for the debates surrounding the authorship and historical setting of the letter? In many ways, a study such as this can add little to these discussions since there is still too little historical information about the apostle Peter (and other possible authors) and the contexts of early Christianity to offer anything more than tentative suggestions. However, whilst the degree of sophistication of the Greek style of 1 Peter is unclear, the use of Scripture is less so. The 'primitive' and 'sectarian' features of the epistle's interpretation of Scripture strongly suggest that it originated within the first decades of the Christian church. There is none of the exegetical sophistication seen in the Epistle to the Hebrews, *1 Clement* or Justin Martyr. Scripture is not read allegorically, nor is there any awareness that interpretation might be contested. Instead, Scripture is applied directly and simply to the communities which the author

---

else a less primitive eschatology than the imminent expectation of the parousia indicated in 1 Peter if the letter belonged to that period. Instead, 1 Peter's optimism about the secular authorities places it alongside Luke–Acts, in terms of dating, Richard suggests. Talbert, 'The Plan of 1 Peter', p. 145, notes that it is not possible to associate 1 Peter with any single known period of persecution, however he does attempt to define the particular social attitudes which may have lead to the persecution suggested in 1 Peter. Talbert draws attention to the known opinion of several early Roman and Hellenistic writers that betrayal of inherited values and religion is socially destructive. Cicero, *De Legibus* 2.19, reads: 'Ad divos adeunto caste, pietatem adhibento, opes amovento. Qui secus faxit, deus ipse vindex erit. Separatim nemo habessit deos neve novos neve advenas nisi publice adscitos; privatim colunto quos rite a patribus cultos acceperint. in urbibus delubra habento. Lucos in agris habento et Larum sedes. Ritus familiae patrumque servanto. Divos et eos qui caelestes semper habiti sunt colunto et ollos quos endo caelo merita locaverint, Herculem, Liberum, Aesculapium, Castorem, Pollucem, Quirinum, ast olla propter quae datur homini ascensus in caelum, Mentem, Virtutem, Pietatem, Fidem, earumque laudum delubra sunto, nec ulla vitiorum sacra sollemnia obeunto.' Cf. Plutarch, *Amatorius* 756. A-B, D and Tacitus, *Historiae* 5.5. Likewise, Cranfield, *Peter*, p. 8, argues that 1 Pet. 4.16 does not imply that Christian faith is illegal: a common assumption made by advocates of a Trajanic *Sitz im Leben*.

78. Moule, 'Purpose of 1 Peter', p. 9; Best, *1 Peter*, pp. 39–42, and Kelly, *Peter*, pp. 29–30.

79. Schutter, *Hermeneutic and Composition*, pp. 14–15. Cf. Kelly, *Peter*, pp. 28–9.

80. Lohse, 'Päranese und Kerygma', p. 72: 'Gegen ein solches konstruktives Verfahren werden immer gewichtige Einwendungen zu erheben sein, weil man sich dabei zu leicht auf das Gebiet von nicht beweisbaren Hypothesen begibt'.

sees as of such significance. The character of this sectarian exegesis, with its eschatological hermeneutic, as has been argued above, resembles the scriptural hermeneutic witnessed in many of the Qumran texts and belongs to a broader apocalyptic Jewish milieu. This suggests that 1 Peter belongs to quite an early period within the development of the primitive Church. As noted above, the approach to Scripture in 1 Peter bears much closer comparison with the treatment of Scripture within the Pauline Corpus, as understood by Richard B. Hayes.[81]

---

81. *Contra* David G. Horrell, 'The Product of a Petrine Circle? A Reassessment of the Origin and Character of 1 Peter', *JSNT* 86 (2002), pp. 29–60.

Chapter 5

1 PETER AND THEOLOGICAL INTERPRETATION
OF SCRIPTURE

The crisis in biblical studies regarding appropriate methodology has long been observed by both biblical scholars and theologians:

> Historical criticism…comprises the congeries of well-known methods such as source criticism, form criticism, grammatical studies, and archaeology, and it attempts to combine them in ways that will produce assured and agreed-on interpretations of the biblical text, whether these be understood as the author's intention, the understanding of the original audiences, or reference to actual historical events.
>
> Postmodernism is characterized by diversity in both method and content and by an anti-essentialist emphasis that rejects the idea that there is a final account, an assured and agreed-on interpretation, of some one thing… What unites this methodological jumble is agreement that no final or essential interpretation of the text is being produced. Other readings are always possible, and often invited.[1]

At the heart of the crisis is the question of how Christian theology, in the broadest sense, relates to other disciplines in the secular university. The fact that many who are interested in the use of Scripture in 1 Peter will not be interested in a discussion of theological hermeneutics in relation to that subject (and indeed may question the place of a more 'theological' chapter in a piece of New Testament research), reveals the depth of this crisis.[2] For the most part, the tendency to view biblical studies as a scientific discipline, employing strict historiographical criteria derived from Enlightenment rationalism, is no longer as obvious. As in other

---

1. George Aichele, Peter Miscall and Richard Walsh, 'An Elephant in the Room: Historical-Critical and Postmodern Interpretations of the Bible', *JBL* 128 (2009), pp. 383–404 (383–4). Cf. B. H. McLean, 'The Crisis of Historicism: And the Problem of Historical Meaning in New Testament Studies', *HeyJ* 53 (2012), pp. 217–40.

2. Cf. Werner G. Jeanrond, 'After Hermeneutics: The Relationship between Theology and Biblical Studies', in *The Open Text: New Directions for Biblical Studies?* (ed. Francis Watson; London: SCM, 1993), pp. 88–9.

disciplines, the methods of modernity are increasingly seen to be philosophically bankrupt: belonging to an age whose claims to progress and neutrality now appear naive and even foolish. In this broader context, biblical scholars and (perhaps more so) theologians have felt at liberty to reconsider the nature of biblical scholarship in new (or more often, old) ways. Behind many recent attempts to redefine methodology in Biblical Studies is the scandal of historical criticism's debt to a philosophy which can be regarded as utterly hostile to theological accounts of both the world as well as the text as revelatory Scripture. This can be seen in statements of the Pontifical Biblical Institute, through to Post-Liberal and Radical Orthodox theology, and right through the broad discipline of Theological Interpretation of Scripture.[3] Each of these approaches or schools share a common aim to re-conceive biblical interpretation as a Christian endeavour, shaped by the history, traditions and values of Christian doctrine.

In the attempt to redefine biblical hermeneutics after the apparent fall of historical criticism, scholars who wish to understand it as a specifically Christian theological enterprise have typically found inspiration in the great traditions of the Church's biblical interpretation prior to the Enlightenment. However, this has rarely featured an engagement with the earliest Christian biblical interpretation witnessed in the use of Scripture in the New Testament. Perhaps surprisingly, then, 1 Peter (and 1 Pet. 1.10-12 in particular) has featured in some discussions of biblical hermeneutics. This chapter will explore some of these discussions before developing an argument that the assumption of the determinate meaning of Scripture in 1 Peter, being derived from a theological account of the status of the scattered communities, offers inspiration towards a reconsideration of determinacy in contemporary biblical hermeneutics.

---

3. See, e.g., Benjamin N. Wambacq, 'Instructio de Historica Evangeliorum Veritate', *CBQ* 26 (1964), pp. 306–7; Rowan Williams, 'Historical Criticism and Sacred Text', in *Reading Texts, Seeking Wisdom* (ed. David E. Ford and Graham Stanton; London: SCM, 2003), pp. 217–28; George A. Lindbeck, 'Postcritical Canonical Interpretation: Three Modes of Retrieval', in *Theological Exegesis: Essays in Honor of Brevard S. Childs* (ed. Kathryn Green-McCreight and Christopher Seitz; Grand Rapids: Eerdmans, 1999), pp. 46–9; John Milbank, 'Knowledge: The Theological Critique of Philosophy in Hamann and Jacobi', in *Radical Orthodoxy: A New Theology* (ed. John Milbank, Catherine Pickstock and Graham Ward; London: Routledge, 1999), pp. 21–37; Daniel J. Treier, 'What Is Theological Interpretation? An Ecclesiastical Reduction', *IJST* 12 (2010), pp. 144–61, and Christopher R. Seitz, *Word Without End: The Old Testament as Abiding Theological Witness* (Grand Rapids: Eerdmans, 1998), p. 104.

1. The Use of 1 Peter in Hermeneutical Discussion

The notion of considering the hermeneutic used in 1 Peter to interpret Scripture in relation to contemporary hermeneutical issues is not particular to this study. Several scholars have attempted to relate the use of Scripture in 1 Peter to contemporary hermeneutics. In a way, this is rather astonishing since so few scholars have been interested in the use of Scripture in 1 Peter as a subject in itself. I. Howard Marshall suggests that 1 Pet. 1.10-12 witnesses the early development of a Christian understanding of the Scriptures of Israel as essentially christological in focus. Whilst Marshall does not want to see the Old Testament read as though it had no meaning in its own time, other than to point to the future, he suggests that this tendency is worthwhile and ought to be continued by Christian readers. Indeed, Marshall maintains that christological reading represents an improvement from the approach used in apocalyptic and rabbinic Judaism, which, he claims, sought to subordinate the text of Scripture to the needs of the community in which it is read.[4] The difficulty with this distinction between 1 Peter's approach and communal focus of other ways of reading Scripture supposedly contemporary with 1 Peter, is that 1 Peter constantly relates Scripture to the needs of the community. Scripture is often the basis for paraenesis in 1 Peter. Indeed, 1 Pet. 1.12 maintains that the Prophets uttered their words in service of the communities now reading the epistle! However, it is not clear that Marshall argues for direct imitation of the hermeneutic of 1 Peter, but simply notes the importance of the christological element of 1.10-12. One scholar who does suggest that the hermeneutic of 1 Peter ought to be imitated is Thomas D. Lea. Lea suggests that, based on his argument that Peter's use of Scripture was learned from the historical Jesus with particular reference to use of the Stone Catena, contemporary readers should similarly attempt to learn from Jesus' own interpretation of Scripture.[5]

Francis Watson argues that 1 Pet. 1.10-12 witnesses to a christological reading of the Old Testament which assumes that its full and complete meaning is found in nothing other than the ministry of God incarnate:

> In the light of Easter Day, the law and the prophets can be seen as preparing the way for what has now come to pass. But this only becomes apparent *retrospectively*: the prophets themselves had only the haziest knowledge of the future event to which, for Christian hindsight, they bore witness (1 Pet. 1.10-12).[6]

---

4. I. Howard Marshall, *1 Peter* (Leicester: Intervarsity Press, 1991), pp. 44–5.
5. Lea, 'How Peter Learned the Old Testament', pp. 101–2.
6. Francis Watson, 'The Old Testament as Christian Scripture: A Response to Professor Seitz', *SJT* 52 (1999), pp. 227–32 (229).

As discussed in Chapter 1, an assessment of 1 Pet. 1.10-12 that notes the view that the Prophets initially spoke in ignorance since their writings referred to a later climax in salvation history, is accurate. Watson uses this idea in support of his own approach to biblical hermeneutics: that the New Testament provides a necessary re-reading of the Old Testament in the light of the fulfilment of God's promises in Jesus Christ.

Joel B. Green provides one of the most interesting discussions of 1 Peter and contemporary biblical hermeneutics. For Green, the primary issue in biblical hermeneutics that a reflection upon the use of Scripture in 1 Peter ought to address – is the status of the Old Testament as Scripture – as a set of texts with their own theological integrity. Green notes that the theological status of the Old Testament has been a persistent problem in biblical interpretation from Gabler and Schleiermacher onwards. For Schleiermacher in particular, as the 'father of Protestant theology', doctrinal claims must have a basis in the New Testament – he says nothing of the Old Testament.[7] In addition to this, Schleiermacher appears to associate the Old Testament with Judaism rather than Christianity.[8] Green suggests that, at least from Schleiermacher onwards, the Old Testament is deprived of a relation to dogmatics that is not mediated through Christology, encouraged by various supercessionist theologies. The pinnacle of the Old Testament's demise as Christian Scripture, according to Green, is its more recent relabeling, largely by historical-critical scholars, as the 'Hebrew Bible': a set of documents to be approached without any reference to Christian concerns. Green rightly points out that there is now a need to make historical criticism the servant, not the master, of Theological Interpretation of Scripture. To understand how 1 Peter affirms the integrity of the Old Testament as Scripture, without aggressively subordinating it to the claims of Christian theology or severing it from any relation to Christian theology, Green discusses 1 Pet. 1.1-10 as an account of Peter's Scripture hermeneutic:

> Peter does speak of the haziness of the prophets, but this is not the point of Peter's theological hermeneutic. Rather the character of the OT witness is documented in Peter's claim that 'the Spirit of Christ which was in them was testifying in advance to the sufferings coming to Christ and his subsequent glories'. Authorial awareness, clarity, or intent aside, the status of the OT as Christian witness was and is determined by the testimony of the Spirit of Christ. That is, Peter's theological hermeneutic does not depend on the competence of the prophets but on the animating presence of the Spirit of Christ.[9]

7. Green, *1 Peter*, p. 247. Cf. F. Schleiermacher, *The Christian Faith* (ed. H. R. Mackintosh and J. S. Stewart; 2d ed.; Edinburgh: T. & T. Clark, 1989), §27.
8. Green, *1 Peter*, p. 247. Cf. Schleiermacher, *Christian Faith*, §12.1–2.
9. Green, *1 Peter*, p. 251.

Because of this, Green rejects Watson's view that 1 Pet. 1.10-12 claims christological interpretation as a re-reading of Scripture, clarifying previous readings. Instead, Green suggests that Peter views the Scriptures of Israel as testifying to Christ, through the inspiration of the same Spirit of Christ at work in his audiences. To this end, Green claims, Scripture is not treated as though it provides predictions to be fulfilled, but rather a narrative of deliverance and redemptive suffering that reaches its climax in the 'sufferings of Christ and the glories after'. According to Green,

> What is problematic is the suggestion that this theological pattern is the consequence of reading with a new lens provided by the advent of Christ. What Peter makes clear, actually, is that this theological pattern is resident already in the Scriptures of Israel themselves. The issue is not that we are taught by the advent of Christ to read the Scriptures retrospectively, but that the Christ in whom Christians place their trust and now worship is the same Christ who long ago revealed the ways of God in the Scriptures. Interpretively, then, Israel's Scriptures are not predictions that Christ would fulfil, but rather testify to the Christ (and none other) who first inspired them.[10]

However, this analysis is difficult in a number of ways. Green's first example of Peter's 'hermeneutical key' applied in practice in 1 Peter is the use of Exodus language. He rightly points out that it would be wrong to say that the Exodus represents a prophecy fulfilled by Christ but argues instead that both God's rescue of his people in the past and his rescue through Christ testify to the character of God and reveal a paradigm for his work of salvation. The problem is that there is no indication that Peter is interested in the Exodus as an historical event, separate from the creation of God's holy nation through Christ, and no indication that his allusions to it can bear the weight of being understood typologically as Green seems to suggest. Green's second example of the 'hermeneutical key' applied to a text is the use of Isaiah 53. Similarly, Green claims that Peter uses the Servant Song material of Isaiah 53 because he sees it as testimony to the same economy of salvation, made in the past in reference to a suffering servant of the LORD, as is known now also through Christ. Again, there is no indication that Peter understands Isaiah 53 as referring in any way to a person or set of events in the past. And yet it is important for Green that he does, since this is the basis upon which he argues that a theological hermeneutic inspired by 1 Peter might take the Old Testament seriously as Scripture without rendering it as a theological footnote to the ministry of Jesus or a mere historical artefact. The trouble is that there is simply too much evidence which

---

10. Green, *1 Peter*, p. 251.

directly contradicts Green's argument that Peter does not understand Scripture to be predictive. As is argued above, Scripture is not simply understood as predictive because it has a primarily paraenetic function in 1 Peter. Yet 1.10-12 implies that a predictive element is important. Even so, the paraenetic element of Peter's biblical interpretation proceeds on the basis of an understanding that Scripture is fundamentally oriented towards his audiences: the Prophets spoke to serve them! A typological understanding of Scripture is simply not possible to demonstrate in 1 Peter; indeed, 1 Pet. 1.10 seems to contradict any sense that Scripture bore witness to any reality prior to the coming of Christ. The Prophets searched diligently for the meaning of their utterances which they only found in the sufferings and glories of Christ. It seems most unlikely that Peter thought of Scripture as having a prior referent, nor in fact any meaning outside the eschatological climax of salvation history for which the Prophets themselves yearned. Furthermore, this is indicated by the use of the participle προμαρτυρόμενον to describe the revealing action of the 'Spirit of Christ' in relation to the sufferings and glories of Christ as the referent of the prophetic witness. Whilst little is known of this term, its etymology and context here indicate a strongly predictive sense, as argued in Chapter 1.

Of considerable importance to Green's analysis of Peter's scriptural hermeneutic is the notion of the *fabula* expressing the divine economy of the redemption of God's people: of unjust suffering vindicated.[11] For Green, Peter's reading of Scripture is ruled by a sense of the unity of God's plan for his people in Scripture, understood on the basis of the Spirit of Christ's trans-historical role in revealing this plan through the Prophets:

> In 1.10-12, Peter recognizes the past testimony of the Spirit of Christ in providing a theological pattern by which to construe the meaning of Scripture. This pattern consisted of a *fabula*, or story behind a story, of the *Vindication of the Suffering Righteous*. What is more, Peter demonstrates that a faithful reading of Scripture traces the story from before creation itself, to the end-time revelation of Christ, *and through the life of the church comprised of aliens and strangers in the world*. Are other readings of the Scriptures possible, even defensible? Of course, but, for Peter, they would not be Christian readings of the Scriptures, since Peter's theological hermeneutic orders our reading of the Bible accordingly.[12]

11. Green, *1 Peter*, pp. 252–3. Cf. Sargent, 'Narrative Structure of 1 Peter', pp. 1–6.
12. Green, *1 Peter*, p. 256. Cf. p. 250, where Green appears to claim Peter's commitment to a limited form of polysemy by referring to the work of Umberto Eco. The comparison of the two is somewhat astonishing in the sophistication it implies for the scriptural hermeneutic of 1 Peter.

However, is it possible to assert that Peter considers other readings of Scripture to have validity, given that 1 Peter ignores such alternative readings and offers an exclusive account of Scripture's meaning in 1.10-12? Green himself notes that it is not really possible to settle the issue of whether 1 Peter is supercessionist or not, despite its application of exclusive titles for Israel to what are most probably Gentile communities, since the purpose of 1 Peter is not to define the relationship of Israel to God's purposes in Christ and his new people, but to confirm the status of the latter.[13]

In general, it would seem that Green ignores the essentially apocalyptic Jewish character of the use of Scripture in 1 Peter, instead seeing it as comparable with or even identical to Patristic biblical interpretation, particularly that of Tertullian and Irenaeus. Green suggests that, like Tertullian, Peter employs a rule of faith, laid out in 1 Pet. 1.10-12. Whilst it is no doubt accurate to regard this passage as establishing, to some extent, a hermeneutical principle, is this the same as a rule of faith? Tertullian employs a rule of faith to be able to reject certain readings of Scripture, whereas Peter shows no interest in other readings of Scripture at all. For Peter, the sufferings of Christ and the glories after are simply the truths to which the Scriptures testify, rather than a set of ideas to be read back onto Scripture to ensure faithful interpretation, even if it could be argued that Peter himself does use them in this way in 1 Peter. Where is the evidence that Peter holds such a complex view of Scripture, rather than understanding it as univocally witnessing to a single reality or directly addressing a particular situation as paraenesis? For Green, 1 Pet. 3.18-22 is the example of typology which gives substance to his claim that other uses of Scripture, such as the application of exodus and election terminology to the communities in 2.9, are also typological, recognising another prior referent of the biblical text. But does this imply polysemy? It is far from clear that the use of ἀντίτυπον here represents typology similar to later Patristic exegesis and could imply that the real value of the account of the Flood is in pointing forward to Baptism, lacking any value apart from this. As is noted in the discussion above on 1 Pet. 3.21, it is an event which is seen to be typological, not a text. Green puts 1 Peter on a par with Tertullian and Irenaeus with regards to the use of the Patristic notion of economy as the basis for typological reading of Scripture.[14] Aside from the fact that it is not possible to evidence the presence of so sophisticated a concept in 1 Peter, it is not clear that such a comparison with Patristic exegesis helps Green establish

13. Green, *1 Peter*, pp. 254–5.
14. Green, *1 Peter*, pp. 256–7.

a theological account of Old Testament interpretation. It must be remembered that even Tertullian did not believe in scriptural polysemy: his opponents were in error: his exegetical tools, such as the rule of faith and typological interpretation, were intended to deny other conflicting interpretations.[15] This is also particularly evident in Justin Martyr's use of typology specifically to undermine Jewish reading of Scripture.[16]

Yet Green also notes the more primitive and eschatological character of the use of Scripture in 1 Peter, though this does not determine his essential definition of Peter's hermeneutic as it does in this study. Green recognises that in 1 Peter, Scripture is seen to have an eschatological bent focused on the ministry of Jesus and the new community he inaugurates. This is seen in the exegetical practice of 'backshadowing', of reading eschatology back onto the Scriptures.[17] However, Green still sees this reading as part of a larger system of typological interpretation, rather than a single exegetical interest overwhelming all other meaning, as has been argued here. Whilst Green's analysis of the use of Scripture in 1 Peter appears to claim an unwarranted sophistication for Peter's hermeneutic, it is without doubt an impressive attempt to relate the use of Scripture in the New Testament to a contemporary debate in biblical hermeneutics.

2. Determinate Meaning in Biblical Hermeneutics

Green's discussion of the use of Scripture in 1 Peter and the theological interpretation of the Old Testament touches upon another significant

15. See, e.g., *De Praescr. Haer.* 19. R. P. C. Hanson, 'Notes on Tertullian's Interpretation of Scripture', *JTS* 12 (1961), pp. 275–7, notes that Tertullian occasionally rejects figurative interpretation of Scripture in favour of literal meaning decided purely by reference to literary context, citing the exegetical maxim 'sed malumus in scripturis minus, si forte, sapere quam contra' from *De Pudicitia* 9.22. In such instances, typological and allegorical reading is something associated with Tertullian's opponents. Cf. *Ad. Haer.* 2.21-24 for Irenaeus' rejection of the heretics' use of typological interpretation of Scripture.

16. For Justin's understanding of Jewish biblical interpretation, see *Dial.* 9., Συγγνώμη σοι, ἔφην, ὦ ἄνθρωπε, καὶ ἀφεθείη σοι οὐ γὰρ οἶδας ὃ λέγεις, ἀλλὰ πειθόμενος τοῖς διδασκάλοις, οἳ οὐ συνίασι τὰς γραφάς. Cf. Tessa Rajak, 'Talking at Trypho: Christian Apologetics as Anti-Judaism in Justin's Dialogue with Trypho the Jew', in *Apologetics in the Roman Empire: Pagans, Jews and Christians* (ed. Mark J. Edwards, Martin Goodman, Christopher Rowland; Oxford: Oxford University Press, 1999), pp. 59–80, and Rodney Alan Werline, 'The Transformation of Pauline Arguments in Justin Martyr's Dialogue with Trypho', *HTR* 91 (1999), pp. 79–93.

17. Green, *1 Peter*, pp. 257–8. This is supported by Hines, 'Peter and the Prophetic Word', p. 234.

issue in contemporary biblical hermeneutics, particularly in relation to recent interest in Theological Interpretation of Scripture: determinate or indeterminate meaning. It is argued above that the primitive and sectarian nature of the use of Scripture in 1 Peter is characterised by an insistence upon interpreting Scripture as though it relates to a single theological reality and the needs of a single community. Whilst other New Testament authors assume this in their use of Scripture, 1 Peter asserts it as the very nature and purpose of Scripture in 1.10-12: Scripture came through the Prophets, who wrote to serve the eschatological communities under the influence of the Spirit of Christ, to refer to nothing other than the sufferings of Christ and the glories after.[18] In a sense, this commitment to a single meaning is not unusual in the New Testament; indeed, it would appear that most interpretation of Scripture in the New Testament assumes a single correct meaning for a text. This is seen most often in the simple use of texts as unambiguous proofs to accompany an author's assertion: 'as it is written'.

Whilst Christian biblical interpretation would go on to embrace polysemy in its use of exegetical methods inspired by rabbinic interpretation and, particularly in its use of figurative and allegorical approaches to Scripture, climaxing in the medieval four-fold emphasis on literal, allegorical, tropological and anagogical senses, some interest in univocity or determinacy has always been present. It is therefore somewhat surprising that determinate meaning is rejected in nearly all contemporary approaches to biblical interpretation. Especially surprising is the total absence of the concept in attempts to redefine biblical interpretation theologically following the perceived demise of historical criticism.

In their recent defences of historical criticism, John Barton and Joseph A. Fitzmyer demonstrate that some of the hermeneutical features of that approach to interpretation are attested before the Enlightenment. Barton argues that a critical approach to Scripture which attempts to discern the 'plain sense' meaning of a text can be seen in Julius Africanus' *Letter to Origen* and in Jerome's *De viris illustribus*.[19] Similarly, Fitzmyer claims that critical interpretation of texts is first seen in the Homeric scholarship of the Alexandrian Grammarians, such as Zenodotus of Ephesus.[20]

---

18. Walter C. Kaiser, 'The Single Intent of Scripture', in Beale, ed., *The Right Doctrine*, pp. 55–67, uses 1 Pet. 1.10-12 and other texts which appear to demonstrate the determinate hermeneutics witnessed in the New Testament as a corrective to subjective interpretation in contemporary Evangelicalism.

19. John Barton, *The Nature of Biblical Criticism* (Louisville: Westminster John Knox, 2007), pp. 131–2.

20. Joseph A. Fitzmyer, *The Interpretation of Scripture: In Defense of the Historical-Critical Method* (New York: Paulist, 2008), p. 61.

A belief in determinate meaning can clearly be seen in the work of Aristarchus of Samothrace in his attempt to define a single authoritative text of the *Illiad*.

Determinacy certainly appears to have been an important feature of the Antiochene School of scriptural interpretation, seen particularly in the works of Theodore of Mopsuestia, Diodore of Tarsus, Theodoret, John Chrystostom, Adrianos and Eustathius.[21] Whilst there is, of course, a great deal of variety in the Antiochene school, the assumption of determinacy appears to have been a common theme in their commentary, despite their well-known development of 'typological' interpretation. The most well-known feature of Antiochene exegesis is the characteristic rejection of the allegorical reading witnessed in the Alexandrian school. The rejection of allegory need not imply the assumption of determinacy, yet the manner in which the Antiochene exegetes addressed allegory suggests that an idea of determinate meaning was a principal motivation. This can be seen most clearly in Theodore's arguments against the claim that St Paul employed Alexandrian-style allegorical interpretation. Theodore argues that Paul meant something quite different by the term 'allegory' in Gal. 4.24:

> qui stadium multum habent interuertere sensus diuiarum scripturarum et omnia quae illuc posita sunt intercipere, fabulas uero quasdam ineptas ex se configure, et allegoriae nomen suae ponere disipientiae; hanc uocem apostolic abutentes, quasi qui hinc uideantus sumpsisse potestatem ut et omnes intellectus diuinae exterminent scripturae, eo quod secundum apostolum per allegoriam dicere nituntus et ipsi, non intellegentes quantum differt quod ab illis et ab apostolo hoc in loco dictum sit.[22]

---

21. Frances Young, 'Alexandrian and Antiochene Exegesis', in *A History of Biblical Interpretation*. Vol. 1, *The Ancient Period* (ed. Alan J. Hauser and Duane F. Watson; Grand Rapids: Eerdmans, 2003), pp. 334–54. Whilst the Antiochene exegetes have been viewed as the forerunners of historical-critical approaches to the Bible, Young points out two important differences. Firstly, the Antiochenes have no interest in historicity: for them, the 'history' recalled in Scripture is theology. Secondly, Antiochene exegetes had a keen interest in tropological interpretation, something utterly alien to much of historical-critical scholarship. Cf. M. F. Wiles, 'Theodore of Mopsuestia as Representative of the Antiochene School', in *The Cambridge History of the Bible* (ed. P. Ackroyd and C. F. Evans; Cambridge: Cambridge University Press, 1970), pp. 489–510 (491).

22. *Ad Galatas* 1.73. Cf. Rowan A. Greer, *Theodore of Mopsuestia: Commentary on Minor Pauline Epistles* (SBLWGRW; Atlanta: SBL, 2010), pp. xiii–xiv; Frederick G. McLeod, *Theodore of Mopsuestia* (London: Routledge, 2009), pp. 19–20, and Young, 'Alexandrian and Antiochene Exegesis', pp. 347–51.

Theodore accuses those who employ allegorical interpretation of dismissing or obscuring a more obvious 'divine meaning'. Though Theodore does not use the term here, Paul's allegory is much closer to typology, he argues. Paul does not deny the historical sense of the text but builds his interpretation on the basis of correspondence between the text and his own argument. This is *theoria*, rather than allegory, according to Theodore. It is an insight built upon the historical and grammatical meaning of the text, rather than a meaning imposed upon the text as he perceived Alexandrian allegorical reading. Yet *theoria* does not supply an additional meaning other than that intended to be understood from the grammar of the text. It is a continuation of grammatical meaning. Likewise, when Theodore interprets the psalms in his early *Commentary on the Psalms*, he uses the notion of Davidic authorship (as well as, at times, the historical context provided by the psalm superscriptions) to present a single meaning of the biblical text.[23] Theodore consistently views the meaning of texts as determinate.

The typical form of Antiochene commentary also suggests a belief in determinate meaning. Prior to detailed exegetical treatment of a text, the meaning of the text is given in an hypothesis or summary paragraph in which the subject matter (πράγμα) is outlined. This summarising tendency in which meaning is limited and expressed in a concise form is antithetical to polysemy, especially as expressed in rabbinic exegesis, in which space is given to a variety of interpretations with no attempt at concise summary. Following the hypothesis, methodical and detailed analysis of the text is conducted. This aspect of Antiochene commentary demonstrates a profound concern for accuracy in interpretation. The commentary expresses an underlying assumption that interpretation must be correct and that the correct reading is the single meaning of the text. Again, this stands in marked contrast to much of rabbinic exegesis, in which a variety of possible interpretations are given, with the suggestion that the reader may make up his or her own mind.

A sense of the determinate meaning of Scripture is also witnessed in some strands of medieval theology. In William of Ockham's treatise on clerical poverty, the clarity and univocity of Scripture is foundational for his arguments. In 1 *Dial*. 2.1-5, Scripture is viewed as the source of theology along with what may be *necessarily* extrapolated from it. In 3.1 *Dial*. 3.19, on the meaning of 2 Thess. 2.7-8, Ockham is happier admitting ignorance of the text's meaning rather than offering an anagogical reading which may go beyond the simple sense of the text:

---

23. Wiles, 'Theodore of Mopsuestia', pp. 497–8.

> Ex quo videtur posse concludi quod de stulta temeritate excusari non possint qui per solos sensus misticos scripture divine, quos nec ex aliis locis scripture possunt argumento evidenti inferre, nec per racionem irrefragabilem possunt concludere, nec per certam et specialem ac miraculosam revelacionem certificati sunt de ipsis, aliqua future contingencia audent predicare, vel quando futura evenient que absque determinacione temporis in sacris literis sunt predicta asserere non formidant, vel queque alia non metuunt affirmare que per aliam viam indubiam et apertam manifestare non possunt.

Ockham does not offer an account of biblical hermeneutics but it is not surprising that he places emphasis upon the 'literal' interpretation of Scripture.[24] For Ockham, Scripture is the primary epistemological resource for making theological assertions. This is because his philosophical definition of reality posits the eternal realm of the divine as utterly transcendent and largely unknowable, since nothing should be posited with necessity. Just as he does not posit abstract theological concepts onto the material world, so he does not consider unnecessary theological interpretations of the material text of Scripture. Of course, for John Milbank and others this is precisely the problem: determinacy is contingent upon an heretical account of reality in which the presence and activity of God is wholly absent, in which the phenomenal and noumenal are utterly separate.[25] Yet to consider Ockham's worldview to be anti-Christian and heretical is to place too limited a definition on what can be appropriately Christian. Ockham's account of the relation of the phenomenal to the noumenal represents a traditionally Christian emphasis upon the majesty and incomprehensibility of God: it is just not Aristotelian. Yet the Medieval period also saw a determinate approach to Scripture in the work of a thinker who consciously rejected nominalism and held to the platonic forms: John Wycliffe. Not only does the 'literal' sense of Scripture offer a challenge to Papal authority for Wycliffe, but he considers the solution to apparent contradictions in Scripture to be a concentration on verbal and grammatical meaning.[26] Wycliffe also associates a dependence upon non-literal meaning with heretical theology.[27]

---

24. Though, as Rowan Williams, 'The Literal Sense of Scripture', *MT* 7 (1991), pp. 121–34, points out, literal meaning is not a constant. Cf. Stephen E. Fowl, 'The Importance of a Multivoiced Literal Sense of Scripture: The Example of Thomas Aquinas', in *Reading Scripture with the Church: Toward a Hermeneutic for Theological Interpretation* (Grand Rapids: Baker, 2006), pp. 53–60.
25. Milbank, *Theology and Social Theory*, p. 18.
26. *De Veritate Sacrae Scripturae*, p. 2.
27. *De Veritate Sacrae Scripturae*, p. 2: 'nam locus ab autoritate scripture non ponderat, nisi de quanto allegatur ad sensum, quem deus flagitat, sed quid sit ille

Of the sixteenth-century Reformers, the Zurich tradition of Huldrich Zwingli and Heinrich Bullinger presents perhaps the clearest evidence of belief in the determinate meaning of Scripture.[28] This is seen particularly in the Helvetic Confessions of Faith which, perhaps unusually for a confessional statement of the Reformation period, feature pronouncement on correct biblical hermeneutics.[29] *Confessio Helvetica Posterior* 2.1 reads:

> Scripturas Sanctas, dixit Apostolus Petrus, non esse interpretationis privatæ. Proinde non probamus interpretationes quaslibet; unde nec pro vera aut genuina Scripturarum interpretatione agnoscimus eum, quem vocant sensum Romanæ ecclesiæ, quem scilicet simpliciter Romanæ ecclesiæ defensores omnibus obtrudere contendunt recipiendum: sed illam duntaxat Scripturarum interpretationem pro orthodoxa et genuina agnoscimus, quæ ex ipsis est petita Scripturis (ex ingenio utique ejus linguæ, in qua sunt scriptæ, secundum circumstantias item expensæ, et pro ratione locorum vel similium vel dissimilium, plurium quoque et clariorum expositæ, cum regula fidei et caritatis congruit, et ad gloriam Dei hominumque salutem eximie facit.[30]

What is interesting here is that a quite developed understanding of what 'genuine' interpretation involves (in relation to the language and setting of biblical texts) is articulated as a statement of faith: of defining beliefs.

The determinate meaning of Scripture also appears to have been of some importance at the beginning of the Enlightenment, as the foundations of historical criticism were laid. Benedict de Spinoza viewed polysemy as a result of theologians' desires to serve themselves and appear to be devout and learned interpreters of Scripture:

> As for theologians, we see that for the most part they have sought to extract their own thoughts and opinions from the Bible and thereby endow them with divine authority. There is nothing that they interpret

sensus, non deducitur nisi per locum topicum, ut puta a testimonio postillantis. Et sic posset proterviens totum sensum scripture subvertere negando sensum literalem et fingendo sensum figurativum ad libitum, ut recitat in libro suo De Heresibus.'

28. Benjamin Sargent, 'Biblical Hermeneutics in the Zurich Reformation', *EvQ* 86 (2014), pp. 325–42.

29. The XXIX Articles of Religion of the Church of England, for example, reveal a principal interest in the sufficiency of Scripture for the Church's doctrine and practice, rather than how the sufficient Scriptures are to be interpreted. However, article XX, 'of the authority of the Church', promotes a form of canonical interpretation in its insistence that 'it is not lawful for the Church to...expound one place of Scripture, that it be repugnant to another'. Determinate meaning is assumed throughout the articles, as in other reformation confessions, insofar as Scripture is seen to deny certain traditional doctrines and practices unambiguously.

30. Note the allusion to 2 Pet. 1.20.

with less hesitation and greater boldness than the Scriptures, that is the mind of the Holy Spirit. If they hesitate at all, it is not because they are afraid of ascribing error to the Holy Spirit or straying from the path of salvation, but rather of being convicted of error by others and seeing themselves despised and their authority trodden underfoot.

If people truly believed in their hearts what they say with their lips about Scripture, they would follow a completely different way of life. There would be fewer differences of opinion occupying their minds, fewer bitter controversies between them, and less blind and reckless ambition to distort our interpretation of the Bible and devise novelties in religion. On the contrary, they would not dare to accept anything as biblical teaching which they had not derived from it in the clearest possible way.[31]

For Spinoza, there is only one method of interpreting Scripture which is 'the clearest possible way' that provides access to Scripture's unambiguous meaning: a persuasive meaning which subdues difference of opinion and controversy. This method is to be derived from the natural sciences, Spinoza argues, constructing a history behind the text and attempting to articulate the mind of biblical authors:

> To extricate ourselves from such confusion and to free our minds from theological prejudices and the blind acceptance of human fictions as God's teaching, we need to analyse and discuss the true method of interpreting Scripture. For if we do not know this, we can know nothing for certain regarding what the Bible or the Holy Spirit wishes to teach. To formulate the matter succinctly, I hold that the method of interpreting Scripture, does not differ from the [correct] method of interpreting nature, but is rather wholly consonant with it. The [correct] method of interpreting nature consists above all in constructing a natural history, from which we derive the definitions of natural things, as from certain data. Likewise, to interpret Scripture, we need to assemble a genuine history of it and to deduce the thinking of the Bible's authors by valid inferences from this history, as from certain data and principles. Provided we admit no other criteria or data for interpreting Scripture and discussing its contents than what is drawn from Scripture itself and its history, we will always proceed without any danger of going astray.[32]

---

31. Benedict de Spinoza, *Theological-Political Treatise* (trans. Michael Silverthorne and Jonathan Israel; Cambridge: Cambridge University Press, 2007), p. 97.

32. Spinoza, *Theological-Political Treatise*, p. 98. One wonders if Spinoza really deserves the rejection he receives from John Milbank, *Theology and Social Theory*, pp. 18–23. From the quotation above, Spinoza clearly possesses a theological understanding of Scripture as argued by Nancy Levine, 'Spinoza's Bible: Concerning How it Is that "Scripture, insofar as it contains the word of God, has come down to us uncorrupted"', *Philosophy and Theology* 13 (2001), pp. 93–142. For Milbank's critique of Spinoza, see Benjamin Sargent, 'John Milbank and Biblical Hermeneutics: The End of the Historical Critical Method?', *HeyJ* 52 (2012), pp. 253–63.

Despite the importance of determinate meaning to Spinoza at the dawn of modernity, polysemy is a profoundly popular concept today. As theologians attempt to restore biblical hermeneutics as a theological enterprise, the certainty of the Enlightenment view of a single historically contingent meaning is being set aside. Indeed, the only scholars arguing for the retention of determinacy do so to prop up the crumbling edifice of historical criticism, a methodological tendency thoroughly dominated by the Enlightenment's idealist vision of scientifically discerned, single meaning upon which all Christians can agree. This idealism centred on determinacy was seen again and again in the last 300 years of biblical scholarship, each time historical criticism was taken up in a new context. For Spinoza, whom one might regard as the father of Enlightenment biblical hermeneutics,[33] his radical and subversive approach to interpreting the Scriptures is a source of hope. Spinoza is optimistic that a 'scientific' approach to Scripture will lay bare the single true meaning of the text and make God known. J. P. Gabler, writing as historical criticism was about to take German universities under its influence, speaks with profound optimism of what this approach might achieve for Christian unity and the pursuit of truth as all the different and contrasting denominational perspectives of Christians are set aside in favour of a single, persuasive and exclusive interpretation.[34] Likewise, as Roman Catholic biblical scholars began to become involved in this approach, long popular in Protestant and non-denominational academic settings, they too glimpsed the vision of a single meaning destroying the barriers separating Christian from Christian. Perhaps the best most recent example of this is seen in Joseph Fitzmyer's defence of the historical-critical method in which he narrates something of the history of the method's use in Roman Catholic biblical scholarship. Fitzmyer's renewed commendation of the method, unlike Barton's (arguably its Protestant counterpart), is interesting because it articulates the same idealism concerning the challenge of a since meaning (stimulating the Church because

---

33. Though one can of course argue, as Barton, *Biblical Criticism*, pp. 117–36, does that biblical criticism has its roots in renaissance humanism or, as Fitzmyer, *Interpretation of Scripture*, pp. 61–3, argues, Antiochene theology and Theodore of Mopsuestia in particular, and before that, Alexandrian scholarship both Christian and pre-Christian. Cf. Benjamin Sargent, '"Interpreting Homer from Homer": Aristarchus of Samothrace and the Notion of Scriptural Authorship in the New Testament', *TynBul* 65 (2014), pp. 125–39.

34. John Sandys-Wunsch and Laurence Eldridge, 'J. P. Gabler and the Distinction between Biblical and Dogmatic Theology: Translation, Commentary and Discussion of his Originality', *SJT* 33 (1980), pp. 139–41.

of its historical alterity), presupposing opposition for whom the method is too radical.[35]

But where does this confident vision come from? It must be recognised that historical criticism's confidence in determinate meaning relates to its presuppositions about the nature of a biblical text (as historically contingent and hence primarily designed for a particular end within a particular historical situation) and the interpreting subject (as rationally and objectively able to discern the meaning which the text was created to convey). Whilst the latter presupposition is difficult to assert without reference to a theological understanding of human personhood,[36] it must be said that this commitment to determinacy is derived, not from a theological understanding of biblical hermeneutics, but from a position which has consciously rejected received theological approaches to biblical interpretation.[37] It is no surprise then that with the end of the Enlightenment project, determinate meaning in biblical interpretation has fallen out of favour. But are the fates of determinacy and modernity inextricably linked? Is it possible to understand determinate meaning as part of a theological approach to biblical interpretation, and how might the use of Scripture in 1 Peter stimulate the development of such an approach? It must be noted that many who have rejected determinate meaning as a feature of historical criticism, perhaps inadvertently, continue to operate as though meaning was in some sense determinate. As John Barton argues, determinacy is taken as given by some feminist biblical scholars who either assume a single patriarchal sense of the text which must be rejected as a text of terror, or assume that a patriarchal mainstream of biblical interpretation has overlooked the true egalitarian meaning of a text. According to Barton,

> the Feminist case...depends on the reader's being able to make a judgement about what the texts mean, on the basis of which he or she can go on to criticize biblical scholars either for the moral failing of not dissociating themselves from a misogynistic Bible or for the exegetical failing (which is surely also a moral one) of reading misogynistic meanings into texts that lack them... Feminist criticism, so far from denying determinate meaning to texts, actually requires it if it is to be coherent. The feminist case is that

---

35. Fitzmyer, *Interpretation of Scripture*, p. 115. In contrast, Barton, *Biblical Criticism*, pp. 141–51 argues for 'Biblical Criticism' in the face of opposition for whom it is too conservative: a product of bygone modernity.

36. Cf. Ian Markham, *Truth and the Reality of God: An Essay in Natural Theology* (Edinburgh: T. & T. Clark, 1998), pp. 47–65.

37. John Milbank, *The Word Made Strange: Theology, Language, Culture* (Oxford: Blackwell, 1997), pp. 126–8. Cf. Sargent, 'Milbank and Biblical Hermeneutics', pp. 255–6.

the text will not support the misogynistic use being made of it; it is not simply that misogyny is unacceptable, which is true but is not a point about biblical interpretation.[38]

The same could perhaps be said for many post-colonial, queer or liberation approaches to the Bible. Similarly, the theological hermeneutic of Stephen E. Fowl, inspired by American literary pragmatism, adopts a form of communally oriented determinism in which the interpretive community may decide clear true and false meanings of a text. This is discussed in greater detail below. Suffice it to say, at this point, that the assumption of determinate meaning is not entirely alien to Christian biblical interpretation. But given that determinate meaning is so closely associated with much-maligned historical criticism, can its use in 1 Peter contribute to a theological understanding of the concept which may grant it some degree of independence from historical criticism?

3. Determinacy in 1 Peter and Today

For Pheme Perkins, the determinate reading of Scripture witnessed in 1 Peter is seen as deeply problematic for contemporary Christians:

> The difficulty that this section of 1 Peter poses for Christians today lies in its appropriation of the Old Testament. The letter never suggests that there is another community of Jewish readers for whom the prophets do not describe Jesus... No doubt persons who had grown up as members of the Qumran sect might say the same about the prophets and their origins.[39]

That exclusive and sectarian emphasis upon a particular group of communities in the interpretation of Scripture witnesses to what many find objectionable about the idea of determinate meaning. It is not suggested here that the scriptural hermeneutic employed in 1 Peter can simply be lifted out of the epistle and appropriated directly into contemporary biblical interpretation. There is much in the use of Scripture in 1 Peter which it would not be wise to imitate: the lack of awareness and engagement with other interpretations of the same texts and the lack of exegetical explanation. Of course, whatever the true motivation behind the composition of 1 Peter, it clearly was not intended as a primer on the interpretation of Scripture! Yet the approach to determinate meaning in 1 Peter may still be instructive as biblical scholars and theologians alike attempt to define biblical hermeneutics in a new era. To appreciate this,

---

38. Barton, *Biblical Criticism*, pp. 160–1.
39. Pheme Perkins, *First and Second Peter, James, and Jude* (Interpretation; Louisville: John Knox, 1995), p. 35.

one needs to identify the distinctive approach to determinate meaning employed in 1 Peter.

Very little work has been done on the assumption of the determinate meaning of Scripture in the New Testament. There are evidently a variety of reasons why determinate meaning is assumed. Hebrews 4.6-8 understands the single meaning of Ps. 95.7-11 to exist diachronically. The meaning the text had in David's time is the same meaning the text has today, since it is the Davidic context of the psalm which determines its meaning. In a similar way, the context of the prophetic authors of Scripture also affects 1 Peter's interpretation of Scripture (since the Prophets are understood as people who serve those who will one day have good news proclaimed to them). Yet in 1 Peter, the single meaning of the Prophets' writings are to be found in a later fulfilment, rather than in the details of the Prophets' historical contexts or the assumed time and place of writing. Similarly, Acts 2.29-31 denies the interpretation of Ps. 16.8-11 witnessed in *Ps. Midr.* 16 by defining the psalm as messianic prophecy, thereby providing its true meaning. One could argue that Paul's assumption of determinate meaning is premised upon his own apostolic identity.[40] This status enables him to offer definitive scriptural interpretation with a sense of authority.

As Achtemeier observes, the application of Scripture to the communities Peter addresses functions upon the basis of a narrative of continuity between the people of God in Israel's past and the people of God in the present: the aliens and strangers reading or hearing the epistle.[41] Yet, as argued above, it is not simply continuity which is important here. Perhaps more significant is the sense in which the communities stand at the climax of salvation history, at the focal point to which God's eternal plan tends: the time longed for by prophets and angels. In a sense, the communities of 1 Peter are not understood simply as a continuation of Israel, they represent the culmination of Israel. These communities are witnesses of things about which the Prophets searched. When the Prophets wrote, they did so to serve these communities. Because these communities stand at the most significant period of time, as prophets and angels testify, it is not surprising that Scripture is thought to be oriented toward them exclusively, describing the things they need to know and exhorting them in areas in which they need exhortation. One might therefore describe the understanding of determinate meaning in 1 Peter as both eschatological and ecclesiological: the meaning of Scripture is

---

40. S. K. Wan, 'Charismatic Exegesis: Philo and Paul Compared', *SPA* 6 (1994), p. 54.
41. Achtemeier, *1 Peter*, p. 110.

determinate because of the status of the community to which Scripture's narrative refers. Since the history of Israel yearns towards the moment of Christ and his people, it is obvious to Peter that Scripture too must share this single focus. Because Peter's audiences are the elect whose knowledge is envied by the angels and who have had revealed to them what was hidden to those in the past, Scripture is understood as something written to serve them. That is why the Prophets spoke (1 Pet. 1.12).

If one wished to reconsider determinate meaning within a theological context, one could follow 1 Peter and seek to define it on the basis of the community or communities for which and in which texts are interpreted. Curiously, a form of determinate meaning appears to be offered on just such a basis in the application of American literary pragmatism to biblical interpretation by Stephen E. Fowl. This is perhaps ironic given the clear rejection of determinate meaning in both literary pragmatism and the work of Fowl. Richard Rorty notes that reading is conditioned by the personal context in which it occurs, the needs of the reader, to the extent that interpretation simply becomes use of a text:

> [Reading] may be so exciting and convincing that one has the illusion that one now sees what a certain text is really about. But what excites and convinces is a function of the needs and purposes of those who are being excited and convinced. So it seems to me simpler to scrap the distinction between using and interpreting, and just distinguish between uses by different people for different purposes.[42]

A reader might think that they have discerned the correct meaning of a text, but what they have probably found is simply the meaning of the text that most meets their needs, suggests Rorty. Pragmatism makes the claim that the interpretation of texts is defined by readers and the particular culture in which they are interpreted. But a hermeneutical question remains: Given that reading will never disclose a permanent and determinate meaning of a text, how can interpretation be done well? What characterises a good reading? For the fullest application of pragmatic philosophy to hermeneutics one needs to look to Stanley Fish. Like Rorty, Fish views meaning as arising in actual use of a text, but adds to this the importance of use within a community in which a particular interpretation can be experienced and recognised as good, or if not, can be debated on the basis of agreed ideas of what good interpretation is. The positive affirmation of a use of a text within a community, insofar as other readings may be dismissed as 'bad' or 'not useful', permits a new form of determinate meaning contingent upon the status and stability of the interpretive community:

42. Richard Rorty, *Philosophy and Social Hope* (London: Penguin, 1999), p. 144.

> This, then, is the explanation for the stability of interpretation among different readers: they belong to the same community. Disagreements... can be debated in a principled way, not because of a stability in texts, but because of a stability in the makeup of interpretive communities.[43]

For Fish, a good reading is one which supplies the particular needs of the interpretive community: a reading which advances what that community considers to be valuable or useful. Good readings are those which are useful and support the community in its understood identity. This approach is taken into theological or biblical hermeneutics by Fowl:

> Christian interpretation of scripture is primarily an activity of Christian communities in which they seek to generate and embody their interpretations of scripture *so that* they may fulfil their ends of worshipping and living faithfully before the triune God.[44]

Fowl argues that Scriptural interpretation ought to reflect the needs, values and ends of the local Church. A good interpretation, according to Fowl, is one which fosters virtue: which promotes the good of the community. Because of this, the mind or ethos of the Christian community has complete control over what readings can be accepted as good. Fowl argues that values of inclusion and hospitality are good for the community and are to be promoted through biblical interpretation. His work has been prominent in the discussion of homosexuality and Christian leadership as he argues that readings which exclude people in some way are to be avoided as not good for the Christian community in which and for which Scripture is read. Whilst Fowl explicitly encourages the assumption of indeterminate meaning in theological interpretation of Scripture,[45] as far as an interpretative community is concerned, the true meaning of Scripture on a subject related to something as fundamental as a human right not to face discrimination because of gender or sexuality, is determinate. The interpretive community will view some interpretations as wrong and others as right in relation to the values they cherish. This is quite distinct from the use of determinate meaning in historical criticism, in which the true meaning of a text may be something quite objectionable to the reading community, but which represents a form of determinate meaning nonetheless. However, meaning is only determinate within a

---

43. Stanley Fish, *Is There a Text in This Class? The Authority of Interpretive Communities* (Cambridge, Mass.: Harvard University Press, 1980), p. 171.

44. Stephen E. Fowl, *Engaging Scripture: A Model for Theological Interpretation* (Eugene, Ore.: Wipf & Stock, 2008), p. 161.

45. Fowl, 'Multivoiced Literal Sense', pp. 35–50.

particular interpretive community: other communities will have a difference sense of what the determinate meaning of Scripture looks like in particular cases. For example, another interpretive community may consider readings of Scripture which others regard as promoting discrimination to be 'useful' and therefore the correct meaning determined by Scripture. Determinate meaning as contingent upon interpretive communities can never claim the universality historical criticism claims for its approach to meaning. Yet here, again, the approach to determinate meaning in 1 Peter is instructive.

Whilst 1 Peter defines determinate meaning in relation to the people for whom Scripture is interpreted, it does so on the basis of a narrative which claims universality. In addition to this, whilst the focus of 1 Peter is sectarian, it is also catholic: it addresses a variety of communities, rather than a single community with a very specific set of issues to negotiate. Peter's application of Scripture is not simply to a single interpretive community who read together: the Cappadocian communities addressed by 1 Peter may have had no real acquaintance with the Christians of Bithynia and Pontus. One might follow 1 Peter in attempting to define a theological approach to determinate meaning on the basis of a theological narrative that encompasses the global Christian community: the Church. This might offer a means of creating a theological understanding of the determinate meaning of Scripture with an appeal to universality.

Of course, one could simply adapt the hermeneutic employed in 1 Peter straightforwardly into a contemporary theological hermeneutic. To do so, one would need to gain some sense of continuity between the communities to whom 1 Peter is addressed and the contemporary church. This would be essential given that the biblical hermeneutics of 1 Peter are entirely dependent upon the theological status of the communities. Elliott's sociological analysis of the communities is particularly unhelpful in this respect, creating an exaggerated distanciation between the text and contemporary readers. Obviously, if the important language of 'aliens' and 'strangers' (or 'resident aliens' and 'visiting strangers' as Elliott renders these terms) refers to the very specific social status of the communities, rather than a purely theological identity to which they are called, then the difference between the text's initial audiences and many of its contemporary audiences is extreme. At the same time, it may be better to speak of 1 Peter's ecclesiology, in which contemporary readers can see themselves, rather than its 'sectarian ideology' if to do so is not too anachronistic.[46] This is the point Green makes regarding the majority of studies of the theology of 1 Peter:

46. Elliott, *Home for the Homeless*, p. 105.

> Rather than bringing the message of the NT more fully to bear on the life and mission of the church, [these approaches tend] instead to segregate that message from the contemporary church. To a large degree, this is because it perpetuates the erroneous claim that these NT materials are written to folks back then and not to the church now. The task of theological interpretation cannot bypass the theological claim that the church is one – one across time and space. The church out of which 1 Peter was written, the church to which 1 Peter was first addressed, the church that received 1 Peter as canon, the church that has engaged in interpretation of 1 Peter, and the church that today turns to it as Scripture – these are all the same church.[47]

If one relates the use of Scripture in 1 Peter in this way, one would have to account for the problem raised by Pheme Perkins above. The eschatological and ecclesiological claim of the narrative of 1 Peter excludes non-Christian readers of the Scriptures of Israel, whilst the actual use of Scripture in the epistle ignores them. A way out of this problem might be to acknowledge openly a variety of narratives that enable different readers of texts to understand themselves as readers of those texts, whether as Jews, Christians or Muslims.[48] Perhaps one need not demand a positive assessment of oneself as a reader within the narrative of another reading community, provided that such a narrative does not promote hostility and isolation.

---

47. Green, 'Narrating the Gospel in 1 and 2 Peter', p. 265. Cf. Benjamin Sargent, *As It Is Written: Interpreting the Bible with Boldness* (LS 75; London: Latimer Trust, 2011), pp. 53–61, on the relation of ecclesiology to the hermeneutical problem of distanciation.

48. Benjamin Sargent, 'Proceeding Beyond Isolation: Bringing Milbank, Habermas and Ockham to the Interfaith Table', *HeyJ* 51 (2010), pp. 819–30.

CONCLUSION

This study has sought to demonstrate that the use of Scripture in 1 Peter may be characterised on the basis of the description of the prophetic ministry in relation to the communities to which the letter is addressed in 1.10-12. The witness of the Prophets is seen here to relate purely to events and people which will not take place within their lifetimes. As the Prophets spoke or wrote they testified in advance to the sufferings of Christ and the glories after, though they were never to know the precise times and circumstances of such things. Primarily, these Prophets are understood to have spoken and written in order to serve a later set of communities, scattered throughout Pontus, Galatia, Cappadocia, Asia and Bithinia, who would stand at the very pinnacle and climax of salvation history. These assumptions concerning the testimony and service of the Prophets influence Peter's actual reference to Scripture in the epistle. The use of Scripture suggests that it is understood to relate directly to the needs of the communities, both as it describes kerygmatically the great recent events of salvation history through which the communities have come into being, and as it operates as paraenesis directly oriented towards the communities.

The analysis of 1.10-12 reveals the theological narrative in and through which Scripture is understood by Peter. The narrative posits a radical separation between the past and the present, because of which the Prophets spoke only of a time and set of circumstances yet to come, using words whose full meaning they did not know. For Peter, the sufferings of Christ and the glories that follow, as well as the community of believers joined to Christ who are served by the Prophets, stand at the grand climax of salvation history. The prophetic witness is oriented towards this climax both in terms of its kerygmatic and predictive testimony to events, as well as its relation to the communities as paraenesis. This understanding of Scripture, derived from a theological narrative of salvation history which stresses climax and discontinuity, leads to a use of Scripture in the epistle which can be described as both primitive and sectarian. The essential orientation of Scripture to Christ and the communities enables it to be interpreted as though its meaning were simply determinate: as though there was no contesting interpretation. Because of this, the use of Scripture in 1 Peter is 'primative' when compared to reading of Scripture in the New Testament which shows a consciousness of other interpretation. At the same time, the theological narrative of 1 Pet. 1.10-12 enables the use of Scripture in the epistle to be 'sectarian'. Because the communities occupy an exclusive place as the people of God at the climax of history, the prophetic witness is essentially oriented towards them and appears to address their concerns and situation directly.

An important hermeneutical principle in 1 Peter is the notion of Scripture's determinate meaning. 1 Peter 1.10-12 suggests that the prophetic utterances or writings lacked meaning in their own time. The Prophets diligently sought this meaning yet discovered, through the Spirit of Christ, that their witness was a service for a later time. There is no sense in 1 Peter here, nor in its actual use in the epistle, that Scripture has two referents, one relating to the Prophets' own times and another relating to a later period. For Peter, Scripture is fundamentally and genuinely oriented towards a single eschatological reality: both a set of events and chosen people. Indeed, it appears to be the eschatological ecclesiology of 1 Peter which establishes this understanding of determinate meaning. Given that the events of Christ's passion, the glories that follow it and the eschatological Christian community are of such significance within the narrative substructure of 1 Peter, a significance which overwhelms all other events in salvation history, it is perhaps obvious to Peter that God's speech through the Scriptures in the past testify to these. As has been noted, this assumption of a single meaning for Scripture is common throughout the New Testament literature. However, whilst it is often assumed without explanation, and other known interpretations of a text are occasionally denied, in 1 Peter determinacy is vigorously asserted on the basis of an account of salvation history and a theological understanding of the communities as the people of God.

That 1 Peter offers a theological account of the determinate meaning of Scripture is worthy of note. Determinacy is a profoundly unpopular concept in the broad field of contemporary biblical studies. Part of this unpopularity can be accounted for by its association purely with the tenets of historical criticism, such that it appears to many to be exclusively wedded to an anti-theological approach to the Bible. Indeed, one can easily see that determinacy has often functioned in an antitheological manner as it has been directed against doctrinal readings of a text which are thought to have no historical warrant. However, the use of determinacy in the New Testament suggests that it is not inherently antitheological. In the case of 1 Peter, it may indeed be articulated theologically. As argued, this raises the question of the enduring value of biblical interpretation that operates on the basis of determinate meaning, even after historical criticism disappears or, at least, is thought to represent a minority interest or approach to the Bible within a much broader field.

Yet many questions remain unanswered, even if one were to agree in principle that scriptural determinacy can function as part of theological interpretation of Scripture. Is determinacy simply a 'primitive' concept, confined principally to first-century documents whose eschatological emphases are often something of an embarrassment to contemporary Christians? Is it the case that determinacy is relatively unattested in the history of Christian interpretation of Scripture so as to be rather uncharacteristic? Even if determinacy is occasionally attested in the history of biblical interpretation (as argued in Chapter 5), can it be theologically, philosophically, or even ethically warranted? It is easy to see that determinacy could be accused of being an expression of theological arrogance or exclusivity, of philosophical naivety or of a violent and insensitive approach to reading texts. It is easy to see why the concept of determinate meaning is repugnant to many, both within theological scholarship as well in other areas. However, it also obvious to many scholars who currently operate within a primarily historical-critical environment, that determinacy provides the foundation for rigorous scholarship and lively disagreement aimed at clarifying a single, historically contingent, meaning of a text. Such scholars might argue that polysemy encourages a culture of scholarly laziness, one in which research does not have to pass the test of historical or literary plausibility. Without a widespread belief in the essentially determinate meaning of Scripture, much of what the academy wishes to express to the Church has little opportunity of being heard, and certainly not heard as coming from an authority. Polysemy can provide a significant obstacle to the quest of the theological academy to serve the Church.

A great deal of further enquiry is needed in order to make a convincing case for the continuation of interpretation proceeding from assumptions of determinate meaning apart from the increasingly unpopular methods of historical criticism. Yet the New Testament use of Scripture, and the use of Scripture in 1 Peter in particular, witness to Christian assumptions that the meaning of scriptural texts is determinate. It remains to be seen whether future generations of Christian interpreters of Scripture will, like the Prophets of 1 Pet. 1.10-11, search diligently for that single meaning.

BIBLIOGRAPHY

Achtemeier, Paul J., '1 Peter 1.13-21', *Int* 60 (2006), pp. 306–8.
———. *1 Peter: A Commentary on First Peter* (Philadelphia: Fortress, 1996).
———. 'The Christology of First Peter', in *Who Do You Say That I Am? Essays on Christology* (ed. Mark A. Powell and David R. Bauer; Louisville: Westminster, 1999), pp. 140–54.
———. 'Suffering Servant and Suffering Christ in 1 Peter', in *The Future of Christology: Essays in Honor of Leander E. Keck* (ed. A. J. Malherbe and W. A. Meeks; Minneapolis: Fortress, 1993), pp. 176–88.
Agnew, Francis H., '1 Peter 1.2 – An Alternative Translation', *CBQ* 4 (1983), pp. 68–73.
Aichele, George, Peter Miscall and Richard Walsh, 'An Elephant in the Room: Historical-Critical and Postmodern Interpretations of the Bible', *JBL* 128 (2009), pp. 383–404.
Attridge, Harold W., *Hebrews* (Hermeneia; Philadelphia: Fortress, 1989).
———. '"Let Us Strive to Enter that Rest": The Logic of Hebrews 4.1–11', *HTR* 73 (1980), pp. 279–88.
Bacher, W., *Die Exegetische Terminologie der jüdischen Traditionsliteratur* (Leipzig: J. C. Hinrichs, 1905).
Balch, David L., 'Hellenization/Acculturation in 1 Peter', in Talbert, ed., *Perspectives on First Peter*, pp. 79–102.
Barr, James, 'בארץ – ΜΟΛΙΣ: PROV. XI. 31, 1 PET. IV. 18', *JSS* 20 (1975), pp. 149–64.
Bartholomew, Craig G., 'Uncharted Waters: Philosophy, Theology and the Crisis in Biblical Interpretation', in *Renewing Biblical Interpretation* (ed. Craig G. Bartholomew, Colin Greene and Karl Möller; Grand Rapids: Zondervan; Carlisle Paternoster, 2000), pp. 1–34.
Barton, John, *The Nature of Biblical Criticism* (Louisville: Westminster John Knox, 2007).
Batten, Alicia J., 'Neither Gold nor Braided Hair (1 Timothy 2.9; 1 Peter 3.3): Adornment, Gender and Honour in Antiquity', *NTS* 55 (2009), pp. 484–501.
Bauckham, Richard J., 'Colossians 1.24 Again: The Apocalyptic Note', *EvQ* 47 (1975), pp. 168–70.
———. 'The Delay of the Parousia', *TynBul* 31 (1980), pp. 3–36.
———. 'James, 1 and 2 Peter, Jude', in *It Is Written: Scripture Citing Scripture: Essays in Honour of Barnabas Lindars* (ed. D. A. Carson and H. G. M. Williamson; Cambridge: Cambridge University Press, 1988), pp. 303–17.
Bauman-Martin, Betsy, 'Speaking Jewish: Postcolonial Aliens and Strangers in First Peter', in Webb and Bauman-Martin, eds., *Reading First Peter*, pp. 144–77.

Bauman-Martin, Betsy, and Robert L. Webb, 'Reading First Peter with New Eyes: An Introduction', in Webb and Bauman-Martin, eds., *Reading First Peter*, pp. 1–7.

Baumgarten, J. M., '4QHalakah^a, the Law of Hadash, and the Pentecontad Calendar', *JJS* 27 (1976), pp. 36–46.

Beale, G. K., ed., *The Right Doctrine from the Wrong Texts? Essays on the Use of the Old Testament in the New* (Grand Rapids: Baker, 1994).

Beale, G. K., and D. A. Carson, eds., *Commentary on the New Testament Use of the Old Testament* (Grand Rapids: Baker; Nottingham: Apollos, 2007).

Beare, F. W., *The First Epistle of Peter: The Greek Text with Introduction and Notes* (3d ed.; Oxford: Blackwell, 1970).

———. 'The Sequence of Events in Acts 9 to 15 and the Career of Peter', *JBL* 42, no. 4 (1943), pp. 295–306.

Bénétreau, Samuel, 'Évangile et Prophétie: Un Texte Original (1 P 1, 10–12) Peut-il Éclairer un Texte Difficile (2 P 1, 16–21)?', *Bib* 86 (2005), pp. 174–91.

Bernstein, Moshe J., and Shlomo A. Koyfman, 'The Interpretation of Biblical Law in the Dead Sea Scrolls: Forms and Method', in Henze, ed., *Biblical Interpretation at Qumran*, pp. 75–87.

Berrin, Shani, 'Qumran Pesharim', in Henze, ed., *Biblical Interpretation at Qumran*, pp. 110–33.

Best, Ernest, *1 Peter* (NCBC; Grand Rapids: Eerdmans, 1971).

———. '1 Peter II:4–10 – A Reconsideration', *NovT* 11 (1969), pp. 270–93.

———. *A Critical and Exegetical Commentary on Ephesians* (ICC; Edinburgh: T. & T. Clark, 1998).

———. 'Spiritual Sacrifice: General Priesthood in the New Testament', *Int* 14 (1960), pp. 280–90.

Betz, Hans Dieter, *Galatians: A Commentary on Paul's Letter to the Churches in Galatia* (Hermeneia; Philadelphia: Fortress, 1979).

Bigg, Charles, *A Critical and Exegetical Commentary on the Epistles of St. Peter and St. Jude* (ICC; Edinburgh: T. & T. Clark, 1902).

Billerbeck, P., *Kommentar zum Neuen Testament aus Talmud und Midrasch*, vol. 3 (Munich: Beck, 1922).

Bird, Jennifer G., *Abuse, Power and Fearful Obedience: Reconsidering 1 Peter's Commands to Wives* (LNTS 442; London: T&T Clark International, 2011).

Block, Daniel I., 'The View from the Top: The Holy Spirit in the Prophets', in Firth and Wegner, eds., *Presence, Power and Promise*, pp. 175–207.

Blomberg, Craig L., 'Matthew', in Beale and Carson, eds., *Commentary on the New Testament*, pp. 1–110.

Boehmer, J., 'Tag und Morgenstern? Zu II Petr i 19', *ZNW* 22 (1923), pp. 228–33.

Boismard, Marie-Émile, *Quartre Hymnes Baptismales dans la Premiere Epître de Pierre* (Lectio Divina 30; Paris: Cerf, 1961).

Boring, M. Eugene, *1 Peter* (Nashville: Abingdon, 1999).

———. 'Narrative Dynamics in 1 Peter: The Function of Narrative World', in Webb and Bauman-Martin, eds., *Reading First Peter*, pp. 7–40.

Bornemann, W., 'Der erste Petrusbrief – eine Taufrede des Silvanus', *ZNW* 19 (1920), pp. 143–65.

Bowker, J. W., 'Speeches in Acts: A Study in Proem and Yelammedenu Form', *NTS* 14 (1967), pp. 96–111.

Boys-Smith, E. P., '"Interpretation" or "Revelation": 2 Pet I. 20, Part II', *ExpTim* 8 (1896–97), pp. 331–2.
Brady, Monica, 'Biblical Interpretation in the "Pseudo-Ezekiel" Fragments (4Q383–391) from Cave Four', in Henze, ed., *Biblical Interpretation at Qumran*, pp. 88–109.
Bratcher, Robert G., *Old Testament Quotations in the New Testament* (London: UBS, 1961).
Brooke, George J., *The Dead Sea Scrolls and the New Testament: Essays in Mutual Illumination* (London: SPCK, 2005).
———. *Exegesis at Qumran: 4QFlorilegium in its Jewish Context* (Sheffield: JSOT, 1985).
———. 'Thematic Commentaries on Prophetic Scriptures', in Henze, ed., *Biblical Interpretation at Qumran*, pp. 134–57.
Brown, Jeannine K., 'Just a Busybody? A Look at the Greco-Roman Topos of Meddling for Defining ἀλλοτριεπίσκοπος in 1 Peter 4.15', *JBL* 125 (2006), pp. 549–68.
Brox, Norbert, *Der Erste Petrusbrief* (EKKNT; Zurich: Benziger, 1979).
Buchanan, George Wesley, *To the Hebrews: Translation, Comment and Conclusions* (AB 36; New York: Doubleday, 1972).
Bultmann, Rudolph, 'Bekenntnis und Lied-fragmente im erste Petrusbrief', in *Exegetica: Aufsatze zur Erforschung des Neuen Testaments* (ed. E. Dinkler; Tübingen: Mohr, 1967), pp. 1–14.
Cahill, Michael, 'Not a Cornerstone! Translating Ps 118,22 in the Jewish and Christian Scriptures', *RB* 106 (1999), pp. 345–57.
Callan, Terrence, 'A Note on 2 Peter 1.19–20', *JBL* 125 (2006), pp. 265–70.
Carson, D. A., '1 Peter', in Beale and Carson, eds., *Commentary on the New Testament*, pp. 1015–45.
———. '2 Peter', in Beale and Carson, eds., *Commentary on the New Testament*, pp. 1047–61.
———. 'James', in Beale and Carson, eds., *Commentary on the New Testament*, pp. 997–1014.
Cavallin, H. C. C., 'The False Teachers of 2 Pt as Pseudo-Prophets', *NovT* 21 (1979), pp. 263–70.
Chalcraft, David J., 'The Development of Weber's Sociology of Sects: Encouraging a New Fascination', in *Sectarianism in Early Judaism: Sociological Advances* (ed. David J. Chalcraft; London: Equinox, 2007), pp. 52–73.
Chin, Moses, 'A Heavenly Home for the Homeless: Aliens and Strangers in 1 Peter', *TynBul* 42 (1991), pp. 96–112.
Clark, W. K. L., 'The Uses of the Septuagint in Acts', in *The Beginnings of Christianity*, vol. 2 (London: Macmillan, 1922), pp. 66–103.
Collins, Adela Yarbro, *Mark: A Commentary* (Minneapolis: Fortress, 2007).
Collins, John J., *The Apocalyptic Imagination: An Introduction to Jewish Apocalyptic Literature* (2d ed.; Grand Rapids: Eerdmans, 1998).
———. 'Introduction: Towards the Morphology of a Genre', in *Apocalypse: The Morphology of a Genre* (ed. John J. Collins; Semeia 14; Missoula: Scholars Press, 1979), pp. 1–20.
Cook, Johann, 'The Greek of Proverbs – Evidence of a Recensionally Deviating Hebrew Text?', in Paul et al., eds., *Emanuel*, pp. 605–18.

Coppens, J., 'Le Don de l'Esprit d'après les Textes de Qumran et le Quatrième Évangile', in *L'Évangile de Jean: Études et Problèmes* (ed. F. M. Braun; Bruges: Desclée De Brouwer, 1958), pp. 209–23.
Cranfield, C. E. B., *The First Epistle of Peter* (London: SCM, 1950).
Cross, F. L., *1 Peter: A Pascal Liturgy* (London: Mowbray, 1954).
Curran, John T., 'The Teaching of II Peter 1.20: On the Interpretation of Prophecy', *TS* 4 (1943), pp. 347–68.
Dalton, William Joseph, *Christ's Proclamation to the Spirits: A Study of 1 Peter 3.18–4.6* (Analecta Biblica 23; Rome: Pontifical Biblical Institute, 1965).
———. 'The Interpretation of 1 Peter 3.19 and 4.6: Light from 2 Peter', *Bib* 60 (1979), pp. 547–55.
Danker, Frederick W., '1 Peter 1 24–2 17 – A Consolatory Pericope', *ZNW* 58 (1967), pp. 93–102.
Dautzenberg, Gerhard, 'Σωτηρία ψυχῶν (1 Petr 1, 9)', *BZ* 8 (1964), pp. 262–76.
Davids, Peter H., *The Epistle of James: A Commentary on the Greek Text* (NIGTC; Michigan: Eerdmans, 1982).
Delling, Gerhard, 'καιρός', *TDNT*, vol. 3, pp. 455–62.
Dibelius, Martin, and Heinrich Greeven, *James: A Commentary on the Epistle of James* (trans. Michael A. Williams; Hermeneia; Philadelphia: Fortress, 1976).
Dimant, D., and J. Strugnell, 'The Merkabah Vision in Second Ezekiel', *RevQ* 14 (1990), pp. 331–48.
Dodd, C. H., *According to the Scriptures* (London: Fontana, 1965).
Doering, Lutz, 'First Peter as Early Christian Diaspora Letter', in *Catholic Epistles and Apostolic Tradition: A New Perspective on James and the Catholic Letter Collection* (ed. K.-W. Niebuhr and R. Wall; Waco: Baylor University Press, 2009), pp. 215–36.
———. 'Gottes Volk: Die Adressaten als "Israel" im Ersten Petrusbrief', in du Toit, ed., *Bedrängnis und Identität*, pp. 81–114.
Driver, S. R., 'Problems in the Hebrew Text of Proverbs', *Bib* 32 (1951), pp. 173–97.
Dryden, J. de Waal, *Theology and Ethics in 1 Peter: Paraenetic Strategies for Christian Character Formation* (Tübingen: Mohr Siebeck, 2006).
Dubis, Mark, *Messianic Woes in First Peter: Suffering and Eschatology in 1 Peter 4.12–19* (SBLSBL 33; New York: Peter Lang, 2002).
Dunn, J. D. G., *The Epistles to the Colossians and to Philemon* (Grand Rapids: Eerdmans, 1996).
———. *Unity and Diversity in the New Testament: An Enquiry into the Character of Earliest Christianity* (London: SCM, 1977).
Elliott, J. H., *1 Peter: A New Translation with Introduction and Commentary* (AB 37B: New Haven: Yale University Press, 2000).
———. *The Elect and the Holy: An Exegetical Examination of 1 Peter 2.4–10 and the Phrase* βασίλειον ἱεράτευμα (NovTSup 12; Leiden: Brill, 1966).
———. *A Home for the Homeless: A Social-Scientific Criticism of 1 Peter, Its Situation and Strategy* (Eugene, Ore.: Wipf & Stock, 2005).
———. 'Ministry and Church Order in the New Testament: A Traditio-Historical Analysis (1 Pt 5,1–5 & plls.)', *CBQ* 32 (1970), pp. 367–91.
———. 'The Rehabilitation of an Exegetical Step-Child: 1 Peter in Recent Research', *JBL* 95 (1976), pp. 243–54. Reprinted in Talbert, ed., *Perspectives on First Peter*, pp. 3–16.

Ellis, Earle, 'Midrash, Targum and the New Testament Quotations', in Ellis and Wilcox, eds., *Neotestamentica et Semitica*, pp. 61–9.
Ellis, Earle, and Max Wilcox, eds., *Neotestamentica et Semitica: Studies in Honour of Matthew Black* (Edinburgh: T. & T. Clark, 1969).
Eriksson, Larsolov, *'Come, Children, Listen to Me!' Psalm 34 in the Hebrew Bible and in Early Christian Writings* (CBOTS 32; Stockholm: Almqvist & Wiksell, 1991).
Evans, Craig A., 'Abraham in the Dead Sea Scrolls: A Man of Faith and Failure', in *The Bible at Qumran: Text, Shape, and Interpretation* (ed. Peter W. Flint; SDSSRL; Grand Rapids: Eerdmans, 2001), pp. 149–57.
Feldmeier, Reinhard, *The First Letter of Peter: A Commentary on the Greek Text* (trans. Peter H. Davids; Waco: Baylor University Press, 2008).
Finkel, A., 'The Pesher of Dreams and Scriptures', *RevQ* 4 (1963–64), pp. 364–70.
Fiorenza, Elizabeth Schüssler, 'Cultic Language in Qumran and the NT', *CBQ* 38 (1976), pp. 173–5.
Firth, David G., and Paul D. Wegner, eds., *Presence, Power and Promise: The Role of the Spirit of God in the Old Testament* (Nottingham: Apollos, 2011).
Fish, Stanley, *Is There a Text in This Class? The Authority of Interpretive Communities* (Cambridge, Mass.: Harvard University Press, 1980).
Fitzmyer, Joseph, 'David, "Being therefore a Prophet..." (Acts 2.30)', *CBQ* 34 (1972), pp. 332–9.
———. *The Interpretation of Scripture: In Defense of the Historical-Critical Method* (New York: Paulist Press, 2008).
Flint, Peter W., 'The Prophet David at Qumran', in Henze, ed., *Biblical Interpretation at Qumran*, pp. 158–67.
Forbes, Greg, 'Children of Sarah: Interpreting 1 Peter 3.6b', *BBR* 15 (2005), pp. 105–9.
Fowl, Stephen E., *Engaging Scripture: A Model for Theological Interpretation* (Eugene, Ore.: Wipf & Stock, 2008).
———. 'The Importance of a Multivoiced Literal Sense of Scripture: The Example of Thomas Aquinas', in *Reading Scripture with the Church: Toward a Hermeneutic for Theological Interpretation* (Grand Rapids: Baker, 2006), pp. 53–60.
France, R. T., *Jesus and the Old Testament* (London: Tyndale, 1982).
———. *Jesus and the Old Testament: His Application of Old Testament Passages to Himself and His Mission* (Grand Rapids: Baker, 1971).
Francis, J., '"Like Newborn Babies" – The Image of the Child in 1 Peter 2.2–3', in *Studia Biblica 1978*. Vol. 3, *Papers on Paul and Other New Testament Authors* (ed. E. A. Livingstone; JSNTSup 3; Sheffield: Sheffield Academic, 1980), pp. 111–17.
Garner, Richard, *From Homer to Tragedy: The Art of Allusion in Greek Poetry* (London: Routledge, 1990).
Gärtner, Bertil, *The Temple and the Community in Qumran and the New Testament* (SNTSMS 1; Cambridge: Cambridge University Press, 1965).
Gillingham, Susan, 'From Liturgy to Prophecy: The Use of Psalmody in Second Temple Judaism', *CBQ* 64 (2002), pp. 470–89.
Goppelt, Leonhard, *Typos: The Typological Interpretation of the Old Testament in the New* (trans. Donald H. Madvig; Grand Rapids: Eerdmans, 1982).
Gréaux, Eric James, '"To the Exiles of the Dispersion...from Babylon": The Function of the Old Testament in 1 Peter' (Ph.D. diss., Duke University, 2003).
Green, Joel B., *1 Peter* (Grand Rapids: Eerdmans, 2007).
———. 'Narrating the Gospel in 1 and 2 Peter', *Int* 60 (2006), pp. 262–77.

Greer, Rowan A., *Theodore of Mopsuestia: Commentary on Minor Pauline Epistles* (SBLWGRW; Atlanta: SBL, 2010).
Grudem, Wayne A., *The First Epistle of Peter: An Introduction and Commentary* (TNTC; Leicester: IVP, 1988).
Grundemann, Walter, 'παρεπίδημος', *TDNT*, vol. 2, pp. 64–5.
Gundry, R. H., *The Use of the Old Testament in St Matthew's Gospel: With Special Reference to the Messianic Hope* (NovTSup 8; Leiden: Brill, 1975).
Hanson, Anthony Tyrrell, *The Living Utterances of God: The New Testament Exegesis of the Old* (London: DLT, 1983).
Hanson, R. P. C., 'Notes on Tertullian's Interpretation of Scripture', *JTS* 12 (1961), pp. 275–7.
Harink, Douglas, *1 & 2 Peter* (London: SCM, 2009).
Harris, J. G., *The Qumran Commentary on Habakkuk* (London: Mowbray, 1966).
Hay, David M., *Glory at the Right Hand: Psalm 110 in Early Christianity* (SBLMS 18; Atlanta: Society of Biblical Literature, 1989).
Hayes, Richard B., *Echoes of Scripture in the Letters of Paul* (New Haven: Yale University Press, 1989).
Heath, Jane, 'Homer or Moses? A Hellenistic Perspective on Moses' Throne Vision in Ezekiel Tragicus', *JJS* 43 (2007), pp. 1–18.
Henze, Matthias, ed., *Biblical Interpretation at Qumran* (SDSSRL; Grand Rapids: Eerdmans, 2005).
Herzer, J., 'Alttestamentliche Prophetie und die Verkündigung des Evangeliums: Beobachtungen zur Stellung und zur hermeneutische Funktion von 1 Petr 1, 10–12', *BThZ* 14 (1997), pp. 14–22.
Hiebert, D. Edmund, 'The Prophetic Foundation for the Christian Life: An Exposition of 2 Peter 1.19–21', *BSac* 141 (1984), pp. 158–68.
Hill, David, '"To Offer Spiritual Sacrifices…" (1 Peter 2.5): Liturgical Formulations and Christian Paraenesis in 1 Peter', *JSNT* 5 (1982), pp. 58–9.
Hillyer, Norman, *1 and 2 Peter, Jude* (Peabody: Hendrickson, 1992).
———. 'First Peter and the Feast of Tabernacles', *TynBul* 21 (1970), pp. 39–70.
———. '"Rock-Stone" Imagery in 1 Peter', *TynBul* 22 (1971), pp. 58–81.
Hines, Paul A., 'Peter and the Prophetic Word: The Theology of Prophecy Traced through Peter's Sermons and Epistles', *BBR* 21 (2011), pp. 227–44.
Holtz, Gruden, 'Rabbinische Literatur und Neues Testament: Alte Schwierigkeiten und neue Möglishkeiten', *ZNW* 100 (2009), pp. 173–98.
Horgan, Maurya P., *Pesharim: Qumran Interpretations of Biblical Books* (CBQMS 8; Washington: Catholic Biblical Association of America, 1979).
Horrell, David G., *The Epistles of Peter and Jude* (Peterborough: Epworth, 1998).
———. 'The Product of a Petrine Circle? A Reassessment of the Origin and Character of 1 Peter', *JSNT* 86 (2002), pp. 29–60.
———. 'The Themes of 1 Peter: Insights from the Earliest Manuscripts (the Crosby-Schøyen Codex ms 193 and the Bodmer Miscellaneous Codex containing P^{72})', *NTS* 55 (2009), pp. 502–22.
———. 'Who are "The Dead" and When Was the Gospel Preached to Them? The Interpretation of 1 Pet 4.6', *NTS* 49 (2003), pp. 70–89.
Horrell, David G., Bradley Arnold and Travis B. Williams, 'Visuality, Vivid Description, and the Message of 1 Peter: The Significance of the Roaring Lion (1 Pet 5.8)', *JBL* 132 (2013), pp. 697–716.

Hort, F. J. A., *The First Epistle of St Peter* (London: Macmillan, 1898).
Jassen, Alex P., 'The Pesharim and the Rise of Commentary in Early Jewish Scriptural Interpretation', *DSD* 19 (2012), pp. 363–98.
———. 'The Presentation of the Ancient Prophets as Lawgivers at Qumran', *JBL* 127 (2008), pp. 307–37.
Jeanrond, Werner G., 'After Hermeneutics: The Relationship between Theology and Biblical Studies', in *The Open Text: New Directions for Biblical Studies?* (ed. Francis Watson; London: SCM, 1993), pp. 85–102.
Jeremias, J., 'Κεφαλὴ γωνίας – Ἀκρογωνιαῖας', *ZNW* 29 (1930), pp. 264–80.
Jervell, Jacob, 'The Future of the Past: Luke's Vision of Salvation History and Its Bearing on His writing of History', in *History, Literature, and Society in the Book of Acts* (ed. Ben Witherington; Cambridge: Cambridge University Press, 1996), pp. 104–206.
Jobes, Karen H., *1 Peter* (BECNT; Grand Rapids: Baker, 2005).
———. 'The Minor Prophets in James, 1 & 2 Peter and Jude', in *The Minor Prophets in the New Testament* (ed. Maarten J. J. Menken and Steve Moyise; LNTS 377; The New Testament and the Scriptures of Israel; London: T&T Clark International, 2009), pp. 135–54.
———. 'The Septuagint Textual Tradition in 1 Peter', in Kraus and Wooden, eds., *Septuagint Research*, pp. 311–33.
Johnson, Dennis E., 'Fire in God's House: Imagery from Malachi 3 in Peter's Theology of Suffering', *JETS* 29 (1986), pp. 285–94.
Johnson, Luke Timothy, *The Letter of James: A New Translation with Introduction and Commentary* (AB 37A; New York: Doubleday, 1995).
Joseph, Abson Prédestin, *A Narratological Reading of 1 Peter* (LNTS 440; London: T&T Clark International, 2012).
Kaiser, Walter C., 'The Single Intent of Scripture', in Beale, ed., *The Right Doctrine*, pp. 55–67.
Kelhoffer, James A., *Persecution, Persuasion and Power: Readiness to Withstand Hardship as a Corroboration of Legitimacy in the New Testament* (WUNT 270; Tübingen: Mohr Siebeck, 2012).
Kelly, J. N. D., *A Commentary on the Epistles of Peter and of Jude* (London: A. & C. Black, 1969).
Kendall, David W., 'The Literary and Theological Function of 1 Peter 1.3–12', in Talbert, ed., *Perspectives on First Peter*, pp. 103–20.
Kiley, Mark, 'Like Sara: The Tale of Terror behind 1 Peter 3.6', *JBL* 106 (1987), pp. 689–92.
Kilpatrick, G. D., '1 Peter 1.11: ΤΙΝΑ Ἠ ΠΟΙΟΝ ΚΑΙΡΟΝ', *NovT* 28 (1986), pp. 91–2.
Klinzing, Georg, *Die Umdentung die Kultus in des Qumrangemeinde und im Neuen Testament* (SUNT 7; Gottingen: Vandenhoeck & Ruprecht, 1971).
Kraft, R. A., 'Para-mania: Beside, Before and Beyond Bible Studies', *JBL* 126 (2007), pp. 11–17.
Kraftchick, Steven J., *Jude, 2 Peter* (ANTC; Nashville: Abingdon, 2002).
Kraus, Wolfgang, and R. Glenn Wooden, 'Contemporary "Septuagint" Research: Issues and Challenges in the Study of the Greek Jewish Scripture', in Kraus and Wooden, eds., *Septuagint Research*, pp. 1–13.
———, eds., *Septuagint Research: Issues and Challenges in the Study of the Greek Jewish Scriptures* (SBLSCS 53; Leiden: Brill, 2006).

Kristeva, Julia, *Desire in Language: A Semiotic Approach to Literature and Art* (New York: Columbia University Press, 1980).
Kruger, Michael J., 'The Authenticity of 2 Peter', *JETS* 42 (1999), pp. 645–71.
LaVerdiere, E. A., 'A Grammatical Ambiguity in 1 Pet. 1.23', *CBQ* 36 (1974), pp. 89–94.
Lea, Thomas D., 'How Peter Learned the Old Testament', *SwJT* 22 (1980), pp. 96–102.
Leaney, A. R. C., *The Rule of Qumran and its Meaning: Introduction, Translation and Commentary* (London: SCM, 1966).
Levine, Nancy, 'Spinoza's Bible: Concerning How it is that "Scripture, insofar as it contains the word of God, has come down to us uncorrupted"', *Philosophy and Theology* 13 (2001), pp. 93–142.
Liebengood, Kelly D., '1 Peter's Fiery Trials and Zechariah 9–14's Pierced Shepherd-King' (SBL 2008 conference paper).
Lieu, Judith, *Image and Reality: The Jews in the World of the Christians in the Second Century* (Edinburgh: T. & T. Clark, 1996).
Lim, Timothy H., *Pesharim* (CQS 3; London: Sheffield Academic, 2002).
Lincoln, Andrew, *Hebrews: A Guide* (London: Continuum, 2006).
Lindars, Barnabas, *New Testament Apologetic: The Doctrinal Significance of the Old Testament Quotation* (London: SCM, 1961).
Lindbeck, George A., 'Postcritical Canonical Interpretation: Three Modes of Retrieval', in *Theological Exegesis: Essays in Honor of Brevard S. Childs* (ed. Kathryn Green-McCreight and Christopher Seitz; Grand Rapids: Eerdmans, 1999), pp. 26–51.
Lohse, Eduard, *Colossians and Philemon* (trans. William Poehlmann and Robert J. Karris; Philadelphia: Fortress, 1971).
———. 'Paränese und Kerygma im I. Petrusbrief', *ZNW* 45 (1954), pp. 68–89.
Longenecker, Richard, *Biblical Exegesis in the Apostolic Period* (Grand Rapids: Eerdmans, 1975).
Lorein, Geert W., 'The Holy Spirit at Qumran', in Firth and Wegner, eds., *Presence, Power and Promise*, pp. 371–95.
Love, Julian Price, 'The First Epistle of Peter', *Int* 8 (1954), pp. 63–87.
Lynch, Chloe, 'Who Are the πρεσβύτεροι and What Is Said about their Role?', *ExpTim* 123 (2012), pp. 529–40.
Mandel, Paul, 'Midrashic Exegesis and its Precedents in the Dead Sea Scrolls', *DSD* 8 (2001), pp. 149–68.
Manns, F., 'Sara, Modèle de l'obéissante: Étude de l'arrière-plan juif de 1 Pierre 3,5–6', *BeO* 26 (1984), pp. 65–73.
Markham, Ian, *Truth and the Reality of God: An Essay in Natural Theology* (Edinburgh: T. & T. Clark, 1998).
Marshall, I. Howard, *1 Peter* (Leicester: Intervarsity Press, 1991).
———. *The Gospel of Luke: A Commentary on the Greek Text* (NIGNT; Carlisle: Paternoster; Grand Rapids: Eerdmans, 1978).
Martin, Ralph P., *James* (WBC 48; Waco: Word, 1988).
Martin, Troy W., *Metaphor and Composition in 1 Peter* (SBLDS 131; Atlanta: Scholars Press, 1992).
———. 'Roaring Lions among Diaspora Metaphors: First Peter 5.8 in its Metaphorical Context', in du Toit, ed., *Bedrängnis und Identität*, pp. 167–79.
———. 'The TestAbr and the Background of 1 Pet 3,6', *ZNW* 90 (1999), pp. 139–46.

Mbuvi, Andrew M., *Temple, Exile and Identity in 1 Peter* (LNTS 345; London: T&T Clark International, 2007).
McCartney, Dan Gale, 'The Use of the Old Testament in the First Epistle of Peter' (Ph.D. diss., Westminster Theological Seminary, 1989).
McKelvey, Robert J., *The New Temple: The Church in the New Testament* (London: Oxford University Press, 1969).
McLay, R. T., *The Use of the Septuagint in New Testament Research* (Grand Rapids: Eerdmans, 2003).
McLean, B. H., 'The Crisis of Historicism: And the Problem of Historical Meaning in New Testament Studies', *HeyJ* 53 (2012), pp. 217–40.
McLeod, Frederick G., *Theodore of Mopsuestia* (London: Routledge, 2009).
Michaelis, Wilhelm, παρακύπτω, *TDNT*, vol. 5, pp. 814–16.
Michaels, J. Ramsey, *1 Peter* (WBC 49; Nashville: Thomas Nelson, 1988).
Milbank, John, 'Knowledge: The Theological Critique of Philosophy in Hamann and Jacobi', in *Radical Orthodoxy: A New Theology* (ed. John Milbank, Catherine Pickstock and Graham Ward; London: Routledge, 1999), pp. 21–37.
———. *The Word Made Strange: Theology, Language, Culture* (Oxford: Blackwell, 1997).
Milgrom, Jacob, 'Qumran's Biblical Hermeneutics: The Case of the Wood Offering', *RevQ* 16 (1994), pp. 449–56.
Mitton, C. L., 'The Relationship between Ephesians and 1 Peter', *JTS* 1 (1950), pp. 67–73.
Moffatt, James, *The General Epistles: James, Peter, and Judas* (New York: Doubleday, 1928).
Moo, Douglas J., *The Letter of James* (Grand Rapids: Eerdmans; Leicester: Apollos, 2000).
Moule, C. F. D., 'The Nature and Purpose of 1 Peter', *NTS* 3 (1956), pp. 1–11.
Moyise, Steve, *Evoking Scripture: Seeing the Old Testament in the New* (London: T&T Clark International, 2008).
———. 'Isaiah in 1 Peter', in *Isaiah in the New Testament* (ed. Steve Moyise and Maarten J. J. Menken; London: T&T Clark International, 2005), pp. 175–88.
———. *The Old Testament in the New: An Introduction* (London: T&T Clark, 2001).
———. 'Quotations', in Porter and Stanley, eds., *As It Is Written*, pp. 15–28.
Muddiman, John, *The Epistle to the Ephesians* (London: Continuum, 2001).
Nauck, Wolfgang, 'Freude im Leiden: Zum Problem einer urchristlichen Verfolgungstradition', *ZNW* 46 (1955), pp. 68–80.
Neyrey, J. H., 'The Apologetic Use of the Transfiguration in 2 Peter 1.16–21', *CBQ* 42 (1980), pp. 504–19.
Nitzan, Bilhah, 'Approaches to Biblical Exegesis in Qumran Literature', in Paul et al., eds., *Emanuel*, pp. 347–65.
Nixon, R. E., 'The Meaning of "Baptism" in 1 Peter 3.21', in *Studia Evangelica*. Vol. 4, *Papers Presented to the Third International Congress on New Testament Studies Held at Christ Church, Oxford* (ed. F. L. Cross; Oxford: Oxford University Press, 1968), pp. 437–41.
Nolland, John, *The Gospel of Matthew: A Commentary on the Greek Text* (NIGTC; Grand Rapids: Eerdmans; Bletchley: Paternoster, 2005).

Osborne, Thomas P., 'Guide Lines for Christian Suffering: A Source-Critical and Theological Study of 1 Peter 2, 21–25', *Bib* 64 (1983), pp. 381–408.

———. 'L'Utilisation de l'Ancient Testament dans la Première Épître de Pierre', *RThL* 12 (1981), pp. 64–77.

Pao, David W. and Eckhard J. Schnabel, 'Luke', in Beale and Carson, eds., *Commentary on the New Testament*, pp. 251–414.

Paschke, Boris A., 'The Roman *ad bestias* Execution as a Possible Historical Background for 1 Peter 5.8', *JSNT* 28 (2006), pp. 489–500.

Paul, Shalom M., Robert A. Kraft, Lawrence H. Schiffman and Weston W. Fields, eds., *Emanuel: Studies in Hebrew Bible, Septuagint and Dead Sea Scrolls in Honor of Emanuel Tov* (VTSup 94; Leiden: Brill, 2003).

Perkins, Pheme, *First and Second Peter, James, and Jude* (Interpretation; Louisville: John Knox, 1995).

Perriman, Andrew, 'The Pattern of Christ's Sufferings: Colossians 1.24 and Philippians 3.10–11', *TynBul* 42 (1991), pp. 62–9.

Pervo, Richard I., *Acts: A Commentary* (Philadelphia: Fortress, 2009).

Piper, John, 'Hope as the Motivation of Love: 1 Peter 3.9-12', *NTS* 26 (1980), pp. 212–31.

Porter, S. E., 'The Use of the Old Testament in the New: A Brief Comment on Method and Terminology', in *Early Christian Interpretation of the Scriptures of Israel* (ed. C. A. Evans and J. A. Saunders; JSNTSup 148; Sheffield: Sheffield Academic, 1997), pp. 79–96.

Porter, S. E., and Andrew W. Pitts, 'τοῦτο πρῶτον γινώσκοντες ὅτι in 2 Peter 1.20 and Hellenistic Epistolary Convention', *JBL* 127 (2008), pp. 165–71.

Porter, S. E., and C. D. Stanley, eds., *As It Is Written: Studying Paul's Use of Scripture* (Atlanta: Society of Biblical Literature, 2008).

Preisker, Herbert, *Das Ethos des Urchristentums* (Darmstadt: Wissenschaftliche Buchgesellschaft, 1949).

Prigent, Pierre, '1 Pierre 2, 4–10', *RHPhR* 72 (1992), pp. 53–60.

Rabinowitz, Isaac, 'Pesher/Pittaron: Its Biblical Meaning and Significance in the Qumran Literature', *RevQ* 8 (1973), pp. 213–32.

Radermacher, L., 'Der 1 Petrusbrief und Silvanus', *ZNW* 25 (1926), pp. 287–95.

Rajak, Tessa, 'Talking at Trypho: Christian Apologetics as Anti-Judaism in Justin's Dialogue with Trypho the Jew', in *Apologetics in the Roman Empire: Pagans, Jews and Christians* (ed. Mark J. Edwards, Martin Goodman and Christopher Rowland; Oxford: Oxford University Press, 1999), pp. 59–80.

Ramsey, William M., *The Church in the Roman Empire Before A. D. 170* (London: Hodder & Stoughton, 1893).

Reicke, Bo, *The Disobedient Spirits and Christian Baptism: A Study of 1 Pet. III. 19 and its Context* (ASNU 13; Copenhagen: Ejnar Munksgaard, 1946).

———. *The Epistles of James, Peter and Jude* (AB 37; New York: Doubleday, 1964).

Richard, Earl, 'The Functional Christology of First Peter', in Talbert, ed., *Perspectives on First Peter*, pp. 121–40.

Richards, E. Randolph, 'Silvanus Was Not Peter's Secretary: Theological Bias in Interpreting διὰ Σιλουανοῦ…ἔγραψα in 1 Peter 5.12', *JETS* 43 (2000), pp. 417–32.

Robertson, Gregory Ray, 'The Use of Old Testament Quotations and Allusions in the First Epistle of Peter' (Ph.D. diss., Anderson University, 1990).

Robinson, John A. T., *Redating the New Testament* (Philadelphia: Westminster, 1976).
Rorty, Richard, *Philosophy and Social Hope* (London: Penguin, 1999).
Rowland, Christopher, *The Open Heaven: A Study of Apocalyptic in Judaism and Early Christianity* (London: SPCK, 1982).
Sanders, E. P., *Judaism: Practice and Belief, 63 BCE–66 CE* (London: SCM; Philadelphia: Trinity Press International, 1994).
Sanders, J. T., 'The Transition from Opening Epistolary Thanksgiving to Body in the Letters of the Pauline Corpus', *JBL* 81 (1962), pp. 348–62.
Sandnes, Karl Olav, 'Revised Conventions in Early Christian Paraenesis – "Working Good" in 1 Peter as an Example', in Starr and Engberg-Pedersen, eds., *Early Christian Paraenesis in Context*, pp. 373–403.
Sandys-Wunsch, John, and Laurence Eldridge, 'J. P. Gabler and the Distinction between Biblical and Dogmatic Theology: Translation, Commentary and Discussion of his Originality', *SJT* 33 (1980), pp. 133–58.
Sargent, Benjamin, *As It Is Written: Interpreting the Bible with Boldness* (LS 75; London: Latimer Trust, 2011).
———. 'Biblical Hermeneutics in the Zurich Reformation', *EvQ* 86 (2014), pp. 325–42.
———. 'Chosen through Sanctification (1 Pet 1,2 and 2 Thess 2,13): The Theology or Diction of Silvanus?', *Bib* 94 (2013), pp. 117–20.
———. *David Being a Prophet: The Contingency of Scripture upon History in the New Testament* (BNZW 207; Berlin: de Gruyter, 2014).
———. '"Interpreting Homer from Homer": Aristarchus of Samothrace and the Notion of Scriptural Authorship in the New Testament', *TynBul* 65 (2014), pp. 125–39.
———. 'John Milbank and Biblical Hermeneutics: The End of the Historical Critical Method?', *HeyJ* 52 (2012), pp. 253–63.
———. 'The Narrative Substructure of 1 Peter', *ExpTim* 124, no. 10 (2013), pp. 485–90.
———. 'Proceeding Beyond Isolation: Bringing Milbank, Habermas and Ockham to the Interfaith Table', *HeyJ* 51 (2010), pp. 819–30.
Schaberg, Jane, 'Mark 14.62: Early Christian Merkabah Imagery?', in *Apocalyptic and the New Testament: Essays on Honor of J. Louis Martyn* (ed. Joel Marcus and Marion L. Soards; JSNTSup 24; Sheffield: Sheffield Academic, 1989), pp. 69–94.
Schelkle, Karl Hermann, *Die Petrusbriefe, Der Judasbrief* (HThKNT 13; Freiburg: Herder, 1961).
Schleiermacher, F., *The Christian Faith* (ed. H. R. Mackintosh and J. S. Stewart; 2d ed.; Edinburgh: T. & T. Clark, 1989)
Schlosser, Jacques, '1 Pierre 3, 5b–6', *Bib* 64.1 (1983), pp. 409–10.
———. 'Ancien Testament et Christologie dans la Prima Petri', in Perrot, *Etudes sur la Première Lettre de Pierre* (LD 102; Paris: Cerf, 1980), pp. 65–96.
Schmidt, Daryl, 'The Historiography of Acts: Deuteronomistic or Hellenistic?', *SBLSP* 24 (1985), pp. 417–26.
Schutter, William L., *Hermeneutic and Composition in 1 Peter* (WUNT 30; Tübingen: Mohr Siebeck, 1989).
Schwank, P. Benedict, 'L'Epître (1 P 3,8–15)', *AsSeign* 59 (1966), pp. 16–32.
Seitz, Christopher R., *Word Without End: The Old Testament as Abiding Theological Witness* (Grand Rapids: Eerdmans, 1998).

Seland, Torrey, 'The "Common Priesthood" of Philo and 1 Peter: A Philonic Reading of 1 Peter 2.5, 9', *JSNT* 17 (1995), pp. 87–119.

———. 'Resident Aliens in Mission: Missional Practices in the Emerging Church of 1 Peter', *BBR* 19 (2009), pp. 565–89.

———. *Strangers in the Light: Philonic Perspectives on Christian Identity in 1 Peter* (BIS, 76; Leiden: Brill, 2005).

Selwyn, Edward Gordon, *The First Epistle of St. Peter: The Greek Text with Introduction, Notes and Essays* (London: Macmillan, 1958).

Shils, Edward, 'The Concept and Function of Ideology', in *The International Encyclopedia of the Social Sciences* (New York: Macmillan, 1968), pp. 66–76.

Shimada, Kazuhito, 'A Critical Note on 1 Peter 1, 12', *AJBI* 7 (1981), pp. 146–50.

Silberman, L. H., 'Unriddling the Riddle: A Study in the Structure and Language of the Habakkuk Pesher', *RevQ* 3 (1961–62), pp. 323–64.

Snodgrass, Klyne R., '1 Peter II. 1–10: Its Formation and Literary Affinities', *NTS* 24 (1978), pp. 97–106.

Snyder, Scot, 'Participles and Imperatives in 1 Peter: A Re-examination in the Light of Recent Scholarly Trends', *Filologia Neotestamentica* 8 (1995), pp. 187–98.

Soards, Marion L., *The Speeches in Acts: Their Content, Context, and Concerns* (Louisville: Westminster John Knox, 1994).

Spence, R. M., 'Private Interpretation', *ExpTim* 8 (1896–97), pp. 285–6.

Spencer, Aída Besançon, 'Peter's Pedagogical Method in 1 Peter 3.6', *BBR* 10 (2000), pp. 107–19.

Spinoza, Benedict de, *Theological-Political Treatise* (trans. Michael Silverthorne and Jonathan Israel; Cambridge: Cambridge University Press, 2007).

Spitta, Friedrich, 'Der Brief des Jakobus', in *Zur Geschichte und Litteratur des Urchristentums*, vol. 2 (Göttingen: Vandenhoeck & Ruprecht, 1896), pp. 1–239.

Spörri, Theophil, *Der Gemeindegedanke im ersten Petrusbrief* (Neutestamentliche Forschung 2/2; Gütersloh: Bertelsmann, 1925).

Stamps, Dennis L., 'The Use of the Old Testament in the New Testament as a Rhetorical Device: A Methodological Proposal', in *Hearing the Old Testament in the New Testament* (ed. Stanley E. Porter; Grand Rapids: Eerdmans, 2006), pp. 26–30.

Stanley, Christopher D., *Arguing with Scripture: The Rhetoric of Quotations in the Letters of Paul* (London: T&T Clark International, 2004).

———. '"Pearls before Swine": Did Paul's Audience Understand his Biblical Quotations?', *NovT* 41 (1999), pp. 124–44.

Starr, James, and Troels Engberg-Pedersen, eds., *Early Christian Paraenesis in Context* (BZNW 125; Berlin: de Gruyter, 2004).

Stern, David, 'Midrash and Indeterminacy', *CI* 15 (1988), pp. 120–39.

Steudal, Annette, 'אחרית הימים in the Texts from Qumran', *RevQ* 16 (1993), pp. 225–8.

Strack, H., and P. Billerbeck, *Kommentar zum Neuen Testament aus Talmud und Midrasch*, vol. 3 (Munich: Beck, 1922).

Strobel, August, *Der Brief an die Hebräer* (Göttingen: Vandenhoeck & Ruprecht, 1991).

Sukenik, E. L., *Study of the Dead Sea Scrolls* (Jerusalem: Mosad Bialik/The Hebrew University, 1951 [Hebrew]).

Sumney, Jerry L., '"I fill up what is lacking in the afflictions of Christ": Paul's Vicarious Suffering in Colossians', *CBQ* 68 (2006), pp. 664–70.

Sylva, D. D., 'The Meaning and Function of Acts 7.46–50', *JBL* 106 (1989), pp. 261–75.